THE CAMBRIDGE COMPANION
MODERN JEWISH PHILC

The Cambridge Companion to Modern Jewish Philosophy is a collection of original essays that examine the work of some of the most important Jewish thinkers of the modern era – the period extending from the seventeenth century to the late twentieth century.

Editors Michael L. Morgan and Peter Eli Gordon have brought together a group of world-renowned scholars to paint a broad and rich picture of the tradition of modern Jewish philosophy over a period of four hundred years. Beginning with the seventeenth century, modern Jewish philosophy developed among thinkers who responded to the new science and modern philosophy in the course of reflecting on the nature of Judaism and Jewish life.

The essays address themes that are central to the tradition of modern Jewish philosophy – language and revelation, autonomy and authority, the problem of evil, Messianism, the influence of Kant, and feminism – and discuss in depth the work of major thinkers such as Spinoza, Mendelssohn, Cohen, Buber, Rosenzweig, Fackenheim, Soloveitchik, Strauss, Levinas, Maimon, Benjamin, Derrida, Scholem, and Arendt.

Michael L. Morgan is Professor of Philosophy and Jewish Studies at Indiana University. In 2004, he was named a Chancellor's Professor. He has published articles in a variety of journals and has written several books, including *Interim Judaism* (2001); *Beyond Auschwitz: Post-Holocaust Jewish Thought in America* (2001); and *Dilemmas in Modern Jewish Thought: The Dialectics of Revelation and History* (1992).

Peter Eli Gordon is Professor of History at Harvard University. He has published widely on topics in modern European intellectual history, modern Continental philosophy, and modern Jewish thought. His book, *Rosenzweig and Heidegger: Between Judaism and German Philosophy* (2003), received several distinguished awards, including the Goldstein-Goren Prize for the best book in Jewish philosophy, the Salo W. Baron Prize for the best first book in Jewish history, and the 2003 Forkosch Prize for the best book in intellectual history.

CAMBRIDGE COMPANIONS TO RELIGION
This is a series of companions to major topics and key figures in
theology and religious studies. Each volume contains specially
commissioned chapters by international scholars that provide an
accessible and stimulating introduction to the subject for new readers
and nonspecialists.

Other titles in the series

THE CAMBRIDGE COMPANION TO CHRISTIAN DOCTRINE
edited by Colin Gunton (1997)
ISBN 978-0-521-47118-3 hardback   ISBN 978-0-521-47695-9 paperback

THE CAMBRIDGE COMPANION TO BIBLICAL INTERPRETATION
edited by John Barton (1998)
ISBN 978-0-521-48144-1 hardback   ISBN 978-0-521-48593-7 paperback

THE CAMBRIDGE COMPANION TO DIETRICH BONHOEFFER
edited by John de Gruchy (1999)
ISBN 978-0-521-58258-2 hardback   ISBN 978-0-521-58781-5 paperback

THE CAMBRIDGE COMPANION TO LIBERATION THEOLOGY
edited by Chris Rowland (1999)
ISBN 978-0-521-46144-3 hardback   ISBN 978-0-521-46707-0 paperback

THE CAMBRIDGE COMPANION TO KARL BARTH
edited by John Webster (2000)
ISBN 978-0-521-58476-0 hardback   ISBN 978-0-521-58560-6 paperback

THE CAMBRIDGE COMPANION TO CHRISTIAN ETHICS
edited by Robin Gill (2001)
ISBN 978-0-521-77070-5 hardback   ISBN 978-0-521-77918-0 paperback

THE CAMBRIDGE COMPANION TO JESUS
edited by Markus Bockmuehl (2001)
ISBN 978-0-521-79261-5 hardback   ISBN 978-0-521-79678-1 paperback

THE CAMBRIDGE COMPANION TO FEMINIST THEOLOGY
edited by Susan Frank Parsons (2002)
ISBN 978-0-521-66327-4 hardback   ISBN 978-0-521-66380-9 paperback

THE CAMBRIDGE COMPANION TO MARTIN LUTHER
edited by Donald K. McKim (2003)
ISBN 978-0-521-81648-9 hardback   ISBN 978-0-521-01673-5 paperback

THE CAMBRIDGE COMPANION TO ST. PAUL
edited by James D. G. Dunn
ISBN 978-0-521-78155-8 hardback   ISBN 978-0-521-78694-2 paperback

THE CAMBRIDGE COMPANION TO MEDIEVAL JEWISH PHILOSOPHY
edited by Daniel H. Frank and Oliver Leaman
ISBN 978-0-521-65207-0 hardback   ISBN 978-0-521-65574-3 paperback

THE CAMBRIDGE COMPANION TO REFORMATION THEOLOGY
edited by David Bagchi and David Steinmetz
ISBN 978-0-521-77224-2 hardback   ISBN 978-0-521-77662-2 paperback

Continued after the Index

THE CAMBRIDGE COMPANION TO

MODERN JEWISH PHILOSOPHY

Edited by Michael L. Morgan
Indiana University

Peter Eli Gordon
Harvard University

CAMBRIDGE
UNIVERSITY PRESS

CAMBRIDGE UNIVERSITY PRESS
Cambridge, New York, Melbourne, Madrid, Cape Town, Singapore, São Paulo

Cambridge University Press
32 Avenue of the Americas, New York, NY 10013-2473, USA

www.cambridge.org
Information on this title: www.cambridge.org/9780521813129

First published 2007

Printed in the United States of America

A catalog record for this publication is available from the British Library.

Library of Congress Cataloging in Publication Data
Morgan, Michael L., 1944–
The Cambridge companion to modern Jewish philosophy / Michael L. Morgan
and Peter Eli Gordon.
  p. cm.
Includes bibliographical references and index.
ISBN-13: 978-0-521-81312-9 (hardback)
ISBN-13: 978-0-521-01255-3 (pbk.)
  1. Philosophy, Jewish. 2. Philosophy, Modern. 3. Jewish philosophers.
  4. Judaism – History – Modern period, 1750–. I. Gordon, Peter Eli. II. Title.
B755.M67   2007
181'.06–dc22   2006031065

ISBN   978-0-521-81312-9 hardback
ISBN   978-0-521-01255-3 paperback

Contents

Contributors

Allan Arkush is Professor of Judaic Studies and History at Binghamton University. He is the author of *Moses Mendelssohn and the Enlightenment* (1994) and numerous articles on modern Jewish history and thought.

Leora Batnitzky is Associate Professor of Religion at Princeton University. She is the author of *Leo Strauss and Emmanuel Levinas: Philosophy and the Politics of Revelation* (2006) and *Idolatry and Representation: The Philosophy of Franz Rosenzweig Reconsidered* (2000). She is also the editor of the forthcoming *Martin Buber: Schriften zur Philosophie und Religion* and, since 2004, the co-editor of *Jewish Studies Quarterly*.

Pierre Bouretz is Professor of Philosophy at the École des Hautes Études en Sciences Sociales (Paris). Among his recent publications are *La tour de Babel*, with Marc de Launay and Jean-Louis Scheffer (2003); *Témoins du futur: Philosophie et messianisme* (2003); and *Qu'appelle-t-on philosopher?* (2006).

Richard A. Cohen is the Isaac Swift Distinguished Professor of Judaic Studies at the University of North Carolina at Charlotte. He is the author of *Ethics, Exegesis, and Philosophy: Interpretation after Levinas* (2001) and *Elevations: The Height of the Good in Rosenzweig and Levinas* (1994); the translator of four books by Levinas; the editor of several books in contemporary thought; and the author of numerous articles in contemporary Continental philosophy.

Paul W. Franks is Professor of Philosophy and a member of the Jewish Studies Program Faculty at the University of Toronto. He is the author of *All or Nothing: Systematicity, Transcendental Arguments, and Skepticism in German Idealism* (2005) and articles on post-Kantian and Jewish philosophy; co-editor and co-translator (with Michael L. Morgan) of *Franz Rosenzweig: Philosophical and Theological Writings* (2000); and associate editor of *The International Yearbook of German Idealism*.

Peter Eli Gordon is Professor of History at Harvard University. He is the author of *Rosenzweig and Heidegger: Between Judaism and German Philosophy* (2003) and *Continental Divide: Heidegger, Cassirer, Davos* (forthcoming).

Lawrence J. Kaplan is Professor of Rabbinics and Jewish Philosophy at McGill University. He is the author of numerous articles on medieval and modern Jewish thought; has co-edited, with David Shatz, *Rabbi Abraham Isaac Kook and Jewish Spirituality* (1995); and has translated Rabbi Soloveitchik's monograph *Halakhic Man* from the Hebrew (1983).

Berel Lang is Visiting Professor of Philosophy and Letters at Wesleyan University. He is the author of, among other books, *Act and Idea in the Nazi Genocide* (1990, 2003); *The Anatomy of Philosophical Style* (1990); *Heidegger's Silence* (1996); and *Post-Holocaust: Interpretation, Misinterpretation, and the Claims of History* (2005).

Michael L. Morgan is Chancellor's Professor of Philosophy and Jewish Studies at Indiana University, Bloomington. He is the author of several books, including *Platonic Piety* (1990) and *Beyond Auschwitz* (2001). Together with Paul Franks, he translated and edited *Franz Rosenzweig: Philosophical and Theological Writings* (2000). He edited *Emil Fackenheim: Jewish Philosophers and Jewish Philosophy* (1996) and *Spinoza: Complete Works* (2002). His book, *Discovering Levinas*, will be published in 2007 by Cambridge University Press.

Steven Nadler is Professor of Philosophy and Max and Frieda Weinstein/Bascom Professor of Jewish Studies at the University of Wisconsin-Madison. He is the author of *Spinoza: A Life* (1999); *Spinoza's Heresy: Immortality and the Jewish Mind* (2002); and the forthcoming *Spinoza's Ethics: An Introduction* (Cambridge) and co-editor of *The Cambridge History of Jewish Philosophy: From Antiquity through the Seventeenth Century*. He also co-edits *Oxford Studies in Early Modern Philosophy*.

Andrea Poma is Professor of Moral Philosophy at the University of Turin. He is the author of *The Critical Philosophy of Hermann Cohen* (1997) and *Yearning for Form and Other Essays on Hermann Cohen's Thought* (2006).

Tamar Rudavsky is Professor of Philosophy at Ohio State University. She is the editor of two books: *Divine Omniscience and Omnipotence in Medieval Philosophy: Islamic, Jewish, and Christian Perspectives* (1984) and *Gender and Judaism: Tradition and Transformation* (1995). Her book, *Time Matters: Time and Cosmology in Medieval Jewish Philosophy*, appeared in 2000. With Steven Nadler, she is co-editor of the forthcoming *The Cambridge History of Medieval Jewish Philosophy*.

Kenneth Seeskin is a member of the Philosophy Department at Northwestern University, where he has served as Chair for more than 15 years. His publications in Jewish philosophy include *Jewish Philosophy in a Secular Age* (1990); *Maimonides: A Guide for Today's Perplexed* (1991); *No Other Gods: The Modern Struggle Against Idolatry* (1995); *Searching for a Distant God: The Legacy of Maimonides* (2000); *Autonomy in Jewish Philosophy* (2001); *Maimonides on the Origin of the World* (2005), and more than thirty scholarly articles and book chapters. In 2001, he won the Koret Jewish Book Award for *Searching for a Distant God*, and in 2005, he edited *The Cambridge Companion to Maimonides*.

Steven B. Smith is Alfred Cowles Professor of Political Science and the Master of Branford College at Yale University. Among his recent publications are *Spinoza, Liberalism, and the Question of Jewish Identity* (1997); *Spinoza's Book of Life: Freedom and Redemption in the* Ethics (2003); and most recently, *Reading Leo Strauss: Philosophy, Politics, Judaism* (2006).

Tamra Wright is Director of Academic Studies at the London School of Jewish Studies and a visiting lecturer in the department of Theology and Religious Studies at King's College, London. She is the author of *The Twilight of Jewish Philosophy: Emmanuel Levinas's Ethical Hermeneutics* (1999).

Acknowledgments

It was nearly seven years ago that Andy Beck at Cambridge University Press first proposed the idea of a *Cambridge Companion to Modern Jewish Philosophy*. We are very happy indeed that his foresight and patience have been rewarded with the publication of this volume, and we are especially grateful to him for all he has contributed to it.

The book has been conceived as a work in the history of philosophy, but one that appreciates the contribution that an encounter with significant historical works and themes makes to contemporary philosophical thinking. And since the philosophy in question is modern Jewish philosophy, the figures and themes explored are taken to be ones that contribute to contemporary Jewish philosophical thought.

Modern Jewish philosophy, as we understand it, is a phenomenon of the seventeenth century to the late twentieth century. It incorporates many more figures and works than could be easily discussed in a single collection of essays, and it addresses a vast array of concepts and issues. Hence, in designing the book, we have had to be selective. It has nonetheless always been our hope that the various essays, some devoted to major figures and others to central themes, cover sufficient terrain to acquaint the reader with the major features of the field.

Anthologies are by nature the product of compromise and collective effort. The essays collected in this volume were written by some of the most accomplished scholars from around the world – from Europe, Israel, and North America – whose work has helped to transform our understanding of modern Jewish philosophy. And they are a diverse group, distinguished one from the other not only by their interests and choices of emphasis but also by their very style of thought and their conception of what Jewish philosophy signifies. Bringing so wide a range of scholars under a single roof has been an exhilarating but by no means simple task. As editors, we have tried to be ecumenical even while the very selection of essays and themes inevitably imposes a certain perspective. Yet we have tried most often to let the essays speak for themselves, and in every case, the results have been far better than had we striven for greater uniformity in vision. It is therefore fitting we begin these acknowledgments by expressing our sincere gratitude to the contributors themselves.

An editorial partnership is itself an act of compromise. The two of us came to this project with different training and our own, unique visions of what a companion to modern Jewish philosophy should look like. No doubt there may have been points about which we disagreed. But from the very start, we found the process of editorial responsibility an enjoyable one. The burdens thereof were lightened considerably by the fact that they were shared. In effect, the two of us became a reading group devoted to the study of modern Jewish philosophy via a scrupulous joint examination of the texts that make up this book; we became conversation partners and indeed friends, a benefit of our collaboration that means a great deal to us both.

Each of us must acknowledge his debts to those who have helped to see this book to completion. What follows are individual statements.

Michael Morgan: For thirty-two years, I have taught modern Jewish philosophy, among my teaching responsibilities, at Indiana University in Bloomington. This volume is a testimony to the hundreds of students who have studied with me and from whom I have learned. It is also a testimony to my wonderful colleagues throughout the university and to the friends of a lifetime that have made my years in Bloomington so rewarding. My thanks to my colleagues, my friends, and to the university are certainly beyond measure.

My life in Jewish philosophy began when I was an undergraduate, but my love for it really first flourished when I was in rabbinical school and then in graduate school. There are teachers and friends who meant a great deal to me then and continue to do so to this day – Sheldon Zimmerman, Michael Cook, Eugene Borowitz, Arnold Wolf, Norbert Samuelson, Michael Stroh, and Kenneth Seeskin. Most of all, as this volume is brought to a conclusion, I think of two people – scholars, friends, and teachers – who have passed away: Emil Fackenheim was my teacher, my friend, and my mentor for nearly forty years; Sam Westfall was my colleague and friend at Indiana for three decades. Both Emil and Sam have always represented for me the ideal combination of scholarship and humanity to which those of us who live both in the university and in the world ought to aspire. Finally, there is no modern Jewish philosophy without modern Jewish life, and mine is so intertwined with my wife Audrey's that they are virtually one.

Peter E. Gordon: For me, the most fascinating features of Jewish philosophy are those that emerge at its many points of contact with the broader tradition of philosophy as such. In matters intellectual, as in so much of life, creativity and human flourishing come about more readily through symbiosis than purification. This may explain why my first published essay (originally written in a seminar for the late Amos Funkenstein) explored some questions in the epistemology of Maimonides, that paragon of intellectual fusion whose thinking represents a potent combination of Judaism, Islam, and the Hellenistic tradition. The crossing of intellectual and disciplinary boundaries has remained a watchword of my own scholarship ever since.

I would like to thank Harvard University for granting me the year's leave during which I could devote myself without interruption to this project. I must also thank my many friends and colleagues at Harvard for making an otherwise forbidding institution into a permanent home. For their ongoing guidance and conversation relevant to this project, I owe a special thanks to the following: Martin Jay, Hilary Putnam, Leora Batnitzky, Warren Breckman, David Biale, Nina Caputo, Hubert Dreyfus, Mitchell Hart, Mark Lilla, Samuel Moyn, Jerrold Seigel, Tommie Shelby, Eugene Sheppard, Dana Villa, and Steven Wasserstrom. Most of all, I would like to thank my wife, Ludmila, for her unsparing support and equally unsparing intellectual criticism.

Finally I would like to recall the memory of my father, whose death after a long and difficult illness coincided with the beginning phase of my academic leave. The year of editing was also a year of mourning. Yet the combination seems somehow apt: My father, a scientist, who as a young man had abandoned orthodoxy for the study of nature, was a scholar of the most humane temperament. It was from him that I learned to appreciate the virtue of dedication to one's profession. He remains a powerful presence in my memory.

We also thank Faith Black at Cambridge University Press, for her consummate dedication and assistance with numerous logistical tasks at the Press; research assistant Nick Alford, for his skillful work on the index; and Ronald Cohen, who edited the manuscript most professionally and with respect for our contributors' work.

Chronology

1492	Expulsion of the Jews from Spain.
1632	Birth of Baruch (Benedict de) Spinoza, Amsterdam, Dutch Republic.
1656	*Cherem* (excommunication) of Spinoza from Amsterdam Jewish community.
1665–66	Sabbatian Heresy.
1670	Anonymous publication of Spinoza's *Tractatus Theologico-Politicus*.
1776	Declaration of Independence and founding of the United States of America. Formal equality of religion for all citizens guaranteed by the U.S. Constitution.
1781	Immanuel Kant, *Kritik der reinen Vernunft* (Critique of Pure Reason), first edition; second edition published in 1787.
1782	Joseph II issues the *Edict of Tolerance*, a step toward Jewish emancipation in Austrian territory.
1783	Moses Mendelssohn, *Jerusalem: Or on Religious Power and Judaism*.
1790	Sephardic Jews in France granted civil rights; applied to Ashkenazim the following year.
1792	Anonymous publication of August Friedrich Cranz's *Search for Light and Right: An Epistle to Moses Mendelssohn*.
1807	G. W. F. Hegel, *The Phenomenology of Spirit*.
1808	Birth of Samson Raphael Hirsch, Hamburg, Germany.
1819	Founding of the Society for the Culture and Science of Jewry (*Verein für Kultur und Wissenschaft der Juden*), by Joseph Hilmar, Isaac Levin Auerbach, Isaac Marcus Jost, Eduard Gans, Moses Moser, and Leopold Zunz.

1822	Immanuel Wolf, "On the Concept of a Science of Judaism," a programmatic essay laying out the basic principles of the "Science of Judaism," published in the inaugural issue of the *Zeitschrift für die Wissenschaft des Judentums*, volume 1, number 1.
1835	Pale of Settlement established by Tsar Nicholas I, demarcating boundaries of Jewish residence in specified areas of Eastern Europe from the Baltic to the Black Sea.
1836	Samson Raphael Hirsch, in *Nineteen Letters on Judaism*, establishes the theoretical foundations for "neo-Orthodox" Judaism.
1842	Birth of Hermann Cohen in Coswig (Anhalt), Germany.
1843	Søren Kierkegaard, *Fear and Trembling*.
1844	Karl Marx (1818–83), *Zur Judenfrage* (On the Jewish Question).
1862	Moses Hess (1812–75), *Rome and Jerusalem*.
1871	Hermann Cohen, *Kants Theorie der Erfahrung* (Kant's Theory of Experience).
1872	Friedrich Nietzsche, *The Birth of Tragedy out of the Spirit of Music*.
1878	Birth of Martin (Mordechai) Buber, Vienna, Austria-Hungary.
1880	Hermann Cohen publishes *"Ein Bekenntnis in der Judenfrage"* in response to anti-Semitic provocation by German-nationalist historian Heinrich von Treitschke.
1881	First wave of pogroms against Eastern European Jews breaks out in the Ukraine, followed by others through 1884; a second wave begins in 1903 in Kishinev, lasting until 1906; a third follows, 1917–21.
1886	Birth of Franz Rosenzweig, Kassel, Germany.
1892	Birth of Walter Benjamin, Berlin, Germany.
1896	Theodor Herzl, *Der Judenstaat* (The Jewish State), Vienna.
1897	Meeting of the First Zionist Congress convened by Theodor Herzl in Basel, Switzerland, declares the aim of Zionism "to create for the Jewish people a home in Palestine secured by public law."
1897	Birth of Gershom Scholem, Berlin, Germany.
1899	Birth of Leo Strauss, Kirchhain (Hesse), Germany.

1904	Hermann Cohen, *Ethik des reinen Willens* (Ethics of Pure Will).
1906	Birth of Hannah Arendt, Hanover, Germany.
1906	Birth of Emmanuel Levinas, Kovno, Lithuania.
1906	Martin Buber, *Die Geschichten des Rabbi Nachman* (The Tales of Rabbi Nachman; English, 1956).
1907	Henri Bergson, *L'evolution créatrice* (Creative Evolution).
1908	Martin Buber, *Die Legende des Baalschem* (The Legend of the Baal Shem; English, 1955).
1911	Martin Buber, *Drei Reden über das Judentum* (Three Speeches on Judaism).
1914–18	World War I.
1916	Birth of Emil Fackenheim, Halle, Germany.
1917	Bolshevik Revolution in Russia.
1918	Official declaration of the Weimar Republic in Germany, November 9. Death of Hermann Cohen.
	Ernst Bloch, *The Spirit of Utopia*, first edition.
1919	Hermann Cohen, *Religion der Vernunft aus den Quellen des Judentums* (Religion of Reason out of the Sources of Judaism), posthumous.
1921	Franz Rosenzweig, *Der Stern der Erlösung* (The Star of Redemption).
1923	Martin Buber, *Ich und Du* (I and Thou; English, 1937).
1925	Franz Rosenzweig, *"The New Thinking."*
1927	Martin Heidegger, *Being and Time.*
1929	Death of Franz Rosenzweig.
1930	Sigmund Freud, *Civilization and Its Discontents.*
1930	Leo Strauss, *Spinoza's Critique of Religion* (German; English edition with Preface, 1962).
1930	Birth of Jacques (Jackie) Derrida, in El-Bair, Algeria.
1930	Theodor Lessing (1872–1933), *Der Jüdische Selbsthaß* (Jewish Self-Hatred).
1933	End of the Weimar Republic; beginning of Nazi dictatorship in Germany.
1935	Leo Strauss, *Philosophie und Gesetz* (Philosophy and Law).
1937	Lev Shestov, *Athens and Jerusalem.*

1939	Sigmund Freud, *Moses and Monotheism.*
1939	World War II begins.
1940	Suicide of Walter Benjamin during his flight from France through the Pyrenees.
1941	Leo Strauss, "Persecution and the Art of Writing."
1941	Gershom Scholem, *Major Trends in Jewish Mysticism.*
1942	Nazi Germany launches the "Final Solution," leading to the murder of six million Jews throughout Europe.
1945	World War II ends.
1947	Emmanuel Levinas, *Le temps et l'autre* (Time and the Other).
1948	Declaration of Independence of the State of Israel.
1951	Theodor W. Adorno, *Minima Moralia* (composition begun during WWII).
1958	Hannah Arendt, *Rahel Varnhagen: The Life of a Jewish Woman* (first draft, 1933).
1958	Hannah Arendt, *The Human Condition.*
1961	Emmanuel Levinas, *Totalité et l'infini* (Totality and Infinity).
1963	Hannah Arendt, *Eichmann in Jerusalem.*
1963	Emmanuel Levinas, *Difficile liberté: Essais sur le judaïsme* (Difficult Freedom: Essays on Judaism).
1965	Leo Strauss, *Natural Right and History.*
1968	Emmanuel Levinas, *Quatre lectures talmudiques* (Four Talmudic Readings).
1973	Death of Leo Strauss.
1973	Gershom Scholem, *Sabbatai Zevi, the Mystical Messiah.*
1974	Emmanuel Levinas, *Autrement qu'être ou au-delà de l'essence* (Otherwise than Being, or, Beyond Essence).
1975	Death of Hannah Arendt.
1982	Death of Gershom Scholem.
1982	Emil Fackenheim, *To Mend the World.*
1983	Susannah Heschel, *On Being a Jewish Feminist.*
1995	Death of Emmanuel Levinas.
2003	Death of Emil Fackenheim.
2004	Death of Jacques Derrida.

MODERN JEWISH PHILOSOPHY

1 Introduction: Modern Jewish Philosophy, Modern Philosophy, and Modern Judaism

MICHAEL L. MORGAN AND PETER ELI GORDON

What is modern Jewish philosophy, and is there such a thing at all? If there is, what makes it modern? What makes it Jewish? And what makes it philosophy? Indeed, who asks such a question and for what reason? Do such questions convey a challenge to the very existence of a species of philosophy that is genuinely Jewish and modern as well? Do they call upon one to respond, perhaps in order to be an advocate on behalf of modern Jewish philosophy and to defend it against its detractors? These questions are puzzling. While they may seem simple in content and easily dispatched, even a moment's scrutiny will expose how difficult they are to answer, and even to understand.

A skeptic might argue that there is no such thing as Jewish philosophy. For philosophy (our bold interlocutor might explain) is the pursuit of universal questions. And the methods we use when posing such questions can display no particular identities and can be bound by no particular commitments other than the devotion to philosophy itself. Julius Guttmann, one of the twentieth century's greatest scholars on this debate, accordingly entitled his 1933 survey *The Philosophy of Judaism* (*Die Philosophie des Judentums*). The title seems to have implied that notwithstanding the particular object in view, the method remained nonetheless universal and purely rational: a philosophy *of* Judaism, but not a *Jewish philosophy*. So our imaginary skeptic may well have a point. If philosophy is simply a human impulse, then "Jewish philosophy" would have to be understood as the application of a general philosophical approach to specific themes (Judaism, Jewish existence, and so forth). But matters are hardly that straightforward. The impulse to approach matters in a philosophical fashion does not arise at all times and in all places. It is a defamiliarizing impulse, an attitude of wonder (in Greek, *thaumazein*) at things normally taken for granted. More recently, in the analytic tradition, philosophy has been understood as the application of logic, or an analysis of ordinary language, to conceptual muddles. Wittgenstein likened it to a therapeutic cure: "showing the fly the way out of the fly-bottle." The image suggests a dislocation or dissolution of conventional error. Philosophy therefore arises most of all, perhaps, when tacitly shared commitments are in some fashion challenged or are cast in an unfamiliar light, such that they seem to require explicit and vigorous justification if they are not to be abandoned.

This notion may help to explain why Jewish philosophy is not timeless but seems on the contrary to be a characteristically *modern* pursuit. To be sure, there were Jewish philosophers as early as Philo of Alexandria. And Maimonides (arguably the greatest Jewish philosopher of them all), whose works synthesize Judaism with Islamic and Hellenistic sources, made his home in Old Cairo in the twelfth century. Jewish philosophy would therefore appear to be as old as the Jewish confrontation with Greece. But in the pre-modern world, the shared understandings that comprised the intellectual background of Jewish life remained largely intact, its changes more or less confined to the normative processes of interpretation (*midrash*) and innovation (*chidush*) under the careful guidance of the rabbinical establishment. It was only with the expulsion from Spain and the ensuing dislocations of the Jewish community throughout the sixteenth and seventeenth centuries that the deeper edifice of Judaism was exposed entirely to scientific and philosophical scrutiny. From that point on, Jewish life could no longer rest comfortably upon a taken-for-granted foundation of shared belief. With accelerating frequency, various challenges arose in a seemingly inexhaustible supply to cast that foundation in doubt: scientific naturalism, the Enlightenment, assimilation, secularism, socialism, and nationalism – all of these accompanied by rising waves of conflict and diversified modes of Jewish response. To be sure, there has always been diversity within the Jewish world. Since its inception, perhaps, Judaism has grown accustomed to frequent challenges, both internal and external. It has not only adapted but also grown stronger because of them. But perhaps the most distinctive feature of Jewish modernity is that such dislocations now seem to be less the exception than the norm. Jewish philosophy – *if*, indeed, it *is* a sign of dislocation – now seems an inescapable feature of the modern Jewish condition.

It has been said that the problem of Judaism and modern philosophy is one dimension of the more general dilemma of "Athens and Jerusalem," or (to invoke a different couplet), "Hellenism and Hebraism." Jewish thinkers such as Leo Strauss, Emmanuel Levinas, and Emil Fackenheim took this relationship to be deep and important, not only for Judaism but indeed for all of Western civilization and culture.[1] Levinas, for example, claimed that the Jewish tradition contained a key insight regarding the fundamentally ethical character of social existence. This insight, however, had been obscured by Greco-Western civilization and needed to be discovered anew. Levinas therefore believed that philosophy and Jewish philosophy were not ultimately distinct enterprises. Rather, traditional philosophy was part of a world that needed to recall its roots, and in this regard, Western philosophy and Jewish philosophy did not differ at the core. All philosophy needed to be refashioned to see its way to a new understanding of human existence and its ethical foundations; all philosophy needed a new first philosophy. But such a view is only one strand in the variegated and complex web that is modern Jewish philosophy. What indeed is the larger pattern of that web?

Suppose we begin with the question that might seem easiest: is there such a thing as modern Jewish philosophy? The simplest response might be to say, "of course there is." And we would then proceed to list figures who appear to fit that categorization – Baruch Spinoza, Moses Mendelssohn, Nachman Krochmal, Samson Raphael Hirsch, Ludwig Steinheim, Hermann Cohen, Martin Buber, Franz Rosenzweig, Julius Guttmann, Samuel Hugo Bergmann, Nathan Rotenstreich, Emil Fackenheim, Emmanuel Levinas, and Horace Kallen. Yet this proposal would immediately generate several demurrals. First of all, the list seems at once too long and too short. It is too long because it includes some who are students of Jewish philosophy but not really Jewish philosophers, and at least one who is neither, but rather a Jew who was also a philosopher. It is too short because it leaves out so many figures of great importance, among them Moses Hess, Isaac Breuer, Moses Maimon, Mordecai Kaplan, Abraham Joshua Heschel, Leo Baeck, Joseph Soloveitchik, Lou Silberman, Bernard Martin, Marvin Fox, Michael Wyschogrod, Louis Jacobs, Steven Schwarzschild, Jacques Derrida, David Hartmann, Eugene Borowitz, and even Gershom Scholem and Walter Benjamin. But one might interrupt: did not the question ask specifically about philosophy and hence for *philosophers*? Surely, many of these figures are not that: Buber, Kaplan, Heschel, Baeck, and Soloveitchik, for example. And if the question were about Jewish philosophers, we must admit that not all of those named merit that title, if to be a Jewish philosopher means to be someone who wrote *philosophical* works specifically addressed to Judaism or Jewish matters. Must we therefore dismiss Buber, Kaplan, Heschel, Baeck, Soloveitchik, Scholem, and Benjamin? If so, our list would have to be considerably reduced indeed.

Constructing such a list is no easy task. Is this to ask what *criterion* to use in selecting who should be on it and who should not? But that means one would need to ask what makes modern Jewish philosophy what it is – modern, Jewish, and philosophical. In order to determine whether there is and has been such a thing as modern Jewish philosophy, perhaps we cannot avoid asking what it is. But even if we felt driven to provide a criterion, where, indeed, would one find it?

As we have suggested, *modern philosophy in general* comes into being with the fitful emergence of the modern-scientific perspective over the course of the seventeenth and eighteenth centuries and the challenge this perspective posed to traditional modes of thought – scientific, philosophical, moral, political, and religious. In terms of influence and importance, the thought of René Descartes marks a, if not *the*, turning point for modern philosophy. A host of others soon followed, either to resist him or to radicalize his claims: Arnauld, Gassendi, Hobbes, Spinoza, Leibniz, and beyond. Jewish philosophy itself long predates the seventeenth century and the rise of modern natural science. But *modern* Jewish philosophy, if it is to be called "modern" in the sense intended here, must surely have something to do with this same confrontation between the new science and traditional habits of Jewish thought.

But what would make such thinking "Jewish" in the relevant sense? What would make it not just philosophy written by Jews but Jewish in character? One suggestion is that to be Jewish it must address Jewish beliefs and concerns; it must be or be part of an attempt to articulate the nature of Jewish doctrine or existence in some way. What would make it Jewish, that is, would be its subject matter: Modern Jewish philosophy would be one kind of effort to say what Judaism is. But need it be the case that such an effort be guided primarily or exclusively toward that goal? What if it were aimed in another direction, if its goals were otherwise, and yet along the way it said interesting or valuable or significant things about Judaism and the Jewish way of life? Would this be sufficient to make such an effort an episode in modern Jewish philosophy? If it were not, then the justification for including someone like Spinoza, for example, would be weak indeed, as would the justification for including Strauss or Levinas or Derrida or Benjamin. Surely, it would require some energy and cleverness to argue that their work, even in part, was *primarily* and *intentionally* aimed at articulating the meaning of Jewish existence. It would be sufficient, then, if the work or figure in question contributed in some interesting and fruitful way to the enterprise of articulating the meaning of Jewish existence, even if it were not aimed at that goal and if the philosopher were not primarily engaged in such a project. But clearly the philosopher's work should touch on provocative and important issues on Jewish matters, and do so in a philosophical way.

With such considerations in mind, we have felt it best to adopt here what might be called a "hermeneutic" or "pragmatic" criterion of modern Jewish philosophy. The latter does not have to meet formal or substantive standards set in advance of its occurrence. It simply must involve a result that is gotten through a broadly construed process of interpretation. Modern Jewish philosophy has been, and continues to be, whatever is the outcome of a multifaceted engagement between, on the one hand, thinking about issues relevant to understanding the Jewish condition or the meaning of Judaism and Jewish life, and, on the other hand, philosophical thinking that is indebted to and responds to the tradition of modern Western philosophy and, perhaps, to the entire tradition of Western philosophy as it has been appropriated and modified in the modern period. Such a definition of Jewish philosophy has several noteworthy marks. First, it is *interpretative,* in the sense that the major exponents of modern Jewish philosophy *have come to be understood as Jewish philosophers* by virtue of an ongoing process of conversation and critique that has developed over time and continues even today to generate its own criteria of inclusion, sometimes, in fact, revising past criteria as well. Second, such a Jewish philosophy is *episodic.* Certain figures contributed to modern Jewish philosophy a vast corpus of work, systematic treatises, and so forth. Others left us only essays, suggestions, or fragments. A thinker such as Gershom Scholem, although he conceived himself as a historian rather than a philosopher, nonetheless made an important contribution to modern Jewish philosophy by means of his historical investigations as well as his occasional reflections on Jewish doctrine. Someone like Franz Rosenzweig, however, is a modern Jewish philosopher in the strong sense, since his major works are richly and self-consciously philosophical and set out to clarify recognizably philosophical questions about Jewish existence.

Characterizing modern Jewish philosophy this way would seem to imply a further assumption: that modern Jewish philosophy, like all Jewish philosophy (indeed, like all philosophy), is a historically changing phenomenon, variable rather than eternal in its marks. How it proceeds methodologically and what topics it explores depend upon the historical context in which it occurs. And such a historical context is itself contingent upon various cultural features and compelling habits of thought, as well as social problems and political events. Modern Jewish philosophy is not the same in all respects as earlier, ancient, or medieval Jewish philosophy. Nor should we expect it to be uniform or self-identical through time and space. What such a philosophy meant for Spinoza or for Mendelssohn is hardly what it was for Rosenzweig or Benjamin,

Fackenheim or Soloveitchik. Such historicity is indeed a common feature of philosophy itself in the West: much of Western philosophy either assumes a historically conditioned notion of what philosophy is or it raises the very question of the nature of philosophy as a contested issue that can only be answered in reference to the values of its time. As Hegel observed, philosophy is its own age reflected in thought. So, too, in the Jewish sphere, the question of what counts as Jewish philosophy and what methods or topics it should embrace has changed with the changes history has brought. Finally, we should note that viewing modern Jewish philosophy in such a historical fashion seems to be a special characteristic of our own situation at the beginning of the twenty-first century. We live in an age when much of our philosophical efforts seem stamped by that panoply of approaches we call "post-foundationalist" or even "post-modern." Whether we welcome such labels or despair of their influence, the hermeneutical and interpretive character of human life is indisputably a touchstone of philosophy – and Jewish philosophy – in our time.

It may not be that all the contributors to this volume would accept this way of defining its boundaries. Individual chapters may imply different and even contrary assumptions concerning both the character of modern Jewish philosophy and the proper manner in which it is to be pursued. But in creating this volume, our approach has been guided by certain basic criteria, as we indicate next.

One such criterion is that modern Jewish philosophy reflect the crisis of scientific naturalism. A central challenge of the new scientific thinking in the seventeenth century was that it introduced the possibility of conceiving human life in an exclusively naturalistic fashion – that is, one that left no obvious room for a non-naturalistic conception of value or for a commitment to a realm other than that of material nature. One of the most distinctive features of modern Jewish philosophy is that it attempts to make Jewish normative commitments intelligible even while it pays explicit acknowledgment to the quintessentially modern vision of scientific naturalism. For some Jewish philosophers, the new naturalism seemed to call into question the trans-historical validity of Judaism itself. Spinoza, to take only the most obvious example, was ready to embrace philosophical naturalism seemingly without qualification. He concluded that Judaism itself was nothing more than a historical-political order specific to the Ancient Near East and no longer binding upon its members. And even the God of the Jews was in Spinoza's eyes susceptible to naturalistic reduction. God was no longer an artificer and legislator standing beyond nature; God was instead identical with nature itself: *Deus sive Natura*. Spinoza's major work, the *Ethics*, lays down its claims against a background of traditional Jewish themes, which it then rejects or modifies. And Spinoza's *Theological-Political Treatise* speaks directly about central Jewish issues – from prophecy and miracles to chosenness and the ritual law – all of which are cast in an unfamiliar and naturalistic light. From his own day to ours, Spinoza's philosophical proximity to Judaism has remained a topic of heated dispute. Some reject his ideas altogether, while others find much in his philosophy that continues to appeal.[2] It therefore seems appropriate that our collection begins with Steven Nadler's contribution to the ongoing discussion as to whether Spinoza is a Jewish philosopher.

In the late eighteenth and nineteenth centuries, Jewish belief was brought into increased contact with the central tenets of the Enlightenment – freedom, rationality, and the principled dissociation between reason and faith. Shortly thereafter, Jewish philosophy found new sources of inspiration in the movements of German Romanticism and German Idealism. How well it negotiated this encounter is the subject of several chapters in this volume. Alan Arkush provides a critique of Mendelssohn's attempt to join Judaism and political liberalism. Kenneth Seeskin discusses the post-Kantian confrontation between autonomy and traditional authority. And Paul Franks explores key Platonic themes in Kantian philosophy and their later resonance in the writings of figures such as Solomon Maimon, Nachman Krochmal, and Isaac Breuer.

It is worth noting that much of modern Jewish philosophy from Mendelssohn through World War II is located in German-speaking culture. Although the German-Jewish relationship has been widely hailed and roundly attacked, its philosophical achievements should not be forgotten. These chapters explore the German-Jewish encounter at a time when the credentials and character of philosophy was changing in intriguing ways, from the formal rationalism of the Leibnizian-Wolffian tradition, through the enormous novelty of Kant's transcendental, critical philosophy, and onward through Romanticism to the grandly systematic philosophies of German idealism in all its forms. The three chapters mentioned mark distinctive moments in this troubled but richly productive encounter.

In the first part of the nineteenth century, modern philosophy as it was being practiced in Germany underwent a series of dramatic transformations, thanks to the chorus of philosophers who arose in rebellion against German Idealism, such as Feuerbach and Marx, Schelling and Kierkegaard. By the last third of the nineteenth century, this diverse group had further fragmented into a host of competing philosophical movements. Neo-Kantianism, one of the foremost trends in academic philosophy, was represented in one of its most characteristic forms at the University of Marburg by Hermann Cohen (the first Jew to hold a full professorship at a German University).[3] Elsewhere in both Germany and France, philosophers such as Wilhelm Dilthey and Henri Bergson developed new theories of human temporality and historicity – popularized as "life-philosophy," "Weltanschauungs-philosophy," and "vitalism." Such theories found a ready audience in a younger generation that was already drawing various and often contradictory lessons from both the Christian existentialism of Dostoyevsky and the corrosive atheism of Friedrich Nietzsche. By the time of World War I, such currents were supplemented by more popular movements such as neo-romantic socialism and socialist Zionism and, in academic philosophy, by new bids for philosophical rigor such as phenomenology, as developed by Edmund Husserl (himself a baptized German Jew).

Here, too, Jewish thinkers sought to understand Judaism in the context of this new intellectual ferment and at a time when urban life was dramatically transformed and people in the cities of Europe were facing new cultural and social crises.[4] It was during this period, from the turn of the century through the Weimar Republic and the rise of Nazism, that Judaism itself faced a new and rapidly changing modernity. In this history, Martin Buber is a central figure at nearly every stage in his long career, from the period of his youthful engagement with Zionism through his recovery of Hasidic texts and profound interest in mysticism in Judaism and throughout world cultures, to the formulation of his dialogical philosophy and his study and translation of the Hebrew Bible. In her wide-ranging chapter on Buber's thought, Tamra Wright demonstrates the integrity of these various strands.

Between World War I and the end of the Weimar Republic, another figure of critical importance for modern Jewish philosophy was Franz Rosenzweig, whose existential vision of Jewish life continues both to inspire and perplex even today. Peter Gordon, in his chapter on Rosenzweig, pays special attention to the nuances and tensions of Rosenzweig's major philosophical system, *The Star of Redemption*. Rosenzweig was only one philosopher within the manifold movement of German-Jewish thought that came to prominence in the 1920s. Another was Leo Strauss, whose influential (and, to some, controversial) political philosophy and unique interpretation of the Jewish tradition are explored in the present volume in the chapter by Steven Smith. Also of central importance for modern Jewish philosophy was the historian of Jewish mysticism, Gershom Scholem, whose historical reflections on the Kabbalah and Jewish messianism left a demonstrable imprint upon the philosophical writings of his friend, Walter Benjamin. In his wide-ranging chapter on the significance of modern Jewish messianism, Pierre Bouretz attempts to distinguish two different kinds of messianism in the writings of Strauss, Rosenzweig, Benjamin, Cohen, and Ernst Bloch.

In the years just prior to World War II, and even in the period that immediately followed, Jewish philosophy in Israel remained largely in the hands of historians. Meanwhile, in North America, the native Jewish thought of Mordecai Kaplan, a blending of sociology and pragmatism and a form of religious naturalism, took root just as America was undergoing the kind of urbanization and secularization that had characterized Europe a half-century before. But at the same time, many immigrant Jewish philosophers and young Jewish intellectuals in the New World were beginning to appropriate the existential philosophy then fashionable in North American intellectual culture for their own purposes. This existentialism had been originally developed in both Weimar Germany and in France by such thinkers as Martin Heidegger, Jean-Paul Sartre, and Albert Camus. In Christian circles, young readers also looked back for inspiration to Karl Barth, Rudolph Bultmann, and Paul Tillich. In the 1950s and 1960s in America, the outcome of this "importation" of French and German existentialism was an interdenominational movement of Jewish theologians, some of them philosophers, whose approach to Judaism was grounded in the historicity and situational rootedness of human existence. Amongst them were Michael Wyschogrod, Lou Silberman, Bernard Martin, and Emil Fackenheim. And there were others, more theological than philosophical, who should be mentioned in association with these developments: Will Herberg, Abraham Joshua Heschel, and Eugene Borowitz. In these early post-war years, alongside naturalist Jewish philosophy and its existential opponents, there were also traditional Jewish philosophers such as Marvin Fox, and traditional Halakhic thinkers such as Joseph Soloveitchik. In his chapter on Soloveitchik for this volume, Lawrence Kaplan clarifies Soloveitchik's significant philosophical debts to both Marburg Neo-Kantianism and to Platonism.

Until the mid- to late 1960s, the shadow of the Nazi death camps was an ever-present but virtually unacknowledged background to Jewish life and belief in Europe, Israel, and North America. But when our attention at last turned to confront that shadow with greater intellectual precision, amongst those who did so were a number of Jewish philosophers. Hannah Arendt was one such philosopher (although she always abjured the title of "philosopher," preferring instead "political theorist"). Indeed,

Arendt was probably the earliest. Her comments on Judaism reflect her complex relation to Zionism, while her probing (if sometimes controversial) reflections on Nazism, the death camps, and the origins of totalitarianism also had roots in political philosophy and existentialism, and continue to be of singular importance for Jewish philosophy today. But the Holocaust also raises a host of more general and strictly philosophical questions about the meaning of Jewish suffering and the significance of evil as such: how can one reconcile the notion of a benevolent God with the experience of unqualified cruelty? Is not God as conceived by Judaism a God of history, and if so, how can we still confirm God's presence in history given the dismal historical record of our own modern era? Does the traditional Jewish explanation for evil still hold true, or must it be revised in light of the Holocaust? Such issues are discussed most fully in Berel Lang's chapter on the role of evil and suffering in modern Jewish philosophy. Related themes were addressed by traditionalist thinkers such as Eliezer Berkovits. But it was undoubtedly Emil Fackenheim who first attempted to raise such questions to a truly philosophical plane. In his chapter on Fackenheim, Michael Morgan discusses Fackenheim's life-long encounter with the Holocaust from the early post-war years through the publication of *To Mend the World* in 1982.

At least two themes in late twentieth-century intellectual culture have forced Judaism to the center of attention of many intellectuals, both European and American. One theme is that of the "Other," a term signifying a person or collective defined by their exclusion from the social whole. Many historians and political theorists have claimed that the Jew has functioned as the traditional paradigm of the Other in the West; this has been the case since the rise of Christianity in antiquity, when the Church defined itself at least in part in opposition to Judaism and Jews.[5] A second and related theme is the special role that the Holocaust and Nazism have come to play as signifying the end of modernity and the so-called end of philosophy as conventionally understood. When one considers these two themes in concert, one can better understand why the image of the Jew-as-excluded-Other has come in philosophical discussion to occupy a fascinating (and, paradoxically, central) position as the primary signifier for alterity, or otherness as such. Such categories – difference, otherness, exclusion – have been especially important for two of the most prominent philosophers of post-war Europe: Jacques Derrida and Emmanuel Levinas. Both were French Jews, although they hailed from different cultures – Derrida was born in Algeria, Levinas in Lithuania. And both of them, albeit in distinctive ways, made creative use of European intellectual traditions in both phenomenology and the philosophy of language. In his chapter on Levinas, Richard Cohen helps us to understand how Levinas's thought represents a special reinterpretation of Jewish monotheism. And in her wide-ranging chapter on language and interpretation, Leora Batnitzky calls attention to the special role that language plays in Derrida's thought.

Yet, notwithstanding the philosophical merits of Jewish difference, we must also admit that one of the most pervasive features of the modern Jewish condition is the simple fact of inclusion. The ideals of the Enlightenment eventually led to civic emancipation, and however ferocious the opposition, the basic provision for civic equality between Jews and non-Jews would now appear to be largely uncontroversial, and in any case inalterable. To an extraordinary degree, modern Jews today now participate (or, at least, are legally and culturally permitted to participate) in the full range of social and intellectual life in the West. This in itself is a fact to be celebrated. But the experience of inclusion has also raised a great number of philosophical questions as to how best to reconcile the singular commitments of Jewish life with the moral-political requirements of universal inclusion: does modernity require Jews to surrender their particularism entirely? Or does there remain the possibility of a more subtle dialectic between universalism and particularism? Philosophers have attempted to negotiate such a dialectic with varying degrees of success. Indeed, Judaism's entry into the modern world is so pervasive a feature of modern Jewish history that one might well argue that the continued tension *between* universalism and particularism is at the heart of all responsible modern Jewish thinking. In his chapter on Moses Mendelssohn, Alan Arkush explains why Mendelssohn's struggle with political liberalism was ultimately unsuccessful. And, in his essay on Hermann Cohen, Andrea Poma examines Cohen's philosophical and political efforts to achieve a reconciliation between Kantian universalism and Jewish distinctiveness.

Zionist aspirations unleashed a great number of intellectual reflections, some of which, such as Hess's *Rome and Jerusalem*, are strongly philosophical in character. But perhaps more importantly, the growth of Zionism as a cultural and political movement among Jews made demands upon Jewish philosophers to come to grips with Judaism's historical and political nature, its conception of messianism, the nature of the relationship between Judaism and the State of Israel, and, indeed, broader questions concerning the very existence of both a Jewish state and Jewish life in the Diaspora. From Buber to Heschel, from Fackenheim to Yeshayahu Leibowitz, Jewish philosophical thinkers have felt moved, if not compelled, to respond to these matters. One might argue that reflections on Israel took on a different sense of urgency and a different content after the Six-Day War and the linkage, in popular Jewish consciousness and imagination, of the rise and defense of the Jewish state with the Holocaust and the destruction of European Jewry. The prominence of Israel in public life after that war, through the 1970s and into the 1980s, made it somehow imperative for Jewish philosophers to come to grips with the state and its meaning for Judaism, both as a historical reality and as an element in Jewish conceptual self-understanding.

Discussion about the roles of women in Judaism has only recently become a central feature of Jewish philosophy. It no doubt drew considerable inspiration from the sophisticated streams of feminist theory that emerged in the wake of the civil rights movement, the New Left, and the ethnicity- and identity-politics of the United States since the late 1960s. The increased sensitivity to issues of gender and general issues concerning human sexuality and the body has had a tremendous impact on both Jewish social experience and Jewish intellectual life as well. Most decisive of all was the impact of Simone de Beauvoir's landmark treatise on feminist theory, *The Second Sex* (1949), which forever dissolved the myth that male experience can be identified with the universal. So, too, much of twentieth-century philosophy has evinced a new seriousness about the gendered or embodied character of human existence. Philosophers such as Heidegger and, even more so, Merleau-Ponty have alerted us to the primacy of existential and affective factors in the constitution of experience. Merleau-Ponty was especially attentive to the role of the body in human perception. Anglo-American philosophy, by contrast, has seemed predominantly rationalist. But we would do well to recall that even philosophers such as Spinoza, Hume, Hutcheson, and the Romantics thought with great nuance about human psychology and its moral implications. Similarly, while modern Jewish philosophy has had its rationalist side, it has also demonstrated a deep appreciation for non-rational features of Jewish life. Yet a pronounced sensitivity to diversity and embodiment has become a central and perhaps even a defining feature of recent feminist work within the orbit of Judaism. In her wide-ranging chapter on Jewish feminist philosophy, Tamar Rudavsky sets out the philosophical dimensions of this discussion and takes special note of its embeddedness in recent social and historical developments within the Jewish world.

Modern Jewish philosophy has not come to an end. But its historical development has perhaps come to a point when reviewing that history and its most significant characteristics might prove to be a rewarding task. Today there are new and emerging ways of understanding the demands of Jewish life and thought that break with some traditions of the past, only to cling to others. Modern Jewish philosophy presents us with an array of attempts to negotiate this challenge. The modern tradition as we see it today is rich, provocative, and adaptive, yet also restive and iconoclastic. It is itself a tradition to be appreciated and examined as efforts are made either to extend that tradition or to call it into question. Looking to the future, it is best to get one's bearings. The present volume is an attempt to help us do just that.

Notes

1. See especially Leo Strauss, "Jerusalem and Athens," in Leo Strauss, *Jewish Philosophy and the Crisis of Modernity*, ed. Kenneth Hart Green (SUNY, 1997), 377–405. And for Levinas, see various essays in *Difficult Freedom, In the Midst of the Nations,* and *Beyond the Verse.* In addition to *Encounters Between Judaism and Modern Philosophy* (Basic, 1973), a notable example of Fackenheim's examination of the shortcomings of modern philosophy and of what Judaism can contribute to it occurs in his book *The Religious Dimension of Hegel's Thought.* See also his essay "Hermann Cohen: After 50 Years," originally a Leo Baeck Institute lecture in 1970, reprinted in Michael L. Morgan (ed.), *Jewish Philosophers and Jewish Philosophy* (Indiana University Press, 1996).
2. For discussion, see Chapters 5 and 4 by Poma and Franks, respectively, in the present volume.
3. Along with the neo-Kantian school centered at Marburg, one should recall the crucial intellectual developments associated with the "Southwest" school (at Heidelberg and Freiburg) led by both Wilhelm Windelband and Heinrich Rickert.
4. The turbulence of the age is reflected, in among other places, the work of thinkers such as Max Weber and Georg Simmel, the latter born a Jew and trained as a philosopher, whose classic work *The Philosophy of Money* (1900) portrays the economic, social, and psychological character of modern urban life.
5. This is a central theme of Steven B. Smith's *Spinoza, Liberalism, and the Question of Jewish Identity* (Chicago, 1997).

2 Baruch Spinoza and the Naturalization of Judaism

STEVEN NADLER

Baruch Spinoza (1632–1677) occupies a somewhat awkward position in the historiography of Jewish philosophy. In the standard story – or at least those versions of it that move beyond the simplistic description of how his philosophy represents a radical and heretical break from what comes before – he is presented either as the culmination of the Jewish medieval rationalist tradition (especially Maimonides and Gersonides) or as the father of modern Jewish thought, and sometimes as both. These are important (but still all too infrequently studied) perspectives for understanding Spinoza's metaphysical, moral, and political ideas, and not just their antecedents and their legacies, but their substantive content as well.[1] While most scholarly attention has been devoted to the seventeenth-century Cartesian background of Spinoza's philosophy, his system also needs to be situated (as Harry Wolfson and others have recognized)[2] in a Jewish philosophical context. But is this enough to give him a rightful place in a "Companion" to Jewish philosophy? After all, Thomas Aquinas was strongly influenced by Maimonides, and our understanding of the *Summa Theologiae* is deepened by a familiarity with the *Guide for the Perplexed*, but no one of course has ever suggested that St. Thomas is a Jewish philosopher. Does the additional fact that Spinoza, unlike Thomas, is Jewish alone qualify him for membership in the canon of "Jewish philosophers"?

A number of significant factors appear to point to, indeed demand, a negative answer to this question. First and foremost, Spinoza was expelled as a young man from the Amsterdam Portuguese-Jewish community with the harshest writ of *cherem* ever issued by the congregation's leaders.[3] This seminal event in his biography is mirrored in the fact that for the rest of his life he clearly did not regard himself as Jewish. One is struck, for example, by the way the Jewish people are regarded in the *Theological-Political Treatise* (published anonymously in 1670; henceforth, TTP) from the third-person perspective. He seems in his writings, including his extant correspondence, to lack all identification and sympathy with Jewish religion and history, and even to go out of his way to distance himself from them. And there is the issue of the content of his philosophy. Spinoza rejected the providential God of Abraham, Isaac, and Jacob as an anthropomorphic fiction; he denied the divine origin of the Torah and the continued validity of the Law of Moses; and he argued that there is no theologically, metaphysically, or morally interesting sense in which the Jews are a chosen people. How, then, can one possibly regard him as a Jewish philosopher without doing a grave injustice to his personal experience, his own sense of identity, and the spirit of his philosophical thought?

However, philosophy (and this is its important difference from religion) never requires one *a priori* to adopt one set of substantive beliefs over another. That is, philosophy never prescribes particular answers in advance. Rather, it demands only that one ask certain kinds of questions and approach them in a certain kind of way (that is, through rational inquiry). And this is as true for Jewish philosophy as it is for, say, the philosophy of mind. Being a Jewish philosopher does not require one to think of oneself as a Jew; nor does it demand that one regard Jews or the Jewish religion or Jewish history in a certain way; nor, finally, does it call upon one to adopt specific theological, metaphysical, or ethical ideas.[4] Being a Jewish philosopher means only that an individual of Jewish descent[5] is, in his or her philosophical thinking, engaged in an honest dialogue with a particular canonical philosophical and religious tradition and wrestling with a certain set of questions.

Some of those questions are about specific Jewish doctrines – What does the election of Israel mean? Is the Law of Moses binding on contemporary Jews? What is the proper way to interpret Torah? What is the relationship between virtue and the world-to-come? Some of the questions, on the other hand, are about Judaism itself, and their answers constitute what Julius Guttmann has called a "philosophy *of* Judaism."[6] Even if a philosopher's answers to the questions differ radically from those provided by other, perhaps more orthodox thinkers, still, this philosopher is addressing the same questions, referencing (for the most part) the same textual canon, and talking across time to the same authoritative figures (for example, Saadya ben Joseph, Maimonides, Gersonides, et al.). According to these criteria, Spinoza is most certainly a Jewish philosopher.[7]

In this chapter, I examine Spinoza's views on some central features of Judaism, primarily with an eye to identifying the ways in which he naturalizes its doctrines, its laws, its texts, and its history. Spinoza had nothing but contempt for organized sectarian religion, Jewish or otherwise,

and for what he saw as its deleterious moral and political effects. To
his mind, the key to mitigating those effects is to understand the phenomenon of religion – religious belief, religious tradition, even the divine
being in which it stands in awe – in purely naturalistic terms, and thereby
demystify it.

I. THE GOD OF ABRAHAM, ISAAC, AND JACOB

The God of Judaism is an all-powerful, all-knowing being. God is a
source of being and the cause of great deeds, and God knows the hearts
and minds of creatures. But beyond these basic metaphysical and epistemological characteristics, God is also endowed with important moral
and even psychological features. God is a wise, just, caring, and providential agent. Like the God of many religions, it is a being to whom one
will pray in times of good and bad fortune. It is also a God who has preferences – and, consequently, becomes pleased, angry, and jealous as those
preferences are fulfilled or thwarted – and who issues commandments.
God demands worship and obedience, and will reward the faithful and
punish transgressors. It is, one might say, a very personal God, both in the
sense of being a kind of person and in the sense of being there *for* a person.

It is this picture of God that Spinoza takes issue with in the very
opening propositions of his philosophical masterpiece, the *Ethics* (begun
around 1663 but not published until after his death in 1677). The God
of Spinoza's philosophy is a far cry from the God of Abraham, Isaac,
and Jacob. Spinoza's God is not some just, wise, good, and providential
being; it is not a personal being whom one would thank or bless or to
whom one would pray or go to seek comfort. It is not a God that fosters
a sense of awe and spiritual piety, nor does it sustain the hope of eternal
reward or the fear of eternal punishment. In the *Ethics*, Spinoza strips
God of all traditional psychological and moral characteristics. God, he
argues, is substance, the ultimate and immanent reality of all things,
and nothing more. Endowed with the infinite attributes of Thought and
Extension, Spinoza's God is identical with the active, generative aspects
of nature. In an infamous phrase that appeared in the Latin but not in
the more accessible Dutch edition of the work, Spinoza refers to *Deus
sive Natura*, "God or Nature."[8] "By God," he says in one of the opening definitions of Part I, "I understand a being absolutely infinite, i.e.,
a substance consisting of an infinity of attributes, of which each one
expresses an eternal and infinite essence." In other words, God is the
universal, immanent system of causal principles or natures that gives
Nature its ultimate unity.

This definition is meant to preclude any anthropomorphizing of the divine being. Spinoza explicitly tells us that he is writing against "those who feign a God, like man, consisting of a body and a mind, and subject to passions... [T]hey wander far from the true knowledge of God."[9] His contempt for the fallacious inference that allows for the anthropomorphizing of God is obvious:

> If will and intellect do pertain to the eternal essence of God, we must of course understand by each of these attributes something different from what men commonly understand. For the intellect and will which would constitute God's essence would have to differ entirely from our intellect and will, and could not agree with them in anything except the name. They would not agree with one another any more than do the dog that is a heavenly constellation and the dog that is a barking animal.[10]

Besides being false, an anthropomorphic conception of God can only diminish human freedom, activity, and well-being, as it tends to strengthen passions such as hope and fear. When understood in the philosophically proper manner, 'God' is seen to refer to nothing but an impersonal, infinite, unique, uncaused causal source of everything else that exists.

> Ip16: From the necessity of the divine nature there must follow infinitely many things in infinitely many modes (i.e., everything which can fall under an infinite intellect).
>
> Dem.: This proposition must be plain to anyone, provided he attends to the fact that the intellect infers from the given definition of any thing a number of properties that really do follow necessarily from it (that is, from the very essence of the thing); and that it infers more properties the more the definition of the thing expresses reality, that is, the more reality the essence of the defined thing involves. But since the divine nature has absolutely infinite attributes, each of which also expresses an essence infinite in its own kind, from its necessity there must follow infinitely many things in infinite modes (i.e., everything which can fall under an infinite intellect).
>
> Cor. 1: From this it follows that God is the efficient cause of all things which can fall under an infinite intellect.
>
> Cor. 2: It follows, second, that God is a cause through himself and not an accidental cause.
>
> Cor. 3: It follows, third, that God is absolutely the first cause.

If God is nothing but the infinite, eternal substance of Nature, endowed with the attributes of Thought and Extension (the natures of mind and matter), then God's causal powers just are the activity of these attributes and the law-like principles that follow immediately from them. And all particular things in nature are nothing but finite modes or effects of these infinite, eternal causes.

It follows that God is not a transcendent creator – that is, a being who spontaneously causes a world distinct from himself to come into being by producing it out of nothing. Spinoza's conception of God strikes right at the heart of the account of creation in Genesis (*Bereshith*, "In the beginning..."), according to which God purposively brings order out of *tohu v'vohu*, chaos. Spinoza's God is the cause of all things, but only because all things follow causally and necessarily from the divine natures – that is, from Nature itself. Or, as he puts it, from God's infinite power or nature "all things have necessarily flowed, or always followed, by the same necessity and in the same way as from the nature of a triangle it follows, from eternity and to eternity, that its three angles are equal to two right angles."[11]

Such a God obviously cannot be endowed with a teleologically conceived freedom of the will. All talk of God's purposes, intentions, goals, preferences, or aims is just an anthropomorphizing fiction.

> All the prejudices I here undertake to expose depend on this one: that men commonly suppose that all natural things act, as men do, on account of an end; indeed, they maintain as certain that God himself directs all things to some certain end, for they say that God has made all things for man, and man that he might worship God.[12]

God is not some goal-oriented planner who then judges things by how well they conform to his purposes. Least of all is God a giver of laws and endowed with moral characteristics. "It is only in concession to the understanding of the multitude and the defectiveness of their thought that God is described as a lawgiver or ruler, and is called just, merciful, and so on."[13] Things happen only because of Nature and its laws. "Nature has no end set before it ... All things proceed by a certain eternal necessity of nature." To believe otherwise is to fall prey to the same superstitions that lie at the heart of most organized religions.

> [People] find – both in themselves and outside themselves – many means that are very helpful in seeking their own advantage, e.g., eyes for seeing, teeth for chewing, plants and animals for food, the sun for light, the sea for supporting fish ... Hence, they consider all

natural things as means to their own advantage. And knowing that they had found these means, not provided them for themselves, they had reason to believe that there was someone else who had prepared those means for their use. For after they considered things as means, they could not believe that the things had made themselves; but from the means they were accustomed to prepare for themselves, they had to infer that there was a ruler, or a number of rulers of nature, endowed with human freedom, who had taken care of all things for them, and made all things for their use.

And since they had never heard anything about the temperament of these rulers, they had to judge it from their own. Hence, they maintained that the Gods direct all things for the use of men in order to bind men to them and be held by men in the highest honor. So it has happened that each of them has thought up from his own temperament different ways of worshipping God, so that God might love them above all the rest, and direct the whole of Nature according to the needs of their blind desire and insatiable greed. Thus this prejudice was changed into superstition, and struck deep roots in their minds.[14]

Divine providence is reduced to the ordinary, law-like course of nature, as it is governed by eternal principles. "By God's direction," he insists in the TTP, "I mean the fixed and immutable order of Nature, or chain of natural events...It is the same thing whether we say that all things happen according to Nature's laws or that they are regulated by God's decree and direction."[15] As for miracles – understood as supernaturally caused exceptions to the course of nature – they are impossible, given the universal, all-encompassing scope of Nature's dominion, along with the deterministic necessity that rules it. As Spinoza notes in the chapter on miracles in the TTP, "nothing can happen in Nature to contravene her own universal laws, nor yet anything that is not in agreement with these laws or that does not follow from them."[16] What we call a 'miracle' is, in fact, simply an event whose explanation happens to surpass our understanding, an event for which we can find no natural cause, even though, strictly speaking, there must be one.

To say that for Spinoza "God exists only philosophically," as his contemporary critics were wont to do, does not even begin to do justice to the radical nature of his conception of God. Descartes's God, it was often said by his religious critics, is a "merely philosophical" God – a dispassionate, infinitely powerful cause whose ways are beyond our comprehension, who is not in any way "close" to human beings with the kind of care often portrayed in Biblical writings. And yet even Descartes's God still has will and understanding,[17] and acts with an indifferent, libertarian freedom but nonetheless with reason.[18] Descartes's God has purposes. For Spinoza, on the other hand, God is not even the kind of being of which it is coherent to speak of will or purpose. Spinoza's God is substance, period, along with whatever else follows necessarily from that claim. The moral and psychological spareness of Spinoza's conception of God goes well beyond anything Descartes could have imagined. It is as profound a naturalization of God as one can imagine.[19]

2. JEWISH LAW

Spinoza's project of naturalization continues with his account of Jewish law. The Torah says that the Law was revealed by God to Moses in a series of commandments (*mitzvot*). Whether the object of a particular commandment regards ethical behavior (the way one human being is to treat another human being), piety (the way a human being is to relate to God), or more mundane matters (a prohibition against combining fabrics in a garment or the numerous dietary restrictions), all of the commandments are, according to tradition, literally divine, and complying with them is obedience owed to God. The changed historical condition of the Jews may have made fulfilling some of the *mitzvot* unnecessary or even impossible (such as those regarding Temple sacrifice), but the suspension of one law or another is brought about by the decision of Jewish *halakhic* or legal authority, not by mere historical or political circumstance per se.

Spinoza sees things otherwise. Not all (or even most) of the laws or commandments of the Torah are divine; consequently, not all of them are of universal scope or perpetual validity. He draws a sharp distinction in Scripture's laws between those that are divine and those that are merely ceremonial. The divine law is very simple, and is concerned only with the "supreme good [*summum bonum*]." What this supreme good consists in is the perfection of the intellect – "the better part of us" – through the acquisition of knowledge. Now, since all true knowledge refers things back to their first and highest causal principles, it ultimately consists in the understanding and the intellectual love of God (or Nature). Consequently, the "divine" law is constituted only by the prescription of those means necessary for the achievement of this intellectual perfection.

> This, then, is the sum of our supreme good [*summum bonum*] and blessedness [*beatitudo*], to wit, the knowledge and love of God. So

the means required to achieve this end of all human action – that is, God in so far as his idea exists in us – may be termed God's commands, for they are ordained for us by God himself, as it were, in so far as he exists in our minds. So the rules for living a life that has regard to this end can fitly be called the Divine Law.[20]

In addition to the epistemic pursuit of the knowledge of God, the Divine Law requires certain types of conduct, but only to the extent to which these are conducive toward that epistemic goal, both for ourselves and for others. These will be the principles of action essential to a good commonwealth and healthy social organization, as well as to the flourishing of our fellow human beings. This part of the law is very neatly summed up in a single phrase: "Love your neighbor as you love yourself." Together with the command to love God – not from fear of punishment or hope of reward, but from the love due to our true good – this exhausts the content of Divine Law.

This law alone is what is universally valid (*universalis*), regardless of time, place, and circumstance, and binding upon all human beings (*omnibus hominibus communem*), regardless of religious persuasion. As the supreme moral law, it can be known through human reason and deduced from human nature, although it is also the message of Scripture. And it demands nothing in the way of beliefs about what did or did not take place with regard to a certain people in the course of time. "It does not demand belief in historical narratives of any kind whatsoever."[21]

All the other commandments found in the Torah relate only to ceremonial practices and sectarian religious rites. Unlike the Divine Law, which is universalistic, a kind of eternal truth, the ceremonial laws are particularistic and of only limited scope and validity. They were instituted by Moses for the ancient Hebrews alone, and thus adapted to their historical and political circumstances. Moses, realizing that devotion was a much better motivator than fear, created a state religion in order to get the people to do their duty. The laws of this state religion are, in fact, social and political regulations. They do not contribute at all to true blessedness and virtue, Spinoza insists, but tend only toward "the temporal and material prosperity" of the community and the peace and security of its government. In and of themselves, "they are of no significance and are termed good only by tradition"; they have, in other words, not intrinsic but only instrumental value.[22] With the end of the Hebrew Commonwealth, moreover, Moses's laws lost their normative force. "The Hebrews are not bound to practice their ceremonial rites since the destruction of their state ... Since the fall of their independent state, Jews are no more bound by the Mosaic Law than they were before their political state came into being" – that is, before Moses issued the Law in the form of the commandments.[23]

Spinoza's views on the Law bear on an important set of related issues. In rabbinic Judaism, there is generally no distinction drawn between law and morality.[24] What God decrees as law is thereby what is moral. There is no independent code of moral behavior distinct from Divine Law (and in accordance with which that law can be judged). Consequently, there is no such thing as natural law – that is, a universally valid law discovered by and justified through reason, without any appeal to the will of God. Spinoza departs from Jewish tradition on this question, and does so once again from a naturalizing standpoint. What he calls Divine Law is the supreme moral law, and it is distinct from Jewish religious (or ceremonial) law. And the Divine Law, while revealed by Scripture, is in principle discoverable and justified by reason alone; in fact, Spinoza insists, it is "innate" in the human mind. Jewish ceremonial law, on the other hand, is a human convention, instituted by Moses and later codified and systematized by Ezra, the Pharisees, and the Mishnaic sages.

3. PROPHECY

The law, according to Jewish tradition, was revealed through prophecy – that is, through a special communication between God and a selected individual, Moses. Later prophets, also benefitting from divine revelation (although not the direct apprehension granted to Moses), were able to convey truths about various other matters. The insights resulting from these highly individualistic exchanges with God are supposed to be beyond what is naturally available to other human beings. Prophetic illumination, in other words, is to be understood as a supernatural phenomenon reflecting the divine will.

Spinoza agrees that there is something special about a prophet. The prophet is above ordinary human beings in certain respects. But, as demanded by Spinoza's metaphysics, there can be nothing literally supernatural about prophecy. The prophet is, to be sure, "filled with the spirit of God." But this means only that he is a person of extraordinary virtue and is devoted to piety with unusual constancy. The prophet is a kind of moral authority, and his teachings – to the extent that they are true – consist only in that simple message of the Divine Law. On the other hand, Spinoza insists, the prophet is not distinguished by any kind of intellectual or philosophical superiority. The prophet is no better endowed with reason than any other human being, and thus can claim no expertise in such subjects as science and philosophy – that is, on matters the knowledge of which is available to all people through the natural light of the intellect.[25]

Prophets excite the admiration and wonder of others only because the latter are ignorant of the causes of prophetic knowledge. When confronted with a person of prophetic powers, the people were amazed and "referred it like all other portents to God, and were wont to call it divine knowledge."[26] In fact, the explanation of prophecy is perfectly natural (although Spinoza confesses his ignorance of the law of our (psychological) nature that make this kind of "revelation" possible; to this extent, he is willing to concede that prophecy is a "gift"). The prophet is simply someone with a highly active and finely tuned imagination. He is, more than the ordinary person, capable of picturing to himself, with words and images, matters that are properly spiritual – that is, "things related to charity and moral conduct."[27] These visions allow the prophet to extend his apprehensions beyond what the intellect alone can convey. The content of prophecies will vary according to the different external circumstances and physical and cognitive endowments of the prophets, and especially differences in their temperaments, beliefs and imaginative faculties. But the core (moral) message embedded in the visions and stories and parables related by the prophets should always be the same.

Spinoza, with his emphasis on the role of the imagination and the natural foundation of prophecy is, to a certain degree, in good Jewish philosophical company. In fact, his position can be seen as a *reductio* of Maimonides' more complex account in the *Guide for the Perplexed*. Maimonides believes that prophecy represents the culmination of the perfection of a person's capacities – in particular, the perfection of his intellect, which receives from the Agent Intellect a divine overflow of cognition (a process accessible to any rational agent), and of his imagination, which represents that general intellectual content in the concrete form of a vision. To this extent, there is nothing miraculous about prophecy; God does not arbitrarily single out a person for prophetic communication. Rather, prophecy is a natural result of the development of the human faculties. It comes about simply when a person reaches a certain level of perfection in his moral and rational capacities and is endowed with a particularly strong and vivid imagination. Prophecy is, Maimonides insists, "a perfection that belongs to us by nature."[28] However, it is not for him an *entirely* natural phenomenon, as it is for Spinoza, because, he adds, it is always up to God to decide if a person who has achieved the appropriate level of perfection is to be denied the gift of prophecy.

4. THE ELECTION OF ISRAEL

Spinoza provides an equally deflationary account of God's election, or the "vocation," of the Hebrews. It is "childish," he insists, for anyone to base their happiness on the uniqueness of their gifts. In the case of the Jews, it would be the uniqueness of their being chosen by God from among all nations and all peoples. In fact, Spinoza insists, the ancient Hebrews did not surpass other nations in their wisdom, their character, or (which amounts to the same thing) their proximity to God. They were neither intellectually nor morally superior to other peoples. Reason and the capacity for virtue are distributed by nature equally among all individual human beings, and the achievement of virtue is found among all nations. "The Hebrews surpassed other nations not in knowledge nor in piety . . . the Hebrews [were] chosen by God above all others not for the true life nor for any higher understanding."[29]

There is, then, no theologically, morally, or metaphysically interesting sense in which the Jews are a chosen people. The only respect in which the Israelites *were* chosen by God (or Nature) is in regard to their social organization and political good fortune. "The individual Jew, considered alone apart from his social organization and his government, possesses no gift of God above other men, and there is no difference between him and a Gentile."[30] This "chosen-ness" is, in fact, nothing but the fortunate external circumstances that came their way from the determinate operations of the ordinary course of nature. The Israelites obeyed the laws that had been set for them, with the natural consequence that their society was well-ordered and their autonomous government long-lived. The process requires no supernatural intervention. If a group is provided with wise and pragmatic laws, and it lives by them, then the result will (naturally) be a secure and prosperous polity.

> The Hebrew nation was chosen by God before all others not by reason of its understanding nor of its spiritual qualities, but by reason of its social organization and the good fortune whereby it achieved supremacy and retained it for so many years. This is quite evident from Scripture itself. A merely casual perusal clearly reveals that the Hebrews surpassed other nations in this alone, that they were successful in achieving security for themselves and overcame great dangers, and this chiefly by God's external help

alone. In other respects they were no different from other nations, and God was equally gracious to all . . . Therefore their election and vocation consisted only in the material success and prosperity of their state . . . In return for their obedience the Law promises them nothing other than the continuing prosperity of their state and material advantages, whereas disobedience and the breaking of the Covenant would bring about the downfall of their state and the severest hardships.[31]

The election of the Jews was thus a temporal and conditional one. With their kingdom now long gone, the distinction has come to an end. "At the present time there is nothing whatsoever that the Jews can arrogate to themselves above other nations."[32] With respect to understanding, virtue and true happiness, with respect to blessedness, there is not, never has been and never will be anything peculiar to the Jews.[33]

5. SCRIPTURE

By analyzing prophecy in terms of vividness of imagination, Jewish election as political good fortune, Jewish law as a kind of social and political expediency, and the belief in miracles as grounded in an ignorance of nature's necessary causal operations, Spinoza naturalizes (and, consequently, demystifies) some of the fundamental elements of Judaism and other religions and undermines the foundations of their external and (to his mind) superstitious rites. At the same time, he thereby reduces the fundamental doctrine of piety to a simple and universal formula involving love of one's fellow human beings and knowledge of God or Nature. This process of naturalization achieves its stunning climax when Spinoza turns to consider the authorship and interpretation of the Bible itself. Spinoza's views on Scripture constitute, without question, the most radical theses of the TTP, and explain why he was attacked with such vitriol by his contemporaries. Others before Spinoza had suggested that Moses was not the author of the entire Pentateuch. But no one had taken that claim to the extreme limit that Spinoza did, arguing for it with such boldness and at such length. Nor had anyone before Spinoza been willing to draw from it the conclusions about the status, meaning, and interpretation of Scripture that Spinoza drew.

Spinoza denies that God is literally the author of Scripture and that Moses (either as God's amanuensis or on his own) wrote all, or even most, of the Torah. The references in the Pentateuch to Moses in the third person; the narration of his death and, particularly, of events following his death; and the fact that some places are called by names that they did not bear in the time of Moses – all "make it clear beyond a shadow of a doubt" that the writings commonly referred to as "the Five Books of Moses" were, in fact, written by someone who lived many generations after Moses. Moses did, to be sure, compose some books of history and of law, and remnants of those long lost books can be found in the Pentateuch. But the Torah as we have it, as well as other books of the Hebrew Bible (such as Joshua, Judges, Samuel, and Kings) were written neither by the individuals whose names they bear nor by any person appearing in them. Spinoza argues that these were, in fact, all composed by a single historian living many generations after the events narrated, and that this was most likely Ezra. It was the post-exilic leader who took the many writings that had come down to him and began weaving them into a single (but not seamless) narrative. Ezra's work was later completed and supplemented by the editorial labors of others. What we now possess, then (according to Spinoza), is nothing but a compilation of human literature, and a rather mismanaged, haphazard, and "mutilated" one at that.

> If one merely observes that all the contents of these five books, histories and precepts, are set forth with no distinction or order and with no regard to chronology, and that frequently the same story is repeated, with variations, it will readily be recognised that all these materials were collected indiscriminately and stored together with view to examining them and arranging them more conveniently at some later time. And not only the contents of these five books but the other histories in the remaining seven books right down to the destruction of the city were compiled in the same way.[34]

As for the books of the Prophets, they are of even later provenance, compiled (or "heaped together," in Spinoza's view) by a chronicler or scribe from the Second Temple period. Canonization into Scripture occurred only in the second century BCE, when the Pharisees selected a number of texts from a multitude of others. Because the process of transmission was a historical one, involving the conveyance of writings of human origin over a long period of time through numerous scribes, and because the decision to include some books but not others was made by ordinary, fallible human beings, there are good reasons for believing that a significant portion of the text of the "Old Testament" is corrupt.

Spinoza was working within a well-known tradition. The claim that Moses was not the author of the entire Pentateuch had already been made in the twelfth century by Ibn Ezra. In his commentary on the Pentateuch, focusing on Deuteronomy 33, Ibn Ezra argued that Moses could not have written the account of his own death. Spinoza knew and admired Ibn Ezra's writings, and there is no question that his views on the authorship of the Torah were influenced by them. But he was also familiar with Isaac La Peyrère's more recent *Pre-Adamitae*, in which the French Calvinist millenarian questioned not only the Mosaic authorship of all of the Pentateuch but also the reliability of the transmission process and, hence, the accuracy of the received Biblical texts. In 1660, Samuel Fisher, the Quaker leader in Amsterdam with whom Spinoza seems to have been acquainted, published *The Rustic's Alarm to the Rabbies*. Scripture as it has come down to us, Fisher insisted, is a historical document, a text written by human beings, and therefore should not be confused with the Word of God, which is ahistorical and eternal. Finally, there is the English philosopher Thomas Hobbes, who, in his *Leviathan* – which Spinoza clearly studied very closely – insists that most of the five books attributed to Moses were actually written long after his time, though Moses did indeed compose a good deal of what appears in them – namely, "all that which he is there said to have written."[35]

To be sure, Ibn Ezra and others who followed him did not question the fact that Moses had written most of the Pentateuch, and denying the Mosaic authorship of the Torah was still an exceedingly unorthodox view. Spinoza noted that "the author [of the Pentateuch] is almost universally believed to be Moses," and he knew that rejecting that dogma would earn an author the condemnation of religious authorities. But there was nothing novel, by 1670, in claiming that Moses did not write all of the Torah, nor even in suggesting that Scripture was composed by human beings and transmitted through a fallible historical process. On the other hand, Spinoza's radical and innovative claim was to argue that this holds great significance for how Scripture is to be read and interpreted. He was dismayed by the way in which Scripture itself was worshiped, by the reverence accorded to the words on the page rather than to the message they conveyed. If the Bible is a historical and thus natural document, then it should be treated like any other work of nature. The study of Scripture – or Biblical hermeneutics – should therefore proceed as the study of nature, or natural science proceeds: by gathering and evaluating empirical data – that is, by examining the "book" itself for its general principles.

> I hold that the method of interpreting Scripture is no different from the method of interpreting Nature, and is in fact in complete accord with it. For the method of interpreting Nature consists

essentially in composing a detailed study of Nature from which, as being the source of our assured data, we can deduce the definitions of the things of Nature. Now in exactly the same way the task of Scriptural interpretation requires us to make a straightforward study of Scripture, and from this, as the source of our fixed data and principles, to deduce by logical inference the meaning of the authors of Scripture. In this way – that is, by allowing no other principles or data for the interpretation of Scripture and study of its contents except those that can be gathered only from Scripture itself and from a historical study of Scripture – steady progress can be made without any danger of error, and one can deal with matters that surpass our understanding with no less confidence than those matters that are known to us by the natural light of reason.[36]

Just as the knowledge of nature must be sought from nature alone, so must the knowledge of Scripture – an apprehension of its intended meaning – be sought from Scripture alone. Spinoza explicitly took issue with Maimonides' view in the *Guide of the Perplexed*. Maimonides, as much of a rationalist as Spinoza, had argued that deciphering the meaning of Scripture is a matter of seeing what is consistent with reason. Because Scripture is the Word of God, its intended meaning must be identical with the demonstrable truth. Therefore, if some passage, when read literally, cannot possibly be accepted by reason as true, then the literal meaning must be rejected in favor of a figurative one. For example, the Bible speaks, on occasion, of divine bodily parts. But reason tells us that an eternal, immaterial God does not have a body. Therefore, any references in Scripture to God's feet or hands must be read metaphorically.[37] For Spinoza, this type of exegesis is illegitimate in so far as it goes beyond Scripture itself – to some external standard of rationality or truth – in order to interpret Scripture. "The question as to whether Moses did or did not believe that God is fire must in no wise be decided by the rationality or irrationality of the belief, but solely from other pronouncements of Moses."[38] There must be a distinction between the meaning of Scripture, which is what one is after when interpreting it, and what is philosophically or historically true. Much of what Scripture relates is not, in fact, true. Scripture is not a source of knowledge, least of all knowledge about God, the heavens, or even human nature. It is not, in other words, philosophy or science, and therefore the principles of reason must not serve as our sole guide in interpreting Scripture. The moral message of Scripture does indeed agree with reason in the sense that our rational faculties approve of it. But *that* Scripture teaches such a message can be discovered only through the "historical" method.

The implementation of that method to discover what the authors of Scripture intended to teach requires a number of linguistic, historical, and textual skills. One should know the language in which Scripture was written, Hebrew, as well as the life, times, and even the "prejudices" of its authors and the nature of their audiences. Only by placing a book in its personal and historical context can one hope to decipher what the writer was trying to communicate.

> Our historical study should set forth the circumstances relevant to all the extant books of the prophets, giving the life, character and pursuits of the author of every book, detailing who he was, on what occasion, at what time, for whom, and in what language he wrote. Again, it should be related what happened to each book, how it was first received, into whose hands it fell, how many variant versions there were, by whose decision it was received into the canon, and, finally, how all the books, now universally regarded as sacred, were united into a single whole. All these details . . . should be available from an historical study of Scripture; for in order to know which pronouncements were set forth as laws and which as moral teaching, it is important to be acquainted with the life, character and interests of the author. Furthermore, as we have a better understanding of a person's character and temperament, so we can more easily explain his words.[39]

One consequence of Spinoza's views is that the interpretation of Scripture is open and accessible to any person endowed with intelligence who is able and willing to acquire the necessary skills. There are, of course, various obstacles standing in the way of even the most well-trained of scholars – the fragmentary knowledge of the Hebrew language as it existed in the seventeenth century; the inherent ambiguities in its alphabet, vocabulary, and grammar; and the difficulty of accurately reconstructing the history surrounding such ancient writings. Nonetheless, Spinoza insists that his method of interpreting Scripture "requires only the aid of natural reason." There is no need for lengthy and complex commentaries or ordained intermediaries such as priests, rabbis, or pastors. "Since the supreme authority for the interpretation of Scripture is vested in each individual, the rule that governs interpretation must be nothing other than the natural light that is common to all, and not any supernatural right, nor any external authority."[40]

6. SALVATION AND THE WORLD-TO-COME

Spinoza, despite his recommendation of the life of reason, argues that human beings, for the most part, live in "bondage" to their passions.[41] We are tossed about by our affective responses to the world and to the comings and goings of the temporal and mutable goods in which we place value. Hope and fear, in particular, direct our behavior as we strive after the things we desire and flee those objects that we believe will bring us harm. These two passions and the subsidiary affects that they ground constitute the greatest natural obstacle to our freedom, well-being, and true happiness. They also cause us to accept a kind of secondary bondage, as hope for eternal reward (in heaven) and fear of eternal punishment (in hell) lead us to submit ourselves to ecclesiastical authority and engage in the superstitious rituals that constitute organized religion. Spinoza believes that an important step in liberating humanity from the grip of these irrational passions and from the voluntary servitude that they engender is to undermine the foundational belief upon which they rest – namely, the belief in the immortality of the soul. For only if one believes that, after bodily death, the soul survives in a robust and personal sense and that the self is the subject of a postmortem divine reward and punishment is one likely to be governed by hopes and fears over its eventual fate.

For Spinoza, there is no personal immortality.[42] There are, to be sure, eternal aspects of the human mind. According to Spinoza's metaphysics, the mind includes, as an essential constitutive element, an idea of the essence of the human body. This extended essence of the body as a material thing is eternal – more precisely, it is an eternal mode of the attribute of Extension – and is independent of the actual existence of the body in duration. Likewise, the 'idea' of the body's essence that forms a part of the mind is eternal, as it constitutes the mind's intellectual understanding of its body's nature and a core feature of its own nature; this idea is an eternal mode of the attribute of Thought. When a person dies, all those aspects of the mind that are dependent on the body's durational existence – its sensations, memories, imaginations, and so on – come to an end. The part of the mind constituted by the idea of the body's extended essence, however, persists eternally. It is in this sense that "the human mind cannot be absolutely destroyed along with the body, but something of it remains, which is eternal."[43] Moreover, the knowledge that the human mind acquires in this lifetime, to the extent that it is a deep understanding of the natures of things, and thus a perception of their essences *sub specie aeternitatis*, is likewise eternal, since it is nothing but a collection of eternal adequate ideas (the content of what Spinoza calls the "third kind of knowledge," which is a rational intuition of the eternal essence of a thing). This part of a person's mental makeup also remains after he has died.

> The essence of the mind consists in knowledge. Therefore, the greater the number of things the mind knows by the second and third kind of knowledge, the greater is the part of it that survives . . . Death is less hurtful in proportion as the mind's clear and distinct knowledge is greater, and consequently the more the mind loves God. Again, since from the third kind of knowledge there arises the highest possible contentment, hence it follows that the human mind can be of such a nature that the part of it that we have shown to perish with the body is of no account compared with that part of it that survives.[44]

Spinoza's doctrine of the eternity of the mind is not a doctrine of immortality. There is nothing personal about what remains of a person after death. It is not a self; there is no consciousness or memory, nor any intrinsic relationship to the life that one led in duration. It is simply a body of ideas and knowledge.[45]

For Spinoza, therefore, the true reward of virtue is not to be sought in eternal benefits in an afterlife. Spinoza rejects the rabbinic eschatological doctrine of *olam ha-ba* (the world-to-come) and a standard Jewish philosophical account of divine reckoning.[46] It is all just another ecclesiastical fiction used to encourage hope and fear (and thus servitude) in the masses. Virtue, he insists, just is the pursuit of knowledge, and the good it does us lies in this life. "Salvation" and "blessedness" are achieved here and now as the knowledge of (God or) Nature provides us with the self-mastery and peace of mind that allow us to navigate the obstacles that this world presents. This naturalization of virtue is the capstone of Spinoza's moral and political project. As Spinoza puts it, "blessedness is not the reward of virtue, but virtue itself."[47] Virtue, that is, is its own reward.

Notes

1. For example, I argue that Spinoza's account of the eternity of the mind cannot be properly understood without considering the views of Maimonides and Gersonides on the active intellect; see Steven Nadler, *Spinoza's Heresy: Immortality and the Jewish Mind* (Oxford: Oxford University Press, 2002).

2. Harry Wolfson, *The Philosophy of Spinoza*, 2 vols. (Cambridge, MA: Harvard University Press, 1934); Warren Zev Harvey, "A Portrait of Spinoza as a Maimonidean," *Journal of the History of Philosophy* 19 (1981): 151–172; Ze'ev Levy, *Baruch or Benedict: On Some Jewish Aspects of Spinoza's Philosophy* (New York: Peter Lang, 1989).
3. For the text of the *cherem*, see Steven Nadler, *Spinoza: A Life* (Cambridge: Cambridge University Press, 1999), p. 120.
4. Although Steven Schwarzschild has argued that what characterizes Jewish philosophy just *is* its primarily ethical orientation (or, as he puts it, "the primacy of Practical Reason"); see "An Agenda for Jewish Philosophy in the 1980s" in Norbert Samuelson (ed.), *Studies in Jewish Philosophy: Collected Essays of the Academy for Jewish Philosophy (1980–1985)* (Lanham, MD: University Press of America, 1987).
5. I know that the qualification "of Jewish descent" begs the question, and I introduce it with hesitation. I am not certain that one needs to be of Jewish descent to engage in Jewish philosophy, but since it is not an issue in the case of Spinoza, I do not want to engage that question.
6. Julius Guttmann, *Philosophies of Judaism* (New York: Holt, 1964).
7. On the question of Spinoza and Jewish philosophy, see Manfred Walther's articles, "Spinozas Philosophie der Freiheit – eine 'jüdische Philosophie'?" *Edith Stein Jahrbuch* 3 (1997): 99–133; "Was/Is Spinoza a Jewish Philosopher? Spinoza in the Struggle for a Modern Jewish Identity in Germany: A Meta-Reflection," *Studia Spinozana* 13 (1997):207–237; and "Spinoza und das Problem einer jüdische Philosophie" in W. Stegmaier (ed.), *Die philosophische Aktualität der jüdischen Tradition* (Frankfurt: Suhrkamp Verlag, 2000). See also Levy, *Baruch or Benedict*; and Geneviève Brykman, *La Judéité de Spinoza* (Paris: J. Vrin, 1972).
8. G II.206/C 544. All references to Spinoza's works and translations are abbreviated as follows:
   G = *Spinoza Opera*, 5 vols. Carl Gebhardt (ed.) (Heidelberg: Carl Winters Verlag, 1972), by volume number, page number.
   C = *The Collected Works of Spinoza*, vol. 1. Edwin Curley (trans.) (Princeton: Princeton University Press, 1984).
   S = *Theological-Political Treatise*, Samuel Shirley (trans.) (Indianapolis: Hackett Publishing, 1998).
   Citations to the *Ethics* are by roman numeral (for Part); p = proposition; s = scholium; c = corollary.
9. *Ethics* Ip15s.
10. Ip17s2.
11. Ip17s1.
12. Part I, Appendix.
13. TTP G III.65; S 56.
14. Part I, Appendix, G II.78–9; C I.440–1.
15. G III.45–6; S 37.
16. G III.83; S 74.
17. Although, as Descartes is at pains to insist, in God will and understanding are one and the same; see his letter to Mersenne of 6 May 1630.

18. On God's reason, see, for example, the letter to Hyperaspistes of August 1641, *Oeuvres de Descartes*, 11 vols., Charles Adam and Paul Tannery (eds.) (Paris: J. Vrin, 1964–75), vol. 3, p. 431. On God's "freedom of indifference," see Sixth Set of Replies, *ibid.*, vol. 7, p. 432–3.

19. This has not stopped some scholars from trying to find in Spinoza a more theologically robust and religiously attractive conception of God; see, for example, Richard Mason, *The God of Spinoza* (Cambridge: Cambridge University Press, 1997).

20. TTP, G III.60; S 51.

21. TTP, G III.61; S 52.

22. TTP, G III.62, 69; S 53, 60.

23. TTP, G III.72; S 62–3.

24. For a discussion of this issue, see Marvin Fox, *Interpreting Maimonides* (Chicago: University of Chicago Press, 1990), chapter 8.

25. TTP, chapters 1 and 2.

26. TTP, G III.27–8; S 20.

27. TTP, G III.42; S 34.

28. *Guide to the Perplexed* II.32.

29. TTP, G III.45; S 37.

30. TTP, G III.50; S 42.

31. TTP, G III.47–8; S 39.

32. TTP, G III.56; S 47.

33. For a discussion of Spinoza on the election of Israel, see David Novak, *The Election of Israel* (Cambridge: Cambridge University Press, 1995), chapter 1.

34. TTP, G III.131; S 121.

35. See *Leviathan*, Book III, chapter 33. For the historical and philosophical background to Spinoza's Bible scholarship, see Richard Popkin, "Some New Light on Spinoza's Science of Bible Study," in Marjorie Grene and Deborah Nails (eds.), *Spinoza and the Sciences* (Dordrecht: Reidel, 1980); "Samuel Fisher and Spinoza," *Philosophia* 15 (1985): 219–36; and "Spinoza and Bible Scholarship" in Don Garrett (ed.), *The Cambridge Companion to Spinoza* (Cambridge: Cambridge University Press, 1996).

36. TTP, G III.98; S 89.

37. See *Guide of the Perplexed* II.25.

38. TTP, G III.100–1; S 91.

39. TTP, G III.101–2; S 92.

40. TTP, G III.117; S 107.

41. See *Ethics* IV, Preface.

42. Not all scholars, however, recognize this; see Wolfson, *The Philosophy of Spinoza*, vol. 2, pp. 289–325; Mason, *The God of Spinoza*, pp. 240–241; Tamar Rudavsky, *Time Matters: Time, Creation and Cosmology in Medieval Jewish Thought* (Albany, NY: SUNY Press, 2000), p. 181.

43. *Ethics* Vp23.

44. *Ethics* Vp38.

45. I argue this point at greater length, including a comparison with medieval Jewish rationalist views on immortality, in Nadler, *Spinoza's Heresy*. I believe, in fact, that Spinoza's doctrine of the eternity of the mind is similar in important respects to Gersonides' doctrine of the acquired intellect.
46. See, for cxample, Saadya ben Joseph (Saadya Gaon), *The Book of Beliefs and Opinions*, Treatise V, chapter 2.
47. *Ethics* Vp42.

3   The Liberalism of Moses Mendelssohn

ALLAN ARKUSH

"Judaism is not Thomas Jefferson." With this terse epigram, Rabbi Meir Kahane contemptuously brushed off an American television interviewer who betrayed more than a little skepticism, back in the 1980s, about Kahane's calls for the revocation of Israeli Arabs' citizenship. As odious and indefensible as Kahane's racist politics were, one has to acknowledge at least the partial validity of his argument. Prior to the Enlightenment, Judaism evinced no recognition of the equal political rights of all men, regardless of their creed or national origin. During the two centuries prior to the advent of Kahane, however, Jewish thinkers of various stripes made strenuous efforts to align themselves with the spirit of modern times. They reinterpreted their religious tradition in the light of the liberal political teachings that had brought them out of the ghetto and had otherwise been so beneficial to themselves as well as others. In the United States, in particular, they succeeded so well at this task that most Jewish viewers of that interview with Kahane must have been shocked and outraged by what sounded to them like a heretical statement.[1]

Nevertheless, however much one might wish to believe that Kahane was an isolated representative of a retrograde attitude, one has to admit that he is far from the only spokesman for traditional Judaism who has in recent years sought to drive a wedge between his religion and modern liberal ideas. The Israeli religious right is well stocked with such figures, and their views have been echoed – albeit rather weakly – in the Diaspora as well.[2] In response to their critiques of liberalism, other traditional Jewish thinkers have grappled with the tension between their heritage and currently regnant political ideologies. That they are engaged in such labors at all might seem quite strange to a great many contemporary Jews, to whom the originally illiberal character of Judaism is often not even a distant memory. Because these thinkers still regard the tradition as authoritative, however, and because they also consider it to be malleable, they feel impelled to revisit it and to develop more liberal options within it in order to fend off threats to the integrity and even the security of the Jewish people.[3]

The thinkers who thus seek to preserve a measure of harmony between traditional Judaism and liberalism are proceeding on a path first traversed in Germany more than 200 years ago by Moses Mendelssohn. Recent scholarship may have deposed Mendelssohn from the position assigned to him by previous generations of historians as "founder of the *Haskalah* (Jewish Enlightenment)," but it has not denied that he was the first Jew to make an important contribution to the European Enlightenment without abandoning his ancestral religion.[4] The product of a traditional Jewish environment and education, the teen-aged Mendelssohn (a name he was only later to select for himself) left the small town of Dessau for Berlin in the 1740s solely in order to continue his talmudic studies. He soon began to supplement them, however, with the study of ancient and modern European languages and literatures, mathematics, and philosophy. By the 1750s, he was composing his own philosophical works, and by the 1760s, his writings on metaphysics, and especially his *Phaedon*, a Leibnizian-Wolffian reworking of Plato's dialogue on the immortality of the soul, had garnered him a European-wide reputation as "the German Socrates."[5]

In his works in German during the earlier stages of his philosophical career, Mendelssohn sought to steer clear of issues directly related to Judaism, although he could not completely escape the task of defending his religion against public challenges from Gentiles who wished to convert him. At the same time, in his Hebrew writings he made limited attempts to explicate biblical texts in the light of his philosophical ideas.[6] Within the Jewish community, he was an agent of change but no revolutionary. His major political battles took place outside its precincts and consisted of efforts to obtain equal rights for his fellow Jews in the polities of late eighteenth-century Europe.[7] Utilizing liberal political-philosophical arguments in the furtherance of this cause brought him into conflict with Gentile critics who opposed the emancipation of the Jews. On one important occasion, however, he also found himself at loggerheads with an anonymous critic who objected not to his goals but to his methods. This man accused Mendelssohn of attempting to improve the status of the Jews by means of arguments incompatible with the fundamental teachings of his own religion. Mendelssohn evidently felt that he could deflect this charge of hypocrisy only by demonstrating that Judaism was, in effect, tantamount to "Thomas Jefferson."

The work in which Mendelssohn undertook to accomplish this task, his *Jerusalem*, has been hailed for more than two centuries as a brilliant response to a malevolent critic. Innumerable historians of Jewish thought have acclaimed Mendelssohn for having shown how neatly the spirit of the Enlightenment could be reconciled with the spirit of Judaism. Liberals themselves (in the broadest sense of the term), and usually faithful Jews, too, these scholars have been only too glad to link the commencement of Jewish modernity with a celebrated philosopher who successfully combined their own disparate loyalties. In my opinion, however, they have been wrong to credit Mendelssohn with an intellectual victory. What he says in *Jerusalem* falls short of achieving his declared purposes. It demonstrates, instead, the vast difference between a real and a merely apparent reconciliation of Jewish and Jeffersonian principles.

Mendelssohn's inability truly to reconcile the principles of liberalism with the tenets of Judaism compels one to wonder where he really stood. Was he at heart a traditional Jew making tactical use of liberal political-philosophical arguments in which he did not really believe? Or was he a sly liberal, masquerading as a believing Jew in order to transform Judaism from within? Or was he perhaps someone who could not choose between two equally attractive alternatives that even his best efforts could not bring into genuine harmony with each other?

Jerusalem's canonical status as the inaugural work of modern Jewish philosophy has earned it a great deal of attention. Scholars have consistently regarded it as the first attempt on the part of a modern Jewish thinker to do the sort of thing that Maimonides had attempted in the twelfth century in his *Guide of the Perplexed*. They have treated Mendelssohn as a philosopher whose primary goal in writing this book was to show in a comprehensive manner that there was no contradiction between the truths attainable through unassisted human reason and what had been disclosed by biblical revelation. In doing so, they have not acted without justification. Although it is by no means a long book, *Jerusalem* encompasses detailed discussions of the nature of the Sinaitic revelation and its contents that are clearly designed to explain why the acceptance of Judaism requires no suspension of human reason. It definitely looks like a book that aims to replicate in a new cultural context the kind of project undertaken by Maimonides and other medieval Jewish rationalists. But one should not overlook the fact that Mendelssohn does not explicitly claim to have written such a work.

Maimonides commenced the *Guide of the Perplexed* with an epistle dedicatory addressed to his former student, Yosef ben Yehudah, in which he identified his target audience. It consisted of young men perplexed by the apparent tension between what they learned from the works of the

philosophers and the contents of the prophetic books.[8] Mendelssohn, for
his part, waited until the beginning of the second section of *Jerusalem*
before he related to his readers what had provoked him to compose this
work in the first place. It was above all, he declared, an objection raised
against one of his earlier publications by an anonymous but unmistakably Gentile pamphleteer (now known to have been a rather unimpor-
tant writer by the name of August Friedrich Cranz), the author of *The
Search after Light and Right*.[9] While most students of *Jerusalem* have
duly noted this fact, they have generally failed, in my opinion, to appreciate its full significance. They have not seen that the necessary point
of departure for any evaluation of the book's success or failure is a careful consideration of the precise nature of Cranz's principal challenge to
Mendelssohn.

This challenge must be seen in the light of what Mendelssohn had
written only a short time earlier in his preface to Menasseh ben Israel's
Vindiciae Judaeorum. In that work, he had cordially taken issue with the
proposal made by his friend Christian Wilhelm von Dohm that Jewish
communities be enabled to maintain a certain measure of internal autonomy, including the right of excommunication. Elucidating his reasons
for opposing the practice of excommunication altogether, Mendelssohn
had briefly set forth some of his own basic ideas concerning the proper
scope of ecclesiastical power. "I know of no rights," he had written,
"over persons and things that are connected to doctrinal opinions and
rest upon them, rights that men acquire when they agree with certain
statements and lose when they cannot consent to them or will not do
so." In general, Mendelssohn had gone on to say, "true divine religion
assumes no authority over ideas and opinions, gives and makes no claim
to earthly goods, no rights of usufruct, possession and property. It knows
no other power than the power to win and convince through reason and
to render happy through conviction." It has need of "neither arms nor a
finger," but consists of "pure spirit and heart."[10]

Genuine religion, by definition, involves no coercion. Nor, said
Mendelssohn, could any human institutions ever possess the legitimate
authority to make people's rights dependent upon their convictions. In
the state of nature, individuals have an absolute right to their own ideas
and opinions, one they do not lose with the signing of the social contract and their entrance into civil society. Mendelssohn therefore saw
no way in which any society could ever acquire the power to connect
civic privileges with religious convictions.[11]

In his public response to Mendelssohn, Cranz professed himself to
be in complete accord with all of this. "In common sense," he agreed,

"religion without conviction is not possible at all; and every forced religious act is no longer such. The observance of divine command-ments from fear of the punishment attached to them is slavery, which according to purified concepts can never be pleasing to God." Yet, he insisted, "Moses connects coercion and positive punishment with the nonobservance of duties related to the worship of God. His statutory ecclesiastical law decrees the punishment of stoning and death for the sabbath-breaker, the blasphemer of the divine name, and others who depart from his laws."[12]

Mendelssohn's espousal of liberal principles was, according to Cranz, incompatible with loyalty to Judaism, for "[a]rmed ecclesiasti-cal law still remains the firmest groundwork of the Jewish polity." He consequently considered himself entitled to pose a sharp question to Mendelssohn. "How can you remain an adherent of the faith of your fathers and shake the entire structure by removing the cornerstones, when you contest the ecclesiastical law that has been given through Moses and purports to be founded on divine revelation?"[13]

Cranz anticipated and ruled out in advance one possible response to this query. He warned Mendelssohn not to attempt to solve the prob-lem by claiming that the old Jewish theocracy was no longer relevant since it had for so long been defunct. He acknowledged that the regime introduced by Moses

> could be carried into practice only so long as the Jews had an empire of their own; so long as their Pontiffs were princes, or such sovereign heads of the people, as created princes, and governed them. But cease it must, as did the sacrifices, upon the Jews having lost territory and power, and, depending on foreign laws, found their jurisdiction circumscribed by very narrow limits. Still, that circumscription is merely the consequence of external and altered political relations, whereby the value of laws and privileges, consigned to quiescence, cannot be diminished. The ecclesiastical law is still there, although it not be allowed to be put into execution. Your lawgiver, Moses, is still the drover, with the cudgel, who leads his people with a rod of iron, and would be sharp after anyone who had the least opinion of his own, and dared to express it by word or deed...[14]

In this manner, Cranz declared that he would not be content with a response that merely obviated *in practice* the apparent contradiction between Mendelssohn's liberal principles and his ancestral religion. He wanted to know how Mendelssohn thought he could do this *in principle*.

This is a challenge that Mendelssohn took much more seriously than have many of his scholarly interpreters, who have often dismissed Cranz as little more than a reincarnation of Johann Caspar Lavater, the Swiss theologian who had in 1769 publicly challenged Mendelssohn to explain his failure to become a Christian.[15] Unfortunately, Cranz himself made the comparison with Lavater virtually inevitable when he suggested that the views expressed by Mendelssohn in the preface to *Vindiciae Judaeorum* indicated that he was drawing closer to what he called "the more rational system" of Christianity. Had he not made these remarks, his challenge to Mendelssohn might not have proved so easy to disparage as the impertinence of a Christian proselytizer. It might more often have been seen as what it was – a fairly cogent statement of the essential opposition between the basic principles of liberalism and the fundamental teachings of traditional Judaism.

As Cranz clearly understood, it is impossible simultaneously to uphold the existence of an inalienable natural right to liberty of conscience and to affirm the absolute, coercive authority of a covenant that requires the worship of the one and only God (while prohibiting the worship of other gods). On the basis of the fundamental premises of liberalism, one would have to conclude that God would *never* have had the will or the power to deprive the ancient Israelites and their descendants of their natural right to practice whatever religion they wished. A consistent liberal would therefore have good reason to agree with Cranz that Judaism merely "purports to be founded on divine revelation."

Unlike many of his later admirers, Mendelssohn seems to have been fully aware of the true importance of Cranz's challenge. It cut him, he said, to the heart, and he wrote *Jerusalem* mainly to respond to it.[16] Still, he did not mention Cranz's pamphlet until the middle of the book. Before addressing directly the issues that Cranz had raised, Mendelssohn dug himself even deeper into difficulties by elaborating at much greater length and formulating much more sharply the views that had provoked his adversary to confront him. In Section I of *Jerusalem*, he explained more thoroughly than he had before why God could never desire coerced obedience and spelled out his own social contract theory, one that precluded any state from impinging in even the smallest way on an individual's inalienable right to liberty of conscience.

Next, in Section II, Mendelssohn recapitulated Cranz's main objections to his earlier arguments and set about responding to them. He did so, however, in a surprisingly leisurely fashion, addressing first the concerns of another critic, a certain David Ernst Mörschel, who had appended a postscript to Cranz's pamphlet, and then venturing into a number of different areas. In these wide-ranging pages, Mendelssohn, among other things, explained why a Jew could be fully respectful of natural religion, set forth the criteria by which one determines the genuineness of a purported revelation, reaffirmed the historicity of the Sinaitic revelation, accounted for the origins of idolatry, speculated about the purpose of the Jewish ceremonial law, insisted upon the non-dogmatic character of the Jewish religion, and described the singular "Mosaic constitution." For our present purposes, we need to pay attention only to the passages in which Mendelssohn expounded on matters that he himself identified as being of relevance to his defense against Cranz.

Only one of the subjects Mendelssohn discussed prior to his account of the constitution introduced by Moses fits this description. Among the laws of the Torah, he maintained, none declare: "*You shall believe or not believe. They all say: You shall do or not do.* Faith is not commanded, for it accepts no other commands than those that come to it by way of conviction." Consequently, according to the law of Moses, "reward and punishment are only for actions, acts of commission and omission which are subject to a man's will . . ." Nowhere are Jews obligated to subscribe to specific articles of faith.[17]

Mendelssohn did not immediately explain the pertinence of these observations to his main concern in *Jerusalem*. Before doing so he observed that in the Israelites' "original constitution, state and religion were not conjoined, but *one*; not connected, but identical." Since God was Israel's Lawgiver and Regent of the nation,

> civil matters acquired a sacred and religious aspect, and every civil
> service was at the same time a true service of God. The
> community was a community of God; its affairs were God's; the
> public taxes were God's; and everything down to the least police
> measure was part of the *divine service*.[18]

This general situation had implications with regard to crimes as well. "Every sacrilege against the authority of God, as the lawgiver of the nation, was a crime against the Majesty, and therefore a crime of state." Under Israel's constitution, such offenses as blasphemy and sabbath desecration (to which Cranz had made specific reference) "could and, indeed, had to be punished civilly, not as erroneous opinion, not as *unbelief*, but as *misdeeds*, as sacreligious crimes aimed at abolishing or weakening the authority of the lawgiver and thereby undermining the state itself."[19]

Mendelssohn then stressed how mild these inevitable punishments actually were. Even the perpetrators of capital crimes such as blasphemy and desecration of the sabbath were treated with great leniency. As a consequence, executions must have been exceedingly rare. "Indeed, as the rabbis say, any court competent to deal with capital offenses and concerned for its good name must see to it that in a period of *seventy years* not more than one person is sentenced to death."

Immediately after this sentence, Mendelssohn abruptly announced that he had effectively refuted his adversaries:

> This clearly shows how little one must be acquainted with the Mosaic law and the constitution of Judaism to believe that according to them *ecclesiastical right* and *ecclesiastical power* are authorized or that temporal punishments are to be inflicted for unbelief or erring belief. *The Searcher for Light and Right*, as well as Mr. Mörschel, are therefore far removed from the truth when they believe I have abolished Judaism by my rational arguments against ecclesiastical right and ecclesiastical power. Truth cannot be in conflict with truth. What divine law commands, reason, which is no less divine, cannot abolish.[20]

But had Mendelssohn really succeeded so completely in reconciling the truth of revelation with the truth of reason, or did he merely assert that he had done so? In my opinion, his arguments against Cranz fell far short of achieving the goals he claimed to have reached.

In distinguishing between the ancient Israelite constitution and an "ecclesiastical law armed with power," Mendelssohn seems to have been suggesting that, as Eliezer Schweid has put it, the fusion of state and religion "is possible and justified only when God himself is the sovereign power in the state." But as Schweid himself has correctly observed, this is a forced and inadequate solution to the problem.[21] It in no way alters the fact that under the arrangements prevailing in ancient Israel, religious offenses, whatever they are called, were subject to punishment in a manner completely inconsistent with Mendelssohn's principles. It was of no essential importance, either, that these punishments were rarely inflicted.[22] "As Mendelssohn himself knew, this answer could only soften but not eliminate the criticism" to which he was responding.[23] Punishment, however infrequent and mild, was still punishment.

Mendelssohn did, to be sure, score one point against Cranz. The laws of Moses, Cranz had claimed, "would be sharp after anyone who had the least opinion of his own, and dared to express it by word or deed." In response to this charge, Mendelssohn had shown that Judaism was far more concerned with deeds than words. What Mendelssohn conveniently overlooked here, however, was that the freedom of expression permitted by Judaism was by no means as absolute as his own principles required it to be. The Torah may have left Jews free to define the principles of their own religion in a variety of different ways, but it did not leave them free to believe in Baal. And even if it contained no punishments for believing in Baal, it did inflict the severest punishments on anyone who worshipped him or any other gods apart from the God of Israel. In doing so it deprived individual Israelites of the unrestricted freedom of religion that Mendelssohn, in his capacity as a political philosopher, listed among the inalienable rights of all human beings.

Despite his confident pose and defiant pronouncements, Mendelssohn himself seems to have recognized the insufficiency of his initial response to Cranz. For after recapitulating his main points one more time, he introduces an additional consideration:

> Moreover, as the rabbis expressly state, *with the destruction of the Temple, all corporal and capital punishments and, indeed, even monetary fines, insofar as they are only national, have ceased to be legal.* Perfectly in accordance with my principles, and inexplicable without them! The civil bonds of the nation were dissolved; religious offenses were no longer crimes against the state; and the religion, as religion, knows of no punishment, no other penalty than the one the remorseful sinner *voluntarily* imposes on himself.[24]

While this may seem, at first glance, to be something of an afterthought, it is clearly much more than that. It is only here that Mendelssohn actually exclaims that he has reconciled Judaism with his own principles and thereby accomplished what he set out to do.

There are, however, two major reasons why even those who are pleased by what he says should not join Mendelssohn in this cry of victory. For these utterances are, first of all, based on faulty history. As Alexander Altmann rather delicately put it, "Mendelssohn's assertion that punitive measures by Jewish courts ceased after the loss of political independence does not fully correspond to the facts."[25] In actuality, as Yirmiyahu Yovel has stated, even in the Diaspora

> Jewish religion was not voluntary in the sense in which modern political theories use this term. It contained an element of coercion, of legal sanction, banning the rebel and subjecting the members of the congregation to rabbinical authority. This was

usually done by decree of the Christian authorities. It was a kind of tolerance, or privilege, which the Jewish congregation enjoyed, but within the community it imposed the authority of a religious law and a semi-theocratic government of the kind which Mendelssohn opposed.[26]

More important, however, than the historical inaccuracy of Mendelssohn's argument is its theoretical inadequacy. For even if it had been true that post-exilic Judaism had entirely abandoned all forms of religious coercion, this would not have changed the fact that what Mendelssohn called "the old, original Judaism" had indeed condoned the use of force to compel Jews to obey religious law. As we have seen, this was a matter of the utmost importance to Cranz. Even if the ecclesiastical statutory law of Judaism, as he put it, was no longer being enforced, it is "still there" – that is, it is present in the Bible and ready to be reinstituted. To explain how the existence at *any* time of such a state of affairs could be reconciled with his rational, liberal principles was precisely the task that Cranz had set for Mendelssohn. How could a God who *never* wished for coerced obedience to His will have revealed the laws of Moses, which called for such behavior? How could He *ever* have laid the basis for a state that deprived its inhabitants of their inalienable right to religious freedom?

These are the questions that Mendelssohn dodged. When he rested his case, at the end of his book, on the fact that the Mosaic constitution had become defunct, he resorted to the very strategy that Cranz had warned him (in a passage not quoted in *Jerusalem*) not to consider using. Why, then, did he think that it would work? He seems to have hoped that his readers would have been thoroughly distracted by all of the other weighty matters discussed in *Jerusalem* and would not notice his failure to develop an adequate response to the challenge that had provoked him to write the book in the first place.

This failure was, in truth, inevitable, for it is simply impossible to reconcile liberalism and traditional Judaism on the theoretical level in accordance with Cranz's demands.[27] In practice, of course, as the experience of the Western world over the past two centuries abundantly attests, it is not at all difficult for the two to arrive at a *modus vivendi*. There is nothing in their religion that would preclude traditional Jews from assuming the responsibilities of citizenship in liberal democratic polities and loyally serving them. It is, indeed, entirely possible for them to prefer such states to any other form of regime – in the Diaspora. Even in

Israel today, people may devise pragmatic justifications for the preservation of the country's existing regime and the postponement of the establishment of a state based on the Law of Moses, a *halakhic* state. But traditional Jews, by definition, can never abandon the hope for the ultimate restoration in the Land of Israel of a state founded on what Mendelssohn called "the Mosaic constitution."

Moses Mendelssohn lived at a time when such a state was a far more distant dream than it is today. It was a dream that he himself displayed no great longing to see realized. Nevertheless, even as he strove to demonstrate the irrelevance of the Mosaic constitution to contemporary politics, he could not consign it to the past as an altogether antiquated institution, and he even felt compelled to speculate vaguely about its recurrence. It existed only once, he remarked, and it "has disappeared, and only the Omniscient knows among what people and in what century something similar will again be seen."[28] It would have been inconceivable for Mendelssohn to have expressly renounced the hope that his own people would once again be fortunate enough to be the recipient of such a blessing. If, on the other hand, he had clearly expressed the hope that they would be the lucky people, his liberal principles would have been exposed as purely provisional, as nothing more than a convenient instrument for espousing what was at the moment in the best interests of the Jews.

At least one of Mendelssohn's later scholarly readers was in any case convinced that his public promotion of liberalism was purely a matter of expediency. According to Ron Sigad, Mendelssohn believed that when the Jews are in exile, living as a minority in less than ideal non-Jewish states, it is in their interest both as men and as Jews to advocate the establishment of barriers between church and state. In the ideal state, however, the one governed by the original Mosaic constitution, he did not consider any such separation to be necessary. Liberty of conscience, in Mendelssohn's eyes, was not something good in itself but something that needed to be upheld only where Jews were living on foreign soil and were not their own masters.[29]

No less a figure than Immanuel Kant drew very different conclusions from his reading of *Jerusalem*. Shortly after the book first appeared, he wrote to Mendelssohn, commending him for having "known how to reconcile your religion with such a degree of freedom of conscience as one would not have imagined it to be capable of, and as no other religion can boast of."[30] But what was the real meaning of Mendelssohn's deft moves? *Jerusalem*, Kant later wrote, covertly signaled to the Gentiles that "if you yourselves remove Judaism from your own religion...we shall consider your proposal" that we formally convert to Christianity.

> (In fact, all that would then remain would be a purely moral religion, without any admixture of statutes.) By throwing off the yoke of external observances our burden is not made easier in the least if another [burden] is imposed on us instead, namely that of articles of faith concerning a sacred history, which presses a conscientious person much harder.[31]

Kant clearly suspected that Mendelssohn's apparent reconciliation of Judaism and liberalism merely cloaked his true intention, which was to subvert Judaism from within.

It may seem quite perverse of Kant to have read *Jerusalem* in a manner so much at variance with Mendelssohn's ostensible purpose of defending and preserving Judaism. But Kant was not being capricious. He himself was a philosopher who was, in the words of Yirmiyahu Yovel, "able, in theory, to dispose altogether of revealed religion and its sacred documents and who looked forward to the replacement of historical forms of religion by a purely rational religion."[32] Nevertheless, while assuming the guise of a respectful interpreter of Scripture, he "used the Bible to reach out to the masses and subvert their longstanding attitudes."[33] He employed "biblical heremenutics as an agent of moral history." If he made frequent references to Scripture, he did so largely in order to "pose as sharing the believer's first principles by appealing to the Bible," a practice that enabled him to "turn the former against themselves."[34] This, Kant thought, was the way in which a rational man ought to deal with the claims of revealed religion, and this, he seems to have believed, is what the eminently rational Mendelssohn must have been doing with respect to the religion of his fathers.

Sigad and Kant are among the very few interpreters of Mendelssohn's *Jerusalem* who have considered the book's reconciliation of Judaism and liberalism to be lacking in solidity.[35] But I believe that they have judged correctly. It does not necessarily follow, however that either of them is correct in his evaluation of the significance of Mendelssohn's inconsistencies. It may be the case that Mendelssohn was at bottom neither a theocrat temporarily disguised as a liberal nor a liberal deviously masquerading as a believer. He may simply have been of two minds, attracted by two theoretically incompatible ways of understanding the world and incapable of choosing between them.

Whatever may have been Mendelssohn's innermost thoughts, the practical ramifications of his ruminations are clear.[36] They provide a rationale for the dissolution of what we might call Judaism's coercive, collectivist dimension and the transformation of the Jewish religion into an entirely *voluntary* matter. Mendelssohn was the first Jewish thinker to declare it to be entirely up to the individual Jew, and not his rabbi or his communal leaders, to determine whether he would fulfill his duty to live in accordance with its demands. He thus showed, for the first time, how one could render the Jewish religion fully compatible with liberalism. For those who found him convincing, Judaism could become "Thomas Jefferson."

To a great many nineteenth- and twentieth-century Jews this was a very welcome message, one that facilitated their full absorption into the liberal polities of the Western world. Milton Konvitz epitomized their thinking when he announced in 1987 that "[w]e pay tribute to Jefferson and to Mendelssohn, because they were pioneers in establishing the link between religion and liberty."[37] The very completeness of the Jews' integration into the Western democracies, however, seems to have obviated the need for any continued reiteration of such sentiments. It has even made it possible for a few contemporary thinkers to raise doubts about the supposed affinities between their religion and the fundamental principles of liberalism without having to fear that they will do anything to weaken the liberal state and thereby place their fellow Jews in jeopardy.

One should consider, for instance, the work of David Novak, a leading student of medieval and modern Jewish philosophy who is also a leading figure in traditional (though non-Orthodox) circles. In his recent book, *Covenantal Rights: A Study in Jewish Political Theory*, Novak has sought to carve out a new path for Jewish political thinking. Disturbed by the contempt for human rights and democratic regimes demonstrated by Kahane and his ilk, he has risen to the defense of liberal democracy. Yet he is unwilling to embrace fundamental liberal principles, which he considers to be both misguided and self-destructive. Novak regards secular social contract theories as intellectual dead ends; he does not believe that they can provide a sound basis for human rights. In his opinion, the only fruitful way "to bridge a commitment to the Jewish tradition and a concern for human rights" is "to locate the concept of human rights *within* the Jewish tradition itself and then develop it from there."[38] Although Novak knows that this will not be an easy task, he makes it the fundamental goal of his "study in Jewish political theory." One of the noteworthy aspects of this study is the complete absence in it of any mention whatsoever of the work of the first Jewish thinker to dwell on the kind of theoretical issues that Novak addresses: Moses Mendelssohn. Novak compensates for this omission in his subsequent and very latest book, *The Jewish Social Contract*, where he discusses Mendelssohn rather extensively. He does so, however, primarily to condemn him for articulating a theological-political position that above all "is inadequate to the Jewish tradition because it renders it subordinate to a non-Jewish universe..." and not to derive any positive message whatsoever from his teaching.[39]

Novak is by no means the only Jewish political thinker to disregard or disparage Mendelssohn in recent years. Very few participants in the renewed discussion in the United States of the role that Judaism ought to play in the public square have made even perfunctory references to him. Nor has he been the object of much attention in Israel, where the theory developed in *Jerusalem* might potentially be of the most use. Beset by the ever-increasing tension between theocratic and liberal conceptions of a Jewish state, many important Israeli religious intellectuals have devoted a great deal of time and effort to the search for a theological-political theory that could provide the basis for more harmonious coexistence between religious and secular Jews. Mendelssohn's *Jerusalem* would seem to be a book well-tailored for their purposes, but, to the best of my knowledge, none of the religious thinkers involved in this pursuit has turned to it for assistance. None of them has echoed what we have seen to be his clinching argument, his contention that "with the destruction of the Temple, all corporal and capital punishments and, indeed, even monetary fines, insofar as they are only national, have ceased to be legal." Instead of looking to Mendelssohn for guidance, compromise-seeking Israelis have turned to a variety of sources, from medieval Jewish political thinkers to the twentieth-century Palestine-born American rabbi Haim Hirschenson to an assimilated European Jewish thinker like Karl Popper.[40]

Mendelssohn's *Jerusalem* has long been recognized as the work that marked the beginning of modern Jewish thought, the first sustained and serious attempt to defend Judaism in terms of modern philosophical teachings. That it still deserves such recognition is beyond question. Nevertheless, before one attempts to summarize and assess *Jerusalem* as a theological treatise, it is necessary to view it in the light of what its author tells us was his primary purpose in writing it. By Mendelssohn's own testimony, the book represents an attempt to respond to what was a very significant polemical challenge, even if it emanated from a rather inconsequential man who cloaked himself in anonymity. Mendelssohn himself apparently considered it to be of the utmost importance to respond to this challenge and thereby to bring his religion into accord with his political philosophy. He did the best that he could do. For many

Jews living in Western liberal democracies in the centuries that followed the publication of *Jerusalem*, this was good enough. Mendelssohn proved the point that they very much wanted to see established. Today, however, when the tension between the provisions of the Torah and the outlook of Thomas Jefferson is once again close to the forefront of Jewish life, one cannot find traditional Jewish thinkers who believe that they can paper over their people's theological-political problems with Mendelssohn's makeshift solution to them. They have to look elsewhere for guidance.

Notes

1. For the historical background to this situation, see Jonathan Sarna, "The Cult of Synthesis in American Jewish Culture," *Jewish Social Studies*, 5, no. 1–2, Fall 1998/Winter 1999, pp. 52–79.
2. For the situation in Israel, see Ehud Sprinzak, *The Ascendance of Israel's Radical Right* (Oxford: Oxford University Press, 1991). For a related case in the Diaspora, see Jerold Auerbach, *Are We One?: Jewish Identity in the United States and Israel* (New Brunswick: Rutgers University Press, 2001).
3. See, for instance, Aviezer Ravitzky, *Ha-im Titakhen Medinat Halakhah?: HaParadox shel ha-Teokratiyah Hayehudit* (Israel Democracy Institute, 2004). See also David Novak, *Covenantal Rights: A Study in Jewish Political Theory* (Princeton: Princeton University Press, 2000), which will be discussed later.
4. See, above all, the work of Shmuel Feiner, especially his *The Jewish Enlightenment* (Philadelphia: University of Pennsylvania Press, 2002) and his "Mendelssohn and Mendelssohn's Disciples: A Reexamination" in *The Year Book of the Leo Baeck Institute*, XL (1995), pp. 133–167.
5. On Mendelssohn's life, see Alexander Altmann, *Moses Mendelssohn: A Biographical Study* (Tuscaloosa: University of Alabama Press, 1973) and, more recently, Shmuel Feiner, *Moshe Mendelssohn* (Jerusalem: Zalman Shazar Center, 2005).
6. See David Sorkin, *Moses Mendelssohn and the Religious Enlightenment* (Berkeley: University of California Press, 1996), pp. 33–89.
7. Shmuel Feiner, *The Jewish Enlightenment*, pp. 166–172. Feiner has highlighted the degree to which Mendelssohn's political writings must also be understood in the context of developments within the Jewish community.
8. Moses Maimonides, *The Guide of the Perplexed*, translated by Shlomo Pines (Chicago: University of Chicago Press, 1963), pp. 3–4.
9. See Moses Mendelssohn, *Jerusalem: Or on Religious Power and Judaism*, edited by Alexander Altmann and translated by Allan Arkush (Hanover and London: University Press of New England, 1983), pp. 84–85. See also Jacob Katz, "To Whom was Mendelssohn Replying in his *Jerusalem*?" in *Zion*, 36, nos. 1–2 (1971), pp. 116f.

10. *Moses Mendelssohn Gesammelte Schriften Jubiläumsausgabe* (Berlin and Stuttgart-Bad Cannstatt: Friedrich Frommann Verlag, 1972), vol. 8, p. 18.

11. Ibid., pp. 19–20.

12. Paul Mendes-Flohr and Jehuda Reinharz, *The Jew in the Modern World* (Oxford and New York: Oxford University Press, 1995), p. 92.

13. Ibid., p. 93.

14. Ibid., p. 92.

15. David Sorkin, for instance, boils Cranz's main argument down to the claim that in opposing excommunication, Mendelssohn had repudiated Judaism. He represents him as having argued that "Since Mendelssohn had called for the abrogation of the ban, what could be left of his faith?" (*Moses Mendelssohn and the Religious Enlightenment*, p. 118). As we have seen, however, the crucial issue for Cranz was not excommunication but religious coercion per se. Jeffrey S. Librett, too, focuses on the question of excommunication in his more extended analysis of Cranz's pamphlet. But he goes on to say "that what is at stake in this debate" between Cranz and Mendelssohn "is not merely or even principally state and religion or Judaism and Christianity, but rather the status of language in its figural and nonfigural dimensions." Cf. his *The Rhetoric of Cultural Dialogue: Jews and Germans from Moses Mendelssohn to Richard Wagner and Beyond* (Stanford: Stanford University Press, 2000), p. 49. Although Librett proceeds to discuss at some length the ways in which *Jerusalem*'s treatment of the relationship between religion and state constitutes a response to Cranz, he loses sight of the fact that Cranz had accused Mendelssohn of adhering to a religion that clearly violated his own rational principles.

16. Moses Mendelssohn, *Jerusalem*, pp. 84–85.

17. Ibid., p. 100.

18. Ibid., p. 128.

19. Ibid., p. 129.

20. Ibid., p. 130.

21. Eliezer Schweid, *Ha-Yehudi ha-Boded veha-Yahadut* (Tel Aviv, 1974), p. 173.

22. Jeremy Dauber has recently pointed out how Mendelssohn manipulated a Talmudic passage in order to make this point. BT Makot 7a has it that "a Sanhedrin that effects an execution once in seven years is branded a bloody tribunal; R' Elazar b. Azariah says once in seventy years." Mendelssohn, in paraphrasing this passage, quotes "the rabbis" as saying that a court must see to it "that in a period of *seventy* years not more than one person is sentenced to death." Dauber shrewdly observes that while the rabbinic language implies that courts may in the past have exceeded the specified limit, "no such impression is given in Mendelssohn's formulation." More importantly, Mendelssohn repeats not the number seven but seventy, "adopting the less normative interpretation for polemical purposes." See Jeremy Dauber, *Antonio's Devils: Writers of the Jewish Enlightenment and the Birth of Modern Hebrew*

and Yiddish Literature (Stanford: Stanford University Press, 2004), pp. 158–159.

23. Isaac Heinemann, *Ta'ammei ha-Mitzvot be-Sifrut Yisrael* (Jerusalem, 1956), Part II, p. 19.

24. Moses Mendelssohn, *Jerusalem*, p. 130.

25. Ibid., p. 232, note to p. 130, lines 24–27.

26. Yirmiyahu Yovel, *Dark Riddle: Hegel, Nietzsche, and the Jews* (University Park: Pennsylvania State University Press, 1998), p. 198, n. 11. Yovel proceeds to argue that Mendelssohn's words on this subject in *Jerusalem* "were intended for the non-Jewish world and are filled with apologetic imprecision."

27. Two of the most recent scholarly treatments of this subject have, in my opinion, mistakenly denied that Mendelssohn's argument was unsuccessful. In *Moses Mendelssohn and the Religious Enlightenment*, David Sorkin argues that the inaccuracy of Mendelssohn's account of an entirely non-coercive post-Biblical Judaism is of little consequence. "Mendelssohn did not make an assertion about history," he maintains, "but about an ideal situation and the principles that should inform it...He did not create a fictional account of the past; instead, he projected a timeless ideal of what should be even if it obviously had not occurred," (p. 138). Here Sorkin loses sight of the unbridgeable difference between Mendelssohn's timeless ideal of freedom of conscience and the "Mosaic constitution's" clear legitimization not only of what he refers to as "the least police measures" but also of the use of lethal force to stamp out such things as idol worship and desecration of the sabbath. In an article on "Mendelssohn's Heavenly Politics" in *Perspectives on Jewish Thought and Mysticism*, eds. Alfred L. Ivry, Elliot R. Wolfson, and Allan Arkush (Amsterdam: Harwood, 1998), Warren Zev Harvey similarly blurs the distinction between the Mosaic constitution and a free society. "In the heavenly politics of the Mosaic constitution," he writes, "God is the King, since the divine King, unlike mortal kings, has no personal needs, His only interest is in the true happiness of His subjects. The Mosaic constitution is thus a constitution of freedom: It liberates human beings from the oppressive rule of other human beings" (407). But freedom and the exemption from subjugation to oppressive rule are not the same thing. Even a well-meaning tutelary government, such as that enjoined by the Mosaic constitution, deprives individuals of much of the freedom to which Mendelssohn considers them to be at all times entitled.

28. *Jerusalem*, p. 131.

29. Ron Sigad, "*Moshe Mendelssohn – Yahadut, Politika Elohit, u-Medinat Yisrael,*" *Da'at*, no. 7 (1981), p. 102.

30. See Alexander Altmann, *Moses Mendelssohn: A Biographical Study* (Tuscaloosa: University of Alabama Press, 1973), p. 517.

31. Immanuel Kant, *Religion Within the Limits of Reason Alone*, translated by T. M. Greene and H. H. Hudson (New York: Harper and Row, 1960), p. 154.

32. Yirmiyahu Yovel, "Biblical Interpretation as Philosophical Praxis: A Study of Spinoza and Kant," *Journal of the History of Philosophy,* XI (1973), p. 193.

33. Ibid., p. 194.

34. Yirmiyahu Yovel, *Kant and the Philosophy of History* (Princeton: Princeton University Press, 1980), p. 216.

35. Michael Morgan is another. For his analysis of the flaws in Mendelssohn's arguments in *Jerusalem,* see chapter 3 ("Liberalism in Mendelssohn's Jerusalem") of his *Dilemmas in Modern Jewish Thought: The Dialectics of Revelation and History* (Bloomington and Indianapolis: Indiana University Press, 1992).

36. For an analysis of Mendelssohn's underlying loyalties that is closer to that of Kant than to that of Sigad, see my *Moses Mendelssohn and the Enlightenment* (Albany: State University of New York Press, 1994), pp. 254–292.

37. See Milton Konvitz, *Torah and Constitution: Essays in American Jewish Thought* (Syracuse: Syracuse University Press, 1998), p. 28. The remarks cited here appear in a chapter entitled "Religious Liberty: The Congruence of Thomas Jefferson and Moses Mendelssohn," which was first published separately in *Jewish Social Studies,* 49, 2 (Spring 1987), 115–124.

38. David Novak, *Covenantal Rights: A Study in Jewish Political Theory,* p. 29. For an extended examination of this work, see my "Conservative Political Theology and the Freedom of Religion: The Recent Work of Robert Kraynak and David Novak" (*Polity,* vol. 37, no. 1, January 2005, pp. 82–107).

39. David Novak, *The Jewish Social Contract: An Essay in Political Theology* (Princeton: Princeton University Press, 2005), p. 183.

40. In his recent book, *Politics and the Limits of Law: Secularizing the Political in Medieval Jewish Thought* (Stanford: Stanford University Press, 2001), Menachem Lorberbaum identifies medieval religious thinkers who "clearly uphold the secularization of politics, rejecting the halakhic polity as untenable" (p. 14). Eliezer Schweid explores the thought of Haim Hirschenson in *Democracy and Halakhah* (Lanham, New York, and London: University Press of America, 1994). Menachem Fisch presents a Popperian model in "Lishlot be-aher – Ha-etgar ha-hilkhati be-hidush ha-Ribonut," in *He-Aher: Beyn adam le-zulato,* ed. Hayim Deutsch and Menahem Ben Sasson (Tel Aviv: Yedioth Ahronoth, 2001), pp. 225–259.

4 Jewish Philosophy after Kant: The Legacy of Salomon Maimon

PAUL W. FRANKS

Blessed be God, who has given of His wisdom to Kant.

Isaac Breuer[1]

Since the end of the eighteenth century, no non-Jewish philosopher has been more central to Jewish philosophy than Kant. The major Jewish philosophers of late modernity have worked out their positions in relation to Kant, sometimes through the mediation of post-Kantians such as Hegel, Schelling, and Schopenhauer – just as the major ancient and medieval Jewish philosophers worked out their positions in relation to Plato, sometimes through the mediation of post-Platonists such as Aristotle, Plotinus and Alfarabi.[2] What is the cause of Jewish philosophy's intimate relation to Kant?

One explanation is that Kant's career coincided with the entry of Jews into German academic and intellectual life, a development to which Kant was openly sympathetic and for which justification could be found in his philosophy, with its doctrine of equal respect for each rational being.[3] When Moses Mendelssohn visited Kant's lectures in Königsberg, Kant is said to have silenced the students' anti-Semitic jeers by greeting the great Jewish philosopher with a show of respect.[4] Kant had several Jewish students, including Markus Herz, whom he chose to defend his (Kant's) inaugural dissertation in 1770. These students, to whom an academic career was open only if they converted to Christianity, chose instead to promote Kantianism from within the Jewish community. After emancipation, when the ban on Jewish professors was formally lifted, Jews such as Otto Liebman and Hermann Cohen – the latter the first Jewish full professor in Germany – were at the forefront of the "back to Kant" movement. In the early twentieth century, when

I gratefully acknowledge the assistance and comments of Robert Gibbs, Peter Gordon, Yitzhak Melamed, Michael Morgan, Hindy Najman, Benjamin Pollock, and Eliot Wolfson.

Neo-Kantianism predominated within the intellectual establishment of Wilhelmine Germany, Isaac Breuer, the intellectual leader of "independent" German Orthodoxy, joined the Kant Society and wrote texts advocating "Torah-true Judaism" at a desk over which Kant's portrait hung.[5]

This explanation has little to do with the details of Kant's thought, so I will offer a complementary but content-based explanation, arguing that between Jewish philosophy and Kant lies a genuine affinity, which is due to Jewish philosophy's longstanding involvement with the Platonic tradition. Kant himself emphasizes his intimate relation to Plato, and this alone suffices for the development of a Kantianism deploying characteristically Jewish terms. However, some distinctive features of Kant's Platonism are especially susceptible to interpretation in terms of such central Jewish concepts as divine unity, law, and messianism. Moreover, Kant's Platonism is quickly radicalized by Salomon Maimon, who explicitly injects Jewish philosophy into post-Kantianism and post-Kantianism into Jewish philosophy. It is Maimon, above all, who facilitates Jewish philosophy's intimate entanglement with post-Kantian traditions such as German Idealism, Neo-Kantianism, and critical theory. While Maimon's role in the development of post-Kantianism is well-known, his centrality in the history of modern Jewish philosophy has hitherto been unacknowledged.[6]

I. FOUNDATIONS OF JEWISH KANTIANISM

Kant's Platonism plays a crucial role in Hermann Cohen's argument for what he calls "inner relations" between Kantianism and Judaism.[7] To acknowledge this point, however, we need not agree with Cohen's particular interpretations of Kant or Plato.[8] We need only note, first, Kant's efforts to position himself as Plato's true heir and, second, the long history throughout which Platonism has been intertwined with both Judaism and Christianity – so closely that someone brought up in either religion can encounter certain Platonic themes for the first time and immediately feel at home.

I.I. Kant and the Ideas

Plato is the author about whom Kant famously remarks in his 1781 *Critique of Pure Reason* "that when we compare the thoughts that an author expresses about a subject, in ordinary speech as well as in writings, it is not at all unusual to find that we understand him even better than he understood himself".[9] When Kant enters uncharacteristically into a polemical controversy in 1796, it is to fend off a competing claim to inherit Platonism.[10]

Kant makes his 1781 remark when he is insisting, at the beginning of Division Two of the *Critique of Pure Reason* (the Transcendental Dialectic), on the distinction between concepts – even those pure or *a priori* concepts called categories – and ideas:

> Plato made use of the expression *idea* in such a way that we can readily see that he understood by it something that not only could never be borrowed from the senses, but that even goes far beyond the concepts of the understanding (with which Aristotle occupied himself), since nothing encountered in experience could ever be congruent to it. Ideas for him are archetypes of things themselves, and not, like the categories, merely the key to possible experience.[11]

In a passage that could easily surprise someone who has been reading the *Critique* sequentially, and for the first time, Kant protests that ideas "that go much too far for any object that experience can give ever to be congruent, but that nonetheless have their reality . . . are by no means merely figments of the brain." The popular portrait of the Platonic republic as "a dream of perfection that can have its place only in the idle thinker's brain" could hardly be further from the truth.[12]

By defending ideas as essential to both epistemology and ethics, Cohen argues, Kant joins the Jewish tradition in opposing both sensualism and materialism.[13] Indeed, (1) Kant himself recognizes an affinity between the Jewish prohibition on representing God and his own insistence on the sublimity of the ideas,[14] which entails a prohibition on the methodological naturalization of reason.[15] But the affinity between Kant and Judaism is not only negative. As we will see, (2) notwithstanding the distinction between theory and practice, the reason whose naturalization Kant opposes is *one*, and he regards this unity as manifest primarily through the concept of *law*. Moreover, (3) Kant's concern for reason as law funds his *teleological conception of history*, which is at once both political and religious.

Kant's defence of Platonic ideas at the beginning of the Dialectic can surprise readers because his argument in the preceding Analytic seems so Aristotelian. He argues that concepts – regarded as *forms of thought* characteristic of the faculty of understanding – can be used to think of objects only in combination with "the matter of cognition", which is given to us humans only through sensibility. Concepts such as "fortune" and "fate," for which there is no appropriate sensible matter, lack objective validity and should, it seems, be jettisoned.[16] In order to save the categories from the fate of "fate," Kant undertakes the torturous task of showing that these *a priori* concepts – of substance, causality, and so on – can be combined with appropriate sensible matter by means of the structures of space and time, which he argues are sensibly given, yet *a priori*. This uncompromising, quasi-Aristotelian *hylomorphism* can leave one unprepared for the quasi-Platonic argument that ideas – *separate forms*, incapable of combination with any sensible matter whatsoever, even if it is *a priori* – are nonetheless essential to our cognition.

An idea, as Kant uses the term, is a representation of a *"totality of conditions* to a given conditioned thing," made possible by an *unconditioned condition* or *absolute.*[17] In other words, it is the representation of some given thing as *intelligible without residue*, so that there is an answer to every possible question as to why the thing is as it is. Though an answer may also invite further why-questions, these too can be answered, until at last an answer is reached that is either self-explanatory or in need of no explanation whatsoever. This final answer gives us a reason that is utterly satisfying, hence unconditioned or absolute. An idea, then, represents *a complete series of answers to why-questions*. Kant maintains that there are three such ideas: God, the world, and the soul.

Now, Kant thinks that only God can be in a position to *know* the absolute totality of reasons for any given thing. No matter how much we humans succeed in developing natural science, some unanswered question, some residue of unintelligibility, will still remain. For human knowledge is indeed hylomorphic: we can think objects only through the combination of conceptual form and sensible matter; we can know only the sensible objects we can think; and the spatio-temporal form of these sensible objects – the handedness of space, the unidirectionality of time – will always remain both fundamental and inexplicable.

Consequently, no idea – no complete series of answers to why-questions – can ever be an object of human knowledge. Yet, Kant argues, without ideas morality would be impossible: "That no human being will ever act adequately to what the pure idea of virtue contains does not prove in the least that there is something chimerical in this thought. For it is only by means of this idea that any judgment of moral worth or unworthy is possible..." Similarly, there could be no judgment of political justice or injustice without the idea of a perfect "constitution providing for the *greatest human freedom* according to laws that permit *the freedom of each to exist together with that of others...*"[18]

Indeed, without ideas, not only morality but also human knowledge would be impossible. For knowledge is not a mere aggregate of isolated perceptions of fact. It is a unified body of interconnected cognitions, representing a world that we can understand, albeit imperfectly. Whence, then, does knowledge get its essential unity? Not from already known principles whereby we can actually explain why the world is as it is. For we come to know such principles only late in our epistemic development, and our ability to explain is always limited. Instead, knowledge gets its essential unity from the *goal* that uniquely orients the pursuit of knowledge. And this goal, Kant argues, can be nothing other than knowledge of *the system of ideas*. This system consists of an infinitely intelligible reality – the thing in itself or the absolute *world* – which is constituted by *God* – the *ens realissimum* or the absolute ground of all reality – who is at the same time the infinite intellect or the absolute *soul*.

To be sure, we can approach this goal "only asymptotically."[19] Nevertheless, Kant argues that, only insofar as we keep our eyes on this prize, can we develop a body of empirical knowledge sufficiently unified to count as natural science. Indeed, his 1790 *Critique of Judgment* can be read as suggesting that, without the unattainable goal expressed in the ideas of reason, we could not even develop the empirical concepts that we employ in our perceptions of empirical objects. On this view, if we were stripped of ideas, we would be left not even with an aggregate of isolated perceptions of fact but merely with "blind intuitions."

Hence Kant rejects the popular notion that ideas are "figments of the brain." Unlike the concepts of fate and fortune, the ideas are neither artificial nor eliminable. Although not, like the categories, *constitutive* of the *object* of knowledge, the ideas are *regulative* of the *project* of knowledge, constituting *reason* itself. Kant's epistemology is quasi-Aristotelian with respect to the faculties of sensibility and understanding, which supply the material and formal ingredients of cognition. But it is quasi-Platonic when he argues for the necessity of the faculty of reason, whose separate forms enable these ingredients to be combined.

Cohen must have been struck by the familiarity of Kant's synthesis of quasi-Aristotelian and quasi-Platonic elements.[20] For a deep impression had been left on Jewish philosophy by the Neo-Platonic doctrine that Plato and Aristotle shared a single view, differing mainly in their mode of expression.[21] Thus – to cite the most famous version – Maimonides' ontology features a hylomorphic, knowable world, grounded in a series of separate forms, culminating in the unknowable yet demonstrably existent God.[22] Such a synthesis combines an Aristotelian focus on natural science and on virtue as the "second nature" of human beings, with a Platonic insistence that the human capacity for science and virtue cannot itself be understood unproblematically as part of the world that is natural science's object. Kant develops a similar synthesis, now in a transcendental register, as an indispensable aspect of his account of the possibility of experience.

1.2. Kant and the Law

Still more striking is the fact that Kant unites epistemology and ethics specifically through the concept of *law*. This concept has been central to Jewish philosophy at least since Philo of Alexandria, the earliest Jewish philosopher still known in any detail, who argued that the *nomos* revealed to Moses on Sinai was equivalent to the law of nature, the supreme norm of both knowledge and virtue.[23]

Kant could not hold Philo's Stoic view of nature since, in accordance with his own understanding of modern physics, he regards *natural laws* as strict necessities, not as norms. To follow laws that cannot be breached is no virtue. As we have seen, perfect virtue cannot be encountered in the natural world whose laws we can know. It can be represented only by an idea that sets an unattainable yet regulative goal. Nevertheless, the concept of law plays an indispensable role in Kant's moral philosophy.   ·

If the standard of morality is to be absolutely valid – obligatory regardless of any sensuous desire we may have – it can be understood only as a *practical law*: not a strict necessity, but an absolute norm. This is possible, Kant argues in the *Critique of Practical Reason*, only if the practical law has no sensuous matter whatsoever. It can only be a separate form – *the form of law or strict necessity itself* – which is the form of forms and which Kant calls *the moral law*.[24] Fundamentally, *practical rationality is action that originates from pure law.*

To be sure, any maxim on which we act involves not only *form* – the concepts whereby it attains the status of a general policy to act in certain ways whenever certain circumstances obtain – but also *matter* – an inclination to fulfill some particular desire, thereby achieving sensuous satisfaction. Maxims, like empirical cognitions, are hylomorphic. But just as knowledge does not consist in an aggregate of perceptions of fact, so practical rationality does not consist in an aggregate of actions performed on the basis of inclination. Both knowledge and practical rationality require *unity*. This unity is grounded, according to Kant, not in prior knowledge of mind-independent reality, but rather in the regulation of rationality's projects by aspiration to the goal of infinite intelligibility, of answering all why-questions. In other words, it is the ideas that secure the unity not only of theoretical but also of practical rationality. Thus, in Kant's ethics, as in his epistemology, quasi-Aristotelian hylomorphism is synthesized with a quasi-Platonic commitment to ideas or separate forms.

Ideas play two roles in Kantian ethics: they regulate both the maxims *on which* the virtuous agent acts, and the goals *for the sake of which* she acts. First, the moral law – the form of forms – serves as the virtuous agent's supreme maxim. She undertakes to act on any maxim whose adoption follows necessarily from adoption of the moral law as supreme maxim, and not to act on any maxim that is incompatible with adoption of the moral law as supreme maxim. The former maxims are moral duties, the latter prohibitions, while all remaining maxims are morally permissible. How is the moral status of a maxim determined? Kant offers several models for a reflection that rises above inclination. For our purposes, this is the most important: I ask myself whether a society of maximally virtuous agents could adopt the maxim in question. Since maximally virtuous agents are perfectly rational and consistent, any maxim they adopt has the force of law for them. So I ask myself *whether I would will a world in which the maxim in question is a law of nature.*[25]

How do ideas regulate the goal of ethical life? One might think that the virtuous agent's supreme goal should be to lead a life of maximal virtue. But, Kant argues, human beings want to be happy, and it is rational for us to pursue happiness, so long as it is subordinate to virtue. Thus, the supreme goal of ethical life – *the highest good* – is a world containing a society of maximally virtuous agents who are *just as happy as they deserve to be*. The highest good makes ethics into a project that is also *political and economical*. For it requires us to do whatever we can to create and support institutions and arrangements that maximally approximate this ideal world. Moreover, the highest good makes ethics into a project that is also *religious*. For, Kant argues, we humans can never *secure* the proportionality of happiness to virtue; only God, who is both creator of the world and has a holy will – a will for which the moral law just *is* a strict necessity – could render this goal attainable. Since the ethical project requires us to *hope* for the highest good, and since this hope is realizable only with divine assistance, it follows that the ethical project requires *belief in God.*[26] *Religion is thus required by reason as part of morality.*

Even committed Kantians have been unconvinced by Kant's argument that rational faith is presupposed by hope for the highest good. Some seek to dispense with religion altogether. Cohen, however, prefers to introduce the idea of God into Kantian ethics, not as the idea of a holy will that guarantees the realizability of the highest good, but rather as the idea of a holy will that is *the absolute ground of virtue*. This way of thinking is also found in Kant, and becomes increasingly prominent in Kant's later writings.[27] Since God altogether lacks inclinations and therefore cannot act immorally, God is even more morally perfect than a maximally virtuous agent who could act immorally but does not. The idea of God is thus the idea of a standard to which even a maximally virtuous agent would aspire. Thus God is "the legislator of the moral law" in the sense that God is the purest instance of the rational will that expresses itself in the moral law. Since a good will is the most valuable thing, indeed the very source of value in an agent's life, it follows that God is maximally valuable and is the ultimate source of all value in the world.

1.3. Kant and History

We have seen, then, that in both Kantian epistemology and ethics, ideas or separate forms set standards that, while unattainable, enable and regulate the project of rendering the natural and human worlds maximally intelligible. Thus Kant provides the foundation for a conception of *history* as goal-oriented and hence rationally assessable. Human history – as the history of science and of society – can and should be seen, in light of the ideas of reason, as moving towards a goal of perfection, which, because it can be approached only asymptotically, can only be hoped for as a future state.

Cohen takes this Kantian view of history to be consonant with Jewish Messianism.[28] Moreover, he sees it as the alternative to a way of thinking that was far more developed in his time than in Kant's – namely, *historicism*, the view that human affairs must be understood in relation to their own local historical contexts. Such a view seems to entail the claim that history can have no global rationality or significance, such as goal-directedness. In contrast, Cohen argues, Kant conceives no history without *the end of history*.[29] No matter how changeable our theories and our moral and political policies – and indeed our concepts – may be, the *goal* of theory and the *goal* of practice remain as unchanging as reason itself, for they are partly *constitutive* of reason.

To summarize what has been argued so far: Kant's quasi-Platonic turn towards ideas of reason, combined with his quasi-Aristotelian account of understanding, though highly novel, can seem to be an epistemological translation of the familiar combination of Aristotelianism and Platonism in the thought of influential Jewish philosophers such as Maimonides. Moreover, the special role of law in Kant's articulation of the unity of reason makes it possible to speak of Kantian reason in terms traditionally ascribed by Jews to God, and of Kantian history as unfolding towards a messianic epoch of justice. Kant's appeal to Jewish philosophers has, then, a content-based explanation.

2. FOUNDATIONS OF JEWISH POST-KANTIANISM

Kantianism's special attraction for Jews has arguably been intensified by major currents of post-Kantianism, notably German Idealism
and two of its successors: Neo-Kantianism and the critical theory of the
Frankfurt school. The close connection between German Idealism and
Lutheranism makes this seem surprising.[30]

To explain what he calls "the German idealism of the Jewish
philosophers," Habermas writes: "It remains astonishing how produc-
tively central motifs of German Idealism shaped so essentially by Protestantism can be developed in terms of the experience of the Jewish tradition. Because the legacy of the Kabbalah already flowed into and was
absorbed by Idealism, its light seems to refract all the more richly in the
spectrum of a spirit in which something of the spirit of mysticism lives
on, in however hidden a way."[31]

Habermas' argument is problematic. He himself excuses it as
"mere reportage" rather than properly philosophical. What he means by
"Kabbalah" is insufficiently determinate and – for the admirable, polemical purpose of refuting an anti-Semitic denigration of the Jewish contribution to German philosophy – he employs his opponent's conception of
Jewishness as determined solely by Jewish descent. Instead of contesting
this conception, he romanticizes it by suggesting that "something of the
spirit of mysticism lives on" in those of Jewish descent, independently
of Jewish identity and knowledge of traditional sources.

Still, there is a kernel of truth here. This is shown by consideration of
the crucial contribution to post-Kantianism made by Salomon Maimon,
who was well-versed in traditional sources, including Kabbalah. After
receiving encouragement from Kant himself, Maimon published a pair
of important works: the *Essay on Transcendental Philosophy* (1790),
written in German, which brought elements of Jewish philosophy to
bear on Kant, and the *Hill of the Guide* (1791), written in Hebrew, a
commentary on the first part of Maimonides' *Guide of the Perplexed*,
which brought elements of modern philosophy, including Kantianism,
to bear on what is arguably the one work of Jewish philosophy that no
Jewish philosopher can afford to ignore.

2.1. Maimon's Reformulation of Kant's Problem

Maimon criticizes Kant's attempt to solve the problem of the possibility of synthetic *a priori* judgments, which Kant calls "the general
problem of pure reason."[32] He argues that Kant's problem is essentially
the problem of the possibility of applying categorial forms to sensuously

given cognitive matter, which is structurally equivalent both to the early modern problem of the possibility of mind-body interaction, which exercised Descartes and his successors, and to the medieval problem of the possibility of creation, which was central to the concerns of those who sought to acknowledge both reason and scripture, among whom the most important for Maimon is Maimonides.[33] What makes Kant's problem distinctive is that it is raised as a *transcendental* question about form and matter as conditions of the possibility of *experience*.

All these problems concern the relationship between form and matter, and none, Maimon insists, can be solved on the assumption of form/matter dualism. Consequently, a range of interconnected Kantian dualisms – between intuition and concept, sensibility and understanding, understanding and reason, theory and practice – must be overcome if Kant's problem is to be solved.

The German Idealists and their post-Kantian successors accept Maimon's criticisms.[34] Even Cohen – who presents himself as returning from the metaphysical and psychological speculation of German idealism to authentic Kantianism – thinks it necessary to overcome the residue in Kant of a dualism of sensibility and understanding.[35]

2.2. Maimon's Radicalization of Kant's Platonism

Maimon draws on Jewish philosophical tradition not only for his reformulation of Kant's problem but also for his alternative proposal, which radicalizes Kant's Platonism.

While defending Plato's conception of ideas that flow "from the highest reason" as necessary for an adequate account of human reason, Kant expresses a reservation. He "cannot follow" Plato's use of these ideas to explain "speculative cognitions, whenever they were pure and given wholly *a priori*, and even...mathematics."[36] Kant explains the validity of mathematics and pure natural science otherwise, appealing not to the ideas of reason but rather to the pure spatio-temporal forms of sensibility and the categorial forms of the understanding.

The implications are indeed significant. If Plato's *single-form* account is correct, then it is possible *in principle* to employ reason for *speculative cognition* beyond the limits of sensible nature. But Kant's *multi-form* account, combined with the assumption that the only cognitive matter available to we humans has the form of sensibility – which is irreducible to the form of reason – entails the *impossibility* of any such rational cognition. Only the forms of sensibility and understanding *constitute* the objects of cognition and can therefore be used to attain knowledge. Meanwhile, the forms of reason or ideas merely *regulate* the cognitive project by setting unattainable goals for infinite approximation. What is at stake, then, is whether the realm of metaphysical speculation – including theology – is accessible to human reason or not.

In his seminal *Essay*, Maimon argues that Kant's multi-form account gives rise to a problematic dualism, leaving an unbridgeable gap between the sensible matter of cognition on the one side, and the forms of understanding and reason on the other. Instead, he proposes to reintroduce, as part of the explanation for the possibility of mathematics and physics, the idea of the infinite intellect or "highest reason" with which "Our understanding is one and the same, but in a limited way." Between the human or finite mind and the divine or infinite mind, there is an identity-in-difference.

This is evident in pure mathematics where, Maimon thinks, we generate objects and are "like gods."[37] In physics, however, where mathematical form is to be applied to *sensible* matter, synthetic *a priori* cognition is possible only if *both* form *and* sensible matter originate in the infinite intellect, where they are somehow identical. So physics presupposes what Maimon calls "ideas of understanding," as underlying our intuitions of sensible qualities. These may be treated *both* as ideas of sensible quality as such *and* as infinitesimal, intelligible quantities. In other words, an identity-in-difference must be assumed between the *qualities* of finite passivity and the infinitesimal *quantities* of infinite intellectual activity. Only then is there no gap of the kind Kant posits between sensible matter and intellectual form. What appears as *matter* from our ordinary, finite perspective is revealed as *form* from an infinite perspective that we can also occupy in mathematics.

Here Maimon draws on several medieval notions: that there is an active intellect that is at once intellectual agent, intellectual activity, *and* intellectual object; that the human finite intellect is the image of this active intellect; and that we humans should aspire to purge ourselves of matter and to achieve unity with this active intellect.[38] These notions figure centrally in Maimonides' interpretation of the Jewish doctrine that the human is created in the divine image, which endows us with creative powers and a vocation unshared by other creatures.

But Maimon is not merely repeating the thoughts of Maimonides. He is *recasting* Maimonideanism – more generally, the synthesis of Aristotelianism and Neo-Platonism characteristic of some medieval Jewish philosophy – in light of modern mathematics, especially calculus. At the same time, Maimon is radicalizing the Kantian notion that reason is unified through the idea as law. Whereas Kant uses the idea of law only to unify theoretical and practical reason, Maimon uses it to unify reason with understanding and sensibility.

This radicalization has had an enormous impact. While the German Idealists reject Maimon's valorization of pure mathematics, they accept his fundamental contention that Kant's reservation must be abandoned and that the possibility of synthetic *a priori* cognition must be explained on the basis of an identity-in-difference between the forms of infinite reason and the forms of finite reason. While Cohen rejects the use of the notion of identity to characterize the relationship between humanity and divinity, his "return to Kant" involves an account of the "infinitesimal method" as overcoming dualism. To a surprising extent, Cohen returns to Maimon.[39]

2.3. Maimon's Renewal of Philosophical Kabbalah

Impressed by the manuscript of Maimon's *Essay*, Kant writes that "none of my critics understood me and the main questions as well as Herr Maimon does." But he also rejects Maimon's alternative proposal, which he calls "Spinozism."[40]

Spinoza's characteristic doctrines – such as denial of teleology and the parallelism of infinite attributes – are nowhere to be found in Maimon's *Essay*. But "Spinozism" had long functioned as the name for various pernicious doctrines, such as fatalism and atheism, notwithstanding lack of any specific connection to Spinoza's thought. When Kant argues against Spinozism in the *Critique of Practical Reason*, his target is *any view involving denial of the transcendence and personality of God and/or of the distinctness of human beings from God*. Let us call this Spinozism$_1$.[41] Thus Kant can regard the idea of an identity-in-difference between the finite and the infinite intellect as an expression of Spinozism$_1$, regardless of whether Maimon is committed to Spinoza's specific view that the human is a finite mode of absolute substance.

But Kant may have something else in mind too. In 1699, Johann Georg Wachter had identified Spinozism with Kabbalah, and Kabbalah with Judaism.[42] Since then, the scandalous accusation of Spinozism, carrying an undertone of anti-Judaism, had been raised against two leading figures of the Enlightenment: Christian Freiherr von Wolff and Gotthold Ephraim Lessing (neither of whom were Jewish). In addition to raising a standard accusation, Kant may be alluding to Maimon's Jewish background.

In fact, Maimon's attraction to Spinozism predates his encounter with Kant. Numerous freethinking intellectuals in Germany are similarly drawn in the 1780s, sometimes thanks to Mendelssohn's widely read apology for him.[43] When, in letters to Mendelssohn published in 1785, Friedrich Heinrich Jacobi exposed Lessing's supposed Spinozism, the *intention* was to show that, pursued consistently, Enlightenment rationalism leads to atheism. But the *effect* was to make Spinozism respectable, at least among Germany's intellectual elite. Maimon must have felt especially close to Spinoza. He too is well-grounded in Maimonides' philosophy, and radicalizes that philosophy in a way that undermined his commitment to traditional Jewish practice.

Jacobi repeats Wachter's identification of Spinozism with Kabbalism, and Maimon himself states that Spinoza's "system had already been suggested to me in Poland by the kabbalistic writings."[44] Since Spinoza dismisses the Kabbalistic writings he has encountered,[45] it is striking that according to Maimon – who is competent to pass informed judgment – "the kabbalah is nothing but expanded Spinozism, in which not only is the origin of the world explained by the limitation [*Einschränkung*] of the divine being, but also the origin of every kind of being, and its relation to the rest, is derived from a separate attribute of God."[46] In other words, *the identity-in-difference between the infinite and the finite intellect, which is central to post-Kantianism after Maimon, can be explicated in either Spinozistic or Kabbalistic terms.*

"Spinozism," as Maimon uses the term here, is the view that every finite thing is in some sense a limitation of God. Let us call this Spinozism$_2$, which is a positive view whereas Spinozism$_1$ is negative. Spinoza's own view that humans are finite modes of absolute substance is *one* instance, but not the only possible one. Maimon identifies Spinozism$_2$ as a restricted version of Kabbalah, regarding the latter as a philosophical attempt to *explain* the origin of the world. He thus invokes a tradition of *philosophical Kabbalah* that originated in Spain and flourished during the Renaissance, a tradition that has been marginalized since the canonization of the *Zohar* and especially since the rise to dominance of the Kabbalah of Isaac Luria.[47] Accordingly, Maimon expresses a preference for the system of Moshe Cordovero,[48] and he understands *tzimtzum* – divine self-contraction – not in mythic terms, but rather as a variant of the rationalist principle of plenitude: "God thinks Himself as limited in every possible way."[49]

Responding to Kant's letter, however, Maimon does not endorse Spinozism or Kabbalah. Instead, he adopts a narrower conception of Spinozism, as the view that "God and the world are one and the same substance." Let us calls this Spinozism$_3$. Maimon denies that he is a Spinozist$_3$ on the ground that – although he makes no mention of it in the *Essay* – his account of the conditions for the possibility of natural science includes a *world-soul*:

> a power inherent in matter in general (the matter of all real objects), a power that affects matter in general in different ways according to the various ways that matter is modified . . . a substance created by God. God is represented as pure intelligence, outside the world. This world-soul, by contrast, is indeed represented as an intelligence but as one that is essentially connected to a body (the world), consequently as limited and as subordinate to the laws of nature. If one speaks of substance as *thing in itself*, one can as little claim that there are several substances in the world as one can claim that there is only one. If we speak of phenomena, on the other hand, I think there are good grounds for deciding in favour of the latter alternative.[50]

Here Maimon reaffirms once again his inheritance of the synthesis of Aristotelianism and Neo-Platonism characteristic of Maimonides. For this tradition identifies the world-soul of Plato's *Timaeus* with the form-bestowing active intellect found by some commentators in Aristotle's *De Anima*. Maimon can be seen as taking sides in a long-standing debate about whether to think of the agency through which God in-forms the world as being identical with God or – as Maimon asserts here – as a divine instrument.[51]

This is not Spinozism$_3$, but seems compatible with Spinozism$_2$. For in speaking of God *creating* the world-soul, Maimon does not rule out the characterization of creation as divine self-limitation. He emphasizes the *difference* between the divine and the natural, but it is unclear whether this excludes a deeper *identity*. Indeed, even if Maimon does not understand creation as divine self-limitation, he has hardly shown that he is not a Spinozist$_1$. For he could still regard human beings as mere limitations of the world-soul. Moreover, Maimon's move is strikingly reminiscent of the Kabbalistic distinction between the divine in itself – the *Ein-Sof* or transcendent infinite – and the sefirotic realm related to human life, a realm described typically as emanated, but sometimes as created.[52]

In short, Maimon explicitly rejects Kant's charge of Spinozism, and hence Kabbalism, which Maimon regards as closely connected. But there are senses in which both terms seem to apply to his views after all![53] Most importantly, Maimon shows, for the first time, not only how to respond to problems within Kantianism by deploying resources from medieval Jewish philosophy to radicalize the Platonic dimension of Kant's thought, but also how the resulting post-Kantianism may be inflected Kabbalistically. The combination of Kant with Kabbalah, which at first sounds so unlikely, becomes characteristic of the Jewish post-Kantianisms that follow.

2.4. Maimon's Messianism

Maimon's thought contains a further twist. As we have seen, Kant argues that, without ideas of reason, there can be no genuine alternative to methodological naturalism, and Maimon extends the argument to include ideas of the understanding. However, Maimon also contends that *transcendental philosophy and methodological naturalism are destined to an eternally unresolved stand-off*.[54]

This is because transcendental philosophy, as Maimon understands it, consists in the investigation of the necessary conditions for the possibility of scientific cognition. But only pure mathematics is indisputably established as a science – which is to say, a body of cognitions grounded in *a priori* principles. To be sure, Kant *assumes* that physics is also a science in this sense, involving the application of mathematics to sensible objects, and Maimon himself offers an alternative account of the conditions for the possibility of natural science. But Kant's assumption remains unproven, and Maimon argues that Newtonian physics as Kant understands it is demonstrably *not* a science.[55] This means not that transcendental philosophy should cease but that it should continue in awareness that it thematizes the conditions of the possibility of an eventuality that has not arrived, hence that it is ineluctably vulnerable to skepticism.

Although few accept Maimon's conclusion, here too his impact is astonishingly widespread. Some German Idealists accept the challenge to develop a presuppositionless version of transcendental philosophy. Instead, Cohen insists on the need to presuppose factual science, which he then seeks to justify through a rational reconstruction of history.[56]

Once again, Maimon draws on Jewish tradition to make his point. He concludes the *Essay* by repeating his claim that "Reason finds that it and its activity are possible only under the presupposition of an infinite reason," distinguishing between infinite, constitutive reason and finite reason, which "approximates the other ad infinitum." He then closes with one of his favourite Talmudic passages:

> Our Talmudists (who, to be sure, occasionally expressed thoughts worthy of a Plato) say, "The students of wisdom find no rest,

neither in this nor in the future life", whereupon they cite the words of the psalmist (84:8): "They flow from power to power [*sie wallen von Kraft zur Kraft*], appear before the Almighty in Zion."[57]

Here Maimon translates "*talmidei chakhamim*" as "students of wisdom" or philosophers, rather than "students of the sages" or recipients of authoritative Jewish tradition. Traditional commentators feel obliged to reconcile this passage with others in which the world to come is said to be "wholly rest."[58] But Maimon is undisturbed by the whiff of heterodoxy coming from the suggestion that the highest human aspiration consists not in the attainment of perfect stasis – in Maimon's terms, the establishment of physics and transcendental philosophy "on the sure path of a science" – but rather in infinite striving for this unattainable goal. By envisaging the dialectical coexistence of naturalism and transcendental philosophy, Maimon transforms the traditional Jewish view that the world is not yet redeemed but will be into the view that the world is always to be redeemed but never will be.

Moreover, since "*Kraft*" is Kant's word for a faculty, this infinite striving would seem to consist in progressing from sensibility to understanding, from understanding to reason, and thence to as yet unknown faculties, ad infinitum. Thus the forms of the faculties may be interpreted as configurations of the divine pleroma – in Kabbalistic terms, *sefirot* and *partzufim* – and human ascent becomes the mirror-image of divine emanation. Transcendental logic becomes a Kabbalistic exposition of the divine emanations.[59]

3. CONCLUSION

I have argued that Jewish philosophy's close involvement with Kant depends, first, on Kant's Platonism – specifically, on Kant's synthesis of Aristotelianism and Platonism, and on his deployment of the concepts of the unity of reason, the fundamental role of law, and the teleological character of history – and, second, on Maimon's radicalization of Kant's Platonism, which explicitly begins the post-Kantian deployment and recasting of Jewish philosophical and Kabbalistic traditions. However, it is important to reflect on the sense in which Jewish post-Kantianisms are thereby rendered possible.

The Jewishness of a philosophy – as I use the term here – depends only on the actual deployment in its articulation of characteristically Jewish terms and traditions. This has three noteworthy consequences. First, it is not necessary that any Jew – self-identifying or other-identified – be involved.[60] Second, the very factors that render a philosophy susceptible to Jewish construal may also render it susceptible to *Christian* construal. For Christianity also involves divine unity, law, and messianism, and there are also Christian syntheses of Aristotelianism and Neo-Platonism, indigenous Christian theosophical traditions, and even Christian versions of Kabbalah. Much of what has been said here could also help to explain the possibility of Christian post-Kantianisms.[61] Third, the Jewishness of a philosophy does not entail any positive relationship to the practice of Judaism.

With respect to the possibility of Christian post-Kantianisms, the following distinction may be drawn, appealing to the disagreement between Christians and Jews about whether divinity can be incarnate or not, and about whether the messiah has already redeemed the world, or is yet to come. Insofar as some post-Kantianism disputes with Maimon by positing a *knowable* principle that *constitutes* nature, it will be more open to Christian inflection. Hence Hegel and early Schelling construe nature as the always already occurring *incarnation* of the infinite. Insofar, however, as some post-Kantianism agrees with Maimon's by taking the infinite principle as a *regulative* idea, it will be more open to Jewish inflection. Hence the insistence in Adorno, Benjamin, and Bloch and Lukács on viewing the world from the perspective of a messianic redemption that is always yet to come, of a distance between God and the world that remains insuperable.[62]

However, it would be wrong to distinguish absolutely between Christian constitutive post-Kantianisms and Jewish regulative post-Kantianisms. To be sure, Cohen presents Judaism as attesting to a difference between God and world that is threatened with erasure, not only by Hegelianism, but also by Spinozism and Christian incarnationism. But others seek to reaffirm the *identity* in Jewish difference. They thereby reenact, on the religious plane, a manoeuvre of Maimon's. Maimon's introduction of the world-soul echoes the Kabbalistic distinction between the divine in-itself and the divine-in-relation-to-the-world, a distinction made possible by a divine self-contraction giving rise not only to nature but also to a history culminating in messianic redemption. Thus Breuer and Rosenzweig invoke further Kabbalistic traditions characterizing the divine-in-relation-to-the-world as especially instantiated by the Torah, which is not only the primordial blueprint for creation but is also revealed to, actualized, and observed by the Jewish people. Indeed it can be argued that Judaism has its own triune structure expressed in the well-known formula that "Israel, and the Torah, and the Holy One Blessed be He, are one."[63] While Breuer sees Judaism as the redemption of creation, Rosenzweig sees it also as the redemption of God.[64] Going beyond the enlistment of demythologized Kabbalah by Maimon, Krochmal, and Breuer, Rosenzweig facilitates the renewal of the mythic thinking of the *Zohar* and Lurianic Kabbalah. Yet even this return to tradition remains post-Kantian, as the self-described fulfillment of Schelling's call for a narrative philosophy of revelation.[65]

Turning to the relationship between Jewish post-Kantianisms and Judaism, it is worth noting that when a philosophy inimical to Jewish practice is couched in Jewish terms, it becomes a greater threat to Judaism's survival since it promises a Jewishness that outlives Judaism. Are Kantianism and post-Kantianism hostile to Jewish practice? Although Kant respects and encourages Jews, he is hostile to Judaism, which "is not a religion at all,"[66] but rather "a *delusion* of religion."[67] When Kant applauds Lazarus Bendavid's proposal – not to grant Jews civil rights until they abolish Jewish law – as a call for the *euthanasia* of Judaism, he misunderstands the proposal's *intention*, but does he correctly discern the probable *effect* of its implementation?[68] Meanwhile, Hegel also encourages Jews but finds it difficult to accommodate Judaism within modernity.[69] His student, Eduard Gans, argues that, from Hegel's viewpoint, "neither can the Jews vanish nor Judaism dissolve." But this applies equally to the ancient Greeks. Of their pagan religion, too, one may say that "in the great movement of the whole it should seem to have perished and yet live on, as the current lives on in the ocean."[70] Is it enough that Jews and Judaism live on, not as flesh-and-blood people practicing a living religion, but only as recollected within the Hegelian system? Whether there can be not only Jewish post-Kantianism but also *post-Kantian Judaism* deserves discussion elsewhere.

In closing, I note that by 1791, when Maimon published his post-Kantian commentary on Maimonides' *Guide*, he had apparently lost the hope of leaving a legacy for the Jewish people.[71] His journey ended in burial outside the Jewish cemetery of Glogau, and this was representative for several generations of Jewish Kantians and post-Kantians, who could comfortably inhabit neither the Jewish community nor the Christian world – even if the Church did not reject them as it did Maimon.[72]

Since then, it has become possible for Jewish Kantians and post-Kantians to carve out their own identities as citizens of a secular state. But it is not only dreams that come true. As an increasingly Jewish Neo-Kantianism emerged, so did an anti-Semitic image of Kant, promulgated by precursors or supporters of Nazism.[73] During the Holocaust, Kant's image of the euthanasia of Judaism became a scene from a living nightmare.

After the murder of European Jewry under (chiefly) German auspices, can Kantianism and post-Kantianism remain vital to Jewish philosophy? On the other hand, can philosophy remain vital after the Holocaust without the witness of Jewish Kantianism and post-Kantianism to the unredeemed and perhaps irredeemable character of modernity? Kant remains the modern philosopher about whom Jewish thinkers cannot evade the question: to recite, or not to recite, a blessing?

Notes

1. Isaac Breuer, *Mein Weg* (Jerusalem and Zürich: Morascha Verlag, 1988), 54, citing the benediction on seeing a Gentile sage. See TB Berakhot 58a.
2. Kantian and post-Kantian ways of thinking are perhaps also detectable within the works of numerous thinkers whose frames of reference and audiences are rabbinic rather than philosophical, such as Israel Salanter, Abraham Isaac Kook, and Eliyahu Eliezer Dessler. This is hard to assess, however, since extra-rabbinic influences are often unacknowledged for strategic reasons, and since these thinkers could sometimes have reached the same formulations on the basis of rabbinic resources alone. Such figures are not considered here.
3. See, for example, Jacob Katz, "Kant and Judaism, the Historical Context," in *Tarbiz* 41 (1971-2). For discussion and more references, see Peter Gordon, *Rosenzweig and Heidegger: Between Judaism and German Philosophy* (Berkeley, CA: University of California Press, 2003), 51-4.
4. See Simon Dubnow, *Weltgeschichte der jüdischen Volkes* (Berlin: Jüdischer Verlag, 1929), 24-5.
5. Isaac Breuer was the grandson of Samson Raphael Hirsch and the son of Joseph Breuer, Hirsch's son-in-law and successor. "Independent" Orthodoxy, founded by Hirsch, insisted on rigorous separation from all institutions involving non-Orthodox movements and on the intrinsic value of both Torah and the surrounding, general culture (*derekh erets*). See Mordechai Breuer, *Modernity within Tradition*, trans. Elizabeth Petuchowski (New York, NY: Columbia University Press, 1992); Alan Mittleman, *Between Kant and Kabbalah* (Albany, NY: SUNY Press, 1990); and Matthias Morgenstern, *From Frankfurt to Jerusalem* (Leiden: Brill, 2002).
6. See, for example, Friedrich Kuntze, *Die Philosophie Salomon Maimons* (Heidelberg: Carl Winter, 1912); Frederick Beiser, *The Fate of Reason* (Cambridge, MA: Harvard University Press, 1987); and Gideon Freudenthal (ed.), *Salomon Maimon: Rational Dogmatist, Empirical Skeptic: Critical Assesments* (Dordrecht: Kluwer, 2004).
7. See Hermann Cohen, *Jüdische Schriften* (Berlin: Schwetschke Verlag, 1924), 1: 283-305.

8. We need not agree, for example, with Cohen's controversial interpretations of Kant's transcendental philosophy as an investigation of the necessary conditions for the possibility of mathematical physics, or of Plato's ideas as scientific hypotheses. This is fortunate since no argument for a genuine affinity should depend on partisan or tendentious construals of either Kantianism or Judaism. Here I follow Cohen only selectively and as a guide.

9. Immanuel Kant, *Critique of Pure Reason* (hereafter *CPR*, cited in accordance with the paginations of the 1781A and 1787B editions), trans. and eds., Mary Gregor, Paul Guyer, and Allen Wood (Cambridge: Cambridge University Press, 1998), A314/B370.

10. See Immanuel Kant, *Theoretical Philosophy after 1781*, trans. and eds., Henry Allison, Peter Heath, Paul Guyer, and Allen Wood (Cambridge: Cambridge University Press, 2002), 8: 387–406. Citations of Kant's works, except for *CPR*, refer to volume and page of *Kants gesammelte Schriften*, ed. Berlin Akademie der Wissenschaften (Berlin: Walter de Gruyter, 1900-).

11. Kant, *CPR*, A313/B370.

12. Kant, *CPR*, A316/B372.

13. Cohen, *Jüdische Schriften*, 1: 290, 2: 239.

14. See Immanuel Kant, *Critique of the Power of Judgment*, trans. and eds., Paul Guyer, Eric Matthews, and Allen Wood (Cambridge: Cambridge University Press, 2000), 5: 274: "Perhaps there is no more sublime passage in the Jewish Book of the Law than the commandment: Thou shalt not make unto thyself any graven image, nor any likeness either of that which is in heaven, or on the earth, or yet under the earth, etc. This commandment alone can explain the enthusiasm that the Jewish people felt in its civilized period for its religion when it compared itself with other peoples, or the pride that Mohammedanism inspired. The very same thing also holds of the representation of the moral law and the predisposition to morality in us."

15. *Methodological naturalism* is the view that the methods of the natural sciences are the only methods capable of yielding knowledge and rationality. It contrasts with *substantive naturalism*, understood as the view that every entity is natural. On competing interpretations of Kant as methodological naturalist and as anti-naturalist, see Paul Franks, "Serpentine Naturalism and Protean Nihilism: Transcendental Philosophy in German Idealism, Anthropological Post-Kantianism, and Neo-Kantianism," in *The Oxford Handbook of Continental Philosophy*, eds., Brian Leiter and Michael Rosen (Oxford: Oxford University Press, forthcoming).

16. Kant, *CPR*, A84/B116.

17. Kant, *CPR*, A321/B379.

18. Kant, *CPR*, A316/B373.

19. Kant, *CPR*, A663/B691.

20. Kant's doctrine of ideas is often neglected. In *The Bounds of Sense* (London: Macmillan, 1966), the most influential Anglophone Kant interpretation of the last forty years, P. F. Strawson attributes to Kant

the exclusively hylomorphic view that thoughts without sensible matter are lacking in significance.

21. See Lenn E. Goodman (ed.), *Neoplatonism and Jewish Thought* (Albany, NY: SUNY Press, 1992).

22. In 1863, shortly after leaving rabbinical school, Cohen won a prize for an essay aiming to find "the true value of Aristotelian psychology in the specialized continuation of Platonic thought." More than fifty years later, in 1910, he said that Maimonides "concealed his religious idealism in his general scientific rationalism. But since his philosophy proceeds from the root of the concept of God, he preserves genuine Platonic idealism in his determination of *God as the unique being* and as *unique cause of all existence*." See Cohen, *Jüdische Schriften*, 2: 244.

23. See Hindy Najman, "The Law of Nature and the Authority of Mosaic Law," *Studia Philonica Annual*, 11 (1999): 55–73, and "A Written Copy of the Law of Nature: An Unthinkable Paradox?" *Studia Philonica Annual*, 15 (2003): 51–60.

24. See Immanuel Kant, *Practical Philosophy*, trans. and eds., Mary Gregor, Paul Guyer, and Allen Wood (Cambridge: Cambridge University Press, 1996), 5:28: "... the mere lawgiving form of maxims is the only sufficient determining ground of the will."

25. See Kant, *Practical Philosophy*, 4: 421: "Since the universality of law in accordance with which effects take place constitutes what is properly called *nature* in the most general sense (as regards its form) – that is, the existence of things insofar as it is determined in accordance with universal laws – the universal imperative of duty can also go as follows: *act as if the maxim of your action were to become by your will a* **universal law of nature**." Kant gives other, supposedly equivalent formulations of the moral law, and there are many views of their interconnections.

26. See Kant, *Practical Philosophy*, 5: 125.

27. See, for example, Immanuel Kant, *Religion and Rational Theology*, trans. and eds., Allen Wood, George di Giovanni, and Paul Guyer (Cambridge: Cambridge University Press, 1996), 6: 153: "*Religion* is (subjectively considered) the recognition of all our duties as divine commands."

28. Cohen is drawing upon Maimonides' naturalistic and political messianism. See Moses Maimonides, *The Code of Maimonides (Mishneh Torah), The Book of Judges*, trans. Abraham Hershman (New Haven, CT: Yale University Press, 1949), Laws of Kings, Ch. 11: 2–3 and Ch.12: 1–2, citing Samuel in TB Berakhot 32b: "The sole difference between the present and the Messianic days is delivery from servitude to foreign powers."

29. Cohen, *Jüdische Schriften*, 1: 301.

30. The three great German Idealists, Fichte, Schelling, and Hegel, were all educated to be Lutheran pastors.

31. Jürgen Habermas, "The German Idealism of the Jewish Philosophers," in Habermas, *Religion and Rationality: Essays on Reason, God, and Modernity* (Cambridge, MA: MIT Press, 2002), 37–8.

32. Kant, *CPR*, B19.

33. Salomon Maimon, *Gesammelte Werke*, ed. Valerio Verra (Hildesheim: Georg Olms Verlag, 1965–76), 2: 62–3.

34. On Kant's alleged dualism, see Paul Franks, "What Should Kantians Learn from Maimon's Skepticism?" in Freudenthal (ed.), *Salomon Maimon: Rational Dogmatist, Empirical Skeptic,* and Paul Franks, *All or Nothing: Systematicity, Transcendental Arguments, and Skepticism in German Idealism* (Cambridge, MA: Harvard University Press, 2005).

35. Cohen believes that this dualism can be overcome thanks to the work of mathematicians after Kant, especially August Cournot. He also regards this dependence on extra-philosophical developments as entirely in Kant's spirit. See Hermann Cohen, *Das Prinzip der Infinitesimalmethode und seine Geschichte,* in Cohen, *Werke,* 5 (Hildesheim: Olms, 1984). Nevertheless, Cohen's position is consequently closer to German Idealism – especially to Fichte's second Jena *Wissenschaftslehre* – than he acknowledges. See Franks, "Serpentine Naturalism and Protean Nihilism: Transcendental Philosophy in German Idealism, Anthropological Post-Kantianism, and Neo-Kantianism."

36. Kant, *CPR,* A314/B371n.

37. Maimon, *Gesammelte Werke,* 4: 442.

38. See Moses Maimonides, *The Guide of the Perplexed,* trans. Shlomo Pines (Chicago, IL: Chicago University Press, 1963), Book 1, Ch. 68, and the commentary on this chapter in Salomon Maimon, *Give'ath ha-Moreh,* eds., Samuel Hugo Bergmann, and Nathan Rotenstreich (Jerusalem: Israel Academy, 1965).

39. See Friedrich Kuntze, *Die Philosophie Salomon Maimons,* 339; and Hermann Cohen, *Kants Theorie der Erfahrung,* in Cohen, *Werke,* 1.1–2 (Hildesheim: Georg Olms Verlag, 1989), 540.

40. Immanuel Kant, *Correspondence,* trans. and ed., Arnulf Zweig (Cambridge: Cambridge University Press, 1999), 11: 48–54. For earlier letters from Herz and Maimon to Kant, see 11: 14–16. For a helpful discussion, see Yitzhak Melamed, "Salomon Maimon and the Rise of Spinozism in Germany," *Journal of the History of Philosophy,* 42: 1 (2004): 57–96.

41. See Franks, *All or Nothing,* 122–8.

42. Strange yet influential, Wachter, *Der Spinozismus im Jüdenthum* (Amsterdam: Johann Wolters, 1699; reprinted, Stuttgart-Bad Canstatt: Frommann-Holzboog, 1994), was directed against Moses Germanus, a convert to Judaism formerly known as Johann Peter Spaeth, who was neither a Spinozist nor a kabbalist. Shortly thereafter, Wachter changed his mind, publicly defending kabbalistic philosophy as he understood it.

43. See Moses Mendelssohn, *Dialogues,* in *Philosophical Writings,* trans. and ed., Daniel Dahlstrom (Cambridge: Cambridge University Press, 1997), 101–11.

44. See Friedrich Heinrich Jacobi, *The Main Philosophical Writings and the Novel Allwill,* trans. and ed., George di Giovanni (Montreal: McGill-Queens University Press, 1994), 233–4; Salomon Maimon, *Autobiography,* trans. J. Clark Murray (Urbana, IL: University of Illinois Press, 2001), 220.

45. Baruch Spinoza, *Complete Works,* trans. Samuel Shirley and ed. Michael L. Morgan (Indianapolis, IN: Hackett, 2002), 486: "I have also read, and

am acquainted with, a number of Cabbalistic triflers whose madness passes the bounds of my understanding."

46. Maimon, *Autobiography*, 105.
47. See Moshe Idel, "The Magical and Neoplatonic Interpretations of the Kabbalah in the Renaissance," in *Jewish Thought in the Sixteenth Century*, ed. Bernard Cooperman (Cambridge, MA: Harvard Center for Jewish Studies, 1983); Moshe Idel, "Jewish Kabbalah and Platonism in the Middle Ages and Renaissance," in *Neoplatonism and Jewish Thought*, ed. Lenn Goodman (Albany, NY: SUNY Press, 1992); and Hava Tirosh-Rothschild, *Between Worlds: The Life and Thought of Rabbi Judah ben David Messer Leon* (Albany, NY: SUNY Press, 1991).
48. Maimon, *Autobiography*, 96.
49. Maimon, *Gesammelte Werke*, 4: 42–3.
50. Kant, *Correspondence*, trans. and ed., Arnulf Zweig (Cambridge: Cambridge University Press, 1996), 11: 174–6.
51. An ancient version of the debate is concerned with whether the ideas are intradeical or extradeical. See Harry Austryn Wolfson, "Extradeical and Intradeical Interpretations of Platonic Ideas," in *Religious Philosophy: A Group of Essays* (Cambridge, MA: Harvard University Press, 1961). In the Middle Ages, Avicenna and Averroes disagree about whether the intellect that moves the first sphere is identical to or distinct from God. See Herbert Davidson, *Alfarabi, Avicenna, and Averroes on Intellect* (Oxford: Oxford Univeristy Press, 1992). Among the kabbalists, the dispute is whether the sefiroth constitute divine essence (*atzmut*) or divine instruments (*kelim*). See Hava Tirosh-Rothschild, *Between Worlds: The Life and Thought of Rabbi Judah ben David Messer Leon*, 207–18; and Moshe Hallamish, *An Introduction to the Kaballah*, trans. Ruth Bar-Ilan and Ora Wiskind-Elper (Albany, NY: SUNY Press, 1999), 159–65. Maimon is certainly familiar with the medieval and kabbalistic controversies.
52. See, for example, the *Iyyun* circle commentary on the *sefirot* cited by Hallamish, *An Introduction to the Kabbalah*, 160.
53. See Maimon, *Gesammelte Werke*, 3: 455 for a "confession" that his intention in the *Essay*, now abandoned, was to combine Kant with Spinozism.
54. See Maimon, *Gesammelte Werke*, 4: 80.
55. See Gideon Freudenthal, "Maimon's Subversion of Kant's *Critique of Pure Reason*: There Are No Synthetic *a priori* Propositions in Physics," in Freudenthal (ed.), *Salomon Maimon: Rational Dogmatist, Empirical Skeptic*.
56. See Franks, "Serpentine Naturalism and Protean Nihilism."
57. TB Berakhot 64a/Moed Katan 29a. Maimon cites this passage at the end of the *Essay*, in his commentary on the *Guide*, and in an unpublished manuscript, *Chesheq Shlomo*, transcribed by Yitzhak Melamed, whom I thank. Since Maimon's interpretation is at stake, I have followed his translation. In Franks, "What Should Kantians Learn from Maimon's Skepticism?" in Freudenthal, ed., *Salomon Maimon: Rational Dogmatist, Empirical Skeptic*, I referred to the commentary of Samuel Eidels

(*Maharsha*) ad loc., who construes the restlessness of the scholars in Maimonidean fashion: as the ceaseless and pure activity of the wholly active
intellect, which is at rest in a higher sense than cessation. More apposite
still is the interpretation of Luria [see Isaac Luria, *Likkutei Shas* (Livorno,
1794)], who states that "just as God, blessed be He, is infinite, so is
His wisdom infinite." Development in wisdom will cease, according to
Luria, only after the resurrection, when each receives a body incarnating
the aspect of the godhead corresponding to the level of wisdom attained.

58. For example, on Shabbat, one adds to Grace after Meals: "May the Merciful One grant us as an inheritance the day that is wholly shabbat and
rest for eternal life." See TB Rosh Hashanah 31a and Sanhedrin 97a.

59. The possibility is realized by Nachman Krochmal, *Kitvei Rabi Naḥman
Krokhmal*, ed. Simon Rawidowicz (Berlin: Ajanoth, 1924), 217. He explicitly interprets human ascent in terms of the first three *sefirot*, construing
what Hegel calls representation – thinking dominated by sensibility –
as *da'at*; what Hegel calls reflection – thinking dominated by understanding and what Kant calls reason – as *binah*; and what Hegel calls
speculation – absolute knowing – as *chokhmah*. See 306 on divine self-
limitation and 422 for a recommendation to read Maimon's commentary on Maimonides for an account of the categories. Krochmal draws
on pre-*Zohar* Kabbalah, especially Abraham ibn Ezra and Isaac ibn Latif,
a pioneer of philosophical Kabbalah who wrote *Sha'ar ha–Shamayim*,
which Krochmal misascribes to ibn Ezra. See Jay Harris, *Nachman
Krochmal: Guiding the Perplexed of the Modern Age* (New York, NY:
New York University Press, 1993), 68; and Sarah Heller-Willensky, "Issac
ibn Latif: Philosopher or Kabbalist?" in Alexander Altmann (ed.), *Jewish
Medieval and Renaissance Studies* (Cambridge: Cambridge University
Press, 1967).

60. See Stephen Schwarzschild, "The Jewish Kant" (unpublished), 5–6: "Not
every Jew is Jewish, as Isaac Deutscher made clear in his well-known
essay 'The Non-Jewish Jew.' In turn I have also made it clear that there
is such a thing as a Jewish non-Jew. (The spectrum extends all the way
from the Jewish Jew to the non-Jewish non-Jew, the 'unJew,' and the non-
Jewish Jew as well as the Jewish non-Jew are only two of the many points
between the end-points of the spectrum . . .) No claim is being made here
that Kant was a Jew. The biographers and the historians are entirely right
on this score. The claim *is* being made that Kant was Jewish – that he was
a Jewish non-Jew." Thanks to Robert Gibbs for showing me this text.

61. Christian post-Kantians draw on Maimon too – as Fichte and Schelling
do explicitly and Hegel implicitly – but they also draw on tradi-
tions to which they have independent access, including Neo-Platonism,
Christian Kabbalah (available primarily through Pico della Mirandola and
Knorr von Rosenroth) and Jacob Boehme's theosophy. See Cyril O'Regan,
The Heterodox Hegel (Albany, NY: SUNY Press, 1994).

62. See Anson Rabinbach, "Between Enlightenment and Apocalypse: Benjamin, Bloch, and Modern Jewish Messianism" in *New German Critique*,
34 (1985): 78–124. Note his comment that "Modern Jewish Messianism
can be found among many Jewish 'ethoses' encompassing a broad cultural

and political spectrum. Above all, it is a Jewishness without Judaism."
(82)

63. This may be considered a kabbalistic reconstrual of the dictum of the philosophers cited by Maimonides, and commented upon by Maimon: "The intellect, the intellection, and the intellected are one and the same." See Maimonides, *The Guide of the Perplexed*, Part I, Chapter 68. The kabbalistic idea was probably popularized by Isaiah Ha-levi Horowitz (known as the *Shelah*, after the initials of his work, *Shenei Luḥot ha–Berit*), who found it implicit in the available work of Moses Cordovero. See Bracha Sack, "The Influence of Cordovero on Seventeenth-Century Jewish Thought," in *Jewish Thought in the Seventeenth Century*, eds. Isadore Twersky and Bernard Septimus (Cambridge, MA: Harvard University Press, 1987), 367: "Had the Shelah had access to Cordovero's commentary on the *Zohar*, particularly to the commentary on the *Zohar* to the Song of Songs, he could have used it as a concise summary of the matter in the following terms: 'The Torah and the *sefirot* and the souls are one matter.'" Cordovero was well known to Maimon, as was Horowitz to Breuer. See Maimon, *Autobiography*, 196; and Alan Mittleman, *Between Kant and Kabbalah: An Introduction to Isaac Breuer's Philosophy of Judaism* (Albany, NY: SUNY Press, 1990), 77. The formula is also frequently cited by Hayyim of Volozhin, on whom see, for example, Emmanuel Levinas, "'In the Image of God' According to Rabbi Haim of Volozhin," in *Beyond the Verse* (Bloomington, IN: Indiana University Press, 1994), 151–167; Levinas, "Prayer without Demand," in *The Levinas Reader*, ed. Seán Hand (Cambridge: Cambridge University Press, 1989), 227–34; and Levinas, "Judaism and Kenosis," in *In the Time of Nations*, trans. Michael B. Smith (Bloomington, IN: Indiana University Press, 1994), 114–32.

64. See Franz Rosenzweig, *The Star of Redemption*, trans. Barbara E. Gallie (Madison, WI: University of Wisconsin Press, 2005), 248, and his citation of a midrash ascribed, like the *Zohar*, to Simeon bar Yohai in *Philosophical and Theological Writings*, trans. and eds., Paul Franks and Michael Morgan (Indianapolis, IN: Hackett, 2000), 23; and in *The Star of Redemption*, 185. See Eliot Wolfson, "Facing the Effaced: Mystical Eschatology and the Idealistic Orientation in the Thought of Franz Rosenzweig," in *Zeitschrift für neuere Theologiegeschichte*, 4 (1997), 69 and 79: "The reappropriation of anthropomorphic and mythical language on Rosenzweig's part to characterize the nature of God in the peak religious experience of beholding the divine face is strikingly reminiscent of the kabbalistic tradition."

65. See Rosenzweig, *Philosophical and Theological Writings*, 121. Schelling's projected philosophy of revelation is a post-Kantian response to Jacobi's opposition of Spinozistic rationalism to natural faith in the revelations of perception.

66. Kant, *Religion and Rational Theology*, 6: 126: "The *Jewish faith*, as originally established, was only a collection of merely statutory laws supporting a political state; for whatever moral additions were *appended* to it, whether originally or only later, do not in any way belong to Judaism

as such. Strictly speaking Judaism is not a religion at all but simply the union of a number of individuals who, since they belonged to a particular stock, established themselves into a community under purely political laws, hence not into a church; Judaism was rather *meant* to be a purely secular state, so that, were it dismembered through adverse accidents, it would still be left with the political faith (which pertains to it through essence) that this state would be restored to it (with the advent of the Messiah). The fact that this constitution of this state was based on a theocracy (visibly, on an aristocracy of priests or leaders who boasted of instructions directly imparted to them from God), and that God's name was therefore honored in it (though only as a secular regent with absolutely no rights over, or claims upon, conscience) did not make that constitution religious."

67. Kant, *Religion and Rational Theology*, 6: 167–8: "The one and true religion contains nothing but laws, i.e., practical principles, of whose unconditional necessity we can become conscious and which we therefore recognize as revealed through pure reason (not empirically). Only for the sake of a church, of which there can be different and equally good forms, can there be statutes, i.e., ordinances held to be divine, though to our purely moral judgment they are arbitrary and contingent. Now to deem this statutory faith (which is in any case restricted to one people and cannot contain the universal world religion) essential to the service of God in general, and to make it the supreme condition of divine good pleasure toward human beings, is a *delusion of religion*, and acting upon it constitutes counterfeit service, i.e., a pretension of honoring God through which we act directly contrary to the true service required by him." See Seeskin (Chapter 10 in the present volume) on Jewish responses to Kant on morality as autonomous and Judaism as heteronomous.

68. See Kant, *Religion and Rational Theology*, 7: 53: "Without dreaming of a conversion of all Jews (to Christianity in the sense of a *messianic* faith), we can consider it possible even in their case if, as is now happening, purified religious concepts awaken among them and throw off the garb of the ancient cult, which now serves no purpose and even suppresses any true religious attitude. Since they have long had *garments without a man* in them (a church without religion) and since, moreover, a *man without garments* (religion without a church) is not well protected, they need certain formalities of a church – the church best able to lead them, in their present state, to the final end. So we can consider the proposal of Ben Davie [sic], a highly intelligent Jew, to adopt publicly the religion of Jesus (presumably with its vehicle, the *Gospel*), a most fortunate one . . . The euthanasia of Judaism is pure moral religion, freed from all the ancient statutory teachings, some of which were bound to be retained in Christianity (as a messianic faith). But this division of sects, too, must disappear in time, leading, at least in spirit, to what we call the conclusion of the great drama of religious change on earth (the restoration of all things), when there will be only one shepherd and one flock." Bendavid – Maimon's friend and Kant's student – actually proposes a reformed Judaism without the law, not the adoption of the

Gospels as Jewish scripture. Perhaps Kant conflates Bendavid, *Etwas zur Charakteristik der Juden* (Leipzig: Stahel, 1793; reprinted, Jerusalem: Dinur Centre, 1994) with David Friedländer, "Open Letter from some Jewish Householders" (1799), in *A Debate on Jewish Emancipation and Christian Theology in Old Berlin*, trans. and eds., Richard Crouter and Julie Klassen (Indianapolis, IN: Hackett Publishing, 2004).

69. See Karl Rosenkranz, *G. W. F. Hegels Leben* (Berlin, Duncker & Humblot, 1844; reprinted, Darmstadt: Wissenschaftliche Buchgesellschaft, 1971), 49, on the "dark riddle" of Judaism; Emil Fackenheim, *The Religious Dimension in Hegel's Thought* (Bloomington, IN: Indiana University Press, 1967); and Fackenheim, *Encounters between Judaism and Modern Philosophy* (New York, NY: Basic Books, 1973); and Yirmiyahu Yovel, *Dark Riddle: Hegel, Nietzsche, and the Jews* (Princeton, NJ: Princeton University Press, 1998).

70. See Eduard Gans, *Eduard Gans (1797–1839): Hegelianer-Jude-Europäer*, in *Texte und Dokumente*, ed. Norbert Waszek (Frankfurt am Main: Peter Lang Verlag, 1991), 67.

71. Maimon was denied entry to Berlin in 1778 because he intended to publish such a commentary. See Maimon, *Autobiography*, 194–5. On Maimon's pessimism, see 285–8.

72. Maimon, *Autobiography*, 253–7.

73. See Hans Sluga, *Heidegger's Crisis: Philosophy and Politics in Nazi Germany* (Cambridge, MA: Harvard University Press, 1993), 82–5, for the controversy surrounding the contrast drawn between the German Kant and the Jewish Cohen in Bruno Bauch, "Vom Begriff der Nation," *Kant-Studien*, 21 (1916): 139–162. Cassirer's reply is soon to be published for the first time.

5 Hermann Cohen: Judaism and Critical Idealism

ANDREA POMA

[Translated by John Denton]

Was Hermann Cohen a Jewish thinker or a German philosopher? Did he belong chiefly to the tradition of Jewish philosophy or instead to the classical tradition of critical idealism, of which Kant is the paradigmatic figure and fundamental reference point? Contemporary opinion of Cohen was marked by controversy. In Jewish circles, although he was respected and acknowledged as an authoritative voice, he was also criticized and accused of denying his Jewish identity. Meanwhile, his philosophical works, notwithstanding respectful attentions, were not always successful in the academic world, where he more than once encountered problems because of his Jewish origins. In this chapter, I shall address the question of Cohen's status as a Jewish philosopher chiefly by examining Cohen's occasional texts on Jewish topics and contemporary controversies that affected the Jewish community in his day.

I. COHEN'S LIFE: A BRIEF SKETCH

Hermann Cohen was born in Coswig (Anhalt) on 4 July 1842, the son of Gerson Cohen and Friederike Salomon. At the age of eleven, he was sent to the grammar school in Dessau. At the age of fifteen, though still enrolled in the grammar school as an external student, Hermann entered the theological seminary in Breslau, where he commenced his rabbinical training. As soon as he had received his school certificate, he also left the seminary, as he was now drawn to philosophy and philology. In 1861, he enrolled in the University of Breslau, and in 1864, he moved to Berlin to study at the University there.

In 1865, Cohen was awarded a doctorate in philosophy at Halle, with a thesis entitled *The Philosophers' Doctrines Concerning the Antinomy of Necessity and Contingency (Philosophorum de antinomia necessitatis et contingentiae doctrinae)*. Although he subsequently continued his research, his efforts to forge an academic career in Berlin met with considerable difficulties. In 1871, he published *Kant's Theory of*

Experience (*Kants Theorie der Erfahrung*), a work that indisputably marked a new and original phase in the interpretation of Kant's philosophy. The book soon attracted the attention of Friedrich Albert Lange (1828–1875), the author of the *History of Materialism (Geschichte des Materialismus)*.[1]

In 1873, Lange, who was teaching at the University of Marburg at the time, invited Cohen there as a "Privatdozent." A few years later, in 1875, Cohen was appointed to an "Extraordinariat" in the same university, and after Lange's death in 1876, was appointed to the chair of philosophy that Lange had held before him. Thus began a long period of teaching at Marburg, during which Cohen developed his philosophical system, founded a veritable "school," and brought renown to the university, becoming one of the more prominent figures on the German philosophical scene between the late nineteenth and early twentieth centuries.

During his years in Marburg, Cohen further developed his interpretation of Kant and also worked out his own philosophical system, a foretaste of which is to be found in his writings on Kant. At the same time, Cohen often found himself called upon to defend the cultural position occupied by his school. Its influence was undoubtedly hampered, both academically and politically, by the fact that some of its leading members were Jews, including Cohen himself. Most unpleasant of all were Cohen's encounters with anti-Jewish propaganda, which was then on the rise both within Germany and beyond. Amongst these episodes the most significant was the controversy begun by Heinrich von Treitschke in 1879–80, in which Cohen also took part.

In 1912, Cohen, at the age of seventy, retired from his chair at Marburg and moved to Berlin, where he began teaching at the "Lehranstalt für die Wissenschaft des Judentums," and continued through published essays to take an active part in the debates concerning German Judaism. It was in this period that Cohen devoted most of his philosophical research to the investigation of religion, a theme related closely to his own Judaism but also linked to his systematic philosophy. The most mature results of this investigation are to be found in *The Concept of Religion in the System of Philosophy (Der Begriff der Religion im System der Philosophie)*, published in 1915, and, especially, *Religion of Reason out of the Sources of Judaism (Religion der Vernunft aus den Quellen des Judentums)*, published posthumously in 1919.

Cohen's final years were a mixture of challenge and triumph. While in Berlin, Cohen met the young Franz Rosenzweig, who was struck by the personality and philosophy of this old teacher, and established a close relationship with him. In 1914, Cohen traveled to Poland and

Russia, where he had the satisfaction of great personal success. But upon his return to Berlin, the momentary light of his success was soon darkened by renewed nationalist disputes, even with his devoted friend Paul Natorp. The outbreak and progress of the war sharpened tensions between Germans and German Jews and enflamed the smouldering embers of anti-Jewish feeling. Cohen again found himself obliged to defend his difficult but deep-rooted belief in an idealized synthesis of Judaism, Germanism, and ethical universalism. For this he was strongly criticised on the German side, not only from the anti-Jewish factions, but also from those invoking German patriotism (a patriotism that Cohen himself claimed to endorse, as can be seen in his dispute with Natorp). He also met with criticism from Jewish circles, who looked upon his sincere adherence to the German cause with suspicion.

Cohen died in Berlin on 4 April 1918, a witness to Germany's impending defeat (it surrendered a few months later). Cohen had already seen the end of his philosophical school, and now he also saw the fall of Germany, a decline due not only to political-military causes but primarily to its deviation from the ideals of "Germanism" to which Cohen adhered. And yet he was spared the greatest tragedy of all, the violent systematic persecution and physical annihilation of German Judaism, a tradition to which he belonged by birth and by choice. This was a persecution to which his wife Martha Cohen was later subjected: she outlived her husband only to die a victim of the Nazis in the Theresienstadt concentration camp.

2. COHEN AND JUDAISM

In his "Introduction" to Cohen's *Jewish Writings*, published by Bruno Strauß in 1924,[2] Franz Rosenzweig offered a compelling portrait of Cohen's relation to Judaism, a portrait many now regard as definitive. In an opening passage, Rosenzweig furnishes this guide to Cohen's relationship to Judaism:

> The road that led to this discovery and self revelation was a long
> one – the two things were parallel, the second even more
> significant than the first – it was a road of further development and
> conversion and return. There is only one Hebrew word that
> describes both the man of conversion and the man of return, and
> the Talmud says that his place in heaven is where not even the
> perfectly righteous are allowed. A speaker at a banquet honoring
> Cohen after his return at the age of nearly 72 from an important

journey to Russia, called him "Baal teshuvah" meaning that he was now once again devoting himself to his brothers in the faith. At that point, with his hearing finely attuned to tones and their underlying harmonics, he interrupted to exclaim: 'Well, I have been a Baal teshuvah for the last thirty-four years!'. He was backdating the beginning of his 'return' to 1880 when he hurled himself into the ongoing controversy, that 'Profession about the Jewish Question' which, on two fronts, against Treitschke on the one hand, and against Graetz and Lazarus on the other, was to provoke more anger in his own party than amongst his anti-Semitic adversaries. But he was aware of having started then along the route he was now still following.[3]

According to Rosenzweig's portrait, although Hermann Cohen had grown up in a religious environment, after quitting the seminary to pursue philosophy he had also neglected his Judaism; he steeped himself in German scientific and philosophical culture and lost all his essential links with Jewish religion and identity, except those ties of affection that bound him to his family. In Rosenzweig's view, only one important "bridge" remained between Cohen and the Jewish tradition: socialism, a political ideal to which Cohen felt an enduring devotion and which he filled with the contents of Jewish prophecy and messianism.[4] His encounter with Friedrich Albert Lange, which had proven decisive for his academic career, also indicated a human agreement beyond their different religious backgrounds, in shared socialist idealism. Rosenzweig recalls a short, significant dialogue as reported by Cohen himself:

> Lange asked: 'Are our views on Christianity different?' Cohen answered: 'No, because what you call Christianity I call prophetic Judaism.' The author of 'Arbeiterfrage' [i.e. Friedrich Albert Lange] understood what he meant, and was able to indicate the passages in the Prophets he had underlined in his copy of the Bible. Cohen finished the story thus: So ethical socialism united us, in one blow, beyond the barriers of our religions.[5]

The year 1880 marked the beginning of Cohen's long "return" to Judaism. Heinrich von Treitschke, a prominent and well-regarded member of the German academic world, started the controversy referred to earlier with an anti-Jewish article, published in 1879. Cohen responded a year later with an essay, "A Profession about the Jewish Question" ("Ein Bekenntnis in der Judenfrage"),[6] which began with the significant phrase: "We are again obliged to bear witness."[7] From this point onwards, Cohen never shirked the responsibility of bearing public "witness" in defence of Judaism with political, academic, philosophical, and other public statements, and also engaged in planning and setting up institutions and promotional activities supporting Judaism. In Rosenzweig's view, Cohen's philosophical writings were also increasingly cognisant of, and in certain cases even inspired by, specifically Jewish concepts. Such was particularly the case for two defining features of Judaism, which Cohen saw as its special contribution to German culture: the uniqueness and spirituality of God, and messianism.

The Ethics of Pure Will[8] (the second part of Cohen's philosophical system, published in 1904, followed by a second edition in 1907), along with other writings from the same period, demonstrate a truly philosophical style of thought strongly influenced by concepts derived from Judaism.[9] In his maturity, then, Cohen had returned to his Judaism to such an extent that Rosenzweig could observe of *The Ethics of Pure Will* that "for the first time in a universal philosophical system the parts dealing with the philosophy of religion are oriented towards the concept of the religion of Judaism."[10] At the same time, Cohen achieved a true synthesis between the newly discovered dimension of Judaism and Kantianism, which for him was philosophically primary, and signified "German" philosophy in the highest sense. Thus Rosenzweig summarized Cohen's stand:

> Towards the end of this period, in 1911, in a commemorative piece for Ludwig Philippson, he gave his opinion on the German Jew's duty to split his activity between work on German culture, without reservations and ulterior motives and work on the survival of his own prophetic-Jewish religion; this split of activity 'endows our spirit alone with true unity and truly our spirit with natural orientation and the core of life'. It was in accordance with these words (. . .) that he lived.[11]

Nevertheless, claimed Rosenzweig, Cohen's return to Judaism remained incomplete. If Cohen had found again (or partially never lost) the philosophical meaning of the conceptual contents of Judaism, and had elaborated a synthesis between these contents and the German philosophical tradition, what was still missing and what this very synthesis risked hiding from view was the *specificity* of the Jewish religion with respect to philosophy. The "historical" return to the concepts of Judaism in philosophy followed the approach of "the great idealists of the beginning of the [nineteenth] century" and was therefore still oriented towards the acquisition of the contents of religion for the sake of philosophy itself, ultimately going beyond religion.[12]

Cohen's further and most decisive step in his "return" to Judaism was only realized in his later years after the move to Berlin. It was there, after retiring from the academic world and even while continuing his philosophical research that Cohen devoted his efforts more intensely to religious thought, and composed his last works on the subject, works in which he formulated a systematic theory of the Jewish religion. Here Cohen offered a profound and original reflection on the correlation between man and God, a correlation by which religion now revealed itself to be the requisite field for conceiving the bond between the living God of faith (a God irreducible to the philosophical Idea) and man as a concretely existing individual (an individual irreducible to abstract, universal humanity).[13]

Yet notwithstanding its nuance and authoritative standing, Rosenzweig's portrait of Cohen as summarized here is in fact quite controversial. It has been challenged (in my view cogently) by a number of scholars, including Alexander Altmann.[14] Indeed, we now realize that in many respects it is more significant as a reflection of Rosenzweig's own biography and philosophical perspective than it is a faithful reconstruction of Cohen's development.

Nonetheless, the parable that characterizes Cohen's life and thought as a long return to Judaism was not only Rosenzweig's creation; it also reflects Cohen's own self-image. This is evident if we recall once again the words with which Cohen began his 1880 pamphlet against Treitschke: "We are again obliged to bear witness."[15] Cohen later claimed that his own return to Judaism dated from that precise moment.[16] Two additional documents serve to mark this new self-awareness with chronological precision. First, as proof of his earlier neglect of Judaism we have a strongly emotional letter from 1872 addressed to Louis and Helene Lewandowsky, in which Cohen described his participation in the family Passover *seder*, yet openly admitted that his "Jewish romanticism" (*jüdische Romantik*) was grounded only in family affections and not truly religious sentiment.[17] Second, we have a report marking his definitive return to Judaism in words uttered when he was old and ill, as related by Rosenzweig: "I can still see him, when he had recovered once again from his illness, lying on the sofa and saying happily:

That I, of all people, I, Ezekiel the thirty sixth – that was his Hebrew name – should come to cause Ezekiel the first to be newly honoured!', then, in Hebrew, almost to himself: 'Repel all your

sins. . . . give yourselves new hearts and new spirits', and again, in a
hardly audible whisper: '. . . . repel . . . and give yourselves . . . give'.[18]

This sketch of Cohen's relation to Judaism is relatively straightforward. Yet we must now admit that the situation was in fact rather
more complex. First, while it is true that the young Cohen decisively
addressed philosophical research, especially on classical idealism (Plato
and Kant), we should also note that he started out in this direction under
the guidance of Chajim Steinthal, and he published his first essays in
the *Zeitschrift für Völkerpsychologie und Sprachwissenschaft*, edited
by Steinthal and Moritz Lazarus. The context was admittedly scientific
rather than religious, but the context was nonetheless Jewish in character. Second, we should not neglect the fact that beginning with his
1880 response to Treitschke, whenever Cohen was called upon to defend
Judaism against outside attacks, he always retained the unambiguous
conviction that Jewish identity is grounded in Judaism's *religious* meaning, and that all attempts to shift the Jewish question in a political or
ethnic direction meant missing Judaism's very essence. Already in *A Profession about the Jewish Question*, Cohen had declared: "My intention
is to treat the Jewish question particularly from this *religious* viewpoint;
not as the spokesman of a Jewish party, but as a representative of philosophy in a German university and as an individual who professes Israelite
monotheism."[19]

A third point to keep in mind (although it may seem to contradict
what has just been noted) is that for a great while, Cohen was convinced
that the most significant contents of the Jewish religion and the profound, inspiring influence of "German" culture would eventually lead
Judaism to its completion beyond the status of a specific religion, ultimately to be absorbed into the general culture of humanity. Only in his
old age did he acknowledge that religion had its own unassailable "pecu-
liarity" (*Eigenart*). But even at that stage, although Cohen conceived of
religion itself as Jewish monotheism and as a religion "from the sources
of Judaism," he also discerned in Judaism a truth of universal value for
the whole of humanity. He therefore considered the survival of Israel for
the indefinite future as a requirement, since Israel was to bear continued
witness to the truth of monotheism and messianism within a culture
where that truth had not yet been wholly absorbed.

Lastly it should be noted that, although one cannot doubt Cohen's
explicit hostility toward Jewish nationalism (which he judged as the
Jews' political-cultural withdrawal from universal culture, especially
the German culture he saw as endowed with a universalist vocation),
he nonetheless fought for the Jews' political identity within a single

pluralist state. To be sure, he remained opposed to all forms of Jewish nationalism, and he strenuously opposed the views of both Heinrich Graetz[20] and Moritz Lazarus.[21] Above all, as illustrated in his clash with Martin Buber, Cohen was always openly hostile to the "Palestinian party" (Zionists).[22] Still, in his last years, Cohen developed a uniquely ethical notion of "nationality" – as distinguished from the naturalistic category of "nation" – which permitted him to endorse the continued persistence of different group-identities (specifically, Jewish identity) within the context of a single, unversalist but pluralist state.[23]

3. THE SYNTHESIS BETWEEN CRITICAL IDEALISM AND JUDAISM

There can be little doubt that an integral synthesis between critical idealism and Judaism was Cohen's lifelong purpose. The whole of Cohen's work testifies to this right from the outset. In the 1869 essay, *Shabbat in its Culture-Historical Meaning* (*Der Sabbat in seiner kulturgeschichtlichen Bedeutung*),[24] Cohen suggested provocatively (and to the horror of some) that the Jewish Sabbath and Christian Sunday should coincide so as to facilitate greater Jewish integration in German society and to spread the ethical and social meaning of the Sabbath more effectively throughout the wider culture. The aforementioned 1880 response to Treitschke also revisits Cohen's persistent theme of an inner accord between Judaism and German culture (even between Judaism and Christianity), an accord grounded ostensibly on the ethical culture of universal humanism.[25] In response to the criticism raised by his friend Rabbi Adolf Moses, Cohen again reiterated his fundamental conviction that faithfulness to the spirit of Judaism did not imply separation, but rather active *integration* within a universalist culture.[26]

However, by the end of his long career and after many years of intense reflection, Cohen had considerably revised his views: he was no longer capable of the earlier suggestion concerning a Jewish Sabbath on Sunday, a change of heart also due no doubt to changes in the historical context.[27] Yet, of the synthesis between Judaism and philosophy he remained as certain as ever before. On 5 February 1918, two months before his death, Cohen reaffirmed in a letter to Franz Rosenzweig's mother Adele his "profession of faith" (*Bekenntnis*) in the unity of the Jewish religion and philosophical culture, a unity he saw just as he had in 1880:

And yet we are living in a new barbarian invasion and a new epoch appears to be bursting upon us. Thus important political disquiet impinges on private worries for me as well. It's an advantage for us that in this confusion we can follow a clear direction. The positive thing about it lies in the fact that our cultural philosophy [*Kulturphilosophie*] is in full agreement with our religion. This is a proof that, first of all, it is authentic and that, besides, it could never be overtaken by any other profession [*Bekenntnis*] with the same clarity and precision.[28]

This theme – that there is a strong agreement between the Jewish religion and philosophy, and especially ethics – recurs throughout Cohen's writings. Such an agreement, he believed, was not merely extrinsic or happenstance, but was clear proof of the founding influence of Jewish monotheism on culture. Cohen was convinced that universal humanist culture, as manifest in the philosophical tradition of German critical idealism, had its deepest roots not only in Greek scientific thought, but equally so in Jewish monotheism and messianism, from which it continued to draw inspiration for its most basic ethical principles.

Given Cohen's devotion to this fundamental theme, we may regard Cohen as both inspired by and a contributor to the great Science of Judaism movement for the reform of Judaism and culture, a movement deriving from Moses Mendelssohn and the Haskalah (Jewish Enlightenment), which was especially active during the first half of the nineteenth century. Cohen was arguably one of its leading members in the generation that followed its founding (by Zunz, Jost, and others).[29] Not only was Cohen a protagonist in its official organizations (for example, *Gesellschaft zur Förderung der Wissenschaft des Judentums*), to which he contributed both lectures and essays,[30] he also assumed an active role in the *Lehranstalt für die Wissenschaft des Judentums* in Berlin. This was not merely labor alongside but incidental to Cohen's philosophical research; the two were in fact closely intertwined. As Dieter Adelmann has noted, Cohen's posthumously published *Religion of Reason out of the Sources of Judaism* was originally conceived and composed as a treatment of the theme, *Ethics and Philosophy of Religion* (*Ethik und Religionsphilosophie*), and was intended as a contribution to the more wide-ranging project, a so-called *Compendium of the Whole of the Science of Judaism* (*Grundriss der Gesamtwissenschaft des Judentums*) under the direction of the *Gesellschaft zur Förderung der Wissenschaft des Judentums*.[31]

Cohen's contribution to the Science of Judaism was not limited to organization and publishing; it was above all theoretical. His chief aim was to demonstrate and further develop the idea of a symbiosis between

Judaism and philosophical culture. This no doubt required a reinterpretation of the entirety of the Jewish religion in the light of the Kantian and critical idealist conception of humanist-universalistic ethics. But for Cohen this did not require draining Judaism of its independent meaning, since on his view philosophical culture *itself*, and especially ethics, had its roots in Judaism. Two complementary tasks – opening Judaism to its universal ethical significance, and revealing the Jewish foundations of universal philosophy – were therefore united as one. The relation between Jewish thought and critical idealism was not merely a matter of Cohen's intellectual biography; it was also the constant theme and the unifying vision for all his work.

Alongside the major publications, this theme makes a constant reappearance in several of the lesser-known works and throughout the various stages in Cohen's development. In *Religious Postulates* (*Religiöse Postulate*),[32] a lecture he presented before the Second Congress of the *Verband der deutschen Juden* in 1907, the aforementioned theme comes out clearly, to the extent of suggesting among the "religious postulates" of German Judaism the setting up of university chairs in the Science of Judaism and Jewish theology and exegesis (one of the priorities of the Science of Judaism).[33]

Foremost amongst the "postulates" Cohen identified was monotheism itself, the postulate of the one and unique God.[34] Monotheism on his view was not only the foundation and essence of the Jewish religion, but was also itself the very source of morality. More specifically, it was the specific meaning of Judaism *inasmuch as* it is the source of morality for the whole of humanity. Here we should recall Cohen's aforementioned claim that the vocation of Judaism is its function as an inspiration for universal culture: Judaism affirms its specificity inasmuch as it functions within culture. Here Cohen explained that the growing indifference of Jewish youth for monotheistic religion was due not to the increasing influence of culture and philosophy (as was widely believed), but rather to a cultural and philosophical *crisis*. "Recently – Cohen wrote – aversion to religion, however, has been on the increase in educated circles, owing to a mistrust and a lack of modesty in respect of philosophy."[35] Moving away from religion was therefore a sign of a "mistrust" in philosophy. This was because the Unique God of Judaism is not, like the mythical gods, a particular belief, in opposition to the universalist trend of culture, but, on the contrary, the inspiring idea of universal ethical culture. Therefore, there is no alternative, rather there is full, unbreakable unity between Jewish monotheism and philosophical humanism.

There is no general culture [Bildung] nor any European culture
[Kultur] nor any ethics without the idea of the Unique God and
the God of morality. There is no foundation and stability of
culture without a *scientifically grounded* morality. For this reason
the idea of the Unique God is necessary. Morality does not need
other gods: but it does need the Unique God. *Therefore there can*
be neither European culture nor ethics without the fundamental
participation of Judaism.[36]

The second "postulate" – Jewish messianism – followed as a direct consequence of the first. Against those who out of concern for the particular identity of the Jewish "people" resisted participation in the German
state and in the universal culture of humanity, Cohen argued that the
authentic sense of Jewish messianism lay in the vocation of the people
of Israel to live amongst other peoples precisely so as to promote universal humanity: "The Unique God has deprived us of our homeland to
return it to us in humanity,"[37] Cohen observed. "If we did not have, or
no longer had, this mission, there would be no *Jewish* sense in preserving our ethnic identity."[38] The core meaning of this statement lay in the
phrase "Jewish sense." This special sense of Jewish identity consisted in
surrendering any conception of this identity as separation and instead
adopting an identity dedicated to the realization of universal humanity.
Today, this claim may be difficult for readers to accept, given our knowledge of the tragedy of the Shoah. Although Cohen was keenly aware of
anti-Jewish persecution, he could never have imagined that there might
be the real risk of the total annihilation of Jewish life and that the historical situation could present itself in which the Jews could consider their
very existence, even in the religious sense, as a "commandment."[39] But
it hardly follows that our new perspective, forced upon us by historical
tragedy, has drained Cohen's argument of all validity.

In 1910, Cohen published an essay, *The Inner Relations of Kant's*
Philosophy to Judaism (Innere Beziehungen der Kantischen Philosophie
zum Judentum),[40] which attempted to demonstrate the thoroughgoing harmony between Kant and Judaism, the latter as represented by
medieval Jewish philosophy. The essay is an apt illustration of Cohen's
particular method: Judaism, Cohen argued, exhibited a fundamental
agreement not only with Kantian ethics but also with the basic, logical premises of transcendental philosophy as such. The very concept of
critical reason corresponds to basic themes that inspired the great Jewish philosophers of the medieval period – that is, the absolute rejection

of blind fideism and absolute trust in the rational character of the contents of revelation.[41] Moreover, Cohen underscored the full agreement between Judaism and Kant's most important ethical themes: the rejection of eudemonism,[42] the conception of the moral principle as law,[43] and the concept of autonomy,[44] which in Kant is also not contradicted by the acceptance of a supreme law-giver, the Unique, spiritual God, and the idea of God.[45] Cohen further emphasized Kant's two-fold thesis concerning the unity of reason and its dualistic application – that (1) reason is the common ground for both natural-scientific knowledge and morality, even while (2) nature and morality remain rigorously distinct. Kant had thereby avoided pantheism, on Cohen's view the antithesis of Judaism and the philosophical error *par excellence*.[46] Cohen made further reference to the ideas of immortality,[47] humanity, cosmopolitanism, political equality, and eternal peace – all Kantian themes that bore a marked resemblance to prophetic and messianic ideals.[48] Even Kant's idea of "radical evil," Cohen claimed, was related to a theme innate to Judaism itself (a unique claim that Cohen had already developed thoroughly in the second, 1910 edition of *Kant's Grounding of Ethics*[49] and to which he returned constantly up until his very last work, *Religion of Reason*).[50]

While we cannot pursue a thorough analysis of Cohen's argumentation here, it is worth pausing to consider its major themes. Let us first consider the framework of this essay (originally a lecture presented on 3 January 1910 at the *Lehranstalt für die Wissenschaft des Judentums*), which will permit us to make explicit a crucial theme in Cohen's notion of the synthesis between Judaism and critical idealism. Cohen admitted that Kant's infrequent remarks on Judaism were largely negative, thus implying that the relation was anything but close. Hence at the beginning of the essay Cohen introduced a distinction between "history of literature" and "history of philosophy, as (...) of the sciences."[51] For in the history of literature, everything written by an author is considered of importance since its purpose is to provide a thorough reconstruction of the entirety of a philosopher's written corpus. For the history of philosophy, however, what counts is only the philosopher's original contribution within his own sphere of expertise. It is thus methodologically defensible to ignore Kant's remarks on Judaism since, in Cohen's words, Kant was not "competent on questions of Jewish religion and the Science of Judaism."[52]

In his *Inner Relations* essay, Cohen was not concerned with an interpretation of Kant's philosophy itself but rather with the "inner relations [*innere Beziehungen*]" between the latter and Judaism. He accordingly put aside not only the history of literature but also the history of philosophy, so as to address a possible comparison at another level – that is, the "philosophy of religion." We should recall here that Cohen was himself a committee-member of the *Compendium of the Whole of the Science of Judaism* and known to be "specialized in the field of 'Ethics and Philosophy of Religion.'"[53] Before his audience at the *Lehranstalt für die Wissenschaft des Judentums*, he spoke of the objectives and fundamental method of the philosophy of religion. The main objective was not to describe religion in all its various historical aspects but to identify the *essence* – the fundamental meaning – of religion. To do so, the method to be pursued was not a neutral or aseptic reconstruction of empirical data in which religion happens to appear but rather the *"conceptual idealization of its fundamental thoughts."* For such a task one could not let the imagination run arbitrarily and subjectively wild. One must instead turn to the critical, philosophical method of the idea.[54]

This was and remained the essence of Cohen's conception of the philosophy of religion. It informed all of his thoughts on the relation between Judaism and culture, between Judaism and philosophy, and between Judaism and Germanism.[55] At this point, we may sum up by noting that *Judaism for Cohen is always the "conceptual idealization" of Judaism*: i.e., prophecy, moral teaching, universalism, and humanism, which, when taken together, constitute the "eternal essence of our religion."[56] Yet we should add that for Cohen, the synthesis between Judaism and philosophical and scientific culture was not only an ideal; its method was also of decisive importance for the continued vitality of Judaism as a living tradition. Cohen's commitment to the Science of Judaism derived from his belief that Judaism cannot be reduced to a static or repetitive preservation of tradition. On his view, there is no alternative between tradition and innovation; they are in fact complementary. If innovation does not have its roots in tradition it is arbitrary, while if tradition is not continually fed with new life by innovation, it will be drained of the very contents it wishes to preserve (and by innovation Cohen meant philosophical culture). The "sources" and "concept" of Judaism are accordingly the two poles between which Judaism as a living faith must proceed.

The 1916 essay *The Polish Jew (Der polnische Jude)*[57] was written to overcome German resistance, even on the part of some German Jews, to Jewish immigration from Eastern Europe. While acknowledging the great suffering of Polish and Russian Jews as well as the religious vitality they might contribute to German Judaism, Cohen also called attention to how the latter (as embodied in the Science of Judaism) might help to improve Eastern European Jewish identity: "I have often had the opportunity of noting that the intellectual sensibility of the Eastern Jew is torn by a spiritual fracture: there is no mediation in it between orthodoxy and religious indifference."[58] At issue, Cohen believed, was an excessively static religious tradition that would ultimately lead to desertion and indifference. Cohen contrasted the "stasis" of Eastern European Jewry with the legacy and ongoing achievements of German Judaism, specifically the Science of Judaism:

> Although this fracture is also present in Jews integrated into European culture [*Kulturjude*], in this case it is, at least partially, compensated for by much despised religious liberalism. Moses Mendelssohn did not only teach us the German language (. . .), but also built up for us a sturdy defence against the attacks of modern culture on our religion. All marginal facts, which would seem to contradict this, fall before the historical fact that it was (. . .) actually we German Jews who alone created *the Science of Judaism*.[59]

Cohen hastened to add that this route was not merely pragmatic. The idealized synthesis between Judaism and culture ("the revelation of the science to our religion and starting off from it")[60] also serves as a regulative idea of history, without which one would be unable to comprehend the special relation between Judaism and German culture: "This is the great example and paradigmatic meaning that the German Jew has for the future of Judaism, for Judaism in the whole world in its religious evolution," he explained. "We were able to posit the interpretation of our history and continuation of our religious practices in harmony with the most intimate motives of our religious tradition and, at the same time, with those of universal culture."[61]

4. THE IDEAL SYMBIOSIS BETWEEN JUDAISM AND GERMANISM

We now briefly consider one of Cohen's most interesting though frequently criticized essays, *Germanism and Judaism* (*Deutschtum und Judentum*).[62] Here Cohen fashioned a true apologia for the intimate relation between Judaism and Germanism. He did so not only to convince Germans and German Jews that they shared a common cultural spirit, but also to invite all the Jews of Europe and America to acknowledge their cultural debt to German Judaism and, consequently, to Germanism itself, to such a degree that even in the midst of war they might be moved to recognize Germany as the bearer of universal humanism, messianic socialism, and perpetual peace (that is, the eternal ideas comprising the essence of Judaism).

Cohen developed this argument by conceiving "Greekness" as a common source or *"tertium comparationis"*[63] between "Germanism" and "Judaism": The Greek spirit (specifically, Platonism) is a source of philosophical idealism, and is accordingly *both* in intimate agreement with Jewish monotheism and messianism *and* an inspiration for Christianity, ultimately leading to the Lutheran Reformation and from there to Germanism. Cohen's larger purpose was to demonstrate that idealism (that is, the critical idealism of Nicholas of Cusa, Leibniz, and Kant) constitutes the very essence of German philosophy and culture and therefore inspires Germany in its special historical vocation to promote universal humanism, socialism, equality, and social justice, a confederation of states, and perpetual peace. At the same time, Cohen wished to demonstrate that for this vocation, Germanism had not only drawn inspiration from Jewish sources, its very realization in the "classical" era was achieved thanks to the decisive contribution of German Jews. By the same token, this Jewish involvement in the development of German classical culture had also encouraged the maturity and reform of German Judaism itself (in the direction of scientific and ethical idealism). Here Cohen assigned the leading role to Moses Mendelssohn and the representatives of the Science of Judaism who were his heirs.[64]

The general thesis presented in Cohen's essay is indeed provocative. Gershom Scholem remarked in his diary: "[Uncle Georg] gave me *Germanism and Judaism* by Hermann Cohen, an impossible piece. The connections he conjured up are [such] that one would like to run away."[65] With few exceptions, reactions to the essay from both Jews and Germans were largely hostile.[66] Jacob Klatzkin's response is particularly noteworthy.[67] It took him little effort to expose the apparent relationship between Greekness and Judaism as an illusion, and he observed that elsewhere in his writings Cohen himself had actually acknowledged the differences between them.[68] Klatzkin made a similar objection to Cohen's arguments concerning the apparent relationship between Judaism and Christianity.[69] Moreover, Klatzkin also noted that to embrace Cohen's claim that idealism was the true source of German culture required that one first confine the meaning of idealism to critical, humanist, universalist, and messianic rationalism, the values in which Cohen saw a point of convergence between Germanism and Judaism. But this meant expelling Hegel from German philosophy and ignoring all other influential figures with divergent tendencies – for example, historical materialism, the historical school of law, Schopenhauer, Nietzsche, and romantic Spinozism.[70] Finally, as for the direct contribution of Jewish intellectuals to German classical culture, Klatzkin objected that any such participation was not crucial, as Cohen had supposed, and that it was no more important than the contribution Jews had always made to different cultures to which they have been assimilated while nonetheless *retaining* a distinctive cultural identity.[71]

If Cohen's contemporaries had no difficulty finding facts by which to refute the arguments in *Germanism and Judaism*, the same is perhaps even easier and more necessary for readers today, burdened as we are by the tragic memory of the Shoah. In Cohen's defence, one might argue that he could hardly have been expected to foresee those future developments. But such a defence would be at once sterile and (partly) false: it would be sterile because it would banish Cohen and his ideas to a dead past with no relevance for the present, and it would be false because even while Cohen could never have foreseen Nazism and the Shoah, he could have realized, like Klatzkin and so many others like him, that the current state of German culture, as of Judaism, certainly did not correspond to his ideal. Cohen's main thesis, for example, was: "German philosophy is idealism."[72] It is this thesis that supports and mediates the ideal-construction of the relation between Germanism and Judaism. But in Cohen's own time, German culture was no longer predominantly guided by the universalist, humanist idealism of Kant and Schiller in philosophy[73] or Bach, Mozart and Beethoven in the arts,[74] but included as significant strands quite different leaders and trends. Of course, Cohen was hardly unaware of such trends. Yet he believed (or perhaps wished to believe) that cultural figures such as Schopenhauer, Nietzsche, and Wagner were ephemeral stars in the German cultural firmament, doomed to fall since they were "unGerman" in Cohen's idealist sense. Of course German history did not transpire as Cohen hoped. And even Judaism as understood in Cohen's era was very different from the concept of Judaism he imagined: trends in the direction of differentiation from European culture and national separatism (represented most especially by Zionism) were not, as Cohen believed, only secondary phenomena, but were instead the predominant course of European Judaism at the time. In sum, at the time Cohen was writing, Germans and Jews, far from uniting in a common idealist spirit, were already on divergent paths.

For such reasons, more recent commentators have remained largely critical of the abstract and historically unreal character of Cohen's essay, a character they have identified with the abstract quality of Cohen's philosophical method overall. Emil Fackenheim, for example, noted "a strange abstractness, a shadowy sort of idealism which ascribes to ideas and ideals far greater power and responsibility than they ever can carry." He further remarks: "Such abstractness, a grave fault in any case, becomes altogether fatal when it assumes a dreamlike quality; when everything is staked on ideas and ideals – in this case, those of Kant, Goethe and Schiller – which, so far as any historical efficacy was concerned, had long vanished into the past."[75]

Against such accusations of intellectual abstraction and historical blindness, Steven Schwarzschild responded in defense of Cohen and reasserted the contemporary relevance of his vision.[76] Schwarzschild brought forth documentary evidence to show that notwithstanding Cohen's idealized conception of a symbiosis between Judaism and Germanism, Cohen himself bitterly acknowledged both publically and privately the unsettling condition of German society at that time.[77] Cohen's theses, then, were not based on an analysis of the actual situation, but were intended programmatically to suggest an ideal paradigm so as to ground both critical judgement in the present and the tasks for the future. "Idealization," therefore, is the interpretative key for properly understanding Cohen's perspective on the relationship between Judaism and Germanism and, more generally, between Judaism and philosophy, and Judaism and culture.[78] Having provided a brief illustration of Cohen's technique of "idealization,"[79] Schwarzschild concludes:

> In this light we can finally translate into our language what Cohen's thesis of 'the German-Jewish symbiosis' was meant to signify. It was not essentially a descriptive proposition but a regulative one. It said in effect: there are a number of social and intellectual forces at work in both the German and the Jewish historical cultures which can and should be used so as to advance as much and as quickly as possible whatever dynamic force they possess toward the goal of a cosmopolitan, humanistic, ethical world society.[80]

The principle of "idealization" recurs throughout Cohen's writings and is perhaps the best means to understand his true intentions. It is not Germany but the "concept" of "Germanism" that concerned him. The latter is an ideal: it is the archetype, critical paradigm and infinite task for German culture, just as Judaism is for Cohen the "concept" of Judaism, gaining its initial definition through "reason" as the primary and a priori source and simultaneously via the "sources of Judaism."[81] Ultimately, the true foundation of Cohen's life and work was critical *idealism*, for which he turned both to the philosophical tradition of Plato and Kant and to the Jewish tradition of monotheism and messianism.

Yet notwithstanding this defense one must squarely acknowledge that Cohen believed (or at least would like to have believed) that the ideal would actually have come about in German culture, and that warped philosophical, artistic, social, and political signals were merely marginal phenomena and would soon be overcome. On this point he was undoubtedly wrong. This does not mean, however, that the relevance for today of Cohen's thought can only be salvaged, as is the case with Schwarzschild, by seeing its realization in other places and other times (for example, the symbiosis between Judaism and American culture)[82] or (and this appears to me to be a more interesting perspective) restating the regulative value of Cohen's ideal for an increasingly more positive co-existence of different "socio-historical entities" in general.[83] Such a prospect could be true, even after the Shoah, for German culture as well.

Notes

1. F. A. Lange, *Geschichte des Materialismus und Kritik seiner Bedeutung in der Gegenwart*, Baedeker, Iserlohn 1866.
2. F. Rosenzweig, *Einleitung*, in H. Cohen, *Jüdische Schriften*, edited by Bruno Strauß, with an introduction by Franz Rosenzweig, Schwetschke, Berlin 1924, Vol. 1., pp. XIII–LXIV.
3. Ibid., pp. XXf.
4. Cf. ibid., pp. XXIIIf.
5. Ibid., pp. XXVf.
6. H. Cohen, *Ein Bekenntnis in der Judenfrage*, in idem, *Jüdische Schriften*, cit., Vol. 2., pp. 73–94.
7. Ibid., p. 73.
8. H. Cohen, *System der Philosophie. Zweiter Teil: Ethik des reinen Willens*, Bruno Cassirer, Berlin 1904, 1907 (second ed.); reprinted in idem, *Werke*, cit., Vol. 7., Georg Olms, Hildesheim – New York 1981.
9. Cf. F. Rosenzweig, *Einleitung*, cit., pp. XXXIff.
10. Ibid., p. XXXVI.
11. Ibid., p. XXXVIII.
12. Cf. ibid., pp. XXXVf.
13. Cf. ibid., pp. XLIIIff.
14. Cf. A. Altmann, *Hermann Cohens Begriff der Korrelation*, in *In zwei Welten. Sigfried Moses zum 75. Geburtstag*, hrsg. von H. Tramer, Bitaon, Tel Aviv 1962, pp. 377–399. See also A. Poma, *Die Korrelation in der Religionsphilosophie Cohens: eine Methode, mehr als eine Methode*, in *Neukantianismus. Perspektiven und Probleme*, ed. by E.W. Orth and H. Holzhey, Königshausen & Neumann, Würzburg 1994, pp. 343–365; Eng. trans. in idem, *Yearning for Form and Other Essays on Hermann Cohen's Thought*, Springer, Dordrecht 2006, pp. 61–85.
15. See note 7.

16. See pp. 83–84, 87–88, this volume. Cohen, *System der Philosophie. Zweiter Teil: Ethik des reinen Willens.*]
17. Cf. H. Cohen, *Briefe*, ausgewählt und herausgegeben von Bertha und Bruno Strauß, Schocken Verlag/ Jüdischer Buchverlag, Berlin 1939, pp. 38ff.
18. F. Rosenzweig, *Einleitung*, cit., p. LII.
19. H. Cohen, *Ein Bekenntnis in der Judenfrage*, cit., p. 74.
20. Cf. ibid., p. 86.
21. Cf. ibid., pp. 81ff.
22. Cf. ibid., p. 85. On Cohen's clash with Buber over Zionism, see H. Cohen, *Zionismus und Religion. Ein Wort an meine Kommilitonen jüdischen Glaubens*, von Geh. Regierungsrat Prof. Dr. Hermann Cohen, in idem, *Jüdische Schriften*, cit, Vol. 2., pp. 319–327; M. Buber, *Begriffe und Wirklichkeit. Brief an Herrn Geh. Regierungsrat Prof. Dr. Hermann Cohen*, in "Der Jude," no. 5, August 1916, pp. 281–289; H. Cohen, *Antwort auf das offene Schreiben des Herrn Dr. Martin Buber an Hermann Cohen*, in idem, *Jüdische Schriften*, cit., Vol. 2., pp. 328–340; M. Buber, *Zion, der Staat und die Menschheit. Bemerkungen zu Hermann Cohens "Antwort,"* in "Der Jude," no. 7, Oktober 1916, pp. 425–433 (all these essays have been reprinted in the new critical and annoted edition of Cohen's *Kleinere Schriften VI*, ed. by H. Wiedebach: H. Cohen, *Werke*, cit., Vol. 17., Georg Olms. Hildesheim – Zürich – New York 2002, pp. 211–275). In the collection of essays containing the Italian translations of these writings (H. Cohen, *La fede d'Israele è la speranza. Interventi sulle questioni ebraiche (1880–1916). Con due lettere di Martin Buber a Hermann Cohen*, ed. P. Fiorato, with a postscript by G. Bonola, Giuntina, Firenze 2000), there are some interesting comments by P. Fiorato on the Cohen-Buber controversy (*Introduzione*, pp. 38ff.) and also by G. Bonola (*Urgenze del lealismo e travagli dell'identità. Dietro le quinte e intorno alla polemica Cohen-Buber*, pp. 283ff.).
23. On this subject, see S. Schwarzschild, *"Germanism and Judaism" – Hermann Cohen's Normative Paradigm of the German-Jewish Symbiosis*, in *Jews and Germans from 1860 to 1933: "The Problematic Symbiosis,"* ed. by D. Bronsen, Carl Winter – Universitätsverlag, Heidelberg 1979, pp. 129–172; H. Wiedebach, *Die Bedeutung der Nationalität für Hermann Cohen*, Georg Olms, Hildesheim – Zürich – New York 1997. See also A. Poma, *La risposta di Hermann Cohen all'antigiudaismo*, in *Atti del II Convegno tenuto a Idice, Bologna, nei giorni 4 e 5 novembre 1981*, "Associazione Italiana per lo Studio del Giudaismo. Testi e Studi n.1," eds. F. Parente and D. Piattelli, Carucci, Roma 1983, pp. 59–75; Eng. trans. in idem, *Yearning for Form and Other Essays on Hermann Cohen's Thought*, cit., pp. 1–20.
24. H. Cohen, *Der Sabbat in seiner kulturgeschichtlichen Bedeutung*, in idem, *Jüdische Schriften*, cit., Vol. 2., pp. 45–72.
25. Cf., for example, H. Cohen, *Ein Bekenntnis in der Judenfrage*, cit., pp. 75ff., 91ff.
26. Cf.. H. Cohen, *Zur Verteidigung*, in idem, *Jüdische Schriften*, cit., Vol. 2., pp. 95–100.

27. In 1912, Cohen stated that he had changed his mind on this point (cf. the note by Bruno Strauß in H. Cohen, *Jüdische Schriften*, cit., Vol. 2., p. 470), although he certainly did not deny the original intentions behind this proposal, as can be seen from a 1917 essay: cf. H. Cohen, *Mahnung des Alters an die Jugend*, in idem, *Jüdische Schriften*, cit., Vol. 2., pp. 175s.; reprinted in idem, *Werke*, Vol. 17., cit., pp. 577s.

28. H. Cohen, *Briefe*, cit., pp. 82f.

29. It should be recalled here that the Breslau seminary, where Cohen studied, was one of the most important centres for the Science of Judaism, and that Cohen's teachers there were among the most important members of the movement.

30. See, for example, H. Cohen, *Die Errichtung von Lehrstühlen für Ethik und Religionsphilosophie an den jüdisch-theologischen Lehranstalten*, in idem, *Jüdische Schriften*, cit., Vol. 2., pp. 108–125; idem, *Zwei Vorschläge zur Sicherung unseres Fortbestandes*, in idem, *Jüdische Schriften*, cit., Vol. 2., pp. 133–141; idem, *Zur Begründung einer Akademie für die Wissenschaft des Judentums*, in idem, *Jüdische Schriften*, cit., Vol. 2., pp. 210–217; reprinted in idem, *Werke*, cit., Vol. 17., cit., pp. 625–635.

31. See D. Adelmann, *Die "Religion der Vernunft" im "Grundriss der Gesamtwissenschaft des Judentums,"* cit., which I have drawn on for much previous material.

32. H. Cohen, *Religiöse Postulate*. Rede, gehalten am Frankfurter Verbandstage der deutschen Juden am 13. Oktober 1907, in idem, *Jüdische Schriften*, cit., Vol. 1., pp. 1–17; excerpted in Hermann Cohen, *Reason and Hope*, Eva Jospe, trans. (W. W. Norton, 1971), 44–51.

33. Cf. ibid., pp. 12ff.

34. Cf. ibid., pp. 1ff.

35. Ibid., p. 2.

36. Ibid., p. 4.

37. Ibid., p. 7.

38. Ibid.

39. Cf. E. L. Fackenheim, *God's Presence in History* (New York University Press, 1970), 85.

40. H. Cohen, *Innere Beziehungen der Kantischen Philosophie zum Judentum*, in idem, *Jüdische Schriften*, cit., Vol. 1., pp. 284–305. Excerpted in Cohen, *Reason and Hope*, 77–89.

41. Cf. ibid., pp. 287ff.

42. Cf. ibid., pp. 290f.

43. Cf. ibid., pp. 291f.

44. Cf. ibid., p. 292.

45. Cf. ibid., pp. 293f.

46. Cf. ibid., pp. 294ff.

47. Cf. ibid., p. 297.

48. Cf. ibid., pp. 297ff.

49. H. Cohen, *Kants Begründung der Ethik*, Dümmler, Berlin 1877; Bruno Cassirer, Berlin 1910 (second ed.); reprinted in idem, *Werke*, cit., Vol. 2., Georg Olms, Hildesheim – Zürich – New York 2001, pp. 335–343.

Previous remarks in this direction are to be found in, for example, H. Cohen, *System der Philosophie. Zweiter Teil: Ethik des reinen Willens*, cit., pp. 303, 626f.

50. H. Cohen, *Religion der Vernunft aus den Quellen des Judentums*, edited by B. Kellerman, Fock, Leipzig 1919; edited by B. Strauß, J. Kaufmann, Frankfurt a.M. 1929 (second ed.); reprinted J. Melzer, Köln 1959, pp. 212f., 372.

51. Ibid., p. 284.

52. Ibid.

53. D. Adelmann, *Die "Religion der Vernunft" im "Grundriss der Gesamtwissenschaft des Judentums,"* cit., p. 20.

54. Cf. H. Cohen, *Innere Beziehungen der Kantischen Philosophie zum Judentum*, cit., pp. 303f.

55. Cf. H. Cohen, *Religion der Vernunft aus den Quellen des Judentums*, cit., pp. 1ff.

56. Cf. H. Cohen, *Innere Beziehungen der Kantischen Philosophie zum Judentum*, cit., p. 304.

57. H. Cohen, *Der polnische Jude*, in idem, *Jüdische Schriften*, cit., Vol. 2., pp. 162–171; reprinted in idem, *Werke*, cit., Vol. 17., cit., pp. 189–202. In the quotations that follow, the page numbers are from *Jüdische Schriften*, followed immediately by those in *Werke*.

58. Ibid., pp. 165/193s.

59. Ibid., pp. 165f/194s.

60. Ibid., pp. 166/195.

61. Ibid., pp. 166/195s.

62. H. Cohen, *Deutschtum und Judentum. Mit grundlegenden Betrachtungen über Staat und Internationalismus*, in idem, *Jüdische Schriften*, cit., Vol. 2., pp. 237–301; reprinted in idem, *Werke*, cit., Vol. 16., Georg Olms, Hildesheim – Zürich – New York 1997, pp. 465–560. Also excerpted in Cohen, *Reason and Hope*, 176–184. In the quotations that follow, the page numbers are from *Jüdische Schriften*, followed immediately by those in *Werke*.

63. Cf. ibid., pp. 237/469.

64. Cf. ibid., pp. 266ff./511ff.

65. G. Scholem, *Tagebücher nebst Aufsätze und Entwürfe bis 1923, I. Halbband 1913–1917*, unter Mitarbeit von H. Kopp-Osterbrink edited by K. Gründer and F. Niewöhner, Jüdischer Verlag, Frankfurt a.M. 1995, p. 207f.

66. See the remarks by Bruno Strauß in the note in H. Cohen, *Jüdische Schriften*, cit., Vol. 2., p. 476, and those by H. Wiedebach, in H. Cohen, *Werke*, cit., Vol. 16., cit., p. XXXIII, note 81.

67. Cf. J. Klatzkin, *Deutschtum und Judentum*, in idem, *Hermann Cohen*, cit., pp. 57–93 (already published by Klatzkin in "Der Jude," 1917, no. 4 and 5/6.: cf. B. Strauß in H. Cohen, *Jüdische Schriften*, cit. Bd. 2., p. 476).

68. Cf. ibid., pp. 59ff.

69. Cf. ibid., pp. 70ff.

70. Cf. ibid., pp. 71ff.

71. Cf. ibid., pp. 79ff.

72. H. Cohen, *Deutschtum und Judentum. Mit grundlegenden Betrachtungen über Staat und Internationalismus*, cit., pp. 239/471.
73. Cf. ibid., pp. 249f./487f.
74. Cf. ibid., pp. 251f./490.
75. E. L. Fackenheim, *Hermann Cohen – After Fifty Years*, Leo Baeck Memorial Lecture 12, Leo Baeck Institute, New York 1969, p. 10.
76. Cf. S. Schwarzschild, *"Germanism and Judaism" – Hermann Cohen's Normative Paradigm of the German-Jewish Symbiosis*, cit., p. 138.
77. Schwarzschild (cf. ibid., p. 139) refers to the preface to the second edition of *Ethik des reinen Willens*, from 1907 (cit., pp. Xf.) and to Cohen's letter to Natorp dated 27 October 1916 (H. Holzhey, op.cit., Bd. 2., pp. 451ff.).
78. Cf. S. Schwarzschild, *"Germanism and Judaism" – Hermann Cohen's Normative Paradigm of the German-Jewish Symbiosis*, cit., p. 142. This obviously has nothing to do with the insinuations by Jacques Derrida that in *Deutschtum und Judentum*, Cohen is in something of a delirium, without even the pretence of objectivity (cf. J. Derrida, *Interpretations at War. Kant, le Juif, l'Allemand*, in *Phénoménologie et politique. Mélanges offerts à Jacques Taminiaux*, Ousia, Bruxelles 1989, pp. 230ff.); here Derrida goes so far as to gratuitously insult Cohen (cf. ibid., pp. 255ff.).
79. Cf. S. Schwarzschild, *"Germanism and Judaism" – Hermann Cohen's Normative Paradigm of the German-Jewish Symbiosis*, cit., pp. 147ff.
80. Ibid., p. 154.
81. This is developed further in A. Poma, *Religion der Vernunft und Judentum bei Hermann Cohen*, in *Zeit und Welt. Denken zwischen Philosophie und Religion*, edited by E. Goodman-Thau, Universitätsverlag C. Winter, Heidelberg 2002, pp. 57–71; Eng. trans. in idem, *Yearning for Form and Other Essays on Hermann Cohen's Thought*, cit., pp. 111–128.
82. Cfr. S. Schwarzschild, *"Germanism and Judaism" – Hermann Cohen's Normative Paradigm of the German-Jewish Symbiosis*, cit., p. 157.
83. Cf. ibid.

6 Self, Other, Text, God: The Dialogical Thought of Martin Buber

TAMRA WRIGHT

What is Martin Buber's legacy to Jewish thought? Buber was certainly one of the most prolific and influential Jewish thinkers of the twentieth century. His writings covered a vast array of disciplines, including several areas of philosophy, mystical traditions from around the world and Hasidism, as well as biblical scholarship, hermeneutics and translation. Above all, he was a visionary thinker, who sought to overcome the 'sickness of the age' by engaging in authentic relationships with others and teaching his students and readers to do the same.[1]

In assessing Buber's legacy to Jewish thought, I will outline the parallels between the development of his approach to hermeneutics and his changing view of the ideal way of relating to others, particularly other human beings and God. I will look in some detail at *I and Thou*, Buber's masterpiece of dialogical philosophy,[2] and explore the extent to which his mature philosophy of dialogue is challenged by the Shoah.

EARLY WRITINGS

Buber was born in 1878 in Vienna. Following the separation of his parents when he was three years old, he was raised until the age of fourteen by his paternal grandparents in Galicia. As a child growing up on his grandfather's estate in Poland, Buber participated in a traditionally observant Jewish life and was also exposed to the Hasidic way of life of some of his Jewish neighbours in Poland. Buber's grandfather, Solomon, was a prominent scholar in the *Haskalah* – Jewish enlightenment movement – whose critical editions of Midrash are still highly regarded.

At the age of fourteen, Buber moved back to Vienna to live with his father. He abandoned Jewish religious practises and became interested in Western philosophy, particularly the thought of Kant and

I am grateful to Michael Morgan and Peter Gordon for their insightful comments on an earlier version of this chapter.

Nietzsche, and went on to study philosophy, German literature, psychology, and history of art at the Universities of Vienna, Berlin, Leipzig, and Zurich.

Buber's interest in Judaism was rekindled through his affiliation with Zionism. He was originally recruited to the Jewish nationalist cause by Theodor Herzl and briefly edited *Die Welt*, the main paper of the Zionist party. Buber soon joined the 'democratic faction' that was led by Chaim Weizmann. Although he sometimes became disillusioned with the political aspects of Zionism, and refrained from practical political activity for extended periods, he remained a passionate advocate of a Zionist renaissance of Jewish culture. In 1916, he began publishing *Der Jude*, a journal of cultural and political Zionism. In political debates from the 1920s to the founding of Israel in 1948, Buber espoused minority opinions based on his philosophy, including pacifism (he argued against arming Jewish settlers) and, perhaps as an outgrowth of his dialogical philosophy, he proposed that a bi-national state should be established in Palestine.

From 1905 onwards, Buber immersed himself in the study of mystical traditions from around the world, and this interest in turn led him to focus on Hasidism, the popular mystical movement that became popular in Eastern Europe in the eighteenth and nineteenth centuries, and which Buber had himself experienced during his childhood visits to Hasidic communities in Galicia. Buber's study of Hasidism resulted in the publication of his well-known collections of Hasidic tales.[3] His earliest collections are free re-tellings of the classic stories, which draw upon the romantic hermeneutics that Buber developed under the influence of Nietzsche, Dilthey, and Schleiermacher.[4]

In his early collections of Hasidic tales and other writings on myth and legend, Buber sought, through empathy, to achieve union with the mind of the author of the text or with that of the original storyteller. Regarding his earliest collection of Hasidic stories, *The Tales of Rabbi Nachman*, Buber writes, 'I experienced...my unity with the spirit of Rabbi Nachman.' Similarly, he writes that his work on the tales of the Baal-Shem Tov involved realizing his 'inborn binding with Hasidic truth' and an attempt to 'construct the inner process in the life of the master.'[5] Buber's romantic hermeneutics led to his belief that his empathy with the Hasidic masters gave him the license to elaborate, embellish, and distort their stories, while remaining faithful to the inner truth of their teaching.[6]

There are striking similarities between Buber's early hermeneutics and his early writings on relation. The 1913 work *Daniel: Dialogues on Realization*, represents the early, mystical period, in which Buber presents union as the ultimate form of relation.[7] His aim in writing *Daniel* was to synthesize the Eastern concept of 'the One' with the Western realms of philosophy, religion, science, and art.[8] Buber describes two ways of being in the world. 'Orientation,' which in many ways prefigures the 'I-It' relation described in *I and Thou*, refers to the world of ordinary experiences, which fit within the laws of causality and the constraints of space and time. 'Realization,' by contrast, 'refers to that enhanced meaning of life which springs from moments of intensified existence and intensified perception.'[9]

In the first of the five dialogues that comprise *Daniel*, Buber focuses on the relationship with nature, using the example of a tree. The same example will recur, with some significant revisions, in *I and Thou*. In the earlier text, Buber presents union with the other as the path of realization. The eponymous Daniel instructs his companion not to think about the tree, not to compare its properties with those of other stone pines, other trees, other plants, but to focus on it exclusively and attempt to draw near it. 'With all your directed power,' he says, 'receive the tree; surrender yourself to it, until you feel its bark as your skin, and the force of a branch spring from its trunk like the striving in your muscles [...] yes truly until you are transformed.'[10] Just as Buber sought to feel 'unity' with Rabbi Nachman, Daniel recommends an extreme form of empathy as the path to true relation.

DIALOGICAL PHILOSOPHY

Both in Buber's later writings on Hasidism and biblical hermeneutics, and in his more mature philosophy, this emphasis on union is replaced by a dialogical model of relation, and it is for his writings on the dialogical, or I-Thou relation, that Buber is best known. While Buber was developing his I-Thou philosophy in the period from 1916 to 1922, his approach to interpreting texts changed radically. He abandoned the romantic quest to unite with the mind of the author, and shifted his focus from the author to the text itself. His 1922 collection of Hasidic tales,[11] and subsequent publications in this area, reflect a new respect for the integrity of the text. The later tales are much sparser, lacking the embellishments, elaborations, and romantic flourishes that earned the earlier tales the punning sobriquet of 'Buber meises' (a play on the Yiddish phrase *booba meises*, old wives' tales).

Buber's new-found respect for the integrity of the text is particularly evident in his biblical scholarship and his collaboration with Franz

Rosenzweig on translating the Bible into German. Buber and Rosenzweig undertook to restrain their own poetic enthusiasm and to retain in their translation as much as possible of the rhythm, semantics, and rhetorical style of the Hebrew text. Rather than creating an eloquent translation, which would read smoothly in German, they deliberately set out to convey the foreignness of the biblical text. In particular, they tried to preserve the oral nature of the Hebrew Bible, seeing it as a work that needs to be heard (*TAT* 43).

In addition to making this profound change in his hermeneutic practice, Buber's approach to religion and spirituality also changed radically during the period leading up to the publication of *I and Thou*. In one of his 'Autobiographical Fragments,' entitled 'A Conversion,' he suggests that the impetus for this move came from personal experience rather than from strictly intellectual considerations. Buber relates that after a morning of "'religious" enthusiasm,' he received a visit from a young man whom he did not know. Although Buber welcomed the visitor and had a friendly discussion with him, he nevertheless was not fully present in the encounter, and he failed to discern that the visit was motivated by the young man's deep existential concerns.

> Later, not long after, I learned from one of his friends — he was no longer alive – the essential content of these questions; I learned that he had come to me not casually but borne by destiny, not for a chat but for a decision. [. . .] What do we expect when we are in despair and yet go to a man? Surely a presence by means of which we are told that nevertheless there is meaning. (*PMB* 26)[12]

Although the episode, as recounted by Buber, might seem to suggest that the visitor committed suicide, he was in fact killed at the front in World War I (*ENR* 80). Buber's point in the fragment is not that he caused the young man's death, but that he was absent in spirit when his full presence was required – 'he failed to make real, insofar as it was up to him, the possibility of genuine dialogue that that hour offered' (*ENR* 81). Had Buber not mentioned that the young man died soon after their meeting, the episode – whilst losing some of its pathos – would still retain its essential message.

It is interesting that the lesson Buber derived from this experience was not a general obligation to be fully present to others whenever they seek us out, but a specific lesson about the dangers of mystical 'religious' experience. 'Since then I have given up the "religious" which is nothing but the exception, extraction, exaltation, ecstasy; or it has given me up.' In place of the pursuit of mystical experience, Buber relates, he was 'converted' to a religiosity of the everyday: 'I possess nothing but the everyday out of which I am never taken. [...] I know no fullness but each mortal hour's fullness of claim and responsibility' (*PMB* 26).

Buber's move from his early romantic philosophy and mystical pursuits to the philosophy of dialogue may also have been triggered by his friend Gustav Landauer's critique of his early enthusiasm for World War I. Like many patriotic German Jews, Buber initially supported the war.[13] He thought that the heroic mood in Germany had 'initiated an epoch of unconditioned action in which one realizes one's *Erlebnisse* in their fullness and thereby gains "a connectedness with the Absolute."' Buber even went so far as to see the tragedy of war as being of 'marginal import compared to the war's metaphysical significance' (*FMD* 18).

Landauer, an opponent of the war, wrote to Buber in May 1916, criticising both Buber's 'perverse' politics and the asocial metaphysics from which they were derived, and his letter seems to have provoked a complete rethinking of Buber's position. All of Buber's public statements subsequent to the receipt of Landauer's letter show him to be completely opposed to the war (*FMD* 102). In addition, following receipt of the letter he began to address one of the themes of Landauer's own teaching, the insistence that any 'change in the quality of spiritual life' must be preceded by a transformation of interhuman relations (*FMD* 19). As we will see later, exploring the connection between the spiritual life and the realm of interpersonal relations is one of the central themes of *I and Thou*.

Another important factor in the development of Buber's dialogical thought was the intellectual influence of Franz Rosenzweig. As Rivka Horwitz has shown, this influence can be seen by comparing the text of Buber's 'Religion as Presence' lectures, delivered at the Frankfurt Lehrhaus in 1922, to the various drafts of *I and Thou* (*BW* 193–205). On the basis of this comparison, Horwitz argues that the dialogical basis of the I-Thou was actually 'one of the very last additions to an already existing structure' (*BW* 194). This argument is not simply of historical interest – according to Horwitz, many of the 'problematical formulations and inconsistencies present in the published version of *I and Thou*' can be explained, at least in part, as arising from the imperfect fusion of two different philosophical approaches (*BW* 194).

Indeed, it is not at all obvious that Buber was primarily concerned with philosophical consistency when he wrote *I and Thou*. Buber often seems to be more concerned with conveying a teaching intended for spiritual guidance than with elaborating a philosophical doctrine.[14] The book is written in a direct, at times intimate, style. No preface or conceptual introduction stands between the reader and the opening words of the work:

> The world is twofold for man, in accordance with his twofold attitude.

> The attitude of man is twofold, in accordance with the basic words which he can speak.

> The basic words are not single words but word pairs.

> One basic word is the word pair I-Thou.

> The other basic word is the word pair I-It; but this basic word is not changed when He or She takes the place of It.

> Thus the I of man is also twofold.

> For the I of the basic word I-Thou is different from that in the basic word I-It.[15]

The general impression created by this style is that the author does not so much have an argument to make as a vision to communicate. Buber himself later described the genesis of *I and Thou* as his response to a 'vision'. In his 1957 'Postscript' to *I and Thou*, he wrote that he had been 'impelled by an inner necessity' to write the book. 'A vision that had afflicted me repeatedly since my youth but had always been dimmed again, had now achieved a constant clarity that was so evidently suprapersonal that I soon knew that I ought to bear witness of it' (*IT* 171).[16]

The opening section of *I and Thou*, which we quoted earlier, sets out the central ideas of the work as a whole. Buber presents a binary system for analyzing and describing the whole of human experience. Our everyday way of relating to objects in the world, and indeed of relating to other people, as a means to an end, as things that we can use, enjoy, and experience, is termed I-It. By contrast, the moments of true encounter with another being, in which the I responds to the whole being of the other with its whole being, are termed I-Thou encounters.[17]

Buber sees I-It as the default mode of human existence. I-Thou encounters do not endure through time. Even with regard to people whom one loves it is impossible to remain in I-Thou mode all, or even most, of the time. Every Thou must become an It again;[18] at the same time, however, every It can potentially be encountered as a Thou (*IT* 69).[19] Moreover, Buber insists that although a person can willingly prevent I-Thou encounters from occurring, it is not possible to create such an encounter through an act of will. Rather, I-Thou encounters happen through 'grace' (*IT* 62).

Buber outlines three different spheres in which I-Thou relations can take place: the natural world, the inter-personal world, and the spiritual/artistic world. Of the three spheres, that of inter-personal relations is the easiest to analyse according to Buber's binary model. Experience teaches us how easy it is to disregard or feel indifferent to the 'whole being' of the other person. (In London, for example, the Underground stations have automatic ticket dispensers that often break down. I would hazard a guess that most commuters who end up purchasing their tickets from a human being do so only because the mechanical dispenser has broken down and that they are not interested in relating to the ticket seller in his or her wholeness.) On the other hand, most people can remember times when they have let go of all plans, presuppositions, and conceptual frameworks and simply responded to the person in front of them.

Of the three spheres in which encounters can take place, only the relationship between self and other allows for a literal 'dialogue.' However, Buber's primary metaphors for the I-Thou relation derive from speech. He uses the terms 'word,' 'speech,' 'dialogue,' and so forth to convey the qualities of presence, dynamism, and reciprocity that are characteristic of I-Thou but not of the I-It relation. For Buber, 'the very act of turning to another in relation is an act of speaking, even when not a word is uttered between them.'[20]

Buber emphasizes the mutuality of the encounter: 'My Thou acts on me as I act on it. Our students teach us, our works form us' (*IT* 67). Although the relationship is reciprocal, it is not necessarily symmetrical – for example, there is a built-in asymmetry to the teacher-student relationship (*IT* 178). In addition, the degree of mutuality that can be achieved will also differ depending on whether the Thou is a plant, an animal, a human being, or a 'spiritual form.'[21]

As an example of relations with the world of nature, Buber presents a fairly elaborate discussion of ways of relating to a tree. Most of the section is dedicated to listing a number of different ways I could approach the tree as It: I can consider it as a picture, as movement, as a botanical sample, as a mathematical object to be counted, or as a material object to be studied according to the laws of physics. To adopt any of these attitudes is to relate to the tree in the mode of I-It. However, it is also possible, without forgetting any of my knowledge of the tree gained in I-It mode, to relate to the tree as Thou. In this mode, I focus exclusively on the tree, and my approach to it is not mediated through any of the conceptual, aesthetic, instrumental, or mathematical categories that characterize the I-It approach. Instead, in relating to the tree I relate to it not according to one or more of its aspects but in its wholeness (*IT* 57–58).

The discussion of the tree in *I and Thou* represents a significant departure from the mystical inclinations of his earlier work. In *Daniel*, Buber had presented the ideal relation with a tree as one in which I would identify with it to the extent that I felt its bark to be my own skin and its sap my own blood. The insistence on mutuality in *I and Thou* makes it clear that mystical union with the other term of the relation is not the goal of I-Thou encounters.

The third sphere Buber discusses is that of relations with 'spiritual beings,' and the example he uses is the form that inspires an artist to create a work. For Buber, the work of art arises when 'a human being confronts a form that wants to become a work through him. Not a figment of his soul but that which appears to the soul and demands the soul's creative power' (*IT* 60). This passage shows a marked contrast with Buber's earlier understanding of the origin of the work of art. Dilthey's hermeneutics, which, as we have seen, influenced Buber's early Hasidic writings, is based on the idea that the work of art results from and expresses the *Erlebnis*, the lived experience, of the author; the understanding of the act of interpretation as the attempt to identify with the author's *Erlebnis* follows naturally from this view of the origin of the work. By contrast, in the passage just quoted, Buber presents the work of art as a response to a 'form of spirit,' a 'Thou,' whose existence is independent of the artist.

The 'spiritual being' that the artist confronts is an intangible form that calls upon the artist to bring it into the world. Buber presents the 'commandment' that arises in such an encounter as a significant difference between other I-Thou encounters and the artist's moment of inspiration. However, the work that the artist is enjoined to produce is but the most concrete manifestation of a feature that is common to I-Thou encounters: I emerge from the encounter changed in some way, and I carry something of it into the world of It.

THE ETERNAL THOU

Following his discussion of the third sphere of relation, Buber introduces a new idea to his presentation of I-Thou relation: each particular I-Thou encounter is simultaneously in some way an encounter with the Eternal Thou. In each Thou, he says, 'we address the eternal Thou' (*IT* 57). The full significance of this idea only becomes clear in the final section of *I and Thou*. It is interesting to note that in 1922, Buber wrote to Rosenzweig about the book he was working on, and told Rosenzweig that it would comprise three sections, 'which can be named: Word, History, God' (*BW* 209). In fact, he omitted these subtitles from the published work, but the tripartite structure remained.

Part Three deals specifically with God, or the 'Eternal Thou.' Buber states explicitly that the special quality of all other I-Thou relations arises from the fact that in each of these encounters, one addresses the Eternal Thou: 'The mediatorship of the Thou of all beings accounts for the fullness of our relationships to them' (*IT* 123). This section of the book presents a radical critique of both theology and traditional religions, insofar as Buber insists that God can only be 'addressed,' never 'asserted' or 'expressed.' God cannot be deduced from either nature or history. Rather, the God of whom Buber speaks is 'what confronts us immediately and first and always' (*IT* 129). To speak about God is necessarily to use It language. But God can never be an It – to worship an It is not to relate to God at all (*IT* 147). Buber acknowledges that a religious person's experience includes not only awareness of God's nearness, but also experiences of his remoteness. However, he insists that 'whoever knows God also knows God's remoteness and the agony of drought upon a frightened heart, *but not the loss of presence. Only we are not always there*' (*IT* 147; emphasis added).[22]

Buber's view of religions is that they grow out of genuine encounters with the Eternal Thou. Human beings are inclined to devise strategies to cope with two of the troubling characteristics of the I-Thou relation – its lack of continuity in both time and space. God becomes an 'object of faith' to fill the temporal gaps between moments of encounter, and cultic practises arise to represent the community's relationship to God. Gradually an objectified 'faith' and communal prayer come to replace, rather than supplement, authentic relation with God (*IT* 162).

In contrast to his earlier writings, Buber explicitly rejects the ideal of renouncing the ego, which is a common theme in mysticism. He insists that 'the I is indispensable for any relation, including the highest, which always presupposes an I and a Thou' (*IT* 126). Nor is renunciation of the world the path to true relation; to actualize the relation with the Eternal Thou, one must not turn away from the world, but see the world in the Thou (*IT* 126).

Revelation takes place in the encounter with the Eternal Thou, but Buber insists that it is a revelation without expressible content. What one receives in this revelation is the guarantee that there is meaning (the affirmation he failed to communicate to the young man in 'A Conversion') – yet nothing is communicated that could be expressed in language.

Nevertheless, Buber insists that the revelation both confirms the mean-
ingfulness of everyday human life and takes the form of a command.
However, the prescription is not a universal – it is a unique call to the
unique person, which must be realised in his own unique way and cannot
be expressed as a universal 'ought' or maxim.

Fackenheim explains the philosophical reasoning behind Buber's
assertions about revelation. Buber is able to reject doctrinal statements
about God and still know that He is eternal and infinite, because these
attributes are not known through speculation but through the encounter
itself. God's eternity and infinity are therefore the minimum content of
any revelation. But there is also specific content to each encounter with
the Eternal Thou, because in each encounter there remains an independent human I, and the I, of course, is finite and temporal. In the
encounter, the divine Thou speaks to the human I in its concrete situation. The specific content of the revelation is a mixture of the divine
speech and human response (*PMB* 287–88).[23]

The concluding pages of *I and Thou* offer an antidote to the 'sickness
of the age.' Buber prescribes 'return' to a life of relation with the Eternal
Thou. In opposition to the misguided strategies that human beings have
developed for trying to preserve continuity by making God an object of
faith and by substituting cults and rituals for true prayer, Buber enjoins
the reader to embody pure relation in 'the whole stuff of life.' That is not
to say that one can leave the world of It behind; this is clearly impossible. However, Buber insists that a person's life can become so permeated
with true I-Thou relations that moments of encounter are no longer like
'flashes of lightning in the dark' – instead, they would be like 'a rising moon in a clear starry night' (*IT* 163). Perhaps surprisingly, given his
emphasis on the importance of I-Thou relationships in the interpersonal
sphere, Buber also suggests that communities achieve authentic existence by placing God at the centre. He portrays the ideal community
by using the image of a circle, at whose centre lies the Eternal Thou.
The periphery is made up of 'I-points,' representing the members of a
community. It is the radii, the lines of relation between each individual
person and the Eternal Thou, that create the true community (*IT* 163).

ETHICS

Buber's ethics, as presented in *I and Thou*, is ultimately based not
simply on the I-Thou relation between self and other, but on the self's
relation to the Eternal Thou. In fact, it is not so much an ethics as a
transcendence of ethics. 'Duties and obligations one has only towards
the stranger,' Buber writes. But a person who has stepped before the

countenance of the Eternal Thou and 'always has God before him' is kind and loving towards others, who are no longer strangers but 'his intimates.' The person who lives this way leaves the third-person dictates of ethics behind, but does not in any way eschew responsibility for others; on the contrary, such a person takes on responsibility for the world before the face of God (*IT* 157).

Neither in *I and Thou*, nor in any of his subsequent writings, does Buber present a systematic account of ethics.[24] In the subsection on ethics in his 'Reply to My Critics,' he acknowledges that supporters and critics alike reproach him for neither endorsing a traditional framework of laws and duties nor creating his own system of ethics. This lack is not accidental: on the contrary, for Buber, filling it would be unthinkable; to do so would be to 'injure the core' of his thought (*PMB* 717). Thus he offers no system of ethics; nor, he emphasises, does he know of any universally valid system.[25]

Buber's contribution to philosophical reflection on ethics and morality is similar to that made by Emmanuel Levinas.[26] Neither thinker provides moral guidelines or a systematic inquiry into the contents of ethical obligation. Rather, Buber's 'I-Thou' and Levinas's 'face-to-face' enrich our understanding of what it means to encounter another human being. Through their respective accounts of the relationship between self and other, they provide answers to a fundamental moral question – why should I be concerned about others at all?

For the Buber of *I and Thou*, as noted earlier, moral responsibility is ultimately based on the relation with God or the Eternal Thou, and God remains central to Buber's thinking about ethics throughout his career. In his 'Reply to My Critics,' Buber re-affirms that he sees moral values as absolute because they come from the Absolute. He writes:

> I have never made a secret of the fact that I cannot hold the decision of a man [...] as to what is right and wrong in a certain situation to be a decision valid *in itself*. In my view, rather, he must understand himself as standing every moment under the judgment of God. (*PMB* 719)

DIALOGICAL PHILOSOPHY AND POST-HOLOCAUST THOUGHT

This discussion of *I and Thou* has shown that Buber's answer to the 'sickness of the age' was not simply for people to open themselves to I-Thou relations with one another. Part Three of *I and Thou* shows that Buber saw a relationship with the Eternal Thou as essential to the highest form of ethics, to authentic communal life, and to providing the individual with assurance that human life is not absurd. Yet the possibility of such a relationship in a post-Holocaust age is called into question by many Jewish thinkers, not least by Buber himself.

Readers often look to Buber's *Eclipse of God* for his response to the Shoah. The phrase 'eclipse of God' evokes the traditional Jewish notion of *hester panim* ('the hiding of the face') and may sound as though it were used by Buber specifically to describe the silence of God at Auschwitz. However, Buber applied it to the entire twentieth century, which he saw as a time of spiritual and moral eclipse. The concluding chapter of *Eclipse of God* repeats the idea first presented in *I and Thou*: the contemporary age is 'sick,' and its sickness consists in the ever-increasing preponderance of I-It.

> The I of this relation, an I that possesses all, makes all, succeeds with all, this I that is unable to say Thou, unable to meet a being essentially, is the lord of the hour. This selfhood that has become omnipotent, with all the It around it, can naturally acknowledge neither God nor any genuine absolute which manifests itself to men as of non-human origin. It steps in between and shuts off from us the light of heaven.[27]

It is interesting to note, however, that Buber did not end the book with this image of despair. Indeed, as Fackenheim observed,[28] the impermanence of an eclipse means that it is, in a sense, a hopeful image. Buber himself wrote, 'The eclipse of the light of God is no extinction; even tomorrow that which has stepped in between may give way' (*EG* 167).

The image of an 'eclipse of God' is, in fact, consonant with a major theme of Buber's biblical hermeneutics, that of the alternation between the presence and absence of God in the history of Israel. According to Buber, the Bible has a unifying theme, which is relevant in all generations. In his 1926 essay 'The Man of Today and the Jewish Bible,' Buber identifies this theme: the Bible is concerned with 'the encounter between a group of people and the Lord of the world in the course of history.' The different genres of biblical text are variations on this theme:

> Either openly or by implication, the stories are reports of encounters. The songs lament the denial of the grace of encounter, plead that it may be repeated, or give thanks because it has been vouchsafed. The prophecies summon man who has gone astray to turn, to return to the region where the encounter took place, promising him that the torn bond shall once more be made whole.[29]

For Buber, the God of the Bible (like the 'Eternal Thou' of *I and Thou*) is a God of personal encounter, not the God of doctrinal belief systems. The biblical stories, songs, and prophecies speak to readers of all generations because they deal with a contemporary concern, the individual and collective relationship with God.

In his 1949 work *The Prophetic Faith*, Buber traces the changing nature of the relationship between God and Israel, emphasizing the intimacy of God with the patriarchs and with Moses, and examining the distancing that occurs at other times, such as when the Israelites sin by worshipping the golden calf (Exodus 32). Moses and subsequent prophets attempt to overcome this distance by bringing the people back to the true service of God. According to Buber, the seeds of Jewish Messianism can be found in the prophecies of Amos, Hosea, and Isaiah, who envision a future return to the nomadic faith of the past. Isaiah in particular prophesies that a descendant of the house of David will establish political kingship over Israel. According to Buber, this is 'not a prediction but an offer' – the Messiah will come when the people have made a decision to return to God.[30]

This section of *The Prophetic Faith*, with its emphasis on the role of human decision-making in bringing the Messiah, remains theodic and, as such, it does not address the issues raised by the Holocaust.[31] However, in the final chapter of the same work, Buber does discuss the suffering of the innocent. In this chapter, he focuses on the 'suffering Messiah' of Deutero-Isaiah, a figure that Buber interprets as the community of Israel rather than as an individual. Buber also draws on the Book of Job and the Psalms to further develop the theme of innocent suffering. Although he does not explicitly link these biblical texts to the Shoah, it seems likely that Buber concluded the work with images of human suffering and separation from God as a way of grappling with the theological issues raised by the Holocaust (*TAT* 136).

However, even in the last chapter of *The Prophetic Faith*, Buber expresses theodic sentiments. His reading of Job does not emphasize the antitheodic moment of protest, but the eventual re-establishment of Job's relationship with God. According to Buber, Job, at the end of the book, 'knows that the friends, who side with God, do not contend for the true God.' Previously, Job had recognized the true God as the 'near and intimate God.' At the end of the book, Job only experiences God 'through suffering and contradiction, but even in this way he does experience God' (*PF* 192). Buber therefore summarises the book as a tale that 'narrates the man of suffering, who by his suffering attained the vision of God (*PF*, 197).' Ultimately, this reading of the book of Job is

theodic in nature; it is not so much about the suffering of the innocent
(*GAA* 64).

By contrast, Buber's 1952 essay 'The Dialogue Between Heaven and
Earth,' which also comments on the Book of Job, explicitly addresses the
post-Holocaust situation, and reaches a much more disturbing conclusion. Buber asks 'how is life with God still possible in a time in which
there is an Auschwitz?' He acknowledges that one might still 'believe in'
a God who permitted the Shoah to happen, but he questions the possibility of hearing God's word, let alone entering into an I-Thou relationship
with Him.

> Can one still hear His word? Can one still, as an individual and as
> a people, enter at all into a dialogical relationship with Him? Dare
> we recommend to the survivors of Auschwitz, the Job of the gas
> chambers: 'Give thanks unto the Lord, for He is good; for His
> mercy endureth forever'?[32]

Buber's question about the possibility of divine-human speech after
the Holocaust is never really answered. The question, however, has
far-reaching consequences for Buber's dialogical philosophy, since, as
Fackenheim has pointed out, 'the centre of Buber's thought is dialogical
speech' and, moreover, it is 'divine-human speech that confers meaning
on all speech.'[33]

Returning to the biblical Job, Buber presents a different perspective
on the end of the book. Instead of emphasizing the re-establishment of
the relationship with God as he had done in the earlier essay, Buber
stresses the inadequacy of the response that Job receives from God, the
fact that God's response not only fails to answer the charges raised by Job,
it does not even touch upon the issues. 'Nothing is explained, nothing
adjusted; wrong has not become right, nor cruelty kindness. Nothing
has happened but that man again hears God's address' (*OJ* 224–25).

The conclusion to Buber's essay focuses on the response of the Jewish
people to the Shoah.

> And we?
>
> We – by this is meant all those who have not got over what
> happened and will not get over it. Do we stand overcome before the
> hidden face of God like the tragic hero of the Greeks before faceless
> fate? No, rather *even now we contend, we too, with God*, even
> with Him, the Lord of Being, whom we once chose for our Lord. We
> do not put up with earthly being, we struggle for its redemption,
> and struggling we appeal to the help of the Lord, who is again and

still a hiding one. In such a state we await His voice, whether it comes out of the storm or out of a stillness that follows it. Though His coming appearance resemble no earlier one, we shall recognize again our cruel and merciful Lord. (*OJ* 225; italics added)

This essay is Buber's most strongly antitheodic piece. He presents Job not simply as the man of faith who awaits the return of God, but as the brave believer who (like Abraham) argues with God, and who protests rather than simply lamenting. Even more radically, God, for His part, is recognized as being cruel as well as merciful. However, despite using the figure of Job to express disappointment and anger at God's hiding, Buber nevertheless appeals to the help of God and awaits His voice (*GAA* 67).

BUBER'S LEGACY

Given the antitheodic motifs expressed in 'Dialogue Between Heaven and Earth,' it seems clear that had Buber published *I and Thou* in the 1960s instead of the 1920s, it might have been a very different work. At the very least, the confident assertions that God is always present[34] would have been formulated in a more nuanced way, taking into account the possibility of an 'eclipse of God,' and the inscrutable – even cruel – divine silence. Nevertheless, Buber never repudiated the philosophy of *I and Thou*; nor, despite the Shoah, did he abandon his biblical conceptual framework. What, then, is Buber's legacy to Jewish religious thought?

Unlike Richard Rubenstein, for whom the Shoah led to the conclusion that 'we stand in a cold, silent, unfeeling cosmos, unaided by any purposeful power beyond our own resources,'[35] Buber saw contemporary Jewish life as a continuation of the dialectic of biblical Israel: the alternation of distance and nearness between God and the Jewish people. Buber's writings do not offer a solution to the theological problems raised by the Shoah. However, they do explore the possibility of maintaining faith whilst awaiting the end of the eclipse of God.

Buber's 1952 book *Good and Evil* includes interpretations of a number of Psalms, each of which relates to the theme of innocent suffering. Without claiming that the Psalms provide complete and satisfying answers to the problem of evil, Buber suggests that sufferers can achieve a renewal of faith and hope through reading them. Buber understands the power of reading Psalms as dependent on an existential exegesis, in which the reader's own life experience is seen 'in and through the psalmist's narrative' (*TAT* 142). This experience involves making a narrative from Judaism's common memory part of the interpreter's personal memory – a movement that Buber saw as essential to the contemporary reader's ability to relate to the biblical text (*TAT* 142).

Although Fackenheim, amongst others, criticizes Buber for not making the breakthrough to a radically new post-Holocaust philosophy, we can nevertheless appreciate Buber's work as a rich resource for the faithful. Buber's understanding of the central theme of the Bible – 'the encounter between a group of people and the Lord of the world in the course of history' – entails that it can be meaningful and accessible to readers in every generation, even that of the 'eclipse of God.' Buber's biblical writings therefore continue to be relevant to religious Jews, and elements of his hermeneutic approach continue to influence translators and educators.[36] If we adopt Buber's approach to biblical hermeneutics, the absence of God does not render the Bible irrelevant or a closed book. Instead, it makes our reading of both the biblical stories that narrate episodes of divine-human encounter and, especially, of the stories and Psalms that lament the absence of such encounter, even more poignant.

Buber understood his task, at least in writing *I and Thou*, as that of 'bearing witness' to a vision. All of his subsequent writings, including those of the post-Holocaust era, ultimately bear witness to Buber's faith that 'God can speak even though He may be silent; that He can speak at least to those who listen to His voice with all their hearts' (*PMB* 296).[37]

Notes

1. Paul Mendes-Flohr has shown, however, that Buber's early work is profoundly asocial in nature. His diagnosis of the sickness of the age in his pre-dialogical period was focused on 'the crisis of *Kultur*, the decline of spiritual and aesthetic sensibilities putatively wrought by industrial, urban *Zivilisation*.' Paul Mendes-Flohr, *From Mysticism to Dialogue: Martin Buber's Transformation of German Social Thought*. Detroit: Wayne State University Press, 1989, p. 15. Hereafter cited as *FMD*.

2. According to Pamela Vermes, *I and Thou* is 'Buber's masterpiece. It is the receptacle into which he pours the learning and wisdom accumulated over the years, and the vessel in which he re-words them to express his own vision of the good life. Everything that he wrote afterwards can be traced back to it.' Pamela Vermes, *Buber on God and the Perfect Man* (London: Littman Library, 1994), p. 27.

3. *Die Geschichten des Rabbi Nachman* (1906) and *Die Legende des Baal Schem* (1908). English translations: *The Tales of Rabbi Nachman* (1956) and *The Legend of the Baal Shem* (1969).

4. For a detailed discussion of the development of Buber's hermeneutics, see Steven Kepnes, *The Text as Thou: Martin Buber's Dialogical Hermeneutics and Narrative Theology* (Bloomington: Indiana University Press, 1992), hereafter cited as *TAT*.

5. Buber, 'My Way to Hasidism,' in Buber, *Hasidism and Modern Man*, trans. Maurice Friedman (New York: Harper, 1966) p. 62.

6. Kepnes elaborates on the connection between Buber's early approach to the Hasidic tales and Dilthey's hermeneutics. For Dilthey, the goal of interpretation in the human sciences is to arrive at 'the mental state, the subjective, personal lived experience of the author, as he or she produced the work' (*TAT* 9). However, in his mature hermeneutics, this is not the final goal of interpretation. Through the process of empathizing with the mental state of the author, a sufficiently adept interpreter can 'not only experience the event as the author experienced it,' but can transcend the text itself by following the line of events 'to a conclusion that did not exist in the mind of the author' (*TAT* 11).

7. Indeed, Mendes-Flohr argues that prior to the development of Buber's dialogical thought (that is, before 1916), all of Buber's writing in different spheres was based on his doctrine of unity. 'All his literary activity, be it as an interpreter of mysticism and folk myths, as a speculative philosopher, or as a Zionist publicist, can be viewed as an elaboration and refinement of his doctrine of unity.' (*FMD* 63)

8. Rivka Horowitz, *Buber's Way to 'I and Thou'* (New York: The Jewish Publication Society, 1988), p. 195. Hereafter cited as *BW*.

9. Maurice Friedman, *Encounter on the Narrow Ridge: A Life Of Martin Buber* (New York: Paragon House, 1991), p. 36. Hereafter cited as *ENR*.

10. *Daniel*, trans. Maurice Friedman (New York: Holt, Rinehart and Winston, 1965), p. 54.

11. *Der Grosse Maggid und seine Nachfolge* (Frankfurt am Main: Rütten and Loening, 1922).

12. Martin Buber, 'Autobiographical Fragments,' trans. Maurice Friedman in Paul A. Schilpp and Maurice S. Freidman, eds. *The Philosophy of Martin Buber* (La Salle, IL: Open Court, 1967), p. 26. Hereafter cited as *PMB*. The idea that what one seeks in an encounter with the other is reassurance that 'nevertheless there is meaning' parallels Buber's assertion in *I and Thou* that the confirmation of meaning is an essential aspect of the I-Thou encounter. (See following.)

13. Pamela Vermes, op. cit., pp. 20–22.

14. Emil Fackenheim asks whether Buber's teaching regarding dialogical relations is a doctrine – 'a body of metaphysical and epistemological assertions' – or pure homily (*PMB* 280). He argues that Buber does indeed present a philosophical doctrine, and that it is this doctrine that distinguishes his work from poems, sermons, and so forth (*PMB* 281). Nevertheless, Fackenheim's essay concludes with the suggestion that Buber is perhaps not really a philosopher after all, but a 'Hebrew sage in modern garb' (*PMB* 296). See note 33.

15. Martin Buber, *I and Thou*, trans. Walter Kaufman (New York: Scribner's, 1970), p. 53. Hereafter cited as *IT*. (All citations of *I and Thou* refer to Kaufman's translation; however, for the sake of consistency, I have followed Ronald Gregor Smith in translating 'du' as 'thou' rather than 'you'.)

16. Buber took this inspiration so seriously that he later refused to revise *I and Thou*, even where the meaning of certain passages was not clear to the author himself! In his 'Replies to My Critics,' Buber explains that he wrote *I and Thou* 'in an overpowering inspiration. And what such inspiration delivers to one, one may no longer change, not even for the sake of exactness.' (*PMB* 706)

17. Franz Rosenzweig criticised Buber's system as overly simplistic. Rosenzweig was particularly concerned that with the I-It, Buber had given the I-Thou 'a cripple for an opponent' (*BW* 208).

18. As we will see later, the one exception to this rule is that God, or the Eternal Thou, can never become 'It.'

19. Buber acknowledges that the process is not always that clear-cut; there can be a confusion and entanglement between I-It and I-Thou (*IT* 69).

20. A. Kohanski, *Martin Buber's Philosophy of Interhuman Relation* (London: Associated University Presses, 198), p. 268.

21. The subject of reciprocity and mutuality has given rise to much discussion. Buber addresses some of the issues in his 1957 Postscript to *I and Thou* and in his 'Replies to My Critics' (*PMB* 707–10). Questions of symmetry, reciprocity, and mutual relation are also very much at issue in the complex dialogue between Levinas and Buber.

22. See what follows for a discussion of whether this claim that it is only human beings (and not God) who absent themselves from the relationship remains valid in Buber's later philosophy.

23. Fackenheim's essay ('Martin Buber's Concept of Revelation,' *PMB* 273–96) is of particular interest not only because it is a carefully argued philosophical analysis of Buber's concept of revelation, but because it pre-dates Fackenheim's criticisms of Buber for failing to respond adequately to the Shoah.

24. Although Buber never presented a systematic account of ethics, his corpus includes many different discussions of moral values and judgments. Bringing together strands from Buber's different writings on the subject, Marvin Fox argues that Buber presents a paradoxical, if not self-contradictory, account. On the one hand, Buber insists that moral values are absolute and that they have their source in the Absolute, in God. On the other hand, he insists that human beings never receive revelation in a completely pure form; rather, it is always modified in some way as it is received. Thus, although Buber's ethics is not ultimately relativistic, as he insists that values are absolute, nevertheless the individual who needs to make a moral decision has no clear method of distinguishing between the true voice of God and his or her own thoughts. Fox therefore charges Buber with presenting a moral philosophy that is 'an attempt to defend moral anarchy while pleading for moral order' (*PMB* 170). Buber's response to Fox, although interesting in itself, is not sufficiently robust to deflect this critique of his ethical teaching.

25. However, he insists that it is both natural and legitimate that 'everyone should accept moral prescriptions, *whatever helps him to go the way*' (*PMB* 718, italics added). Nevertheless, according to Buber's philosophy,

there is no set of rules, no way of knowing in advance when it will be sufficient to act in accordance with traditional moral prescriptions and when one will need to forge one's own response to a unique situation. Ultimately, whether I choose to follow traditional teachings or to create my own response, I am equally responsible for the course of action I choose.

26. Despite – or perhaps because of – the important similarities between the two thinkers, Levinas repeatedly expressed significant reservations about Buber's account of the I-Thou relation. Although the precise content of his various critiques of Buber varied, it would be fair to summarise Levinas's position as asserting that the I-Thou relation is insufficiently 'ethical.' Robert Bernasconi surveys Levinas's numerous studies of Buber in his essay '"Failure of Communication" as a Surplus: Dialogue and Lack of Dialogue between Buber and Levinas.' This essay has recently been re-printed in Atterton et al. (eds.), *Levinas and Buber: Dialogue and Difference* (Pittsburgh, PA: Duquesne University Press, 2004). Michael Morgan's review of that volume highlights some of the main issues in the debate between dialogical philosophy and Levinasian ethics. (*Notre Dame Philosophical Reviews*, www.ndpr.nr.edu, first published 17 November 2005.)

27. Martin Buber, *Eclipse of God*, trans. Maurice Friedman et al. (Atlantic Highlands, NJ: Humanities Press, 1988), p. 167. Hereafter cited as *EG*.

28. Fackenheim, *God's Presence in History*, 61. Fackenheim argues that although the image of an eclipse of God can sustain Jewish faith when it is confronted with modern secularism, its very hopefulness may render it insufficient to sustain faith when confronted with Auschwitz – perhaps hope itself has been destroyed (GPH pp. 78–79). Fackenheim's dialectical explication of the '614th commandment' reinstates not hope itself, but the 'commandment to hope' (*GPH* 88).

29. Martin Buber, *On the Bible*, ed. Nahum N. Glatzer (New York: Schocken, 1982), p. 1.

30. Martin Buber, *The Prophetic Faith* (New York: Harper and Row, 1949), p. 144. Hereafter cited as *PF*.

31. I am following Zachary Braiterman in distinguishing between theodicy (discourse that attempts to justify, explain, or accept 'the relationship between God and evil') and its opposite, antitheodicy. Zachary Braiterman, *(God) After Auschwitz* (Princeton: Princeton University Press, 1998), p. 20. Hereafter cited as *GAA*.

32. Martin Buber, *On Judaism*, (New York: Shocken Books, 1967), p. 224. Hereafter cited as *OJ*. Buber is quoting a verse from Psalms that is one of the refrains of *Hallel*, a liturgical expression of praise of God the Redeemer.

33. Emil Fackenheim, *To Mend the World* (Bloomington: Indiana University Press, 1994), p. 196.

34. See the earlier discussion of Part Three of *I and Thou*, particularly the idea that the Eternal Thou confronts us 'immediately and first and always' and that only human beings, not God, can be at fault when there is an absence of relation with God.

35. Richard Rubenstein, *After Auschwitz* (London: The Johns Hopkins University Press, 1992) p. 172.
36. For example, Everett Fox's translations of the Bible into English follow many of the principles of the Buber-Rosenzweig translation. See, for example, *In the Beginning: New English Rendition of the Book of Genesis* (New York: Schocken, 1989).
37. The quotation is from Fackenheim's final sentence in the essay 'Buber's Concept of Revelation.' Fackenheim's conclusion leaves open two possibilities: (1) Buber's position is that philosophy, at its most profound, is not I-It knowledge but a dialectical critique of I-It knowledge that points to the commitment of the I-Thou standpoint. In this case, the doctrine of I-Thou is properly philosophical. (2) Buber's position is that philosophy is only I-It knowledge and the doctrine of I-Thou is derived from I-Thou knowledge. In the latter case, Buber would not be a philosopher but a 'Hebrew sage in modern garb' because 'the ultimate basis of his doctrine is an unargued commitment to the dialogue with the ancient of God of Israel, a commitment the reader is called upon to share' (*PMB* 295–96).

7 Franz Rosenzweig and the Philosophy of Jewish Existence

PETER ELI GORDON

The thought of Franz Rosenzweig is arguably the twentieth century's most enduring monument to Jewish philosophy. Yet its deeper meaning continues to elude comprehension. No doubt this is chiefly due to the difficulty of Rosenzweig's major work, *The Star of Redemption* (1921). Composed in the heat of inspiration, it overflows with effulgent metaphor and sometimes extravagant claims to religious insight. More challenging still, it presumes the reader's intimate knowledge of Judaism and Christianity, along with much of the German intellectual tradition, not to mention a basic familiarity with both Hellenistic thought and Scholasticism. In style as well as substance it is a book that forbids immediate understanding.

A more helpful place to begin is Rosenzweig's 1925 essay, "The New Thinking: A Few Supplementary Remarks to the *Star*."[1] The essay represents Rosenzweig's contribution to a spate of philosophical manifestos that appeared in the era of intellectual ferment during the short-lived Weimar Republic (Germany's first experiment with democracy, lasting from 1919 to 1933). And it signals his conscious participation in a trend then called "the resurrection of metaphysics."[2] Specifically, it announces in programmatic fashion the various themes already familiar to a new generation tutored in Kierkegaard, Nietzsche, Dilthey, and Bergson: the primacy of poetic language, the bankruptcy of rationalist and idealist philosophy, the constitutive-existential function of temporality, the linguistic, spoken, and always intersubjective grounding of human meaning, the paradigmatic import of religious revelation, and, perhaps most of all, the turn from theoretical knowledge to "life" itself as the chief field of hermeneutic inquiry. These are the foundational

For helpful suggestions on this chapter in its various stages of development, I am grateful to my co-editor Michael Morgan as well as to Martin Jay, Dominick LaCapra, Michael P. Steinberg, Vicki Caron, Mitchell Hart, Nina Caputo, Samuel Moyn, Eugene Sheppard, and Leora Batnitzky.

themes of Rosenzweig's "new thinking," summarized in the demand that there be a more cooperative – or "sibling-like" – relation between philosophy and religion.

The new thinking was a philosophical movement and hardly confined to Judaism alone. Of course, Rosenzweig was an acknowledged source of inspiration for younger Jews seeking to reclaim their heritage. And, along with Martin Buber (Rosenzweig's senior by eight years and his partner in the translation of the Hebrew Bible into modern German), Rosenzweig helped to create what Michael Brenner has called a "renaissance" of Jewish culture in Weimar Germany.[3] But, unlike Buber, whose philosophy was more accessible and dialogical in style, Rosenzweig's contribution to the "new thinking" was bristling with intellect and verged on impiety. And while Buber willingly served as a popularizing writer on Jewish doctrinal themes and became a sage for national and spiritual renewal, Rosenzweig was a philosophical modernist, a principled non-Zionist, and an esoteric thinker without apology. Even while Rosenzweig was dedicated personally and intellectually to the re-creation of modern Judaism, his work was not in any obvious sense continuous with prior traditions in Jewish religion. Philosophically, Rosenzweig is recognizable as a member in that broader stream of modern thinkers who staged a Nietzschean rebellion against German idealism. Religiously, he was largely sui generis. The opening lines of "The New Thinking" conclude that

> [*The Star*] is not a "Jewish book" at all, at least not what those buyers who were so angry with me take for a Jewish book. It does deal with Judaism, but not any more exhaustively than with Christianity and barely more exhaustively than Islam. Neither does it make the claim to be a philosophy of religion – how could it do that when the word "religion" does not occur in it at all! Rather, it is merely a system of philosophy.[4]

Its author's protest notwithstanding, *The Star* has been received chiefly as a Jewish book, and Rosenzweig himself has been widely commemorated as a paradigm of Jewish authenticity.[5] It may be precisely because of Rosenzweig's enduring appeal that his actual philosophy remains so poorly understood.

AN INTELLECTUAL SKETCH

Rosenzweig was born in the town of Kassel on 25 December, 1886. He enjoyed a comfortable childhood immersed in German music and literature, thanks chiefly to the encouragement of his mother, Adele, with whom he felt a deep personal affinity. His father was a man of business, and the young Franz was acutely aware of their difference in temperament.[6] From his grand-uncle Adam, the young Franz derived an enduring passion for the Jewish religion, even while others in his circle, including his cousin Hans Ehrenberg (1883–1958) and his companion Eugen Rosenstock-Huessy (1888–1973), had converted to Christianity. Throughout his life, Franz attempted to navigate, both personally and intellectually, between the worlds of Judaism and the German-Protestant establishment. The distinctive character of his thought is due in no small measure to their uneasy union.

After some hesitation, rejecting by turns both the medical profession and dreams of becoming a Goethe scholar, Rosenzweig decided upon a plan of historical and philosophical study at Freiburg under Germany's then-leading practitioner of *Geistesgeschichte*, or "history of ideas," Friedrich Meinecke. Taking his initial cue from Meinecke's studies in German political thought, Rosenzweig wrote a dissertation on the genesis of Hegel's theory of the state.[7] He finished his doctoral study by 1913.[8] *Hegel and the State* was Rosenzweig's most enduring contribution to German academic literature. Some interpreters have read the mature philosophy of Judaism in isolation from, or even in opposition to, the earlier Hegel book. But a careful reading reveals the continuity between them: one of the book's chief concerns is the irreconcilable conflict between political and religious existence, a theme that would reappear in the *Star*.[9]

This perceived rift – between politics and religion – also helps to explain Rosenzweig's admiration for the early-nineteenth-century German Idealist philosopher, Friedrich Schelling. In the summer of 1914, Rosenzweig made a fortuitous discovery of a fragmentary manuscript – dated from around 1800 and apparently written in Hegel's hand – and now known as the "Oldest System-Program of German Idealism." Rosenzweig concluded that the true author of the system-program was Schelling (a conclusion now generally discredited). The fragment calls for philosophers to forge a new alliance with poetry, and it ends with the ringing phrase, *"Wir müssen also auch über den Staat hinaus!"* ("We must therefore rise out and beyond the state!"),[10] a declaration that anticipates Rosenzweig's own turn from politics.[11]

The roots of this transformation were twofold – religious and political. Religiously, Rosenzweig was compelled to face the question of his Judaism and to resolve consciously upon his theological identity. During the night of 7 July, 1913, in Leipzig, Rosenzweig found himself in a heated conversation over the relative merits of Christianity and

Judaism with his friend, the philosopher Eugen Rosenstock, who had converted to Christianity. Rosenstock challenged Rosenzweig either to give a coherent defense of his faith or to undergo baptism. Rosenzweig accepted this challenge, but he promised to convert only once he had reckoned with his Judaism. The correspondence between Rosenstock and Rosenzweig lays bare their profoundest theological disagreements, and it continues to inspire those who are interested in the possibilities for Jewish-Christian dialogue.[12]

But Rosenzweig's passage beyond Judaism did not go as planned. As he reexamined his faith over the next three months, he came to the conclusion that Judaism required no "completion" in Christianity. Nahum Glatzer, Rosenzweig's first biographer for the post-war American audience, claimed that Rosenzweig owed this new perspective to his spiritual awakening at a Yom Kippur service in a small, orthodox synagogue in Berlin frequented by Eastern European Jews. (The accuracy of this claim remains uncertain.) Rosenzweig's change of heart was far-reaching in its philosophical consequences. He now reasoned that "the development of Judaism bypasses the Jesus to whom the pagans say 'Lord' and through whom they 'arrive at the Father.' It [Judaism] does not pass through him."[13] By the end of October 1913, Rosenzweig had determined to revoke his former decision as "no longer necessary, and "in my case, no longer possible." In a simple and now famous phrase, he concluded that "I shall therefore remain a Jew." [*Also bleibe ich Jude.*][14]

Along with this personal trial of faith, Rosenzweig also underwent a trial of political disillusionment. For many of the "generation of 1914," the war experience was an apocalypse of near-theological proportions. Death now seemed of greater moment than cultural erudition, and intellectuals were newly attuned to the sheer facticity of everyday life as an object of metaphysical inquiry. This new intellectual sensibility was surely intensified by the very fractiousness of political life in the fledgling Weimar Republic: Politics seemed, to some thinkers at least, a merely technological maneuver without philosophical import. For Rosenzweig in particular, the war brought the German Idealist tradition of political speculation into disrepute: He now looked upon the Hegel book as an artifact of a world destroyed.

These two transformations, religious and political, conspired to persuade Rosenzweig that he must break with a great many of his prior philosophical and theological assumptions, most especially the logic of narrative-fulfillment that supported both Christianity and Hegelianism.[15] Once this rupture was achieved, the way was open for the development of a new philosophical perspective.

Already during the war, Rosenzweig had begun to write what he would call his "system of philosophy." The metaphysical architecture for the book was first laid out in a 1917 letter to Rudolf Ehrenberg, known as the "germ cell." Its contents followed soon afterward in a rush of inspiration. While guarding an anti-aircraft outpost in the Balkans, Rosenzweig sketched out the initial portions of the book on mail-grams that he sent homeward to his mother. Drawing sustenance from the rebellious tradition of anti-idealism – especially from Kierkegaard, Schelling, Schleiermacher, Feuerbach, and Nietzsche, as well as from the later religious philosophy of Hermann Cohen – Rosenzweig drafted the basic chapters for what he called '*The Star of Redemption, A World-Picture [Ein Weltbild]*' (the subtitle was eventually dropped).

Little in Rosenzweig's previous academic labors would have prepared his readers for the finished work, first published in 1921. A curious mixture of metaphysical speculation, religious history, sociological excursus, poetic analysis, and biblical commentary, *The Star of Redemption* comprises an affirmation of religious existence, both Jewish and Christian, against the oppressive tradition of idealism spanning Western thought from Parmenides to Hegel. It ranges across topics as diverse as Homer and Saint Augustine, Spinoza and Darwin, Luther and Goethe, Maimonides and Machiavelli. Its claims, taken in sum, guide the reader, both Jewish and Christian, toward the precipice of a this-worldly leap into religious commitment. But beyond this, there is little agreement upon the book's proper interpretation. *The Star* has been read variously as a manifesto of existential theology, a highly encrypted personal confession, a belated contribution to the Kabbalah, and, most recently, as a supplement to themes now flourishing in psychoanalysis and post-modernism. The dual offspring of German expressionism and Jewish belief, it is surely one of the most forbidding artifacts of Weimar culture. In its pastiche of styles and its very polyphony, it resembles perhaps nothing so much as a theoretical counterpiece to Mahler's *Song of the Earth*. Rosenzweig himself later called it "this great world-poem."[16]

The Star was to be the only substantial book of original philosophy Rosenzweig would ever write. By January 1922, he had been diagnosed with a rare form of progressive paralysis (amyotrophic lateral sclerosis), which affected his speech, his hands, and his legs, and eventually imprisoned him inside his own body. Within a year, he could no longer leave his house of his own initiative. Doctors did not expect him to survive. Quite miraculously, however, he endured in this condition until the end of the 1920s, although he always considered *The Star* his sole contribution to modern philosophy. Yet even while *The Star* was his magnum opus, Rosenzweig remained intellectually productive until the final months of his life. Aided by his wife, and outfitted with an ingenious writing machine, he authored numerous shorter and more accessible texts on matters such as Jewish theology and the theory and practice of translation, as well as critical reflections on the contemporary intellectual trends of his time.

He wrote a shorter, polemical work, *Das Büchlein vom gesunden und kranken Menschenverstand* (available in English with the title 'Understanding the Sick and the Healthy'), an allegory that portrays the philosopher's misguided search for essence as a paralysis. He also forged a close bond with the neo-Kantian philosopher Hermann Cohen, whose final work, *Religion of Reason out of the Sources of Judaism* (published posthumously in its complete form in 1919), came to occupy a special place in Rosenzweig's imagination.[17]

Like such figures as Leo Baeck and Nehemiah Nobel, Rosenzweig also became a charismatic force for the interwar flourishing of German-Jewish culture. His paralysis itself added poignancy and a martyr's prestige to his thought, and a small circle gathered at his home to explore the meaning of their neglected Judaism. He assumed a leading role in the founding of the famous Frankfurt *Lehrhaus*, an institute of adult Jewish education that drew many younger and often assimilated Jews toward a more sustained and substantive Jewish identity. In 1924, he produced a volume of German translations on the medieval Hebrew poetry of Judah Halevi, accompanied by an erudite philosophical commentary. And beginning in 1925, he undertook the monumental task of translating the Hebrew Bible into German in collaboration with Martin Buber.

Such acts of linguistic mediation expressed a more general ideal of diasporic identity, a way of being simultaneously a Jew and a German. In a remarkable letter from 1923, Rosenzweig relates that during an interview for a position at a Jewish school, he was asked to take a stand on the vexed question of German or Jewish allegiance:

> I retorted that I would refuse to answer this question. If life were at one stage to torment me and tear me into two pieces, then I would naturally know with which of the two halves the heart – which is, after all, asymmetrically positioned – would side. I would also know that I would not be able to survive the operation.[18]

To be sure, what Paul Mendes-Flohr has called the "dual identity" of German Jewish intellectuals could be sustained only so long as other Germans judged it admissible.[19] Yet the "German" side of Rosenzweig's identity was hardly contingent upon political conditions. In a letter composed in the autumn of 1929, just months before his death, Rosenzweig declared: "my Germanness would be exactly what it is today, even if there were no longer a German Reich. Language is indeed more than blood."[20]

One may consider it Rosenzweig's good fortune that he did not survive long enough to see a new and more brutal German Reich destroy this ideal. In his last days, Rosenzweig was still at work translating the Bible into the language he loved. He was concentrating his remaining strength upon a section of Isaiah 53 that includes the famous passage concerning God's suffering 'servant.'[21] His final extant letter, dated just one day before his death, is addressed to Buber. It breaks off in mid-sentence: "and – now it comes, the point of all points, which the Lord had granted me in sleep: the point of all points for which it . . ." Rosenzweig died, at forty two years of age, on 10 December, 1929.

THE STAR OF REDEMPTION: AN OVERVIEW

The Star is a work that forbids easy summary. Its basic aim is to provide a philosophical portrait of the deep structures that inform human religious experience. But the difficulty of this task is extraordinary. The philosophers' traditional view of religion, Rosenzweig suggests, has almost always failed to capture what religion truly means within the finite, this-worldly terms of human life. Philosophers habitually describe religion according to all the deficiencies of idealism. But here it is crucial to note that "idealism" for Rosenzweig is not the name for a specific movement: It characterizes the entirety of the metaphysical tradition from Parmenides to Hegel, or – in his phrase – "from Ionia to Jena." This tradition is animated by what Rosenzweig regards as a self-deception: Idealism conceives being as conceptual being only, and thereby loses sight of that difference beneath thought, the pre-conceptual existence upon which our thought must always depend. So "philosophy," at least as it has been conventionally practiced, seems to have obstructed our understanding of how we actually experience religion within the overall structure of human *existence*.

The book begins on a dramatic note, with a broad indictment of Western philosophy that borrows several phrases without acknowledgement from Friedrich Schiller's poem, *"Das Ideal und das Leben"* ("The Ideal and Life"):

'From death, from the fear of death, there begins all knowledge of the Whole. To cast off the fear of earthly things, to rob death of its poisonous sting, and Hades of its pestilential breath, in this task philosophy deceives itself.'[22]

For Rosenzweig, Schiller's model of transcendence seems to typify our customary image of redemption.[23] We construe redemption as a kind of metaphysical release, as if it required a casting aside of finitude and a flight from time to eternity. For Rosenzweig, however, philosophy after Hegel has reached a point of exhaustion and can at last recognize the spuriousness of this metaphysical dream. In a letter to Margrit Rosenstock written during the heat of composition, Rosenzweig remarked that "idealism simply *knows* nothing of redemption."[24] Philosophy, beginning with Nietzsche, Rosenzweig tells us, has admitted the priority of finitude over and against the nihilistic longing for release. Humanity thus always "remains [*bleibt*] within the bounds of creatureliness [*innerhalb der Grenzen der Geschöpflichkeit*]." The metaphysical-idealist tradition, which regards thought as the height of being, would have us strive for transcendence. But to be human is to cherish one's finitude and to *remain* always *in-the-world: The Star* thus aims at something like a redemption of philosophy *from* the philosophical tradition.

The first paragraph of the book ends by offering a direct rejoinder to Schiller, which again calls upon the poet's imagery:

> Man is not to throw off the fear of the earthly; he must remain in the fear of death, but he must remain. [*Der Mensch soll die Angst des Irdischen nicht von sich werfen; er soll in der Furcht des Todes – bleiben.*][25]

Rosenzweig therefore wishes to develop a better understanding of religion that accords with the post-metaphysical and eminently human desire to remain in the world. One might also be tempted to read the *Star* as the transposition into philosophical language of a biographical protest – Rosenzweig's personal decision several years before to "remain" (*bleibe*) a Jew. But this act of defiance is now staged not merely despite Christianity, but also despite the Christian-metaphysical vision of redemption as a passage beyond mortality. Indeed, the desideratum of the entire work is that since religious experience can never grant access to a realm beyond time, redemption itself must be reconceived such that eternity *itself* is understood as *eternity-in-time*, as a life within the bounds of human community.[26]

To portray human religious experience in this temporal form, Rosenzweig must undertake something like a descriptive "phenomenology." He must lay out the basic structures of religious life as they are manifest in both Christianity and Judaism. But he must take care not to indulge in philosophical talk about the "essence" of religious phenomena if they do not actually present themselves within the historical and cultural horizon. Rosenzweig wants to pursue the description from the 'inside,' since human finitude forbids our trespassing beyond the mortality-constraints to discourse upon the "ideas" of revelation, redemption, and so forth. One of *The Star*'s many challenges is that it is so rich in interpretative detail: It contains a wealth of commentary on history, poetry, and religious ritual, phenomena described with a sympathy and precision that seems almost to invite the reader to imagine she is experiencing them herself. The method owes much to Dilthey's *Lebensphiloso-phie* and its hermeneutic strategy of *nacherleben*.[27] Here, Rosenzweig's original subtitle, "a world-portrait" (*ein Weltbild*), proves helpful, since *The Star* is meant as nothing less than a portrait of our own religious world. Such a portrait would be impossibly complex were it not carried out in small and systematic steps. Accordingly, Rosenzweig breaks up the life-world of religious experience into its basic constitutive elements – God, Man, and World. Each of these is subjected to careful description, first in separation and then in temporal relation with the others.

The first part of the *Star* consists in a preliminary analysis of this structure and its three constitutive points – God, Man, and World – now shorn of their conceptual meaning. Rosenzweig calls them "irrational" objects. To pursue this analysis, Rosenzweig borrows creatively from the neo-Kantian "principle of origins," a logical instrument, modeled upon the calculus, which Hermann Cohen deployed to show reason's ability to generate finite magnitudes out of the thought of negation.[28] In Rosenzweig's hands, the principle of origins metamorphosed into an anti-idealist device: In an argument that anticipates Heidegger's thoughts concerning being-toward-death, Rosenzweig suggests that when we become alive in anxiety to our own mortality, we gain a unique glimpse into the nothingness that distinguishes our thoughts of being from being itself. And by thinking this nothingness, we can then perform a negation upon each of the three elements of our experience.

God, for example, is disclosed to be what Rosenzweig in his wholly modern usage calls the "metaphysical." Man is accordingly the "meta-ethical" and the world is the "metalogical." Each of the elements is found to emerge from a place of ontological independence, and each is therefore grounded in its own distinctive "nothingness" prior to any and all conceptual elaboration. Thus, before God is properly an object of knowledge, God is for human experience a sheer object of *privation* – an object of which we can say nothing. But since this nothingness is a nothingness distinctively of God, Rosenzweig discloses this divine being in its *difference from thought*. Pursuing the same strategy, Rosenzweig claims that the essence of "meta-ethical" man is itself *nothing*. That is, no essence lies behind our concerned way of being-in-the-world: To be human is ultimately grounded upon nothing deeper than its own existential investment. Meta-ethical man is therefore a creature whose being is always – as Heidegger would say – "at issue." Or as Rosenzweig put it, drawing upon a biblical image, meta-ethical man is like "Jonah without the palm branches."[29]

In the second part of the *Star*, Rosenzweig aims to show how these distinctive elements emerge on the plane of temporality. They are, as Kant would say, "schematized," one with another, so as to form the three bridges comprising lived experience: God meets World in creation, God meets Man in revelation, and Man meets world in redemption. The resultant six "points" thus form the eponymous *Star*, the symbol famously associated in Jewish tradition with the shield of David. While the quasi-geometric 'star' system may seem little more than a contrivance, Rosenzweig exploits the structure to emphasize that the locus of our religious experience must necessarily be life-in-time. (In "The New Thinking," Rosenzweig reminds us that his new approach to philosophy differs from the traditional sort precisely in "taking time seriously.") The three coordinates of the book thus indicate the three basic temporal "tenses." *Creation* denotes the irrecoverable past (facts into which we are born), *revelation* signifies the immediate present (of divine as well as human love), and *redemption* points to the future (that is, the divine completion of our necessarily purposive but necessarily finite activity). It should be noted that Rosenzweig's breakdown of temporality into its three religious axes anticipates in some measure what Heidegger later calls temporal "ecstases" in *Being and Time*. When reassembled, the entire coordinate system of creation, revelation, and redemption allows us to orient ourselves within the space of religious experience. And Rosenzweig performs a hermeneutic description of that space.

Revelation holds a pivotal position in the book, since it is God's love that lays down the model for human love and community. Humanity pursues the "work" of redemption, although it is important to note that "redemption" itself is neither a mere extension of human love nor in any sense a purely human achievement. "Actual" redemption, Rosenzweig tells us, emanates from God alone: It is an event of which humanity "knows neither the day nor the hour."[30] Given this emphasis on divine as against human agency, Rosenzweig's theism remains largely unqualified. Indeed, it can be fearsome: In a decision imposed from beyond, God separates friend from foe, a choice that casts the enemies of the divine into a void.[31] Ethics, then, which some interpreters would assign a vital position in Rosenzweig's philosophy, seems in fact consigned to its periphery.

Here we may pause to reconsider the much-discussed relation between Rosenzweig and Levinas.[32] An obvious point of comparison is Rosenzweig's insistance that God, Man, and World cannot be collapsed into a metaphysical unity: According to the *Star*, "God alone plants the sapling of his own eternity . . . utterly beyond time into eternity."[33] God therefore remains in an important sense "other" to the intraworldly realm of human experience. This Rosenzweigian stricture anticipates Levinas's idea that the human "other" exceeds all totalization.[34]

But the resemblance between Rosenzweig and Levinas is misleading on several counts. First, it is crucial to note that *The Star* never violates the hermeneutic principle that any and all philosophical description of the religious life-world must remain fully *within* the world. In a letter to Margrit Rosenstock, written in 1918 while he was composing *The Star*, Rosenzweig affirmed this principle:

> [I]t becomes now more clear to me, what I meant when I said to you that *love does not overstep the bounds of life* [my emphasis]. In life, I love the neighbor, into whose eyes I look, who looks in my eyes, and love him, perhaps, 'sitting within the shadow of God,' and love him "in" God. Indeed, I love him more than I love or can love God. For it must be so. God's face "can no man see and remain living [*bleibt leben*]."[35]

Although Levinas cited Rosenzweig as an important influence, Rosenzweig's doctrine of love appears critically distinct from Levinas' later notion that the self's relation to the face of the other somehow captures a phenomenon beyond all ontological horizons. Levinas surely borrowed from Rosenzweig's philosophy, but Rosenzweig himself saw love as constrained always to the holistic bounds of life, and he insists that human love can appear only within this field as it is staked out by the divine. In *The Star*, either the face of the other is experienced as being-in-the-world or it cannot be experienced at all. To "remain," in Rosenzweig's dictum, "within the bounds of creatureliness" applies to the human experience of divine love no less than to the experience of other created beings.

Specifically, Rosenzweig reserves the term "revelation" to describe only how God attains a mode of worldly and experiential being, quite apart from any mystical or non-experiential facets of God's "secret being."[36] Revelation for Rosenzweig is a movement *into-the-world*, a movement from God to the human soul that does not shatter but rather confirms the coherence of human life. Rosenzweig elsewhere complains that "anthropomorphism" is a misnomer since it exaggerates God's "infinite" and ineffable being: God's ability to conform to human experiential categories, claims Rosenzweig, should more correctly be termed "theomorphism."[37] Revelation is therefore an event that is destined to become *a piece of the world*:

> [God's] revelation to the soul has now entered the world and become a piece of the world. Not that something strange is entering the world with it. [*Indem aber Gott so tut, ist seine Offenbarung an die Seele nun in die Welt getreten und zu sinem Stück Welt geworden. Nicht als ob mit ihr etwas Fremdes in die Welt träte.*] Rather revelation remembers back to its past, while at the same time remaining wholly of the present; it recognizes its past as part of a world passed by. But thereby it also provides its presentness with the status of something real in the world.... The presentness of the miracle of revelation is and remains its content; its historicity [*Geschichtlichkeit*], however, is its ground and its warrant.[38]

Rosenzweig seems explicitly to deny the metaphysical view of revelation as an awakening to alterity. On the contrary: Revelation becomes "a piece of the world." Rosenzweig will argue later in the book that redemption itself is that event whereby God becomes "like time." Here he argues that God's love becomes like the world. Revelation, therefore, begins from alterity but ends by conferring unity upon temporal experience.

But why does Rosenzweig wish to *deny* that revelation introduces "something strange" into human experience? Doesn't a Jewish philosophy require some idea that revelation is a transformative event? The surprising answer is that for Rosenzweig, revelation brings *consolation rather than disruption*. It effects a peculiar state of "quiet" defiance, and it lends the otherwise anxious soul a pride for merely existing, a pride "which spreads out under and around man like the still waters and supports him instead of transforming him beyond recognition." Revelation accordingly becomes a piece of human experience and it inspires in humanity a special kind of pride that "can simply – be; and nothing more."[39] Revelation for Rosenzweig is therefore quite different from the trauma Levinas imagines it to be, since it is revelation which grants one the security of being sheltered: The soul enriched by revelation "knows that nothing can befall it" and that "no power can rob it of this consciousness which carries it wherever it may go and by which it is perpetually surrounded."[40] Divine love prepares the soul for the possibility of a life of splendid isolation – an existence wholly in-the-world but nonetheless set free from the distortions of worldly attachment. Revelation, one might say, is the precondition for peace.

It is also important to note that even while Rosenzweig sees revealed love as lending the soul an unworldly character of "quiet defiance," revelation itself remains essentially compatible with history. Rosenzweig has been interpreted as an "anti-historicist," as if in his abandonment of Hegelian political thought he came to share Kierkegaard's antipathy for history in general. But this neglects Rosenzweig's peculiar ability to unite in his thinking seemingly contradictory intellectual positions. In fact, revelation does not contradict the historical nature of being human but actually serves as its justification: In Rosenzweig's words, while the "presentness" of the revealed miracle is its "content," its historical facticity is its "ground." To live in accordance with a revealed tradition naturally requires that revelation become a living inheritance that may be passed on from generation to generation, not only through history but actually gaining its truth-status *in and through* its historical transmission. Revelation finds its highest validation not in opposition to the past but instead in what Rosenzweig expressly called its "historicity" (*Geschichtlichkeit*). This generously historical perspective on the nature of divine revelation would seem to suggest that Rosenzweig was as much an heir to German historicism as a rebel against it.

It is redemption alone that provides *The Star* with unambiguous purpose, since it is necessary to live with some anticipatory sense of redemption if one's religious life-world is to be structurally complete. (This claim also applies to the system itself: Without some sense of "meaning" the star-shape would be merely symmetrical and would lack a definite orientation.) Rosenzweig argues that one can only live out the experience of redemption within a community. So the last third of the *Star* lays out a detailed reconstruction of Christianity and Judaism as the two basic communal systems in which redemption comes to be a lived experience. (There are also some rather crude passages concerning Islam, which Rosenzweig failed to grant almost any positive theological importance.)[41] Perhaps one of *The Star*'s most famous ideas is that Christianity and Judaism are internally incompatible but mutually reinforcing religious life-worlds, both of which stand as necesssary witnesses to redemption. Christianity, claims Rosenzweig, construes redemption as an activity unfolding through history, and it is therefore progressive, forging God's kingdom in worldly action. Judaism, on the other hand, Rosenzweig regards as uniquely capable of experiencing redemption in the present, and it is therefore conceived as cyclical, the collective figure of eternity within time. The remaining portions of the book offer a multifaceted discussion of both Judaism and Christianity, justifying the distinctive roles each is meant to play in human affairs. The *Star* ends with a famous exhortation that the reader should leave the book aside and return to the serious work of redemption in life.

JUDAISM AND ETERNITY-IN-TIME

The *Star* can hardly be understood as emerging out of an unambivalent and organic bond to the Jewish tradition. But the reader should note that its tripartite structure recapitulates the liturgical order of the Jewish Day of Atonement, or *Yom Kippur*: It opens in a mood of abjection, exposing the human being in radical separation from God and in fear of her possible death. But through the encounter with divine love, we pass from abjection to reconciliation, and at the end of the text we find ourselves inscribed once more in the book of life. In its closing pages, the text moves through a "gate" (*Tor*) which recalls the gates of repentance mentioned in the *Yom Kippur* liturgy. Here Rosenzweig constructed a visual pun: The text points, quite literally, beyond itself such that the reader is enjoined to close the "book of life" and pass "into life" itself (*ins Leben*). The *Star* is unmistakably a work of modern philosophy, but it is modeled on an unmistakably traditional remnant of Jewish ritual.

The centerpiece of the *Star* – what Rosenzweig called the 'fire' at its core – is its striking portrait of Jewish life. The Jews are the light unto the nations, the exemplary community from which redemption radiates to the perimeter of the world. In a conceptual analysis recalling his Hegel book, Rosenzweig sees the Jews as ontologically torn from world history. (For Hegel, Judaism represented the so-called "religion of sublimity" in that their theology is ostensibly torn between God and World.) Rosenzweig calls the Jews a *Schicksalsgemeinschaft*, a community of fate: Their very existence constitutes a breach in the historical continuum, an irruption of the future into the present. But against Hegel, Rosenzweig considers this fate an ontological privilege, since it grants to the Jews alone an anticipatory taste of the world's future redemption.

Rosenzweig offers several conjoined explanations for the privileged status of the Jews. Because they remain open to the eternity of future-redemption, they exhibit a profound indifference to history. They alone seem to discern that the surrounding nations in their struggle for security place undue trust in political and geographical roots. Regimes rise and fall, while the Jews persist beyond the war-plagued chaos of secular time.[42] But precisely because they remain eccentric to history, they come to occupy the central role in the narrative of redemption, since they alone now dwell at the gathering place where all nations will eventually arrive. The Jews alone come to live *in-and-from* their experience of redemption, and they do so with such intensity that their presence in history is evacuated of all meaning. Living wholly for the sake of the always "not-yet" of the future, they draw strength from what Rosenzweig calls the "terrestrial repetition" of yearly and weekly ritual.[43] This unique temporality sets them free from the flow of secular history. Uprooted from land and state, they seek rootedness wholly in themselves – *"Verwurzelung im eigenen Selbst."*[44] The sole mark of their belonging lies in what Rosenzweig provocatively calls "the dark wellsprings of the blood."[45]

In this portrait of the Jewish condition, great emphasis is placed upon the Jews' exemplary status. The Jews remain separate and utterly unique, but it is this very fact that grants them an unparalleled universality. It would thus be wrong to construe the notion of "blood community" along the lines of race or ethnicity.[46] It is, instead, a form of nomadic group-identification, a "self-rootedness" that evokes the self-enclosed and circulatory structure of the Jewish liturgical calendar itself. It therefore provides a bold illustration of Rosenzweig's belief that the Jewish community has "its temporality" apart from the time of the nations.[47] Here one must note the critical distinction between temporality and history: The Jews, too, are fully in time. But because they detach themselves from political events, they experience time not as succession but instead as cyclical. The Jews are therefore self-rooted while lacking roots in political history. They are, in other words, "uncanny," or *unheimlich* – that is, not at home.[48]

One may find it surprising to read Judaism described as a religion "without a history." Judaism is more customarily seen as a *narrative* religion, as the unfolding romance between God and His Chosen People. But history to Rosenzweig meant political struggle, while the Jews are "chosen" precisely so as to consecrate themselves without compromise or distraction to God alone. In their conspicuous indifference to secular time, they exemplify the Christian-Stoic ideal of this-worldly-asceticism, a mode of being "in the world" but not "of the world."[49] The peculiarly ascetic quality of the Jewish people in *The Star* prompted Leo Strauss to remark that for Rosenzweig, "the truly central thought of Judaism" is Israel's chosenness, since "he looks for a Jewish analogue to the Christian doctrine of Christ."[50]

It is the Jews' separation, then, that permits them to fulfill their unique role as "light unto the nations."[51] Because they resist the idolatry of history, they never yield to the lustrous vagaries of power and the arrogance of identifying redemption with their own, all-too-human political narrative. To be sure, in the eyes of the nations, such resistance can only appear as a kind of "constriction."[52] Rosenzweig freely grants that the Jews' claim to exceptionalism can make them at times the object of fierce resentment. But he remains sufficiently Hegelian to believe that current strife is the precondition for future unity. The Jews are the embodiment of hope: the present sign of the world's final and complete reconciliation. Nothing could be further from Rosenzweig's purposes, therefore, than a post-modern surrender to fragmentation. He insists that there is a singular and coherent truth that will eventually be revealed to all humanity, and he accordingly described *The Star* as a "messianic theory of knowledge." The true aim of the book, therefore, is to recuperate within the landscape of human experience that "totality" that idealist philosophy failed to achieve.[53] Judaism's very quiescence is the projection within history of the eternal peace that shall come to all nations only at history's end.

CONCLUDING REMARKS

Rosenzweig's legacy has been marked by controversy. His clear indifference to Jewish politics earned him the opprobrium of many Zionist thinkers, who found it scandalous if not unintelligible to maintain that in the modern period Jews dwell in some imaginary precinct "outside" of history. His rather fanciful star-shaped "system" and his thirst for the 'primordial' in religion aroused the strong antipathy of modernist Marxists such as Georg Lukács, who condemned Rosenzweig as an irrationalist reactionary, or modernist culture-critics such as Siegfried Kracauer, who scorned his poetic style as anti-modernist if not archaic.[54] Gershom Scholem regarded Rosenzweig's Germanic brand of Judaism as predestined for failure: The Buber-Rosenzweig Bible seemed to typify the naiveté of the German-Jewish experience, since, Scholem believed, it would be shunned by other Germans and would reach no audience except the German Jews themselves.[55] Others made Rosenzweig into a post-war icon for Jewish "existential" identification, although this posthumous celebrity did not always require a rich understanding of his philosophy.

Walter Benjamin considered *The Star of Redemption* one of the most enduring works of the 1920s.[56] One detects a Rosenzweigian strain in Benjamin's thinking, most especially in the "Theses on the Philosophy of History," which condemns the evolutionist model of history as barren, and portrays history itself as ceaseless catastrophe. Benjamin's view of revolution as a "messianic" rupture into the "homogenous," "empty" continuum of political history pays homage to Rosenzweig's notion that genuine redemption is something altogether discontinuous with historical progress. And via Benjamin, this same notion is sustained, however faintly, in the late dialectics of the Frankfurt School, which bears witness to redemption only as if in a photographic negative, as the "messianic light" that enables us to see without deception the "cracks and fissures" of historical catastrophe.[57]

A more obvious inheritance can be found in the philosophical ethics of Emmanuel Levinas, who explicitly credited *The Star* for inspiring his own metaphysical opposition to totality and the associated idea that ethical obligation binds the self to the "other" as an always untotalizable "exteriority."[58] But whether Rosenzweig himself was similarly allergic to philosophical totality is far from obvious. Although he insisted that the ontological separation between God, Man, and World cannot be fully sublated into an idealist whole, he nonetheless affirmed that they are brought into a stable yet always temporal "relation," which he called "the new unity" (*neue Einheit*) and "the new whole" (*neue Allheit*). Indeed, the often-cited phrase at the beginning of *The Star* should not be understood as a thoroughgoing rejection of holism as such. *Rosenzweig rejects only knowledge of the whole; he does not reject holism as such.* He merely suggests that the "all" of the cosmos cannot be grasped as a single and self-contained object of *knowledge*. The attempt to seize the unity of being in an Absolute idea is tantamount to believing that one might view the world from "outside" – that is, from an Archimedian point of safety beyond the "flow of life." There is, accordingly, within the human perspective at least, no possibility of knowledge of the all (*Erkennen des All*), but it does not follow that there is no unity to the very fabric of things. On the contrary, Rosenzweig most signals his continued allegiance to monotheism when he affirms that the whole of the cosmos can indeed be subsumed under a single, redemptive principle leading to an ultimate and ultimately unified peace.[59]

But it is critical to note that Rosenzweig distinguished between the "work" of redemption (humanity's task) and redemption itself (a divine achievement). The distinction implies that the first may serve only as an *anticipation* of the second and not as its cause. Just as Rosenzweig's "messianic theory of knowledge" looks forward to the unity brought to the world by God, so, too, Rosenzweig can be said to hold a messianic theory of redemption, in that human action can only *anticipate* but cannot *bring about* the peace of the world. And we should also note that for Rosenzweig the activistic, the social-political work of transforming the world is chiefly a Christian task, not a Jewish one: The Jews are meant to "embody" redemption precisely by remaining *inactive*. Rosenzweig's reduction of ethics (which is confined chiefly to a meaningful but wholly interpersonal love) and his stringently theological claim that "true" redemption comes from God alone frequently pass without notice in readings that wish to categorize his new thinking as a variant of activistic or socially-responsible humanism.

Rosenzweig was a philosopher who struggled to reconcile the conflicting demands of Athens and Jerusalem (in the terms made famous by Leo Strauss), to live and to think "between two worlds" (to cite a classic essay on Rosenzweig by Levinas).[60] He remained passionately committed to the Jewish religion even while striving also to embrace the riches of modern, secular philosophy. More specifically, Rosenzweig's thought appears as a testament to the possibility of religion even in the wake of Nietzsche's pronouncement that "God is dead." Indeed, one might gauge the true modernity of *The Star* by the generous view it takes of Nietzsche, who is named the "first real human being among the philosophers."[61] It is Nietzsche, as no philosopher before him, who first contemplates the meaning of divine existence in terms of human *life*. But he finds that God's will, if truly infinite, must conflict with the human will to power. Nietzsche's atheism thus follows upon the insight that any concession to divine freedom would mean compromising human sovereignty. *The Star* concludes: "The first real human being among the philosophers was also the first who beheld God face to face – even if it was only in order to deny him."[62] For Rosenzweig, therefore, the scandal of atheism is not specifically its denial of God but its failure to recognize that dimension of human experience which escapes human control. In one of his earliest essays, Rosenzweig criticized Jewish nationalists for seeking salvation exclusively in communal power and thereby losing sight of revelation, an error he called "atheistic theology." His mistrust of Zionism bears comparison with Nietzsche's critique of German nationalism: Like Nietzsche, Rosenzweig regards with suspicion any thinking that would exalt the momentary achievements of political history as the sign of divine favor.

The prominent position that *The Star* assigns to Nietzsche's atheism may serve as a warning against those interpretations that wish to install Rosenzweig within an uninterrupted and venerable tradition of Jewish thought. He was unmistakably modern in outlook. But if he resists facile classification as exclusively a "Jewish" thinker, it is also because he remained open, as very few Jewish philosophers before him or since, to the fullest merits of "paganism." One should not find it at all surprising, then, that in one of his last essays, Rosenzweig drew a favorable comparison between his own philosophy and that of Martin Heidegger.[63]

But here, one suspects, the partnership between religion and philosophy was not quite so balanced as Rosenzweig claimed. Rosenzweig's search for the most "primordial" elements of faith brought him to the paradoxical insight that Judaism and Christianity were not "originally" religions at all: The former was a "fact" (*Tatsache*), the latter an "event" (*Ereignis*). This would appear to validate Rosenzweig's claim that *The Star* is not a philosophy of religion, since its true object of inquiry is that deeper stratum of human experience he called "the earthly path of revelation" (*der Erdenweg der Offenbarung*).[64]

Yet this experience in Rosenzweig's opinion could be found equally in Judaism, Christianity, and paganism as well (at least among the pagans who abjure their "official" Hellenistic philosophies).[65] We might conclude that Rosenzweig was a philosopher of Jewish existence, even if he did not create an essentially *Jewish* philosophy. At the end of "The New Thinking," he affirmed that "this is a Jewish book" but only in as much as "I received the new thinking in these old words, thus I have rendered it and passed it on." But he admitted that "to a Christian, instead of mine, the words of the New Testament would have come to his lips; to a pagan [. . .] although not words of his holy books [. . .] perhaps entirely his own words. But, to me, these words." *The Star* was indeed a Jewish book, but not one that dealt exclusively or essentially with only "Jewish matters." Rather, it was

> one for whom the old Jewish words come in order to say what it
> has to say, and precisely for the new things it has to say. For Jewish
> matters are, as matters generally are, always already past; but
> Jewish words, even if old, take part in the eternal youth of the
> word, and the world is opened to them, and they will renew the
> world.[66]

The question as to whether Rosenzweig was truly a "Jewish" philosopher admits of no determinate answer. He struggled to embrace simultaneously the particularism and the universalism at the heart of the Jewish faith. He cherished the Jews' incommensurable singularity, and he found messianic significance in the requirement that they remain utterly distinct among the nations of the world. But he also looked upon the seeming variety of religious experience as merely provisional, since he believed that all faiths must essentially share the single vision of a future without strife.

These two facets of Rosenzweig's philosophy are not easily reconciled. On the one hand, it could be argued that Rosenzweig remained
so bound to the specific, messianic core of the Jewish tradition that he
was willing to pursue its logic even to the point of breaking from the
non-redeemed world. His particularism would thus be a sign of just how
jealously he guarded the purity of the universal. But if so, this would
seem to be a particularism indefensible in universal terms, and untrans-
latable into the lexicon of another culture or religion. On the other hand,
it might be inferred from the passage just quoted that he believed this
messianic message can be found in various "words" or creeds. Judaism
then, like all religion, would possess its true significance less for its
doctrinal content than for its capacity to sustain for humanity that common experience of wonder – "the earthly path of revelation" – which the
Greeks believed to be the origin of philosophy itself. This might seem
an appealing solution, and it seems most in harmony with Rosenzweig's
own claim that the new thinking is an ecumenical movement. But if so,
the availability of a common language would appear to threaten the last
remaining justification for Jewish exclusivity. Rosenzweig's philosophy
is perhaps most fascinating for the way it portrays Jewish existence itself
as the living embodiment of this unresolved – and, perhaps, unresolv-
able – dilemma.

Notes

1. Franz Rosenzweig, "The New Thinking," hereafter, ND. For English, I
   cite the new anthology, *Franz Rosenzweig's "The New Thinking,"* Alan
   Udoff and Barbara Galli, trans. and eds. (Syracuse: Syracuse University
   Press, 1999); 67–102. I have amended the translation where needed and
   indicate accordingly.
2. See, for example, Peter Wust, *Die Auferstehung der Metaphysik* (Leipzig:
   Felix Meiner, 1920); and Heinrich Kerler, *Die auferstandene Metaphysik,
   Eine Abrechnung.* 2. Auflage (Ulm: Verlag Heinrich Kerler, 1921).
3. Michael Brenner, *The Renaissance of Jewish Culture in Weimar Germany* (New Haven: Yale University Press, 1996). Also see Asher Biemann, "The Problem of Tradition and Reform in Jewish Renaissance
   and Renaissancism," in *Jewish Social Studies,* Vol. 8, No. 1 (Fall, 2001),
   58–87.
4. ND, 69.
5. His own misgivings about such categorization (in the lines just quoted)
   were omitted from the version of "The New Thinking" that was
   published in the English-language anthology as edited by his student
   Nahum Glatzer, in *Franz Rosenzweig: His Life and Thought.* Nahum N.
   Glatzer, ed., 3rd edition (Indianapolis: Hackett, 1998). On the politics of
   the post-war reception, see my "Rosenzweig Redux: The Reception of

German-Jewish Thought," *Jewish Social Studies*, Volume 8, No. 1 (Fall, 2001), 1–57.

6. Franz Rosenzweig, *Die "Gritli"-Briefe: Briefe an Margrit Rosenstock-Huessy*. Inken Rühle und Reinhold Mayer, eds. (Tübingen: Bilam, 2002), hereafter GB. In this chapter, I provide only the dates of each letter. GB, April 29, 1918.

7. After the war, Rosenzweig emended his dissertation for publication as *Hegel und der Staat* (München and Berlin: Verlag R. Oldenbourg, 1920). A one-volume edition was prepared in 1937 but destroyed by the Gestapo before publication; it was later printed in photostat (Aalen: Scientia Verlag, 1962). In what follows, I cite the 1962 edition, hereafter HS.

8. About Meinecke's *Cosmopolitanism and the Nation-State*, Rosenzweig observed in 1908 that "To have written such a book I would well give ten years of my life." In Franz Rosenzweig, *Briefe*. (Berlin: Schocken Verlag, 1935). No. 32. An die Mutter. (November 13, 1908, Freiburg), 41.

9. On Rosenzweig's relation to Hegel, see Ulrich Bieberich, *Wenn die Geschichte göttlich wäre: Rosenzweig's Auseinandersetzung mit Hegel* (St. Ottilien: Verlag Erzabtei St. Ottilien, 1989); Gérard Bensussan, "Hegel et Rosenzweig: le franchissement de l'horizon" in *Hegel et l'Etat*. Trans. Gérard Bensussan. (Paris: Presses Universitaires de France, 1991), xix–xliii; Paul-Laurent Assoun, "Avant-propos, Rosenzweig et la politique: postérité d'une rupture," in *Hegel et l'Etat*, Bensussan, trans., v–xvii; Shlomo Avineri, "Rosenzweig's Hegel Interpretation: Its Relationship to the Development of his Jewish Reawakening," in *Franz Rosenzweig*, International Kassel Conference, vol. II (1986), 831–838; Otto Pöggeler, "Rosenzweig und Hegel," *Franz Rosenzweig*, International Kassel Conference, Vol. II (1986), 839–853; Otto Pöggeler, "Between Enlightenment and Romanticism: Rosenzweig and Hegel," in *The Philosophy of Franz Rosenzweig*, Paul Mendes-Flohr, ed. (Hanover, NH: University Press of New England, 1987), 107–123; and Miriam Bienenstock, "Rosenzweig's Hegel," *The Owl of Minerva* 23.2 (Spring) (1992), 177–182.

10. "Das Älteste Systemprogramm des Deutschen Idealismus, Ein handschriftlicher Fund," reprinted in *Franz Rosenzweig, Der Mensch und sein Werk. Gesammelte Schriften* (Dordrecht: Martinus Nijhoff, 1984) GS, III, 3–59. Written in the summer of 1914 in Berlin, this analysis was first printed by the Heidelberger Akademie der Wissenschaften in 1917, 5. Abhandlung (under the direction of Heinrich Rickert). Against the Schelling-attribution, see, for example, the essays in *Hegel-Studien*, "Das älteste Systemprogramm, Studien zur Frühgeschichte des deutschen Idealismus," Beiheft 9 (1973). Rosenzweig's relationship to Schelling is discussed at length in Else Freund, *Die Existenzphilosophie Franz Rosenzweigs* (Hamburg: Felix Meiner, 1959).

11. See especially Rosenzweig's "Concluding Remark" as translated in the excellent volume, *Frank Rosenzweig, Philosophical and Theological Writings*, translated and edited with Notes and Commentary by Paul W. Franks and Michael L. Morgan (Indianapolis and Cambridge: Hackett, 2000), 79.

12. On dialogue, see Leora Batnitzky, "Dialogue as Judgment, Not Mutual Affirmation: A New Look at Franz Rosenzweig's Dialogical Philosophy," *Journal of Religion*, 79:4 (October, 1999), 523–544.
13. *Briefe*, 57. An die Mutter [Berlin] October 23, 1913.
14. *Briefe*, 59. An Rudolf Ehrenberg. [Berlin] October 31, 1913, p. 71.
15. See especially Stéphane Mosés, *L'Ange de l'Histoire. Rosenzweig, Benjamin, Scholem* (Paris: Éditions du Seuil, 1992); and David N. Myers, *Resisting History: Historicism and its Discontents in German-Jewish Thought* (Princeton: Princeton University Press, 2003).
16. ND, 150.
17. Rosenzweig, "Einleitung" in *Hermann Cohens Jüdische Schriften* (Berlin: Schwetschke und Sohn, 1924); Vol. I, V–LXIV. Although scholars, then and now, have disputed its accuracy, Rosenzweig's romantic portrait of his old teacher remains deeply appealing. Steven Schwarzschild, "Franz Rosenzweig's Anecdotes About Hermann Cohen" in *Gegenwart im Rückblick: Festgabe für die Jüdische Gemeinde zu Berlin 25 Jahre nach dem Neubeginn*. (Heidelberg: Lothar Stiehm Verlag, 1970), 209–218, especially n. 10 and n. 13. For the dispute over Cohen's image, see Jacques Derrida, "Interpretations at War: Kant, the Jew, the German," *New Literary History*. 22 (1991), 39–95; and the first chapter of my book, *Rosenzweig and Heidegger: Between Judaism and German Philosophy* (Berkeley: University of California Press, 2003).
18. See Rosenzweig, *Briefe*, Letter No. 364, An Rudolf Hallo (Ende Januar, 1923), 472–473; and comments by Karl Löwith, in *Mein Leben in Deutschland vor und nach 1933*. (Stuttgart: J.B. Metzlersche Verlagsbuchhandlung und Carl Ernst Poeschel Verlag, 1986), 138–139.
19. See Paul Mendes-Flohr, *German Jews, A Dual Identity* (New Haven: Yale University Press, 1999).
20. *Briefe*, 539. An die Mutter. October 6, 1929, 631.
21. See Martin Buber, "Zu einer neuen Verdeutschung der Schrift: Beilage zum ersten Band," in Martin Buber and Franz Rosenzweig, *Die fünf Bücher der Weisung*, Vol. I (Berlin: Lambert Schneider, 1956), 44.
22. Franz Rosenzweig, *Der Stern der Erlösung*, 4th edition. (Frankfurt am Main: Suhrkamp, 1993). In English as *The Star of Redemption*. William W. Hallo, trans. (Notre Dame: University of Notre Dame Press, 1985). Hereafter SE. All citations are from the 4th German edition; the number in parenthesis refers to the corresponding passage in the English translation.
23. The line occurs in the third stanza of the poem, "Das Ideal und das Leben," in Friedrich Schiller, *Werke, Band III: Gedichte, Erzählungen*. (Frankfurt am Main: Insel Verlag, 1966), 99–103. Rosenzweig also cites the poem in his lecture notes from 1924, "Glauben und Wissen," first published only in FR, III, 581–595; and recently translated as "Faith and Knowledge" in Franz Rosenzweig, *God, Man, and the World*. Barbara Galli, ed. and trans. (Syracuse: Syracuse University Press, 1998), 97–121. For a discussion, see my book, *Rosenzweig and Heidegger: Between Judaism and German Philosophy*, esp. pp. 143–150.

24. Franz Rosenzweig, *Die 'Gritli' Briefe: Briefe an Margrit Rosenstock-Huessy*. Inken Rühle and Reinhold Mayer, eds. (Tübingen: Bilam Verlag, 2002), letter dated November 27, 1918; 200–201, emphasis in original.
25. SE, 4 (4).
26. SE, 463 (416).
27. Rosenzweig's debt to Dilthey extends back to *Hegel and the State*, the opening pages of which praise Dilthey's hermeneutic method for disclosing the *Weltanschauung* of the young, religiously minded Hegel. See my comments earlier on the Hegel book and in the list of secondary literature in the Bibliography in the present volume.
28. On Rosenzweig's use of Cohen's "principle of origin," see Amos Funkenstein, *Perceptions of Jewish History* (Berkeley: University of California Press, 1993), esp. pp. 257–305.
29. Rosenzweig, "Urzelle" in *Kleinere Schriften* (Berlin: Schocken Verlag, 1937), 359.
30. SE, 269 (242).
31. SE, 264 (237).
32. The relation between Rosenzweig and Levinas is discussed in Robert Gibbs, *Correlations in Rosenzweig and Levinas* (Princeton: Princeton University Press, 1992), and in Richard A. Cohen, *Elevations: The Height of the Good in Rosenzweig and Levinas* (Chicago: University of Chicago Press, 1994).
33. SE, 290 (260).
34. On alterity as a point of continuity between Rosenzweig and Levinas, see Samuel Moyn, *Origins of the Other: Emmanuel Levinas between Revelation and Ethics* (Ithaca: Cornell University Press, 2005).
35. GB, 13.4.1918.
36. SE, 182 (203).
37. Franz Rosenzweig, "Bemerkungen über Anthropomorphismus," in *Franz Rosenzweig: Der Mensch und sein Werk, Volume III: Zweistromland* (Dordrecht: Martinus Nijhoff, 1984), 735–746.
38. SE, Hallo trans., 183.
39. SE, 167 (186).
40. SE, 168 (187).
41. As Gil Anidjar has noted, although *The Star* is often praised for religious ecumenicism, it displays a quite poor and stereotypical understanding of Islam.
42. In a dual exploration of theological themes in psychoanalysis and psychoanalytic themes in Rosenzweig, Eric Santner notes that Rosenzweig offers a critique of "Egyptomania" – that is, a critique of neurotic attachment to various "false" investments, such as the investment in state power. See Santner, *On the Psychotheology of Everyday Life: Reflections on Freud and Rosenzweig* (Chicago: University of Chicago Press, 2001).
43. SE, 323 (291).
44. SE, 339 (305).
45. SE, 338 (304); Hallo omits the word "dark" in his translation.

46. The claim that Rosenzweig's notion of blood community might be read as ethnicity can be found in the indispensable commentary by Stéphane Mosès, *System and Revelation: The Philosophy of Franz Rosenzweig*, Foreword by Emmanuel Levinas. Catherine Tihanyi, trans. (Detroit: Wayne State University Press, 1982).

47. On the Jews' special kind of internal and independent temporality, see especially SE, 364 (328).

48. The Jews are thus never "entirely at home" (*in keinem andern Land mehr ganz heimisch*). Elsewhere he characterizes them as "uncanny" (*unheimlich*), SE, 333 (300). For commentary, see Leora Batnitzky, "Rosenzweig's Aesthetic Theory and Jewish *Unheimlichkeit*," *New German Critique*, 77 (Spring-Summer, 1999): 87–112; and Susan Shapiro, "The Uncanny Jew: A Brief History of an Image," *Judaism* 46, 1 (1997): 63–78.

49. It is worth noting that Rosenzweig believed his philosophical portrait of the Jews bore a close resemblance to Weber's sociological portrait of the "*Pariah-Volk*" in Max Weber, *Ancient Judaism*, Hans H. Gerth and Don Martindale, eds. and trans. (Glencoe: The Free Press, 1952), esp. ch. 13, "The Pariah Community," 336–355.

50. Leo Strauss, *Spinoza's Critique of Religion*. Trans. E. M. Sinclair (New York: Schocken Books, 1965), Preface, 13.

51. On the messianic and mission-theory element in Rosenzweig, see Batnitzky, *Idolatry and Representation*, esp. p. 11.

52. On "constriction," see Richard Cohen, *Elevations: The Height of the Good in Rosenzweig and Levinas* (Chicago: The University of Chicago Press, 1994), 21–22.

53. SE, 283 (254).

54. Siegfried Kracauer, "Die Bibel auf Deutsch: Zur Übersetung von Martin Buber und Franz Rosenzweig" Part 1: *Frankfurter Zeitung*, 70, no. 308 (April 27, 1926). Part 2: *Frankfurter Zeitung*, 70, no. 311 (April 28, 1926). In English in Siegfried Kracauer, *The Mass Ornament*. Thomas Y. Levin, trans. (Cambridge: Harvard University Press, 1995). Martin Jay, "Politics of Translation: Siegfried Kracauer and Walter Benjamin on the Buber-Rosenzweig Bible," in LBIY, XXI (1976), 3–24. From Walter Benjamin, *Briefe an Siegfried Kracauer*. Edited by Theodor Adorno Archiv. (Marbach am Neckar), 1987, 16n. On Benjamin's hostility to Buber, see Momme Brodersen, *Walter Benjamin, A Biography*. Malcom R. Green and Ingrida Ligers, trans. (London: Verso, 1996); and Gershom Scholem, *Walter Benjamin, The Story of a Friendship*. Harry Zohn, trans. (New York: Schocken Books, 1981), esp. circa July 1916. For George Lukács' critique, see Lukács, *Der junge Hegel* (Berlin: Hermann Luchtenhand Verlag, 1966).

55. Gershom Scholem, "On the 1930 Edition of Rosenzweig's *Star of Redemption*," originally published in *Frankfurter Israelitisches Gemeindeblatt*, X (1931), 15–17, reprinted in *Judaica* (Frankfurt am Main, 1963), pp. 226–234, trans. Michael Meyer, Reprinted in Gershom Scholem, *The Messianic Idea in Judaism and Other Essays on Jewish Spirituality* (New York: Schocken Books, 1971), 320–324.

56. Walter Benjamin, "Bücher, die Lebendig Geblieben Sind." Originally published in *Die Literarische Welt*. May 17, 1929 (Jahrgang 5, Nr. 20), p. 6. Reprinted in Walter Benjamin, *Gesammelte Schriften*. III (Frankfurt am Main: Suhrkamp Verlag, 1972), 169–171.

57. See, for example, Theodor Adorno's celebrated remark that "the only philosophy which can be responsibly practised in face of despair is the attempt to contemplate all things as they would present themselves from the standpoint of redemption." From the entry, "Finale," in Adorno, *Minima Moralia, Reflections from Damaged Life*. E. F. N. Jephcott, trans. (London: Verso, 1978), 247.

58. Levinas, cited from *Totality and Infinity*, Alphonso Lingis, trans. (Pittsburgh: Duquesne University Press), 28.

59. As Rosenzweig explains, "the eternal people" must "*look upon the world, its own world* as complete." SE, 364 (328), my emphasis.

60. Emmanuel Levinas, "Entre deux mondes. Biographie spirituelle de Franz Rosenzweig," in Amado Levy-Valensis, Eliane, ed. *La Conscience juive. Données et débats* (Paris: Pressses Universitaires de France, 1963), 121–149. Reprinted in *Difficile Liberté*. 3rd ed. (Paris: Albin Michel, 1984), 253–281; and "Franz Rosenzweig. L'Étoile de la Rédemption" in *Esprit*. 6, 3 (1982), 157–165.

61. SE, 20 (18).

62. SE, 20 (18).

63. On the Heidegger-Rosenzweig comparison, see Peter Eli Gordon, *Rosenzweig and Heidegger: Between Judaism and German Philosophy* (Berkeley: The University of California Press, 2003). Rosenzweig's essay contains remarks on Heidegger in the context of the 'Davos encounter' with Ernst Cassirer. See Rosenzweig, "Vertauschte Fronten." Originally published in *Der Morgen*, Vol. VI, No. 6 (April, 1930), 85–87. Reprinted in *Franz Rosenzweig, Der Mensch und sein Werk*, III., 235–238. Also see Leo Strauss, *Spinoza's Critique of Religion* (New York: Schocken Books, 1965), 13. Significantly, Strauss dedicated this book to the memory of Franz Rosenzweig. Also see Karl Löwith, "M. Heidegger and F. Rosenzweig, or, Temporality and Eternity," in *Philosophy and Phenomenological Research*, Volume III, No. 1. (September, 1942), 53–77, and the German version (with variations), "M. Heidegger und F. Rosenzweig, Ein Nachtrag zu *Sein und Zeit*" in *Zeitschrift für Philosophische Forschung*, 12, 2 (1958), 161–187. Heidegger, too, one may recall, saw Nietzsche as "*the sole true believer*" of the nineteenth century. See Martin Heidegger's 1943 lecture, 'The Word of Nietzsche: "God is Dead."' Quoted from Karl Löwith, "The Political Implications of Heidegger's Existentialism" in Richard Wolin, ed., *The Heidegger Controversy, A Critical Reader*. (Cambridge, Massachusetts: MIT Press, 1993), 172.

64. Rosenzweig, "Das neue Denken," in *Kleinere Schriften*, 155.

65. ND, German text, in Franz Rosenzweig, *Kleinere Schriften* (Berlin: Schocken, 1937), 391.

66. ND, cited from Galli and Udoff, trans. 92.

8 Leo Strauss and Modern Jewish Thought

STEVEN B. SMITH

"I believe I can say, without any exaggeration, that since a very very early time the main theme of my reflections has been what is called the 'Jewish Question.'"[1]

Was Leo Strauss a modern Jewish thinker? Was this even a category that Strauss recognized? The question is not an idle one. It is not self-evident that Strauss belongs to the canon of modern Jewish thinkers in which one might expect to find names like Hermann Cohen, Franz Rosenzweig, Martin Buber, Gershom Scholem, and Emmanuel Levinas. His work dealt characteristically with the philosophical tradition rather than the Jewish tradition. His studies on Jewish thinkers and themes occupy a relatively small portion of his total corpus of writing. And his most important (or at any rate, his most widely read) book, *Natural Right and History*, contains scarcely a word about any Jewish topic. Given these considerations, what has Strauss contributed to modern Jewish thought?[2]

Before trying to answer these questions, some biography.[3] Leo Strauss was born in the Hessian village of Kirchhain in 1899. He was brought up in an observant household, where he remarked later that the Jewish laws "were rather strictly observed." After graduating from a humanistic Gymnasium and a brief service in World War I, Strauss attended the university at Marburg that was then the center of the neo-Kantian revival inspired by Hermann Cohen. Strauss received his doctorate from the University of Hamburg in 1921, where he prepared a dissertation under the direction of Ernst Cassirer. A year later, he spent a post-graduate year in Freiburg, where he went to study with Edmund Husserl. It was during this year that Strauss first heard Husserl's student, Martin Heidegger, who left a deep, even a life-long, impression on him.

Strauss worked as a research assistant at the Academy of Jewish Studies in Berlin from 1925 to 1932, where his principle duties were to assist with editing the Academy's jubilee edition of the works of Moses

Mendelssohn. During this period, Strauss published some of his earliest writings on Zionism and other Jewish themes in Martin's Buber's journal *Der Jude* and in the *Jüdische Rundschau*. His first book *Die Religionskritik Spinozas* [Spinoza's Critique of Religion] (1930) was dedicated to the memory of Franz Rosenzweig, who had died the year before its publication.

Strauss left Germany in 1932 under the auspices of a Rockefeller Foundation grant and he spent a year in Paris before moving to England. There he wrote a book on Maimonides and his predecessors titled *Philosophie und Gesetz* [Philosophy and Law] (1935) and a book on *The Political Philosophy of Hobbes* (1936). Unable to find a permanent position in England, Strauss emigrated to America in 1938, where he joined the faculty of the New School for Social Research, which was then a haven for academics in exile from Hitler's Germany. Strauss's New School years was a remarkably productive period in his life in which – we are now beginning to learn fully – his major ideas began to germinate. It was there that Strauss first became a "Straussian."[4]

In 1949, Strauss accepted a position at the University of Chicago, where he spent almost the next twenty years and where his most important books – *Persecution and the Art of Writing* (1952), *Natural Right and History* (1953), *Thoughts on Machiavelli* (1958), and *What is Political Philosophy?* (1959) – were written. It was during the Chicago years that Strauss exercised his greatest influence and attracted a remarkable cadre of students. At the invitation of Gershom Scholem, he spent a year at the Hebrew University in Jerusalem, but otherwise devoted himself almost exclusively to teaching and writing. His later works focused increasingly on ancient political philosophy, especially Plato, Xenophon, Aristotle, and Thucydides. Upon his retirement, Strauss spent his last years in Annapolis, Maryland, where he went to join his old friend Jacob Klein on the faculty of St. John's College. His last completed work, *The Argument and Action of Plato's Laws* (1975), was published two years after his death. Since his death, several volumes of previously uncollected essays, lectures, and a sizeable philosophical correspondence have been published. His work, always controversial, has continued to generate debate arguably more today than during his lifetime. It remains a remarkable monument to twentieth-century scholarship and philosophy.

THE THEOLOGICO-POLITICAL PREDICAMENT

Strauss was a product of his times. What else could he be? In the 1965 Preface to the English translation of *Spinoza's Critique of Religion*, he describes his context as that of "a young Jew born and raised in Germany who found himself in the grip of the theologico-political predicament."⁵ Strauss's description of himself as both a German and a Jew defines the precise parameters of this predicament. The theologico-political problem was meant to describe, but was not confined to, the predicament of German Jewry.

Politically speaking, the Germany of Strauss's early adulthood was the Weimar Republic. Weimar was a liberal democracy created in the wake of Germany's defeat in World War I. It was Weimar's attempt to strike a tenuous balance between adherence to the liberal principles of the French Revolution and to Germany's deepest traditions that accounted for its weakness. Liberalism was weaker in Germany, or at least came later than to many other European states. This weakness accounts for the inability of Weimar to protect its most vulnerable minority, its Jewish citizens. Above all, German Jewry owed its emancipation to Weimar. It was no coincidence that the attack upon Weimar from both the Left and the Right was an attack upon German Jewry. The failure of Weimar came to represent for Strauss a failure endemic to liberalism.

Theologically speaking, Strauss's predicament turned on what form or shape Judaism would take under a liberal republic. German Jewry, perhaps more than Jews of any other nation, wedded themselves to the fate of modern liberalism. The result, as Strauss analyzed it, was a mixed blessing. The triumph of liberal democracy brought civil equality, toleration, and the end of the worst forms of persecution, even if not all forms of private discrimination. Yet at the same time, liberalism requires that Judaism – as it requires all faiths – undergo the privatization of belief, the relegation of Jewish law from a communal authority to the precincts of individual conscience. Arguably, this makes harder demands on Judaism than on many other religions. Judaism understands itself in the first instance not as a faith or set of beliefs, but as a body of laws intended to regulate social and political life. The liberal principle of the separation of state and society, of public life and private belief, could not but result in the "Protestantization" of Judaism.

Strauss addresses the condition of German Jewry as shaped by the Enlightenment in the introduction to his *Philosophy and Law*.⁶ By the term Enlightenment, Strauss means the efforts of those seventeenth- and eighteenth-century writers such as Hobbes, Spinoza, Bayle, and Voltaire to overthrow the reigning systems of orthodoxy, or what Hobbes tellingly called "the kingdom of darkness." The authors of these theologico-political treatises attacked not just clerical abuses of religion – they were not just religious reformers – but the very foundations, the "roots," of the law. The Enlightenment strategy was to turn religion from a universal bond of society and morality into an essentially private affair. This strategy need not result in the extirpation of religion, but in the "internalization" of the basic concepts of orthodoxy – revelation, miracles, creation. This process of internalization or privatization was intended to deprive historical or positive religion of its traditional meaning by warding it off, quarantining it, as it were, into its own independent zone of "culture."

The quarrel between orthodoxy and the Enlightenment – an anticipation of Strauss's later interest in the quarrel of the Ancients and the Moderns – resulted in various rearguard attempts to preserve religion in a modern guise. Moses Mendelssohn's *Jerusalem* (1783) attempted to construct a Judaism amenable to philosophy, a rational Judaism, or as Hermann Cohen would later call it, "a religion of reason from out of the sources of Judaism." What Mendelssohn did for Judaism, Kant attempted for Protestantism – namely, fashioning a *Religion from Within the Limits of Reason Alone* (1793). These various attempts to mediate or reconcile the differences between orthodoxy and Enlightenment whose greatest exponent was Hegel came over time to appear increasingly thin and unconvincing. "It must necessarily remain the case," Strauss writes, "that not just every compromise but also every synthesis between the opposed position of orthodoxy and Enlightenment proves to be untenable."[7] Why?

Strauss was intellectually and temperamentally a splitter, not a lumper. He believed in keeping alive certain fundamental distinctions, and remained deeply suspicious of attempts to bridge the gap or find a middle way between inherently irreconcilable points of view and ways of life. As he would put it much later: "There are many people who believe that there can be a happy synthesis which is superior to the isolated elements: Bible on the one hand, philosophy on the other. This is impossible. Syntheses always sacrifice the decisive claim of one of the two elements."[8] The attempt to synthesize the claims of reason and revelation could not but lead to a blurring of important differences, of either the subordination of theology to philosophy or the transformation of theology into a private faith cut off from the authoritative character of law. In either case, one side would be sacrificed to the other. The Enlightenment effort to divest religion of its public or legal character could not but result in theological asphyxiation. "These reconciliations," he avers, "always work ultimately as vehicles of the Enlightenment, not as dams against it."[9]

There is a deeper reason for Strauss's resistance to the Enlightenment's critique of orthodoxy. The Enlightenment, at least in its Spinozistic form, takes its departure from the principle of the self-sufficiency of reason. By "the self-sufficiency of reason" is meant the belief that reason alone is sufficient to make us autonomous, the masters and possessors of nature. But the belief in rational self-sufficiency is precisely that – a belief. It is no less a faith than orthodoxy. Atheism and orthodoxy are equally systems of belief that can neither understand nor refute one another. Strauss concluded that the philosophical tradition had failed in its effort to refute the possibility of revelation. Its reliance on mockery and ridicule provided at least an "indirect proof" of its failure to penetrate the bridgehead of orthodoxy. Revelation remains a possibility, and thus an open question. The Enlightenment's "Napoleonic" attack upon revelation was beaten back by successive waves of Counter-Enlightenment theology and the call for a return to orthodoxy.[10]

The conflict between orthodoxy and Enlightenment was brought to a crisis situation by Nietzsche with his demand for honesty or probity (*Redlichkeit*).[11] Nietzsche demonstrated the necessity to choose between orthodoxy and a resolute atheism. Intellectual honesty makes clear that the various efforts to reconcile orthodoxy and Enlightenment have demonstrated a failure of nerve, a tendency toward self-deception, and a refusal to "endure fearful truth." It is this impasse that defines the situation of the modern Jew:

> For a Jew who cannot be orthodox and must hold unconditional
> political Zionism (the only possible 'solution to the Jewish
> problem' on the basis of atheism) to be a highly honorable but in
> the long and serious run unsatisfactory answer, the situation
> created by that alternative, the contemporary situation, seems to
> allow no way out.[12]

It might seem here that Strauss is describing himself and his own situation. We know from letters and other sources that Strauss had already ceased to be an observant Jew.[13] Yet his statement that the situation faced by contemporary Judaism only "seems to allow no way out" suggests that this is not a self-description. The impasse is more apparent than real. The requirement to choose between orthodoxy and atheism is necessary if and only if the situation as described by Nietzsche and the Enlightenment is the only possible one. But what if the Enlightenment's critique of orthodoxy has failed? Could a return to an earlier pre-modern Enlightenment represented by Maimonides be possible? In other words, must Enlightenment be modern Enlightenment? Strauss was aware that the idea of a return to an ancient pre-modern Enlightenment would appear to his contemporaries as impossible or absurd or possibly both, yet the idea began to dawn on him. As he put it thirty years later, it became necessary to ask "whether what seems to be an impossibility is in fact only a very great difficulty."[14]

JERUSALEM OR ATHENS

The situation of German Jewry was a local, albeit vivid, expression of a theme that would occupy Strauss's life's work. He refers to this theme metaphorically by the names Jerusalem and Athens.[15] Let us see what these names imply.

Strauss intermittently describes these two cities and what they represent as the "core" or the "nerve" of the Western tradition. The conflict between biblical faith and Greek philosophy is said to be the "characteristic of the West" and "the secret of its vitality." The Bible and philosophy represent two fundamentally different "codes" or ways of life that defy final reconciliation.[16]

Athens means for Strauss the city of philosophy, the philosophical city. By its nature, philosophy is the attempt to understand the whole, of everything that is, by means of unaided reason alone. Philosophy must submit – and submit ruthlessly – everything to the bar of critical rationality. It was this emphasis on reason, the "examined life" in Socratic language, that led philosophy to believe that contemplation is the highest life for a human being. Philosophy only comes into being with the discovery of "nature" or essences. To inquire into the nature of things is to ask about their causes or principles. Strauss likes to remind his readers that there is no word for nature in Biblical Hebrew that approximates the Greek *physis*. The Hebrew *mishpat* indicating "way" or "custom" is at most a pre-philosophical anticipation of nature.[17]

Jerusalem, by contrast, represents the holy city, the city of faith. Biblical thought begins not from the experience of intellectual curiosity but from a sense of awe or fear of the Lord. According to the Bible, human life is best characterized not by intellectual self-sufficiency but by a sense of our radical dependence upon God. Not contemplation, but piety, obedience, and love are the highest human powers. The God of the Bible – whatever else He might be – is not the God of Aristotle. The God of Abraham, Isaac, and Jacob is not the unmoved mover.[18]

From the beginning, the differences between Jerusalem and Athens expressed two fundamentally different ways of life. These differences are

at heart political, a question of political authority. Does authority ultimately rest with human reason or revelation as the most fundamental
guide to life?[19] Philosophy as represented by Socrates, finds its natural
home in the city or *polis*. Philosophy presupposes a context of urban-
ity, wealth, and leisure to sustain it. The life of simple piety or humble
awe as extolled by the Bible is unequivocal in favor of the pastoral life.
According to the Bible, the first murderer was also the founder of the
first city and the arts necessary to sustain it. It is no accident that it was
not Cain, the tiller of the soil, but Abel, the keeper of sheep, who found
favor in the eyes of God.[20]

To be sure, Strauss is not oblivious to the profound areas of agreement between Jerusalem and Athens. Although Strauss often writes
about Jerusalem and Athens as two incompatible alternatives, he also
presents them as two limbs of the same tree that have nourished and sustained each other. There is, he asserts, a broad agreement regarding the
place of morality in the overall economy of life. The locus of morality for
both Greek philosophy and the Bible is located in the patriarchal family.
And both agree that the core of morality is justice supported by some
notion of divine sanction. Indeed, Strauss claims that what Plato says
about the power of divine retribution in the *Laws* is "virtually identical"
with certain verses of Amos and Psalm 139.[21]

It is only natural to ask where Strauss stood. Was he a citizen of
Jerusalem or Athens? Where did his fundamental loyalties lie? Strauss
played his cards close to his chest. His close readings of various texts in
both the philosophical and theological traditions have often been called
"Talmudic," generally by people who know little of Talmud. What is true
is that he read philosophical works as though they were sacred texts and
sacred texts as philosophical works. He treated the opening chapters of
Genesis as if they were a companion to Plato's *Timaeus*.

Strauss's answer to this situation is not to choose one side or the
other, but to maintain a full and free recognition of these two contending
claims on our allegiance. Western history is replete with examples of
competing loyalties as well as efforts to reconcile faith and reason. It is
unnecessary to repeat this history. Strauss advised his readers that it is
more necessary than ever to remain thoughtfully alive to both Jerusalem
and Athens without becoming exclusively a partisan of either:

No one can be both a philosopher and a theologian, nor, for that
matter, some possibility which transcends the conflict between
philosophy and theology, or pretends to be a synthesis of both. But

every one of us can be and ought to be either one or the other, the philosopher open to the challenge of theology or the theologian open to the challenge of philosophy.[22]

Strauss's answer to his theologico-political predicament that he said at one time seemed to offer "no way out" was in fact to maintain a lively awareness of the powers of both Jerusalem and Athens without becoming a citizen of either. It is not a matter of opting for one or the other, either orthodoxy or atheism. All such decisions rest upon arbitrary premises or willful choices that resist ultimate justification. Perhaps Strauss's belief that our commitments ultimately require rational justification implies that in the final analysis he had opted for Athens. Or, just as likely, his belief that such commitments can never be fully justified and remain necessarily an act of faith suggests the victory of Jerusalem. In either case, rather than opting for easy solutions, Strauss preferred a life of permanent exile from both Jerusalem and Athens – perhaps akin to the Athenian Stranger in Plato's *Laws*. Finding himself in America, he may well have believed that he had landed on Crete!

THE CASE OF SPINOZA

When Strauss published his *Die Religionskritik Spinozas*, the Jewish world was in the throes of preparation for the commemoration in 1932 of the tercentennial of Spinoza's birth. Throughout Europe and Palestine, events were planned to welcome Spinoza back into the fold of Jewish history. For many who were participating in this event, it represented an unprecedented opportunity to right what was seen as a deep historical injustice – namely, the excommunication of Spinoza from the Sephardic community of Amsterdam and from the Jewish world more generally. The rehabilitation of Spinoza had, of course, been underway for more than a century. Beginning in the last quarter of the eighteenth century, Spinoza was canonized by the German romantics as the "God-intoxicated man," and by the first third of the nineteenth century he was being treated by the German Jewish community as a forerunner of the liberal, cosmopolitan, "man-in-general." Spinoza may have been seen as a heretic, but he was still a Jewish heretic, and his heresies were seen as vital steps toward the age of emancipation. Into this garden party – ironically on the eve of Hitler's ascension to power – Strauss lobbed a grenade.[23]

Strauss's intervention in the Spinoza controversy was in part a response to the work of the aged Hermann Cohen (1842–1918) who had continued an older line of Spinoza criticism as guilty of a "humanly incomprehensible betrayal" of Judaism. Cohen, who had been an early role model for Strauss ("the center of attraction for philosophically minded Jews"),[24] had excoriated Spinoza throughout his long career, but it was only in his old-age that his work took on a bitter and *ad hominem* tone. Spinoza stood condemned as a betrayer and falsifier of his own people. This for Cohen was an especially grievous sin as it demonstrated a lack of fidelity. It is loyalty to one's family, friends, and religious tradition that is one of the crucial virtues in Cohen's understanding of Judaism, and that explains his aversion to Spinoza. Spinoza's betrayal consisted among other things in his denigration of the prophets, his identification of God and nature (*deus sive natura*) leading to a doctrine of "might makes right," and his treatment of Judaism as a purely national or political religion. Spinoza's depiction of Judaism as a civic religion, Cohen argued, was based on a profound misunderstanding of the universalism of the monotheistic idea as well as the ethical idealism of the prophets. Spinoza's misleading caricature of Judaism as a purely civil legislation, Cohen argues, was deliberately constructed to deny its ethical content. Perhaps most dangerously, Cohen claimed that Spinoza created certain negative stereotypes about Judaism and biblical religion that were later to influence Kant, who depended upon Spinoza's research. Spinoza thus stands accused of being the chief "prosecutor" of Judaism before a hostile Gentile world.[25]

Strauss devoted a lengthy essay titled "Cohens Analyse der Bibel-Wissenschaft Spinozas" (1924) both to attacking and also deepening Cohen's case against Spinoza.[26] Strauss vindicates Spinoza from Cohen's charge by arguing at length that Spinoza's critique of Judaism was carried out neither from malice nor animus against the Jewish people, but derived from the "objective conditions" of seventeenth-century Holland. Cohen failed to see the forces of persecution prevalent at the time of Spinoza. Consequently, "he understood Spinoza too literally" because "he did not read him literally enough."[27] Strauss spends a considerable part of his analysis showing that Spinoza's motives for writing the *Theologico-Political Treatise* cannot be inferred from the biographical facts of his excommunication or some psychological desire for revenge, but derive from his desire to liberate philosophy from ecclesiastical supervision.[28]

There is a further reason that Strauss takes issue with Cohen's Spinoza criticism. For Cohen, the core of Judaism is the messianic idea by which he understands the notion of Israel's universal mission. Cohen interprets the prophets in the light of Kant's moral idealism. Thus the distinctive mission of Judaism is to create an ethical culture of reason that Cohen associates with socialism and the idea of an almost infinite moral progress. Spinoza's claim that Judaism was merely a tribal religion could not but appear as "satanic" to Cohen, whereas Strauss adds sardonically that Cohen would have regarded it not as satanic but "divine" if Spinoza had said that the sole purpose of Judaism was the establishment and preservation of the socialist state.[29]

Strauss's later judgment on the Kantian-Cohenian idea of ethical socialism was dispositive:

> Cohen's thought belongs to the world preceding World War I.
> Accordingly, he had a greater faith in the power of modern Western culture to mold the fate of mankind than seems warranted now.
> The worst things he had experienced were the Dreyfus scandal and the pogroms instigated by Czarist Russia; he did not experience Communist Russia and Hitler's Germany.[30]

The upshot of Strauss's critique of Cohen is both a vindication and a condemnation of Spinoza. On the one hand, Strauss exonerates Cohen from the charge of acting out of pure malice, yet on the other he does so by severing entirely the principles of Spinoza's biblical criticism from Jewish sources and tradition. At the time when the Jewish world was just preparing to reinstate Spinoza within the Jewish canon, Strauss could conclude his critique of Cohen with the following pronouncement: "The *Tractatus* is a Christian-European, not a Jewish event."[31] In a single sentence, Strauss confers on Spinoza a more powerful and permanent *cherem* than could ever have been delivered by the rabbis of Amsterdam.

Strauss's Spinoza critique was developed further in a short essay, "Das Testament Spinozas," written in the same year as the Spinoza tercentennial.[32] He begins the essay by surveying the reception of Spinoza from condemnation after his excommunication, to partial vindication at the hands of Mendelssohn, to canonization by Moses Hess and Heinrich Heine, to the scholarly neutrality of the twentieth century. Strauss admits straight out that "Spinoza was a Jew," but then goes on to ask rhetorically: "But should we mention the names of other men, perhaps of equal rank with Spinoza, who were likewise born and educated as Jews, and whom scarcely any Jew would dare to remember proudly and gratefully as a Jew?"[33] One may wonder who Strauss has in mind in raising the specter of other now-forgotten figures who were of equal rank with Spinoza. His point is that it is not enough to have been born and educated as a Jew to be considered a great or venerable member of the Jewish tradition. How, then, are we to understand Spinoza?

It is not as a Jew, but as a member of that "small band of superior minds" that Strauss, following Nietzsche, calls "the good Europeans" to which Spinoza properly belongs:

> To this community belong *all* the philosophers of the seventeenth century, but Spinoza belongs to it in a special way. Spinoza did not remain a Jew, while Descartes, Hobbes, and Leibniz remained Christians. Thus it is not in accordance with Spinoza's wishes that he be inducted into the pantheon of the Jewish nation. Under these circumstances it seems to us an elementary imperative of Jewish self-respect that we Jews should at last again relinquish our claim on Spinoza. By so doing, we by no means surrender him to our enemies. Rather, we leave him to that distant and strange community of "neutrals" whom one can call, with considerable justice, the community of the "good Europeans."[34]

Strauss went on further to deconstruct Spinoza's alleged influence on the creation of the Zionist movement. Spinoza had been feted in Jewish circles as a founder of Zionism on the basis of his statement that if the foundations of their religion had not "effeminated their mind," it would still be possible to recreate a Jewish state, "so changeable are human affairs," and thus gain God's election "a second time."[35] Regarding Spinoza's reference to God's election as nothing more than an "empty phrase," Strauss argues on the basis of this passage that it would be "risky" to assign to Spinoza a privileged role in the Zionist movement. Spinoza does not so much endorse the creation of a Jewish state as consider it a condition of possibility (*Möglichkeitsbedingung*). "As if condescending from the height of his philosophical neutrality," Strauss writes, "he leaves it to the Jews to liberate themselves from their religion and thus to obtain for themselves the possibility of reconstituting their state."[36]

Strauss also casts doubt on Spinoza's claim that the loss of Jewish sovereignty was due to the "softening" or effeminating of the Jewish mind. He wonders why the same law that was said to lead to a weakening of political resolve could also be responsible for the strength to preserve and survive even under the most adverse circumstances – for example, the Inquisition. Just as Spinoza's "teacher," Machiavelli, had attributed to Christianity the corruption of Roman virtue, so does Spinoza make Judaism responsible for the impossibility of creating a Jewish state.[37]

So what, then, is the testament of Spinoza? Strauss distinguishes his position from the villifiers (Cohen) and the celebrators. Asking whether we still owe Spinoza our veneration, Strauss answers as follows: "Spinoza

will be venerated as long as there are men who know how to appreciate
the inscription on his signet ring (*caute*) or, to put it plainly: as long as
there are men who know what it means to utter [the word]: *independence (Unabhängigkeit).*"[38] The independence that Strauss is referring
to here is not the freedom to live as a Jew, but the freedom to live apart
from or outside one's own theologico-political community. It is the
freedom of the philosopher.

ZIONISM AND ISRAEL

Jerusalem meant for Strauss more than a metaphor for revelation;
it represents the spiritual and historical home of Judaism and the Jewish people. Whatever reservations he may have had about the case for
orthodoxy, he believed that Jewish survival required the existence of a
Jewish polity. The Weimar experience demonstrated the necessity for a
Jewish state if only for the sake of Jewish survival. He once referred to
the establishment of the state of Israel as "the only bright spot for the
contemporary Jew who knows where he comes from."[39]

Strauss reports that he was "converted" to Zionism as a teenager.
This meant originally "simple, straightforward political Zionism" of
the kind found in Pinsker's *Autoemanzipation* [Autoemancipation] and
Herzl's *Judenstaat* [The Jewish State].[40] He was not very forthcoming on
the details of his involvement with the Zionist movement of his youth,
although he recounted a memorable meeting with Vladimir Jabotinsky
(1880–1940), the founder of the Revisionist wing of the movement. From
an early time, however, Strauss came to have certain misgivings about
the ability of political Zionism to put an end to the Jewish question.
To be sure, Zionism sought to rescue Jewish honor from centuries of
degradation, but it did so on the basis of an assimilation of its own,
assimilation to the norms and culture of the modern secular state. The
Zionist slogan "a state for a people, for a people without a state" was
itself dependent upon the world of liberal assimilationism that it was
trying to escape. The state it promised was not necessarily the state of
Israel, but could have just as easily been founded in Canada or Katmandu.

The problem with political Zionism was its failure to think through
the problems of the modern liberal secular state. Herzel's solution to the
Jewish question was to establish a version of the modern liberal secular state that could put an end to discrimination and provide full civic
equality for the Jews. The problem with such a solution is that it lacked
connection to the moral and spiritual world of the Jews it was seeking to
save. Strauss voiced his first concerns about the poverty of this liberal

solution in an essay on the Zionism of Max Nordau (1923) that appeared in Martin's Buber's journal *Der Jude* [The Jew]:

> Zionism is a child of the nineteenth century. Instead of the "volcanic" conception of Jewish history, which orients itself by the great national catastrophes, Nordau demands a "Neptunian," less melodramatic conception which sees in the accumulation of minor political and economic facts the cause of large revolutionary changes. Both the plight of the Jews and its alleviation lose all semblance of the miraculous. We are not dealing any more with the coming of the Messiah, but with "a long, difficult common effort" of the Jewish people. In Zionist matters, theology has no say; Zionism is purely political.[41]

In a cruel aside, Strauss compares Nordau's attitude to that of the apothecary Homais in *Madame Bovary* who puts his scientific knowledge in the service of cider making while never ceasing to proclaim his own virtues.[42]

Despite his misgivings, Strauss remained loyal throughout his life to the achievements of Zionism for its efforts to restore a sense of Jewish "self-respect" in an age characterized by assimilation and the progressive leveling of tradition. After spending the academic year 1954–1955 at the Hebrew University in Jerusalem, Strauss sent a letter to the conservative weekly *The National Review* protesting the magazine's "anti-Jewish animus." Strauss defended the Labor Zionists who then ran Israel, not because they were trade unionists but because they were "pioneers," like the American Pilgrim fathers who form the "natural aristocracy" of the country. "The moral spine of Judaism was in danger of being broken by the so-called emancipation which in many cases had alienated them from their heritage and yet not given them anything more than merely formal equality," he wrote. "Political Zionism was the attempt to restore that inner freedom, that simple dignity, of which only people who remember their heritage and are loyal to their fate are capable."[43]

The problem with political Zionism was best revealed by cultural Zionism with the claim that a Jewish state separated from Jewish tradition and sensibilities would be nothing more than an "empty shell." Ahad Ha'am (1856–1927), the founder of the cultural Zionists, regarded the secular liberal state as merely perpetuating the condition of "external freedom and internal servitude." A Jewish state would need to be rooted in vibrant Jewish culture, of Jewish arts and letters, language and literature. If political Zionism was a product of the liberalism of the Enlightenment, cultural Zionism was a product of European romanticism. It understood Judaism as a culture that, as such, must be merely one out of any number of possible cultures. The problem here should be self-evident. Cultural Zionism conceived of the Jewish tradition not as a divine gift or divine revelation, but as the product of the national mind or national genius of the Jewish people. By turning Judaism into just one culture among others, cultural Zionism failed to reflect adequately on the foundations of its culture. If it had done so, it would have discovered that the foundation of Jewish culture is a faith in revelation, in God's gift of the Torah at Mount Sinai. This – not Israeli folk music or dance – is the true basis of Jewish culture. It is only when we consider this foundation that cultural Zionism turns into religious Zionism.[44]

Strauss was not a religious Zionist, and he never for a moment confounded politics with redemption. In an enigmatic passage from his lecture "Why We Remain Jews," he argues that the Jewish people have been chosen to prove the absence of redemption, that redemption is not possible in this world.[45] The creation of the Jewish state may be the most important fact in Jewish history since the completion of the Talmud, but it should not be confused with the coming of the Messianic age and the redemption of all people. So what, then, is the function of the Jewish state? If it is not to be understood as a purely secular democratic state, what is its purpose?

In the final analysis, Strauss was grateful for the Jewish state, which he called "a blessing for all Jews everywhere regardless of whether they admit it or not."[46] But the Jewish state should not be regarded as a solution to the Jewish question. "The establishment of the state of Israel," he wrote, "is the most profound modification of the *Galut* which has occurred, but it is not the end of the *Galut*; in the religious sense, and perhaps not only in the religious sense, the state of Israel is a part of the *Galut*":

> Finite, relative problems can be solved; infinite, absolute problems cannot be solved. In other words, human beings will never create a society which is free from contradictions. From every point of view it looks as if the Jewish people were the chosen people, at least in the sense that the Jewish problem is the most manifest symbol of the human problem, as it is a social or political problem.[47]

Passages like this one – actually it is unique in Strauss's writings – call to mind Franz Rosenzweig (1886–1929), "whose name," Strauss would acknowledge, "will always be remembered when informed people speak about existentialism."[48] For Rosenzweig, the Jewish question was something that ultimately stood outside of politics and history. Judaism is a repository of certain revealed, trans-historical truths that cannot be reduced to politics or culture. Like Cohen, Rosenzweig was a passionate anti-Zionist. The Jewish calling was to remain a people of prayer and study and to resist the entrapments of political power. It is the destiny of the Jewish people both to live in the world but to remain apart from it as part of a unique covenantal community. Rosenzweig's establishment of the *Freies Jüdisches Lehrhaus* (Free Jewish House of Learning) in Frankfurt devoted to the study and translation of traditional Jewish texts could well have served as a model for Strauss's creation of an interpretive community in Chicago many years later. Strauss's claim to stand apart from both Jerusalem and Athens and to remain an attentive interpreter of each to the other was an echo of Rosenzweig's argument that the modern Jew is torn between two homelands (*Zweistromland*), between faith and reason, law and philosophy, *Deutschtum* and *Judentum*.[49]

Rosenzweig's "new thinking" exercised a profound influence on Strauss. By this term Rosenzweig meant to signal a type of thinking that would be neither philosophical nor theological, but both together. The new thinking, so called, formed the basis of both the Jewish existentialism of Rosenzweig and its opposite, the atheistic existentialism of Heidegger. Which was right? Heidegger's continued use of the language of fallenness, guilt, and conscience showed an unwitting dependence on theological categories. This seems to make Rosenzweig a more reliable guide to the new thinking. Yet, as Strauss relates, the new thinking was the product of the subjectivist philosophies of Kierkegaard and Nietzsche. Rosenzweig allowed his own subjective experience to determine which elements of orthodoxy he would either accept or reject, thus turning it into a matter of free choice. For Strauss, this brought out the inadequacy of Rosenzweig's experiential approach to the Torah: it had to be a matter of all or nothing. The new thinking thus remained as external to orthodoxy as the old thinking. Rosenzweig admitted as much: he described his opus the *Star of Redemption* (1921) not as a Jewish book but as a "system of philosophy."[50]

There was a further danger to the new thinking that Strauss addresses at the very end of his preface to Spinoza. The attempt to validate orthodoxy on the basis of free choice or experience could not guarantee the victory of Jewish orthodoxy. Rather it could validate only a groundless existential commitment or what came to be called "decisionism." "The victory of orthodoxy through the self-destruction of rational philosophy was not an unmitigated blessing," Strauss wrote. He worried that the return to orthodoxy unbounded by reason would sanction the emergence of new forms of irrationalism and fanatical obscurantisms.

"Other observations and experiences confirmed the suspicion that it would be unwise to say farewell to reason" he warned.[51] It was this self-destruction of the tradition of modern rationalism in particular that led Strauss to consider a return to pre-modern, medieval Jewish rationalism.

A RETURN TO ORTHODOXY?

On the basis of his survey of the currents of modern Jewish thought – Cohenian neo-Kantianism, Zionism, Rosenzweig's "new thinking" – Strauss considered anew the ground of orthodoxy. It was in this context that he put forward what at first appeared a fantastic thought-experiment – namely, the return to "medieval rationalism," a term Strauss coined to describe the Maimonidean Enlightenment. In what did this consist?

Strauss's discovery of medieval rationalism meant returning to the traditional or at least the pre-modern meaning of revelation. Works like Maimonides' *Guide of the Perplexed* were not philosophical books in the manner of Spinoza's *Ethics* or Rosenzweig's *Star*. The former were Jewish books insofar as they accepted the primacy of revelation as their absolute point of departure. In contrast to the moderns, who regard revelation as a subject for the "philosophy of religion," Strauss sees it as a branch of law. The prophet, in its original meaning, is a lawgiver, and prophecy is the purest science of the law. The prophet is the creator of the moral and political community within which philosophy is even possible. "The philosopher," he writes, "is dependent on Revelation as truly as he is a man, for as a man he is a political being thus in need of a law."[52] It follows, then, that revelation belongs to the study of political science. Strauss's awareness of the primacy of politics was the first fruit of his turn to medieval rationalism.

It is often claimed that the centrality Strauss accorded to politics was the result of the influence of Carl Schmitt's *Concept of the Political* (1923) with its picture of humanity divided into hostile camps of "friend and enemy" struggling over matters of ultimate consequence.[53] This is false. It was not through Schmitt but from the reading of Maimonides and the medieval Arabic *falasifa* that Strauss came to his awareness of the primacy of the political. Strauss read Maimonides first and foremost as a Platonist rather than an Aristotelian. This distinction, easy to overlook, had profound implications. Aristotle is identified with the complete freedom of philosophizing, while Platonic philosophy, even though it is also committed to the freedom of philosophizing, always takes place within a legal context, within a community bound by law.

"Socratic questioning regarding the right way of life," Strauss wrote in an early essay, "is a communal questioning (*Zusammenfragen*) regarding the right way of living together (*des rechten Zusammenlebens*)." Socratic political philosophy is essentially political ("Das Fragen des Sokrates ist wesentlich *politisch*").[54] This Platonic requirement was only fulfilled by the medieval Judeo-Arabic philosophers, who sought to justify philosophy from within the context of the revealed law.

At least two consequences follow from this discovery. The first is his assertion of the fundamental difference between revelation-as-politics and philosophy. Unlike his senior colleague, Julius Guttmann (1880–1950), who understood the purpose of revelation as the vehicle for the communication of truth, Strauss understood it as the proclamation of law.[55] This put him deeply at odds with those interpreters who stressed the unity, or at least the compatibility, of faith and reason. The belief in the unity of faith and reason is evidence of a "Thomistic" tendency that may hold true for Christian thought, but does not hold for the Judeo-Arabic writers. In fact, Strauss's discovery of Avicenna's statement that "the teaching of prophecy and the Divine Law is contained in [Plato's] *Laws*" contains his first and decisive inkling that theology means fundamentally political theology.[56]

The second consequence of Strauss's return to Maimonides and the medieval Enlightenment appears to be merely a literary problem. This concerns the complex and often ambiguous manner of writing in which the ancient and medieval writers chose to reveal, or rather conceal, their deepest and most important teachings from public scrutiny. This doctrine of esotericism or the "double truth" had certainly been noted by Strauss's scholarly predecessors, but none had accorded it the centrality that Strauss attributed to it. Unlike the modern Enlightenment that set itself the task of removing prejudices and undermining foundations, "a race in which he wins who offers the smallest security and the greatest terror" – a kind of race to the abyss – Strauss found in the medieval Enlightenment a different mode of philosophy, one that set out not to destroy society but to maintain religion's political role while indicating obliquely that which favors philosophy.[57]

Strauss's study of the medieval Enlightenment led him to a new understanding of the political. The word "political" as a modifier of philosophy can be understood in two ways.[58] It can designate a distinct branch of philosophy alongside ethics, logic, and metaphysics or it can designate an attribute of all philosophy. Every philosopher insofar as he desires to communicate to others does so in a way that must take into account the political situation of philosophy, what can be said and what needs to be concealed. It is in this sense of the term "political" that one can speak of the primacy of political philosophy. Such a strategy was undertaken in the past in part out of a need to avoid persecution at the hands of society, but more seriously out of the desire to safeguard society from the dangerous, even malignant, truths to which philosophy adheres. The medieval Enlighteners took upon themselves the paradoxical task of protecting society from themselves. It was as a result of their highly elliptical manner of writing that Strauss developed a hermeneutic of his own, characterized by "a scrupulous, almost pathological attention to detail" down to the smallest words and articles as containing clues to the deep structure of an author's thought.[59]

Strauss regarded this recovery of the esoteric tradition in Judaism not only as a historical or philological finding, but as a key to his own understanding of orthodoxy. By orthodoxy, Strauss did not mean the black hat Haredi community that lives in sections of Crown Heights or Borough Park in Brooklyn. Orthodoxy does not refer to the Naturei Karta ("Watchers of the City of Jerusalem") or Agudat Israel, but to a "Maimonidean" strategy that professes outward fidelity to the law and the community of Israel, with an inward or private commitment to philosophy and a life of free inquiry. This dual strategy allows one to maintain respect for, even love of, the tradition as a prophylactic to the alternatives of atheism and assimilation. The doctrine of the double truth remains the only way of preserving the viability of Judaism in a post-Nietzschean world that demands intellectual probity at all costs.

It is almost impossible not to read Strauss's understanding of orthodoxy as intended to apply to the situation of contemporary Jewry. To be sure, fundamental differences exist between the twelfth-century and the twentieth-century theologico-political predicaments. To state only the most obvious, we no longer occupy a world where the primacy of revelation and the immortality of the soul are taken for granted. For this very reason it has been a source of deep consternation for some readers that Strauss decided to imitate Maimonides by adopting similar modes of expression and practicing the same reticence and deliberate caution in an altogether different world. Why? What purpose could this serve in the modern "disenchanted world"? Strauss's defense of orthodoxy as little more than a Platonic noble lie – a "heroic delusion" he once called it – violates the one cardinal rule we expect from philosophers: intellectual honesty.[60]

People who live in glass houses should not throw stones. Strauss, who took such evident glee in exposing others, cannot in good conscience complain when the same trick is played on him. Does Strauss's defense of orthodoxy as civil theology escape the problem that he so ably diagnosed in others? Does his attempt to turn orthodoxy into a legal fiction fulfill the basic requirement of his hermeneutic method: to understand the thought of the past as it understood itself? Or does he import a kind of neo-Maimonideanism, even Averroism, into his understanding of orthodoxy? Gershom Scholem may have been correct when he wrote to Walter Benjamin about Strauss's bid for a chair in Jewish studies at the Hebrew University that "only three people at the very most will make use of the freedom to vote for the appointment of an atheist to a teaching position that serves to endorse the philosophy of religion."[61]

Notes

1. Leo Strauss, "Why We Remain Jews: Can Jewish Faith and History Still Speak to Us?" *Jewish Philosophy and the Crisis of Modernity*, ed. Kenneth Hart Green (Albany: SUNY Press, 1997), 312.

2. For some attempts to put Strauss in a Jewish context, see Alan Udoff, ed., *Leo Strauss's Thought: Towards a Critical Engagement* (Boulder: Lynne Rienner, 1991); Kenneth Hart Green, *Jew and Philosopher: The Return to Maimonides in the Jewish Thought of Leo Strauss* (Albany: SUNY Press, 1993); Kenneth L. Deutsch and Walter Nicgorski, eds., *Leo Strauss: Political Philosopher and Jewish Thinker* (Lanham, MD: Rowman & Littlefield, 1994); Steven B. Smith, *Reading Leo Strauss: Politics, Philosophy, Judaism* (Chicago: University of Chicago Press, 2006).

3. Information about Strauss's biography has been culled from different sources, among them Leo Strauss and Jacob Klein, "A Giving of Accounts," *Jewish Philosophy and the Crisis of Modernity*, 457–64; "Why We Remain Jews," 311–29; and the "Preface to Spinoza's Critique of Religion," *Liberalism Ancient and Modern* (New York: Basic Books, 1968), 224–59. Regarding his preface to the Spinoza book, Gershom Scholem wrote the following to Strauss: "Have no doubt you have my blessing and most likely I will form with maybe five or six other readers what might hardly attain to a Hessian minyan, the only legitimate nucleus of readers for this opuscule. For you should not have any illusions that these pages will be practically impenetrable to American readers. Naturally, if an institution exists that is willing to publish it, then let it be praised. What amazes me is that you are actually prepared to put these sentences on paper." Letter from Scholem, December 13, 1962, in *Leo Strauss Gesammelte Schriften*, vol. 3, *Hobbes' politische Wissenschaft und zugehörige Schriften – Briefe*, ed. Heinrich Meier (Stuttgart: Metzler, 2001), 749; my translation.

4. A growing literature has developed around Strauss's so-called Weimar years, among which see David Biale, "Leo Strauss: The Philosopher as Weimar Jew," *Leo Strauss's Thought*, 31–40; David Janssens, "Questions and Caves: Philosophy, Politics, and History in Leo Strauss's Early Work," *The Journal of Jewish Thought and Philosophy*, 10 (2000): 111–44;

166   *Steven B. Smith*

Michael Zank, "Introduction," *Leo Strauss: The Early Writings (1921–1932)*, trans. Michael Zank (Albany: SUNY, 2002), 3–49. Similar attention should be paid to the New York years, where Strauss first perfected his manner of "close reading" and his attention to the distinction between ancients and moderns.

5. Strauss, "Preface to Spinoza's Critique of Religion," 224.
6. Leo Strauss, *Philosophy and Law: Essays Toward the Understanding of Maimonides and his Predecessors*, trans. Fred Baumann (Philadelphia: Jewish Publication Society, 1987), 3–20.
7. Strauss, *Philosophy and Law*, 7.
8. Leo Strauss, "On the Interpretation of Genesis," *Jewish Philosophy and the Crisis of Modernity*, 373; see also Leo Strauss, *On Tyranny Including the Strauss-Kojève Correspondence*, eds. Victor Gourevitch and Michael S. Roth (Chicago: University of Chicago Press, 2000) 191.
9. Strauss, *Philosophy and Law*, 14.
10. Leo Strauss, "Preface to Hobbes Politische Wissenschaft," *Jewish Philosophy and the Crisis of Modernity*, 453: "The reawakening of theology, which for me is marked by the names of Karl Barth and Franz Rosenzweig, appeared to make it necessary to investigate how far the critique of orthodox theology – Jewish and Christian – deserved to be victorious." For the reawakening of this Counter-Enlightenment theology, see Mark Lilla, *The Stillborn God: Religion and the Modern Experiment* (New York: Knopf, 2007).
11. The importance of Nietzsche for Strauss is frequently acknowledged and easily overstated. In a letter to Karl Löwith, Strauss remarked: "Nietzsche so dominated and charmed me between my 22nd and 30th years that I literally believed everything I understood of him," in "Correspondence of Karl Löwith and Leo Strauss," *Independent Journal of Philosophy* 5/6 (1988): 183. Readers who rely on this letter often overlook the fact that Strauss goes on to reproach Löwith for failing to see Nietzsche's faults. For the claim that Strauss was a secret Nietzschean, see Laurence Lampert, *Leo Strauss and Nietzsche* (Chicago: University of Chicago Press, 1996).
12. Strauss, *Philosophy and Law*, 19.
13. See letter from Strauss to Kojève (early 1930s, undated), *On Tyranny*, 222: "we have the wonderful English breakfast – the hams taste too good as to consist of pork, and therefore they are allowed by the Mosaic law according to atheistic interpretation."
14. Strauss, "Preface to Spinoza's Critique of Religion," 231.
15. See Leo Strauss, "Jerusalem and Athens: Some Preliminary Reflections," *Studies in Platonic Political Philosophy*, ed. Thomas Pangle (Chicago: University of Chicago Press, 1983), 147–73; "Progress or Return," *Jewish Philosophy and the Crisis of Modernity*, 87–136; "On the Interpretation of Genesis," 359–76.
16. Strauss, "Progress or Return," 116.
17. Strauss, "Progress or Return," 111–12.
18. Strauss, "Jerusalem and Athens," 165–66; *Philosophy and Law*, 108 where Strauss quotes Cohen: "All honor to the god of Aristotle; but he is truly not the God of Israel."

19. Leo Strauss, *Natural Right and History* (Chicago: University of Chicago Press, 1953), 74–6.
20. Strauss, "Progress or Return," 108–09.
21. Strauss, "Progress or Return," 105–06.
22. Strauss, "Progress or Return," 116.
23. This chapter is being written during the 350th anniversary (1656) of the excommunication of Spinoza; for some recent discussions of Spinoza's heresy, see Yirmiyahu Yovel, *Spinoza and Other Heretics: The Marrano of Reason* (Princeton: Princeton University Press, 1989); Steven B. Smith, *Spinoza, Liberalism, and the Question of Jewish Identity* (New Haven: Yale University Press, 1997); Steven Nadler, *Spinoza's Heresy: Immortality and the Jewish Mind* (Oxford: Oxford University Press, 2004).
24. Leo Strauss, "Introductory Essay to Hermann Cohen's 'Religion of Reason out of the Sources of Judaism,'" *Studies in Platonic Political Philosophy*, 233.
25. Hermann Cohen, "Spinoza über Staat und Religion, Judentum und Christentum," *Jüdische Schriften*, ed. Bruno Strauss (Berlin: Schwetschke, 1924), vol. 3: 360–61, 363–64, 370–72; for an excellent account of Cohen's Spinoza critique, see Ernst Simon, "Zu Hermann Cohens Spinoza Auffassung," *Monatsschrift für Geschiche und Wissenschaft des Judentums* 79 (1935): 181–94; Franz Nauen, "Hermann Cohen's Perceptions of Spinoza: A Reappraisal," *AJS Review* 4 (1979): 111–24.
26. Leo Strauss, "Cohens Analyse der Bibel-Wissenschaft Spinozas," in *Gesammelte Schriften*, vol. 1, *Die Religionskritik Spinozas und zugehörige Schriften*, ed. Heinrich Meier (Stuttgart: Metzler, 1996), 363–86; trans. Michael Zank, "Cohen's Analysis of Spinoza's Bible Science," *The Early Writings*, 139–72.
27. Strauss, "Preface to Spinoza's Critique of Religion," 257.
28. Strauss, "Cohen's Analysis," 143, 148, 152, 159.
29. Strauss, "Cohen's Analysis," 144.
30. Strauss, "Jerusalem and Athens," 168.
31. Strauss, "Cohen's Analysis," 158.
32. Leo Strauss, "Das Testament Spinozas," *Gesammelte Schriften*, vol. 1: 414–22; trans. Michael Zank, "The Testament of Spinoza," *The Early Writings*, 216–23.
33. Strauss, "The Testament of Spinoza," 219.
34. Strauss, "The Testament of Spinoza," 220; the phrase "good European" comes from Friedrich Nietzsche, *Beyond Good and Evil*, trans. Walter Kaufmann (New York: Vintage, 1966), Preface.
35. Baruch Spinoza, *Theologico-Political Treatise*, trans. Samuel Shirley (Indianapolis: Hackett, 1998), 42.
36. Strauss, "The Testament of Spinoza," 221.
37. Smith, *Spinoza, Liberalism, and Jewish Identity*, 101–03.
38. Strauss, "Spinoza's Testament," 222.
39. Leo Strauss, "An Introduction to Heideggerian Existentialism," *The Rebirth of Classical Political Rationalism*, ed. Thomas Pangle (Chicago: University of Chicago Press, 1989), 31.
40. Strauss, "A Giving of Accounts," 460.

41. Leo Strauss, "Der Zionismus bei Nordau," *Gesammelte Schriften*, vol. 2, *Philosophie und Gesetz – Frühe Schriften*, ed. Heinrich Meier (Stuttgart: Metzler, 1997), 320; trans. Michael Zank, "The Zionism of Nordau," *The Early Writings*, 87.
42. Strauss, "The Zionism of Nordau," 87.
43. Leo Strauss, "Letter to the Editor," *Jewish Philosophy and the Crisis of Modernity*, 414.
44. Strauss, "Preface to Spinoza's Critique of Religion," 229–30; "Why We Remain Jews," 319–20; for the varieties of messianic Judaisms, see Aviezer Ravitzky, *Messianism, Zionism, and Jewish Religious Radicalism*, trans. Michael Swirsky and Jonathan Chipman (Chicago: University of Chicago Press, 1996).
45. Strauss, "Why We Remain Jews," 327.
46. Strauss, "Preface to Spinoza's Critique of Religion," 229.
47. Strauss, "Preface to Spinoza's Critique of Religion," 230.
48. Strauss, "Heideggerian Existentialism," 28.
49. Franz Rosenzweig, *The Star of Redemption*, trans. William Hallo (Notre Dame: University of Notre Dame Press, 1985), part 3; see also Paul Mendes-Flohr, *German Jews: A Dual Identity* (New Haven: Yale University Press, 1999), 66–88; Peter Eli Gordon, *Rosenzweig and Heidegger: Between Judaism and German Philosophy* (Berkeley: University of California Press, 2005), 132–41.
50. Strauss, "Preface to Spinoza's Critique of Religion," 237.
51. Strauss, "Preface to Spinoza's Critique of Religion," 256–57.
52. Strauss, *Philosophy and Law*, 51; Guttman's reply to Strauss was not published during his lifetime, but for a useful analysis of the debate, see Eliezer Schweid, "Religion and Philosophy: The Scholarly-Theological Debate Between Julius Guttmann and Leo Strauss," *Maimonidean Studies*, vol. 1, ed. Arthur Hyman (New York: Yeshiva University Press, 1990), 163–95.
53. The most thorough account of the Strauss-Schmitt connection is Heinrich Meier, *Carl Schmitt and Leo Strauss: The Hidden Dialogue*, trans. Harvey Lomax (Chicago: University of Chicago Press, 1995); the influence of Schmitt is usually trotted out by those who want to tar Strauss with the brush of Schmitt's later National Socialism; for an example of this, see John McCormick, "Introduction" to Carl Schmitt, *Legality and Legitimacy*, trans. Jeffrey Seitzer (Durham: Duke University Press, 2004), xlii–xliii.
54. Leo Strauss, "Cohen und Maimuni," *Gesammelte Schriften*, vol. 2: 412; for the importance of this early work for Strauss, see Janssens, "Questions and Caves." 111–44; Corine Pelluchon, *Une autre raison, d'autres lumières. Essai sur la crise de la rationalité contemporaine* (Paris: Vrin, 2005), 129–57.
55. Strauss, *Philosophy and Law*, 52.
56. Strauss, *Philosophy and Law*, 101; Leo Strauss, *The Argument and Action of Plato's 'Laws'* (Chicago: University of Chicago Press, 1975), 1.
57. Strauss, "Preface to Spinoza's Critique of Religion," 235.
58. Strauss, "Cohen und Maimuni," 412–13.

59. Rémi Brague, "Strauss and Maimonides," *Leo Strauss's Thought*, 97.

60. For Strauss's views on the social responsibility of philosophers, see *Persecution and the Art of Writing* (Chicago: University of Chicago Press, 1980), 17–19, 33–37; *On Tyranny*, 205–06.

61. Letter to Walter Benjamin, March 29, 1935 in *The Correspondence of Gershom Scholem and Walter Benjamin, 1932–1940*, trans. Gary Smith and André Lefèvre (New York: Schocken, 1989), 157.

9 Messianism and Modern Jewish Philosophy
PIERRE BOURETZ

We raise a question that is anything but self-evident. As an initial step, both sides of the "and" in our title must first be scrutinized. On one side, two main misunderstandings have to be removed concerning Messianism. The notion can be taken in a purely metaphorical sense; hence, for example, Marxism can be considered a messianic phenomenon inasmuch as it includes an utopian view of the best society. But, even while each one of the numerous forms of messianism incorporates utopian elements, every utopia is not by itself messianic. Alternatively, there is the risk of obsessing over the diverse contents of the very words – "messianism," "messiah," or "messianic" – in order to bring forth the underlying idea. At issue is a combination of discontent vis-à-vis the current world and a preoccupation in favour of a future inspired by the Jewish conception of redemption.

On the other side of the "and" is the existence of a "Jewish philosophy," which can be neither presupposed nor simply proven. The field of our inquiry is the encounter between philosophy as such and Jewish tradition, two more or less conflicting discourses about the truth, each one expressed through a particular language belonging to a specific history. Before explaining how this encounter with respect to Messianism does exist and what it means, we must ask when, where, and why it has been possible.

Answering the first of these three questions requires taking into account opposite relations between philosophy and Jewish tradition during the medieval and modern ages. At the time of Maimonides, philosophy was regarded as an intruder, an alien element whose introduction into the tradition was controversial. The conflict between philosophy and the Jewish tradition was mostly focussed on the question of creation versus the eternity of the world. Messianism was not seen as the key issue. The chief concern was to codify the beliefs about the coming of the Messiah in order to allay people's anxiety and impatience. In the framework of modernity, however, it is Law that has become external to Reason, and the major theological categories nowadays stay with contrasting statuses: creation is irrelevant from the point of view of science, and philosophy seems recurrently embarrassed about the idea of revelation. Redemption appears to be less uncomfortable; it is puzzling enough to impress even the most unreligious minds. However paradoxical it might seem, Messianism is perhaps more accessible to philosophical speculation today than it has ever been in the past.

In modern times, the specific location for the most fruitful encounter between philosophy and the Jewish tradition has been Germany, for many reasons that deserve explanation. It is due first and foremost to the particular historical situation of German Judaism – between French Judaism, which was too much involved with assimilation to question seriously its dilemma, and Eastern Judaism, which was still confined within "the magic circle of tradition."[1] Brief biographical sketches demonstrate this point: Leo Strauss, for example, in reflecting upon his youth, characterized his experience "in the grips of the theologico-political predicament," stressing at the same time the precarious social position of the Jews and their ambiguous relation to the tradition.[2] When judging the phenomenon of assimilation, Gershom Scholem was more severe: he recalled a "desire for self-relinquishment" and a capacity for "self-deception" bordering on self-hatred.[3] A term created for his diary (November 1916) perfectly summarizes his profound repulsion towards the alleged "German-Jewish symbiosis": *Golusjudentum* (*Galut*, or, exile Judaism). His feelings reflect a combination of amazement and shame about exile much like that depicted by Franz Kafka's *Letter to the Father*.[4] For Kafka and Scholem alike, the rediscovery of Judaism was similar to a revolt of sons against their fathers' generation, a revolt inspired by what Heine named *himmlische Heimweh* (a heavenly homesickness) and a "desire for Jerusalem." Kafka, in depicting "true men of the transition," captured the experience of Jews writing in German with this poignant image: "[T]heir hind legs were still stuck to their father's Judaism and their forelegs were unable to find new ground."[5] Scholem, more strongly still, regarded the whole of German Judaism as a "wasteland."[6]

To appreciate how powerful was the temptation to immerse oneself in German society and to understand what the "return" should have meant, the most evocative evidence derives from the biography of Franz Rosenzweig, between the time when he planned to become a Christian, considering that "there did not seem to be any place for Judaism," and the moment of his decision to "remain a Jew."[7] An aura of mystery surrounds his night-long conversation with Eugen Rosenstock on July 7,

1913, in Leipzig. His later report of this event characterizes the occurrence as the experience of a double-bind. Rosenzweig's account makes clear what would occur later: his own "faith in philosophy" characterized by relativism had been attacked step by step by Rosenstock's "faith based on revelation." But Rosenzweig's Judaism was at this point still quite fragile, and he could not be prevented from considering conversion as the price of his new conviction. The consolidation of his Jewish identity through a fierce epistolary confrontation three years later would lead him eventually to a "new thinking" that would contest the entire history of philosophy "from Thales to Hegel."[8]

The exchange between Franz Rosenzweig and Eugen Rosenstock epitomizes the theological substratum of a long-term German-Jewish confrontation. Rosenstock wrote: "He [the Jew] is a paragraph of the Law, *c'est tout*" / "The synagogue has been talking for two thousand years about what she had, because she really has absolutely nothing" (Rosenstock, October 30, 1916). To this, Rosenzweig replied: "It lies within my power to determine whether I as an individual take upon myself the metaphysical destiny, 'the yoke of the Kingdom of Heaven,' to which I have been called from my birth" (Rosenzweig, November 8, 1916). "To the 'naïve' laying claim to an inalienable right before God corresponds, you forget, just as naive a taking up of a yoke of inalienable sufferings, which we – 'naively' – know is laid upon us . . . 'for the redemption of the world'" (Rosenzweig, November 7, 1916).[9]

Yet Rosenzweig would never wholly repudiate whatever a "symbiosis" between German and Jewish cultures might provide. He continued until his death to imagine at the very least an elective affinity between the two: "let us be Germans and Jews, both together, without being preoccupied by the *and*, without speaking too much about it, but truly *both*."[10] Even more striking, perhaps, he proclaimed of his major book: "*The Star* will one day be considered for good reasons as a gift the German spirit would owe to its Jewish enclave."[11] This approximates Scholem's later statement of dissatisfaction with the translation of the Bible realized by Buber and Rosenzweig, which Scholem called "a kind of *Gastgeschenk* [guest's gift] which German Jewry gave to the German people, a symbolic act of gratitude upon departure."[12]

Franz Rosenzweig's intimate adventure is like a primal scene of what could be called the *Teshuvah* (both "return" and "repentance") of German Judaism. Furthermore, his intellectual experience helps us to understand why a critical encounter between philosophy and Jewish tradition would probably have been impossible anywhere else but in Germany. According to his own account, the new thinking had been conceived in the effort to triumph over relativism, while Scholem, alluding to the celebrated allegory of the four Sages going through Paradise, suggests that he had entered "the magical circle" of German idealism before leaving it safe and sound.[13] More generally, one could say that what Scholem had discovered was the human cost of the "disenchantment of the world" and the philosophical costs of nihilism.

In this chapter, I shall explain what was required to confront this darker aspect of Western modernity, how some elements of Jewish Messianism might have been helpful, and why the thinkers who have devoted themselves to such a task might well be called "witnesses for the future."[14] In brief, from a philosophical point of view, three classic statements express what was to be challenged: The first is Hegel's request to renounce thinking what the world ought to be, and to assign philosophy a purely retrospective task, of painting reality "grey in grey," as if history could be understood "only with the falling of the dusk."[15] The second is Nietzsche's announcement concerning God's death. Third is Heidegger's interpretation of that same assertion as indicating a definitive erasure of the supra-sensible world.[16]

We must now investigate one side of our question with greater precision. Because of its clashing components, the messianic idea has always evoked disquiet within the Jewish tradition. Its source could be located in an acutely ambiguous prediction from the Talmud: "The son of David will come only in a generation that is either altogether righteous or altogether wicked" (*Sanhedrin*, 98a). Needless to say, such a paradoxical conjecture is akin to a bombshell, and it is all the more threatening insofar as there exists in the same literature forecasts corroborating each one of the two facets, decency or iniquity: "(the Messiah will come) today, if ye will hear his voice" / "Jerusalem shall be redeemed only by righteousness"; and "in the generation when the Messiah comes, young men will insult the old, and old men will stand before the young" / "the people shall be dog-faced, and a son will not be abashed in his father's presence. . . . "

In his own discussion of messianic doctrines, Gershom Scholem proposed several typologies that differentiated them according to their distinctive impacts upon Jewish history. These typologies can be reduced to a key antagonism, as summarized in an essay from 1919, between two theoretically and historically opposed forms of messianism. On the one hand, there is a "revolutionary" messianism (as illustrated by the war between Gog and Magog, a conflict that would pave the way to a Last Judgment and the end of the world); and, on the other hand, there is an "evolutionary" (*verwandelnde*) messianism, which neutralizes that image of conflict and in its stead proposed an idea of purification.[17] Scholem's later statements, whatever their variations, reiterate this basic antagonism as the most dramatic and consequential rift in Jewish thought. From a theological point of view, Scholem foregrounds two main conflicts: between (1) "apocalyptic tendencies and those aiming at their abolition," and (2) between "restorative" and "utopian" outlooks.[18] Sometimes, he superimposes a social aspect on this tension: Thus, in depicting the background of the Sabbatai Zevi episode, Scholem contrasts a popular tradition nourished by myths with a strictly rational one associated with a philosophical elite.[19] Finally, in his most comprehensive essay on the subject, Scholem emphasizes a kind of Messianism related to this striking characterization of redemption: "a transcendence breaking in upon history, an intrusion in which history itself perishes, transformed in its ruins because it is struck by a beam of light shining into it from an outside source."[20]

Scholem remained somewhat vague about what should be considered the "utopian" elements in Messianism. Indeed, he came close to denying their effectiveness other than in the apocalyptic-catastrophic doctrines.[21] Because our own task is to identify those messianic concepts that left the strongest impression upon modern philosophy, we need first to refine Scholem's typology. Let us assume from the outset that every Messianism is familiar with the concept of utopia. We can therefore distinguish two major conceptions: The first involves some kind of rationalization of the idea of the future. The second takes cognizance of its erratic quality, and resorts to images of catastrophe or apocalypse. In more metaphorical terms, such a distinction suggests two contrasting ways of construing the traditional imagery of the "light of the Messiah." The image can be understood either as: a star shining faraway but guiding men looking forward to an age of peace and wisdom; or as a flash of lightning that breaks in upon the temporal course of events without any predictable outcome. At the heart of this contrast lies a basic debate concerning the character of the future as utopia.

Maimonides has been perhaps Judaism's most trustworthy advocate for the first conception. In a major text on the subject, he observed: "To believe that the Messiah will come and not to consider him late (...); set no time limit for his coming (and) do not make conjectures based on Scripture to conclude when (he) will come." Scholem is incontestably right when he notes that such an injunction neutralizes the apocalyptic aspect of Messianism. Yet we should also recognize that Maimonides takes into consideration what looks like a double future incorporated in a renowned Talmudic statement: "All the prophets prophesied only in respect of the Messianic era; but as for the World to Come, *the eye hath not seen, O Lord, beside thee"* (*Sanhedrin*, 99a). Maimonides explained this difference by reducing the messianic epoch properly understood to be the recovery of political freedom and the attainment of peace. And there is no doubt that his primary concern was to prevent his people from becoming frustrated with a repeatedly delayed event. Yet the notion of a World to Come seems to imply a post-messianic time, and it suggests that Maimonides, too, distinguished between the two concepts of utopia.

The second, apocalyptic-catastrophic tradition is more difficult to identify, precisely because it is by definition associated with recurrently concealed events and is transmitted through a marginal or even secret literature. One can wonder whether the Lurianic Kabbalah should be included. What is noteworthy is its sophisticated way of interpreting history from the beginning (Creation) to the end (Redemption) as the narrative of an exile of the divinity into the world. Although this is not per se associated with images of dissolution or devastation preceding the coming of the Messiah, we know from Scholem that this interpretation assumed inspirational power especially during times of dereliction. Particularly following the disastrous failure of the Sabbatian adventure, it served as a convenient means for fashioning paradoxical ideas such as that of "redemption through sin."[22]

Thanks to its astonishing diversity, the messianic idea has indeed exerted a strong influence upon the most prominent figures in modern Jewish philosophy, such as Hermann Cohen, Franz Rosenzweig, Walter Benjamin, Ernst Bloch, and Emmanuel Levinas. The philosophers we will take into consideration here are obviously less concerned about the troubles related to a long desired and long delayed event than they are concerned to find notions or images within that messianic legacy that might be deployed so as to challenge philosophical systems obstructing the future. The Hegelian philosophy is for this reason crucial. Twentieth-century philosophers attempting to restore this dimension of human experience could hardly avoid a confrontation with Hegel's legacy. Yet the problem with Hegel has to be precisely established, which is possible by looking to some of his early writings (as Franz Rosenzweig himself did).[23] Some of these texts show evidence of a theological hostility toward the Jewish people. In one, Hegel describes Abraham as spurning the "beautiful relationships of his youth" in order to submit himself and his descendants to the external law of a "jealous God."[24] In another one, Hegel speaks of a "mania for segregation" and denounces a pleasure to remain "on its solitary pinnacle."[25] Elsewhere he stigmatises Judaism with an "ineffective messianic hope," by which he means a longing for the recovery of freedom unable to achieve its end.[26] Nevertheless, such a manifest lack of sympathy for Judaism might not be the key issue.

Through a scrupulous reconstruction of the inner movement of Hegel's thought from the beginning, Franz Rosenzweig's *Hegel und der Staat* shows how such writings consist of embryonic forms of the mature philosophy, like this proposition, which metaphorically formulates the Hegelian project as it will progressively be realized: "to vindicate, as human property, the treasures formerly squandered on heaven."[27] In Bern around 1795, such a claim expressed a wish to reject monotheism at large, insofar as it involved submitting men to the externally imposed law of Abraham's God. At that time, Hegel was seized by a nostalgia for the Greek religion, which he construed as harmonious with the everyday life of free citizens. But he would quickly come to conceive his philosophical problem differently, and discover a new solution in Christianity. By 1800, he had arrived at the following question: how can a division generated by the Jewish Law be overcome so as to promote a "reconciliation" (*Versöhnung*) with the world? The solution was conceived by reconsidering the historical foundations of Christian experience, now conceived as a dialectical process that opened with the annihilation of an initial beautiful unity, proceeded through a moment of warlike division, and continued onward via a movement of sublation (*Aufhebung*), thus achieving the ultimate reconciliation.

When describing the genesis of Hegel's thought from the inside, Rosenzweig sought to identify what is wrong in such a final system by differentiating the various levels of the anticipated "reconciliation" between the individual and the State; the Spirit and the world; the Heaven and and the Earth. First of all, Rosenzweig declared, Hegel's political philosophy calls for the sacrifice of individual freedom on the altar of a State magnified as the rational expression of a conflictual civil society. More consequential is the meaning of Hegel's pronouncement of the end of History: philosophy is but a retrospective Reason; the world as it runs must be recognized as the whole of human life. Last is the meaning of a presumed identity between the real and the rational: the withdrawal of the future as the proper time of hope and thus the deletion of messianic perspective. These discoveries might very well have inaugurated the philosophical twentieth century.

If we follow Rosenzweig's example of looking back to "1800" as inaugurating a genuine epoch of Western culture symbolized by Goethe and Hegel, one might think about 1918 as being at the same time the end of an age of philosophy and the beginning of a new one: as if the war had definitively made the Hegelian system irrelevant in a Germany similar to a "field of ruins."[28] Three major books published around this date confirm such a hypothesis, all of them related to some form of struggle against Hegel imbued with fragments of Jewish messianism: Hermann Cohen's *Religion of Reason*, Franz Rosenzweig's *Star of Redemption*, and Ernst Bloch's *Spirit of Utopia*.

At first glance, Hermann Cohen's position seems self-evident. He was philosophically immunized against Hegel's system and its consequences by Kantianism, but socially and politically involved in the German-Jewish "symbiosis." Hence, two conclusions follow – that Cohen's *Religion of Reason* proceeds from a "return" to Judaism, and that this book represents the modern version par excellence of the rational form of messianic utopia. But at least two of these claims call for serious examination. Asserting that Cohen's final thought results from a "great Teshuvah," Rosenzweig paradoxically forgets the crucial importance of the *Jüdische Schriften* of which he was in fact the editor.[29] For these three volumes are made up of around seventy texts, the first one being devoted as early as 1867 to "Heine und das Judentum," with many of the others enlightening both Cohen's enduring attachment to Jewish thought and his anxiety about the awkward situation of the Jews within modern societies. A further sort of commonplace about Cohen rests on the presumption that his attempt to promote a synthesis of Jewish tradition and German idealism is the intellectual manifestation of an unquestioned assimilation. No doubt Cohen saw himself as the Maimonides of his time, attempting to "harmonize" the prophetic message with Kant's philosophy, as did his predecessor with Aristotle. Nonetheless, some of his "Jewish" writings are clearly committed to challenging racial anti-Semitism or political animosity towards Jewish people, while at the same time the *Religion of Reason* clearly refutes classical allegations of deliberate self-isolation and more discretely criticizes Spinoza, considered as a denigrator of Jewish people.

As might be expected, Hermann Cohen's Messianism is a universalist one. It tends to erase the apocalyptic eschatology and to favor instead the traditional doctrine that bears greater affinity with the modern Enlightenment. From this point of view, Cohen's hero among the Prophets seems to be Isaiah, who enlarges the Covenant to all the nations prior to looking at the coming of the Messiah as opening an age of peace and wisdom, prefiguring the Kantian cosmopolitanism. This conception of Messianism includes a corollary that was unacceptable to young Zionists like Scholem: the Jewish people must come to terms with the loss of its state and the lack of political autonomy, Israel as a nation being "the mere symbol for the desired unity of mankind."[30] It must be added that such a view introduces an idea difficult to endorse after the destruction of the European Jews: "The historical suffering of Israel gives it its historical dignity, its tragic mission, which represents its share in the divine education of mankind."[31] Nevertheless, these assertions neither could nor would mask the almost revolutionary significance of Cohen's thought.

We must draw special attention to the structure of *Religion of Reason* at its midpoint. The two chapters devoted to Messianism (XIII and XIV) are preceded by another, dedicated to the Day of Atonement. Considering this festival as an anticipation of Redemption from the religious point of view and a symbol of the future among the categories of time, Cohen emphasizes the "only purely moral" aspect of the sins confessed, what it means that transgressions between man and man are more significant than the ones between man and God.[32] Linked to the conceptual distinction established earlier between "fellowman" (*Mitmensch*) and "next man" (*alter ego*), this statement leads to an argument that is the core of Cohen's philosophy: "The correlation of man and God cannot be actualised if the correlation of man and man is not first included."[33] Here it is critical to note what differentiates Cohen from Kant and how Cohen's thought opens horizons unknown to his predecessor. Cohen's religion is not confined "within the limits of reason alone," as it was more or less through his earlier *Begriff der Religion im System der Philosophie* (1915). Furthermore, less than an effort to demonstrate that the connection between man and God is reason, as was the Active Intellect for medieval philosophers inspired by Aristotle, Cohen's main concern, embodied in the concept of "correlation," is with man's ethical responsibility for the other fellow. From this point of view, Cohen's successor, more than Rosenzweig, is Emmanuel Levinas, who describes the face-to-face with the Other as instituting a transcendental relation to God that surmounts modern atheism.[34]

Finally, Cohen's decisive contribution to a modern recovery of Messianism coincides with his conception of its utopian aspect and the way in which it is conceived from the point of view of man's relation to the world and experience of time. We might be surprised by Cohen's claim that "messianism defies the whole present political actuality."[35] No doubt such a declaration grounds his distrust of Zionism, but it does have a very deep meaning, related to his philosophical rejection of eudemonism at large: "The messianic future is the first conscious expression of the opposition to moral values derived only from empirical sensibility."[36] In saying this, Cohen rejected the Hegelian idea of a reconciliation with the world and reintroduced the concept of the supra-sensible within contemporary thought. In this way, Cohen's conception of Messianism as promising the pure idea of the future permits an expansive vision of human experience, one no doubt inspired by Kant's notion of cosmopolitanism, but enriched also by the notion of a "World to Come," a notion substantially different from that of an age of "perpetual peace."

Dissatisfaction with the present world and attraction for a more or less undetermined future also characterize a strictly contemporary book: Ernst Bloch's *The Spirit of Utopia* (1918, 2nd ed. 1923). Readers familiar with Bloch may be puzzled over its appearance at this point in my discussion. As commonly perceived, many of Ernst Bloch's numerous works deal in many ways with questions related to Marxism, at least a heterodox one. However, it seems to me that his first book, which he never disowned, was premised on a Kantian critique of Hegel's philosophy, drafting a utopian point of view unconnected to materialism of any kind. Let us be attentive to this affirmation: "Hegel's theory that everything rational is already real concludes a premature and total truce with the world, but Kant's only approximative infinity of reason (...) makes of the world an ocean without a shore."[37] Asserting at a later point that in Hegel, "philosophy becomes a headmaster, or indiscriminate lawyer for the Being that hired him," whereas it was in Kant "a solitary light meant to burn up the night of this world," Bloch offers the most precise and profound formalization of the intellectual space in which a utopian Messianism should take place in times when metaphysics has long been declared irrelevant. This proposal may seem too defiant, but in its defense it must suffice to take note of Bloch's most thought-provoking category, "not-yet," which emerges from the chapter of *The Spirit of Utopia* entitled "The Shape of the Inconstruable Question," and which would eventually structure the whole of the later *Principle of Hope* (1953, 2nd ed. 1959). Alluding to something possible without being assured, the "not-yet" would appear to have its origins in the Kantian "as-if." But it may be perceived as more secretly echoing the metaphysical idea of the World to Come.

At this point, I must briefly clarify an option that might be discussed – to develop substantially the parallel of Rosenzweig's *Star of Redemption* with Levinas' *Totality and Infinity*.[38] One type of argument might be developed on the basis of Levinas' declaration about the considerable influence of Rosenzweig's book on his own. The ultimate argument rests, however, on the assumption that, because of their respective complexity, these two works enlighten one another. We thus turn to the last of the three books to which I propose to draw special attention – the one proclaiming the most resounding rupture with Hegel. Unlike Bloch, Rosenzweig does not enlist Kant, whom he considers to be the midwife to Hegel's concept of universal history, in this epoch-making struggle. The reason why the Hegelian system appears to be his main target is grounded on the conviction that, less than being the product of an individual philosopher's mind, this philosophical system is the culmination of the whole body of Western philosophy.[39]

Let us attempt to extract what is clear from what remains more ambiguous and consequently controversial in Rosenzweig's philosophical endeavour. One of the opening propositions of *The Star of Redemption* belongs to the first category: Western philosophy is a system of the "All," meaning that it has presupposed the unity of the logos, has been for a century devoted to a disputation between knowledge and belief, and reaches its goal when "the old quarrel seems settled, heaven and earth reconciled." The same with this reverse proposition: whatever its denomination, "a self-contained unity rebelled against this totality which encloses the All as a unity"; in front of the singular person's uniqueness, "the All can no longer claim to be all." Without any doubt, Rosenzweig takes seriously Hegel's allegation that his system accomplishes the oldest dream of philosophy. Yet Rosenzweig judges that such an achievement belongs henceforth to the past, his own task or the one of his epoch being to promote a "new thinking."[40] Most significant from our perspective is the description of the Jewish experience of the world and time as a quarrel with the experience of other peoples as subsumed into Hegel's philosophy of history. This figure is all the more fascinating insofar as it looks nearly systematic: other peoples are rooted in the earth, convinced that they are masters of time and confident about the ability of the state to guarantee their continuity; the Jewish people knows that the true nature of the state is war and its last word "violence," and it considers its own foremost ritual as an anticipation of redemption and the entire holy year as prefiguring eternity.

This feature, that knowingly counterbalances the individual-subjective aspect of Rosenzweig's "system," raises the difficult question of the status to be assigned to the irksome image of a blood-community. It is conversely clear that the Jewish people's exceptionality is neither rooted in an essential superiority nor due to historical precedence, but rather it refers to the idea of an "ontological priority" linked to "a privileged experience of eternity in the world."[41] Correlated with a desire to remain in the world, such a concept of redemption may look like what survives from Hegel into Rosenzweig's thought. It also determines Rosenzweig's historical-political conception of the Jewish people's destiny: if not assimilation to the nations, "dissimilation" among them, something that explains his mistrust of Zionism. Lastly, it yields a partially troubling interpretation of the messianic event: it may occur at any time, even "today," but it will concern nothing more than a "remnant" of Israel resulting from a process of "subtraction."[42]

Although less spectacular than Rosenzweig's rebuttal of Western philosophy, Levinas' philosophy might appear more radical in the strict sense of the word. From the very beginning, it was bound up with an ontology premised on the idea that war is "the pure experience of the pure being," an objective reality from which nobody could escape and which morality is unable to defeat. Its main concept is therefore the one of "totality," covering a process by which otherness is reduced to sameness. The opening pages of *Totality and Infinity* are devoted to contesting both the assumption and the result of such a conception of philosophy, perfectly accomplished through Hegel's system, whereas the major part of the book endeavours to promote an alternative view. Contrary to Rosenzweig, Levinas does not consider the individual's rebellion against totality as the trustworthy foundation of a new way of thinking, but at the same time he dislikes Heidegger's predilection for Angst and his novel project of ontology – the inquiry into Being. His disagreement with the former has to be related to an uncompromising commitment to the idea of alterity, which is the core of his own philosophy: far from being free, for example, from the point of view of moral autonomy, the subject is affected by an insomniac responsibility for the Other that makes him similar to a hostage.[43] But more closely linked to our issue, his discontent towards Heidegger authorizes him to go straight to the key point: rejecting ontology as such, Levinas puts forward the messianic concept of peace as the only one capable of weakening the system of Totality, one of his main philosophical purposes being to describe the human face as reflecting the infinite.

Levinas's idea of Messianism prompts us to the following remark (much as Scholem observed of Rosenzweig): even if the Levinasian idea is not identical to a pure revival of the classical-rational conception, at the very least it seems to erase the apocalyptic-catastrophic aspect of the phenomenon. This point deserves more precise consideration. If Rosenzweig's theory of Messianism is neither inspired by an ideal of contemplation nor enclosed within the vision of a historical accomplishment, the same is true concerning Levinas's. Scholem depicts Rosenzweig's idea perfectly: "The power of redemption seems to be built into the clockwork of life lived in the light of revelation, though more as restlessness than as potential destructiveness."[44] Levinas' position may look more complex. Emphasizing the endless disturbing being-there of the Other, he appears to be reluctant to consider redemption as an almost silent event, and accordingly preserves a partly disruptive dimension of Messianism. The point remains, however, that both authors are disposed to "remove the apocalyptic thorn from the organism of Judaism."

Fond of the iridescent views of the Kabbalah rather than the disembodied concepts of philosophy, Scholem was to be sure inclined to favour the kind of Messianism he described through the image of a transcendence that burst into history and unpredictably disrupts its course. This never appears more clearly than when he quotes and comments on a metaphorical assertion coming from Moses of Burgos: "You ought to know that these philosophers whose wisdom you are praising, end where we begin" ... "[the Kabbalists] stand on the shoulders of the philosophers and it is easier for them to see a little farther than their rivals."[45] Considering that the philosophers had converted the living realities of Judaism into abstract allegories while the Kabbalists were comparable to magicians of symbolism, stressing their unequal aptitude to arouse and sustain popular enthusiasm towards the *mitzvot* and underlining incommensurable imprints on Jewish life, Scholem was much more than a pure scholar, and he brilliantly contributed to the modern reflection about Messianism. In many respects, his description of this phenomenon as a never-ending dialectical process comes close to a genuine philosophy of history. More accurately, it generates a concept of meta-history that renders thoroughly irrelevant any idea of linear progress or absolute fate.

Were we to attempt to outline Scholem's interpretation of Jewish history, we ought precisely to appreciate his art of questioning what he called the "price of Messianism," something he scrutinized anxiously with regard to the political adventure of Zionism, the legacy of the *Wissenschaft des Judentums* toward which he was an enfant terrible, or the destiny of the Hebrew language within a secular society.[46] Yet we also might wonder whether some elements of his understanding of messianism could be discovered in the works of his best friend, Walter Benjamin, who one day said to him that if he ever had a philosophy of his own, it somehow would be a "philosophy of Judaism."[47] At a time when Benjamin has become an object of almost fetishistic attention, Scholem remains the finest guide for anyone who wants to explore Benjamin's undeniable contradictions. As Scholem discerned, Benjamin could never decide definitively between his attraction for Marxism, kindled by Brecht or Adorno, and his own more personal fascination for

Messianism.[48] Here we are chiefly concerned with the second of these two interests, the metaphysical dimension of Benjamin's personality and works. To understand this metaphysical dimension more fully, two major topics must be taken into account: his theory of language and his philosophy of history.

The influence of messianic ideas on Benjamin's mind is authenticated through his two essays on language more than it is by the celebrated "Work of Art in the Age of Its Technological Reproducibility." Although we would be mistaken to seek some kind of systematicity within Benjamin's work, these pieces are at the very least symmetrical, the one describing a desperate process of degeneration, the other an expected movement of restitution. Dealing with language as such, and partly elaborated around a commentary of Genesis 2, the 1916 text proceeds in two moments: an interpretation of the power to denominate given by God to man as meaning that man's "spiritual essence" is transmitted to God within the name; and an explanation of Adam's fall and expulsion out of Paradise through its consequence – that is, a disruption of the link between words and things generating an unfathomable nostalgia of mankind for the Adamic tongue.[49] Benjamin was not reluctant to introduce this essay, equally focused on Babel's narrative, as a "metaphysics of language," and one can assume that it echoes discussions with Scholem about Kafka or Kabbalah. The fact remains that it incorporates, even if between the lines, the idea of a disastrous scattering of tongues waiting to be both mended and gathered in order to restore an original unity. This is precisely what Benjamin will illustrate by analysing the phenomenon of translation.

The essay devoted by Benjamin to that everlasting controversial issue is deliberately enigmatic if not esoteric.[50] Written seven years after the previous essay, this one is more clearly inspired by the mystical concept of *tikkun*, which relates to a process of both return and reinstatement of an initial harmony. Rather than considering the almost technical aspect of the question of translation, Benjamin has in mind a nearly metaphorical signification from the point of view of how the true nature of the work of art must be understood, and why an accomplished conjunction of two alien languages might prefigure the future of humanity. These questions are answered by way of a paradox: however good the translation of a literary work may be, it plausibly has no significance as regards the original; yet, the mere fact of being translatable ensures its life and hints at an eternal afterlife in succeeding generations. The core of this enigma lies in the fact that translatability, as expressing a reciprocal relation between languages, remains hidden as long as each one retreats into silence, but is unveiled as soon as they open one to the other. On such a view, the problem is not with freedom or loyalty for the translator, let alone with similarity between adaptation and original concerning words or sentences. What matters is that, despite their separation, languages concord in their intention and supplement each other as by a supra-historical affinity (*überhistorische Verwandtschaft*). Against all conventional conceptions, therefore, the authentic task of the translator is to express an intimate relation between various tongues and more profoundly to release (*erlösen*) in his own (language) a pure language, which was "exiled" inside of the singular work of art. As innovative as it may appear, this argument is hardly Benjamin's last word.

The most fascinating aspect of the essay lies in its culminating elaboration, conceptually grounded in the difference between languages (tongues) in the plural and a singular pure language (*reine Sprache*), something that affords a messianic perspective. In a narrow sense, this last concept might seem to correspond to an old dream of philosophers from Plato to Leibniz, to promote what would be the perfect language of truth. But Benjamin has something different in mind when he says that the translator's task consists in "ripening the seed of pure language," the interlinear version of the Scriptures being the prototype of all translation. His idea is that a seemingly practical activity supports "the allowed growth of languages" and furthermore moves them towards "the messianic end of their history." One might be tempted to observe in this idea some sign of optimism about a forthcoming reconciliation of humanity through successful translations. It nevertheless would be better to distinguish a more or less serene aspect of Benjamin's metaphysical if not theological messianic inspiration, something that disappears within his philosophy of history.

Regularly perceived as a symbol of his tragic destiny, Benjamin's almost ghostly fragments "On the Concept of History" only serve as an approximate statement of his actual thesis on this topic.[51] I suggest they be read with caution, in a conjectural fashion, hypothetically but not deductively. First let me raise some questions relating to the general purpose of "On the Concept..." and my assumptions about Benjamin's work. Must we take seriously the assertion that historical materialism helps us to understand that every generation is "endowed with a *weak* messianic power?" How should we appreciate this claim: "Only for a redeemed mankind has its past become citable in all its moments. Each moment it has lived becomes a *citation à l'ordre du jour*. And that day is Judgment Day?" What should we see in the *Angelus Novus* figure Benjamin left with Scholem, the depiction of an angel of history appearing eyes wide, mouth open, wings spread, which would like to stay but is pushed towards the future by a storm blowing from Paradise – that is progress? To be sure, all these statements and some others testify to contradictory aspirations and irresolute tensions at the core of Benjamin's thought. In the light of modern philosophies of history, one might recognize a clearly anti-Hegelian theme in the image of "the triumphal procession in which current rulers step over those who are lying prostrate." But what about the idea that "every document of culture is at the same time a document of barbarism?" Is it as evident as asserted that the historical materialist will have such knowledge? In order to pursue this point a little further, we should say that what look like scattered elements of heterodox, if not truly bizarre, Marxism conflict with no less strange pieces of messianic ideas.

Yet the most puzzling point remains the fact that, even from this point of view, Benjamin's last fragments appear to be torn between the opposed forms of Messianism under discussion here: on the one hand, the more expected and "apocalyptic" one, as expressed through the view of "splinters of messianic time" breaching the present; and, on the other hand, and more surprisingly, the multi-faceted "rational" one, as expressed in his saying that the Jewish predilection for remembrance and hostility to inquiries into the future convert every second into "the small gateway in time through which the Messiah might enter," an idea that neutralized the catastrophic aspect of Messianism. Such a tension might prompt us to consider Benjamin's work as definitely erratic or to suggest that our initial categorization was too cut and dried and ought to be refined. Otherwise, it might suggest for philosophy unsolved problems with the messianic idea.

The second half of the twentieth century raised the last question in such a paroxysm that only radical statements now seem relevant. We have in mind Adorno's assessment that to write poetry after Auschwitz is "barbarism." Yet, regardless of the fact that literary works like Celan's do contradict Adorno's judgment, one might wonder whether such a conviction would not paradoxically afford a posthumous victory to the murderers. The best outcome would be to suggest that Auschwitz's shadow possibly causes the very idea of the future to fade. Adorno has also put forward a less uncompromising idea: "The only philosophy which can be responsibly practised in the face of despair is the attempt to contemplate all things as they would present themselves from the standpoint of redemption."[52] This clearly echoes Benjamin's own fascination with little, bizarre, unusual objects or gestures, at the same time that it lends warrant to a kind of fragmentary philosophical writing. Needless to say, nothing remains from Hegelian and Marxist outlooks when it is suggested that we "displace and estrange the world" in order to imagine how it would appear in the messianic light. Astonishingly, the most evocative aspect of such a view could be what it is not, either a neo-apocalyptic picture of the end of history, or some quasi-Kantian representation of its asymptotic accomplishment.

Another attempt to radically question the idea of the future comes from Hans Jonas. Looking like a refutation of Bloch's *Principle of Hope*, his late *Imperative of Responsibility* (1979) proposes an openly anti-utopian view, and this antagonism between two major books gives us the opportunity to construct an antinomy. Jonas' concept of responsibility is clearly devoted to rebuffing all the classical or contemporary philosophies of history and politics that promote an image of the best society, and it subsequently gives priority to an ontological enquiry about being-into-the-world, something that erases the messianic perspective. On the other side, we can be confirmed in our opinion that, whatever the manifestations of its influence on modern thought, the messianic idea puts forward some form of supra-sensible or meta-historical reality. Concerning the philosophical debate specifically focused on responsibility, Jonas substitutes the face-to-face between individuals for a commitment in favour of forthcoming generations that gives advantage to the preservation of nature over its adaptation to man's purposes. On a more speculative level, such an endeavour may nevertheless seem forgetful of a fundamental component of human experience.

The question will long remain how much to narrow or to enlarge the human hope for the future. Ultimately it may appear that amongst the notions gleaned from the Jewish messianic tradition, the most fruitful is also that which is the least determined: the notion of the World to Come. Admittedly, it concerns a future no eye has yet glimpsed. But it is clearly related to peace, and in this respect, at least, it resembles the Kantian idea of cosmopolitanism: For Kant, "peace is a concept which overflows the *strictly* political thought."[53] Yet one might ask nevertheless whether the messianic concept does not go further than the philosophical one. As Jacques Derrida suggested, the latter is still political, since Kant restricts cosmopolitanism to what makes possible a universal hospitality, whereas the former invokes something *beyond* the end of wars and the actualisation of human fraternity.[54] What to call this sort of post-history is not crucial for our purposes, and neither Derrida nor Levinas will tell us. What matters is that here we do possess ultimate evidence of the enduring ability of the messianic idea to alter the landscape of philosophy.

Notes

1. Y. H. Yerushalmi, *Zakhor: Jewish History and Jewish Memory* (Seattle and London: University of Washington Press, 1982), 96.
2. See L. Strauss, "Preface to *Spinoza's Critique of Religion*," in *Jewish Philosophy and the Crisis of Modernity: Essays and Lectures in Modern Jewish Thought* (Albany: State University of New York Press, 1997), 137. Similar to a piece of intellectual biography, this text offers an acute reflection upon the German-Jewish philosophical milieu during the 1920s.
3. See G. Scholem, *From Berlin to Jerusalem: Memories of my Youth*, trans. H. Zohn (New York: Schocken Books, 1980), 25–26. This book must be read in its definitive version: *Von Berlin nach Jerusalem: Jugenderinnerungen*, Erweiterte Fassung (Frankfurt a. Main: Jüdischer Verlag, 1994).
4. G. Scholem, *Tagebücher: Nebst Aufsätzen und Entwürfen bis 1923*. Vol. 1: 1913–1917 (Frankfurt a. Main: Jüdischer Verlag, 1995), 437. The second volume (1917–1923), published in 2000, is an extraordinary document; for further discussion, see P. Bouretz, "*Yichouv* as *Teshuvah*: Gershom Scholem's Settling in Jerusalem as a Return from Assimilation," in B. Greiner (ed.), *Placeless Topographies: Jewish Perspectives on the Literature of Exile* (Tübingen: Max Niemeyer Verlag, 2003), 89–101.
5. Kafka's Diary, December 24, 1911, in F. Kafka, *Tagebücher*, edited by H. G. Koch, M. Müller, and M. Pasley (Frankfurt a. Main: Fischer Verlag, 2002), 311; Kafka's letter to Max Brod, June 1921, in *Briefe 1902–1924* (Frankfurt a. Main: Fischer Verlag, 1958), 337.
6. G. Scholem, "Franz Rosenzweig und sein Buch "Der Stern der Erlösung,"" in F. Rosenzweig, *Der Stern der Erlösung* (Frankfurt a. Main: Suhrkamp Verlag, 1988), 526.
7. F. Rosenzweig, Letter to Rudolf Ehrenberg, October, 31, 1913, in F. Rosenzweig, *Briefe und Tagebücher*, edited by R. Rosenzweig and E. Rosenzweig-Scheimann, Vol. 1, 1900–1918 (The Hague, Netherlands: Martinus Nijhoff, 1979), 134.
8. See the whole letter quoted earlier and A. Altmann, "Franz Rosenzweig and Eugen Rosenstock-Huessy: An Introduction to Their "Letters on Judaism & Christianity,"" in A. Altmann, *Essays in Jewish Intellectual History* (Hanover, New Hampshire, and London: University Press of New England, 1981), 246–265.
9. Letter from E. Rosenstock to F. Rosenzweig, October, 30, 1916, in F. Rosenzweig, *Briefe und Tagebücher*, 280 and 279; Letters From F. Rosenzweig to E. Rosenstock, November 8 and November 7, 1916, idem, 287 and 284.
10. Letter from F. Rosenzweig to Helene Sommer, January 16, 1918, in *Briefe und Tagebücher*, 508.
11. Letter from F. Rosenzweig to Rudolf Hallo, January 1923, in *Briefe und Tagebücher*, Vol. II, 887.
12. G. Scholem, "At the Completion of Buber's Translation of the Bible," trans. M. A. Meyer, in *The Messianic Idea in Judaism* (New York: Schocken Books, 1971), 318. See Jacques Derrida's commentary in *Le monothéisme de l'autre* (Paris: Galilée, 1996), 92–100.

13. See "Franz Rosenzweig und sein Buch "Der Stern der Erlösung,""
527 (allusion to *Hagiga*, 14b). From a more general point of view, see
Jürgen Habermas' thought-provoking essay: "Der deutsche Idealismus
der Jüdischen Philosophen," *Philosophisch-politische Profile* (Frankfurt
a. Main: Suhrkamp Verlag, 1984), 39–64.

14. See my *Témoins du futur. Philosophie et messianisme* (Paris: Gallimard,
2003), a book that deals with all the thinkers I discuss here, and some
others, such as Martin Buber and Leo Strauss. The image is taken from
the "Idea for an Arcanum" drafted by Walter Benjamin in November
1927, where he pictured a human court established because of the non-
appearance of the promised Messiah and deciding to hear "witnesses
for the future": "the poet who senses it, the sculptor who sees it, the
musician who hears it, and the philosopher who knows it." See this
little piece in Gershom Scholem, *Walter Benjamin: Story of a Friendship*,
trans. H. Zohn (Philadelphia: The Jewish Publication Society, 1981), 144–
145. *Témoins du futur* is to be read with George Steiner's commentary:
"Zion's Shadows," *The Times Literary Supplement*, February 27 2004,
3–5.

15. *Hegel's Philosophy of Right*, trans. T. M. Knox (London, Oxford, New
York: Oxford University Press, 1967), 13.

16. See M. Heidegger, "Nietzsches Wort "Got ist tot,"" *Holzwege* (Frankfurt
a. Main: Vittorio Klostermann, 1977), 209–267.

17. See a note about Messianism (written between August 1918 and August
1919) in *Tagebücher*, Vol. 2: 1917–1923 (Frankfurt a. Main: Jüdischer
Verlag, 2000), 380. This opposition between "revolutionary" and "evolutionary" forms of Messianism was formulated in the vocabulary of the
post-war period. In his mature work, he will prefer less openly political
terminology.

18. G. Scholem, "Reflections on Jewish Theology," trans. G. Shalit, in *On
Jews and Judaism in Crisis*, ed. W. J. Dannhauser (New York: Schocken
Books, 1976), 284.

19. See G. Scholem, *Sabbatai Zevi. The Mystical Messiah*, trans. R. J.
Werblosky (Princeton, New Jersey: Princeton University Press, 1973),
Chap. 1.

20. G. Scholem, "Toward an Understanding of the Messianic Idea in
Judaism", trans. M. A. Meyer, in *The Messianic Idea in Judaism*, 10.

21. See, for example, his appreciation of Maimonides' eschatology in *Sabbatai Zevi*, 12–15.

22. See G. Scholem's eponymous paper, in *The Messianic Idea in Judaism*,
78–141.

23. See F. Rosenzweig, *Hegel und der Staat* (München and Berlin: Verlag R.
Oldenbourg, 1920), sect. 3, 4, and 6; P. E. Gordon, *Rosenzweig and Heidegger: Between Judaism and German Philosophy* (Berkeley, Los Angeles, London: University of California Press, 2003), chap. 2.

24. G. W. F. Hegel, *Der Geist des Christentums und sein Schicksal*, in
Herman Nohl, ed. *Hegels Theologische Jugendschriften* (Tübingen: J.
C. A. Mohr, 1907), 246 and 248. In English: G.W.Friedrich Hegel, *On*

Christianity: Early Theological Writings (New York: Harper Torchbook, 1961; orig. University of Chicago Press, 1948), 185, 188.
25. G. W. F. Hegel, *Die Positivität der christlichen Religion* (1795), in Herman Nohl (ed.), *Hegels Theologische Jugendschriften*, 148; English, *Early Theological Writings*, 178.
26. G. W. F. Hegel, "Jedes Volk...," in *Frühe Schriften I*, ed. F. Nicolin and G. Schüler (Hamburg: Felix Meiner Verlag, 1989), 371; in English: Hegel, *On Christianity*, 159.
27. G. W. F. Hegel, *Frühe Schriften I*, 372; in English: Hegel, *On Christianity*, 159. See Rosenzweig's remarks in *Hegel und der Staat*, 43–44. Rosenzweig describes Hegel's program as "recovery of the lost unity of Greek man."
28. *Hegel und der Staat*, XII, 1920, Preface to the book, which was completed before the war and "could no longer (be) written." The idea of "1800" as the symbol of an epoch is recurrent in Rosenzweig's corpus, but was formulated for the first time in a page of his diary dated February 9, 1926 (*Briefe und Tagebücher*, Vol. 1, 25).
29. See F. Rosenzweig's letter to Jakob Horovitz dated April 1924 (*Briefe und Tagebücher*, Vol. 2, 958) and his Introduction to the three volumes of Hermann Cohen's, *Jüdische Schriften* (Berlin, C. A. Schwetschke & Sohn/Verlagsbuchhandlung, 1924), Vol. 1, XIII–LXIV.
30. H. Cohen, *Religion of Reason Out of the Sources of Judaism*, trans. S. Kaplan, Introductory essay by Leo Strauss (Atlanta: Scholars Press, 1995), 253.
31. *Religion of Reason*, 283.
32. *Religion of Reason*, 218. Cohen has in mind a passage from *Yoma*, 85b, which will be commented on by both Rosenzweig and Levinas: "Transgressions as between man and the omnipresent the day of atonement procures atonement, but transgressions as between man and his fellow the day of atonement does not procure any atonement until he has pacified his fellow."
33. *Religion of Reason*, 114.
34. I have in mind the inner movement of the second chapter (*Séparation et discours*) of *Totalité et infini. Essai sur l'extériorité* (The Hague, Netherlands: Martinus Nijhoff Publishers, 1961); *Totality and Infinity. An Essay on Exteriority*, trans. A. Lingis (Pittsburgh, Pennsylvania: Duquesne University Press, 1969). One could find a less formal explanation in "Une religion d'adultes," *Difficile liberté* (Paris: Le livre de poche, 1988), 24–42. I adopt the convention proposed by the translator of *Totalité et infini* and accepted by the author, consisting of translating "*autrui*" as "Other" and "*autre*" as "other."
35. *Religion of Reason*, 291.
36. *Religion of Reason*, 249.
37. E. Bloch, *The Spirit of Utopia*, trans. A. Nassar (Stanford: Stanford University Press, 2000), 178.
38. From the point of view of Rosenzweig's reception, some other proximities can be underlined – for example, with Heidegger – as proposed by Peter Gordon. On the other hand, the question of the springs from which

Levinas drinks is controversial. For further discussion, I refer to the chapter devoted to Levinas in my *Témoins du futur*.

39. Hence his celebrated claim that he wished "to throw down the gauntlet to the whole honorable company of philosophers from Ionia to Jena." F. Rosenzweig, *The Star of Redemption*, trans. W. Hallo (London: Routledge & Kegan Paul, 1970), 12.

40. See "Das neue Denken," in *Zweistromland. Kleinere Schriften zu Glauben und Denken* (Dordrecht, Netherland, Boston, Lancaster: Martinus Neijhoff Publishers, 1984), 139–161. Another explanation of the *Star*, so to speak, is to be found at the same place (125–138): ""Urzelle" des *Stern der Erlösung*." See *Franz Rosenzweig: Philosophical and Theological Writings*, translated and edited by Paul W. Franks and Michael L. Morgan (Indianapolis and Cambridge, MA: Hackett Publishing), 48–72 and 109–139.

41. P. E. Gordon, *Rosenzweig and Heidegger: Between Judaism and German Philosophy*, 208. Gordon clarifies precisely the disconcerting notion of *Gemeinschaft des Bluts* (community of blood).

42. *The Star of Redemption*, 404.

43. This is the main theme of Levinas' most radical book: *Autrement qu'être ou au-delà de l'essence* (Paris: Le livre de poche, 1990).

44. G. Scholem, "On the 1930 Edition of Rosenzweig's Star of Redemption," in *The Messianic Idea in Judaism*, 323. It must be added that Scholem perceives virtually the same idea in Martin Buber's work. See "The Neutralization of the Messianic Element in Early Hasidism" and "Martin Buber's Interpretation of Hasidism," *The Messianic Idea in Judaism*, 176–202 and 227–250.

45. G. Scholem, *Major Trends in Jewish Mysticism* (New York: Schocken Books, 1954), 24. One can find a meticulous and respectful discussion of those views by Leo Strauss in "How to Begin to Study Medieval Philosophy" in *The Rebirth of Classical Political Rationalism* (Chicago and London: University of Chicago Press, 1989), 212–215. No doubt Scholem was particularly fascinated by the Lurianic Kabbalah, in which he discovered a sophisticated system of concepts and a narrative of God's exile into the world, echoing the Jewish people's circumstances within history.

46. I have in mind a disenchanted, if not desperate, 1944 paper in which Scholem allegorically describes a "hidden relation" between destruction and salvation, *tohu* and *tikkun*, within current Jewish history. See G. Scholem, "Überlegungen zur Wissenschaft vom Judentums," in *Judaica 6. Die Wissenschaft vom Judentums* (Frankfurt a. Main: Suhrkamp Verlag, 1997), 7–52, and my "Gershom Scholem und das Schreiben der Geschichte," in *Gershom Scholem. Literatur und Rhetorik*, eds. Stéphane Mosès and Sigrid Weigel (Köln, Weimar, and Wien: Böhlau Verlag, 2000), 93–123.

47. See G. Scholem, *Walter Benjamin: Story of a Friendship*, 32.

48. Beside Scholem's *Story of a Friendship*, which should be read like a two-hero *Bildungsroman*, one must look at Hannah Arendt's sensitive portrait, which does have the same quality: to illustrate Benjamin's conflicting aspirations rather than compel one to make a choice. See Arendt's

Introduction to Walter Benjamin, *Illuminations*, trans. H. Zohn (New York: Harcourt, Brace & World, 1955), also published in Hannah Arendt, *Men in Dark Times* (New York: Harcourt, Brace & World, 1968), 153–206.

49. W. Benjamin, "Über Sprache überhaupt und über die Sprache des Menschen," in *Gesammelte Schriften*, Vol. II, 1 (Frankfurt a. Main: Suhrkamp Verlag, 1977), 140–157; "On Language as Such and on the Language of Man," trans. E. Jephcott, in W. Benjamin, *Selected Writings*, Volume 1, 1913–1926 (Cambridge, MA, and London: The Belknap Press of Harvard University Press, 1996), 62–74.

50. Walter Benjamin, "Die Aufgabe des Übersetzer," in *Gesammelte Schriften*, Vol. IV, 1 (Frankfurt a. Main: Suhrkamp Verlag, 1972), 9–21; "The Task of the Translator," trans. H. Zohn, in *Selected Writings*, Volume 1, 1913–1926, 253–263 (this translation is far better than the one included in *Illuminations*). The most thoughtful views on Benjamin's theory of language and translation are to be found in George Steiner's *After Babel* (New York and London: Oxford University Press, 1975) and *Language and Silence* (London: Faber and Faber, 1967). I also refer to my "22 variations sur Babel," in P. Bouretz, M. de Launay, and Jean-Louis Schefer, *La tour de Babel* (Paris: Desclée de Brouwer, 2003), 9–108.

51. W. Benjamin, "On the Concept of History," trans. H. Zohn, in *Selected Writings*, Vol. 4: 1938–1940 (Cambridge, MA, and London: The Belknap Press of Harvard University Press, 2003), 389–411.

52. Theodore Adorno, *Minima Moralia. Reflexions on a Damaged Life* (London, New York: Verso, 2005), 247.

53. E. Levinas, "Politique après !" in *L'au-delà du verset* (Paris: Les éditions de Minuit, 1982), 228.

54. See Jacques Derrida, *Adieu à Emmanuel Levinas* (Paris: Galilée, 1997), 134–176 and my "Adieu, Jacques Derrida," *Les Temps Modernes*, no. 629, November 2004 / February 2005, 231–233.

10 Ethics, Authority, and Autonomy

KENNETH SEESKIN

The crux of the doctrine of autonomy is easy to state: "Man," as Kant tells us in *Religion within the Limits of Reason Alone*, "must make or have made himself into whatever, in a moral sense, whether good or evil, he is or is to become."[1] Simply put, God can command us to obey certain laws and threaten us with punishment if we refuse; but only we bear responsibility for what we do. In the words of Ezekiel (18:20): "the righteousness of the righteous shall be his own, and the wickedness of the wicked shall be his own." Though God bids us to turn from wickedness and sanctify ourselves, sanctification cannot be vicarious: it makes sense only if it comes from within.[2]

What kind of being is able to do this? The answer is a moral agent, something that can take responsibility for its actions and change direction when it decides that its actions are not what they should be. Although it is easy for us to take moral agency for granted, it is worth recalling that at one point it was a revolutionary idea. The first formulation of the Ten Commandments (Exodus 20:5) claims that God *will* punish children for the iniquity of their parents. Ezekiel's point is that this cannot be right: each person must answer for her own actions. To understand the doctrine of autonomy is to recognize, with Hermann Cohen, that it is nothing more than an extension of Ezekiel's insight.[3] Once a person becomes responsible for herself, she becomes master of herself. She cannot inherit someone else's sin, and if she commits a sin of her own, only she has the power to atone for it.

I. DUTY AND RESPONSIBILITY

By arguing that we must make ourselves what we are to become, Kant took moral responsibility to its logical conclusion: the moral subject is both an end *in* itself and capable of legislating morality *for* itself. This means (1) that every moral subject must be treated with dignity and can never be used solely as a means to a greater end, and (2) a moral subject can only be bound by a law it imposes on itself. It is with the latter claim that problems arise. According to Kant, previous theories failed not because they were unable to advance a plausible view of how to live but because they did not account for the primary fact of duty:[4]

> If we now look back upon all previous attempts which have ever been undertaken to discover the principle of morality, it is not to be wondered at that they all had to fail. Man was seen to be bound to laws by his duty, but it was not seen that he is subject only to his own, yet universal, legislation, and that he is only bound to act in accordance with his own will, which is, however, designed by nature to be a will giving universal laws.

Suppose God commands me to do something, and I ask why I should obey. There is no question but that God can destroy me if I refuse. Still the question is not "What is it in my interest to do?" but "What am I *obliged* to do?"

By saying that I am subject only to the laws of my own legislation, Kant means that neither God nor anything else can create an obligation *for* me. Rather than saying "Do this" and "Don't do that," a person in authority must give me the chance to see for myself that some actions are right and others wrong. An animal can be trained to respond to commands if it is offered positive and negative reinforcement. Kant's contention is that it is degrading to treat a moral agent this way. Unlike an animal, a moral agent is not only subject to law, but, in a sense that needs to be clarified, subject in a way that allows it to also be the source of law.

To return to Kant:

> The will is thus not only subject to the law but subject in such a way that it must be regarded also as self-legislative and only for this reason as being subject to the law (of which it can regard itself as the author).[5]

Once we can regard ourselves as authors of our own behavior, reward and punishment no longer matter. If we obey a law, we do so not to gain an advantage but because we are convinced it is right. This is another way of saying that the law we impose *on* ourselves is a sufficient motive for action *in* itself, that instead of resting on incentives, it is something we are willing to do on principle.

For Kant, a moral principle is distinguished by its generality: if an action is right for me, it must be right for every other person as well. As he goes on to say, a rational agent "must regard itself as giving universal law through all the maxims of its will."[6] To legislate for myself is, then, to legislate for all humanity, to say that the action is right not just for me but for everyone else as well. It follows that moral legislation does not involve personal matters, such as whom to marry, what career to choose, or how to get ahead in the world. At bottom it involves only one thing: how to treat all of humanity with the respect it deserves. On this basis, Kant concludes that one is obliged to keep promises, tell the truth, respect the sanctity of human life, and assist people less fortunate than oneself.

At one level, autonomy poses no threat to Judaism or any other revealed religion. A famous passage from the Mishnaic tractate *Pirke Avot* (1.3) says that one should not serve God like a servant who expects a reward. Commenting on this and similar passages, Maimonides argues that references to blessings and curses in the Bible cannot be taken literally. While one may bribe a child with rewards and punishments in order to instill good habits, in Maimonides' opinion, anyone who continues to think that good behavior can be motivated by personal gain "destroys the glory of the Torah and extinguishes its light."[7]

The problem arises with the idea of self-legislation. For some people, the essence of revealed religion *is* the heteronomy of divine commands: God tells us what to do, and out of love of God, we have no choice but to obey. Once we view ourselves as legislators in Kant's sense, the objection runs, we make ourselves superior to God. According to this view, human consent is irrelevant: we must obey God whether we agree or not. Did the Israelites not say this when they responded (Exodus 24:7), "We shall do and [then] hear?" By introducing the doctrine of autonomy, Kant touched off a debate in Judaism that rivaled that over Aristotelian metaphysics in the Middle Ages. I should say at the outset that I am a partisan in that debate for I believe that heteronomy is objectionable in any form, and that Judaism has always seen this. That is not to say that the classical texts of Judaism assert the doctrine of autonomy as clearly as Kant does, but that they contain insights that lead to much the same result. But enough introduction; it is time to get to substance.

2. MISCONCEPTIONS

The first job is to clear up some common misconceptions. When Kant says that I legislate morality for myself, he does not mean that I am at liberty to reject the moral law or alter its content. While the doctrine of autonomy is a powerful affirmation of human freedom, it does not mean

I can do as I please.[8] For Kant, the moral law is determined by reason a priori with no consideration for personal preference. In the *Critique of Practical Reason*, he calls it "stern, unindulgent, truly commanding."[9] It is the irrelevance of personal factors that allows it to bind categorically and permits a single individual to say that everyone should do likewise. As the etymology of the word suggests, autonomy (*auto+ nomos*) means self-rule or the self-imposition of law. Without an objectively valid law we could instigate behavior but not be masters of it in the sense just described.

Thus Kant does not mean by autonomy what existentialists such as Martin Buber or Eugene Borowitz mean by it. For the latter two, universal laws are abstract and do not address the concrete factors that determine the situations in which we find ourselves. It is all very well to say that we should treat humanity as an end in itself, but this leaves unaddressed the issue of how, when, or with whom. Since every situation is different, the attempt to rely on fixed rules of any kind is misguided. In a famous passage, Buber tells us that an I-Thou knowledge that can be held fast, preserved, and factually transmitted is impossible.[10] Rather than autonomy's being the imposition of a law determined by reason a priori, Buber regards it as the freedom of every individual to engage in her own spiritual search and find meaning in the uniqueness of her own life. In this way, autonomy becomes personal, with the emphasis moving from the suffix to the prefix.

Against Buber and Borowitz, it may be objected that Kant never regarded the moral law as a fixed rule that leaves no room for personal discretion. His point is that no matter how much discretion is involved, the intention must still be pure. The only way for this to happen is if a person wills the moral law for its own sake. So once again there can be no autonomy in Kant's sense without an objectively valid law.

Another misconception involves authorship. Since the moral law is known a priori, it cannot have an author in the way that King Lear does. As members of the kingdom of ends, everyone is an author; as empirical beings responding to sensuous influences, no one is. Accordingly, Kant maintains that the supreme condition of the will's harmony with reason is "the idea [my emphasis] of the will of every rational being as making universal law."[11] This means that the author of the law is not John Doe acting as an individual but our conception of ourselves as beings capable of legislating for all humanity. Emil Fackenheim makes this point by saying that while I am the author of the law in the sense of being able to appropriate it freely, it does not follow that I am (or have to be) the author of the law in fact.[12]

Consider an example. The Fifth Amendment to the U.S. Constitution says that the government cannot force someone to testify against himself, which means that it cannot use torture to elicit a confession. Though I was not present when the Constitution was written, I have no trouble regarding myself as its author because it expresses my deepest conviction of how a civilized nation should behave. By calling us authors, Kant means that the moral law acquires its validity not because someone orders me to obey it but because my own reason tells me it is right.

By saying that autonomy is based on the *idea* of the will of every rational being, Kant implies that it is something we have to strive for. Simply put: we do not possess autonomy in the way we possess a circulatory system. By the same token, the rationality Kant is talking about has nothing to do with intelligence tests or mastery of technical subjects such as physics or metaphysics. He was convinced that every person has the rationality to see that it is wrong to treat other people in a manner inferior to the way you want to be treated, wrong to lie and expect others to tell the truth, wrong to steal and expect others to respect property.

From a religious standpoint, the crux of autonomy is that no obligation can result from a purely external revelation such as a voice from heaven or a set of inscriptions on a tablet. Kant never denies that external revelation can occur; his point is stronger: even if it did, it could not oblige us to do anything. Voices from heaven are addressed to people in specific circumstances and thus cannot bind humanity as a whole. To have a message binding on all humanity, we would first have to decide that the content of the message was worth acting on. But then the real authority would not be the voice itself but the moral judgment of the people who approved of it.

Does this mean that revelation is a sham? Kant's answer is no. In addition to external revelation, there is also internal revelation: God's act of endowing every agent with the ability to distinguish right from wrong. As we saw, each of us is "designed by nature" to be a will-giving universal law. In a moment of eloquence, Kant goes further, saying that the moral law is engraved on the heart, a passage that calls to mind Deuteronomy 30:11–14, where Moses says the same thing of the Torah.[13] If this is right, the duties we impose on ourselves are no different from the duties God imposes on us in the moment of revelation.

The idea of internal revelation is hardly new; any number of medieval rationalists, including Maimonides, espoused something similar.[14] What is new, and therefore problematic, is Kant's view of priority, for rather than start with the knowledge that something is a divine command and infer that it is a duty, Kant thinks we start with the knowledge that it is a duty, and infer that it is a divine command.[15] In other words, our idea of God is derived from our idea of moral perfection, not the other way around. Moral perfection can be known by reason alone. So it would seem that for Kant, reason, not God, is the supreme authority in religious matters.

Another way to see this is to recognize that while Kant believes that God commands us to do our duty, *the fact that* God commands it is of no moral significance. As Fackenheim remarks, the fact that the law originates with God has no more bearing on our sense of duty than a remark about the weather. As in geometry, the question is not where we get the law but whether it is valid in its own right. It is in this sense that autonomy poses a threat to traditional religion. If all that matters is the validity of the law and not its origin, why not do what reason requires and forget God altogether?

3. COVENANT AND CONSENT

The question just posed goes to the heart of the idea of authority. What is the important factor in the divine/human encounter – the commanding presence of God or the appropriation of divine commands by human beings? From a traditional perspective, it must be the former. As David Novak puts it: "It is divine offering, not human acceptance, that creates the obligation."[16] There is ample evidence in the Torah for either view. If one wishes to stress commanding presence, one will point to Abraham as he is about to slay Isaac. Unless God asks something Abraham would not do on his own, which is to say, unless Abraham could *not* regard himself as the author of his action, there is no test of his love. So the question becomes: is Abraham willing to please God even at the cost of subverting his conscience?

In Fackenheim's view, the answer is yes. The freedom Abraham displays in this episode is not rational self-legislation but the opposite: the freedom to love God and say "Here I am, send me." As we saw, this is one way of interpreting Israel's response to God at Exodus 24:7. "But," continues Fackenheim, "this entails the momentous consequence that, if and when a man chooses to accept the divine commanding Presence, he does nothing less than accept the divine Will as his own." The formula "Accept the divine will as your own" derives from *Pirke Avot* (2.4) and is a classic statement of heteronomy. In effect, it asks us to do as God says without hesitation.

If, however, one wishes to stress human appropriation, one will point to passages where Abraham and Moses protest to God in the name of what is right. First there is the passage where Abraham challenges God over the destruction of Sodom and Gomorra (Genesis 18:23–25):

> "Will you actually sweep away the righteous with the
> wicked? . . . Far be that from you! Shall not the judge of all earth do
> what is just?

Rather than make God's will his own, Abraham argues that the proposal falls short of a standard to which God too must adhere.[17]

In a similar way, Moses protests God's decision to destroy Israel as a punishment for disobedience. In the first instance (Exodus 32:13–14), he uses two arguments: the Egyptians will form the wrong impression of God's intentions, and God will break the promise made to the patriarchs. The passage clearly assumes that promise-breaking is as wrong in heaven as it is on earth. In the second (Numbers 14:13–19), he again uses two arguments: the nations of the world will form a mistaken impression of God's saving power, and God will break the promise made to Moses, according to which God is supposed to be slow to anger, abounding in love, and willing to forgive iniquity.

It is not just that these characters say no to God, but that they rise in our – and presumably God's – estimation by doing so. In both cases, God backs down. According to David Hartman: "The creation of a being capable of saying no to divine commands is the supreme expression of divine love, insofar as God makes room for humans as independent, free creatures."[18] Without the ability to say no, humans could be agents *of* God but not genuine partners *with* God. The difference is critical. As normally understood, a partner is more than an extension of oneself. Rather than someone who always says "Here I am, send me," a partner is someone who is given the privilege of exercising his own judgment – even if that judgment issues in a question or contrary opinion. If autonomy runs the risk of introducing anarchy, heteronomy runs the risk of legitimating fanaticism.

There is little question that the Torah tries to avoid both. The typical way for God to establish the rule of law is not to make an edict but to enact a covenant (*brit*).[19] There is a covenant with Noah (Genesis 99.1–17), with Abraham (Genesis 15:1–21, 17: 1–27), and with the Jewish people as a whole (Exodus 19:5–6). Obviously God could have imposed the divine will by force, saying: "Here is what I want, and if you don't obey, I will exact a price." Despite a number of misconceptions about "the God of the Old Testament," this is not the way the narrative is written. Again from Hartman, the important point is that God *invites* Israel to enter a partnership at Sinai: *if* you obey my covenant," not "Here is why you have to obey."[20]

An objection will be raised that there are well-known passages in Leviticus (26) and Deuteronomy (28) where God promises blessings and curses for obedience and disobedience. It is significant, however, that the blessings and curses do not accompany the original list of commandments given in Exodus. Instead of the usual "If you breach the agreement by doing *X*, I will retaliate by doing *Y*," these commandments are expressed in categorical form with no mention of threats. According to Nahum Sarna:[21]

> The motivation for observing the law is not fear of punishment but the desire to conform to the will of God. The Decalogue thus becomes a self-enforcing code in that its appeal is to the conscience, not to enlightened self-interest, and its enforcing mechanism is the spiritual discipline and moral fiber of the individual, not the threat of penalty that is imposed by the coercive power of the state.

Sarna's interpretation runs counter to a well-known Midrash according to which God held the mountain over the people's heads and threatened to destroy them unless they pledged their loyalty.[22] As the Rabbis saw, this view, taken literally, would nullify the agreement because it would mean that the people acted under duress. It would also mean that God entered into a covenant by threatening violence against the weaker party. In fact, the opposite is true. Rather than being a despot whose word becomes law the minute it is uttered, God both needs and asks for human consent. In addition to Sinai, the covenant is offered to Israel in the plains of Moab, near Mount Gerizim, at Joshua 24, and 2 Kings 23. In the view of Jeremiah (31), it will be offered yet another time when a sinful Israel is restored to its innocence. Repetition is a sign of importance. The covenant is offered on many occasions and read back to the people to emphasize that there can be no question that they acted of their own accord.

The implication is that unless the people accept the law and enter a partnership with God, there is a sense in which God will have failed. According to another Midrash: "You are my witnesses, says the Lord, and I am God. That is, when you are my witnesses, I am God, and when you are not My witnesses, I am, as it were, not God."[23] Without consent, both parties would lose the most important feature of the relationship: the recognition of the other party. God would still be the most powerful force in the universe, and while every nation would have to defer to that power, no nation would have accepted God's law as its own; no nation, that is, would be able to regard itself as author of the law in Kant's sense.

4. DUTIES AS DIVINE COMMANDS

With the doctrine of autonomy in mind, one can say that the purpose of Sinai is to establish a sacred community in which the law expresses the considered judgment of every member. While Kant may not have been aware of Deuteronomy 30:11–14, the import of the passage is clear: though the law may have originated in heaven, it is not in heaven any longer. It is written on the heart of every person who stood at Sinai so that he may do it. "Duty, as Lenn Goodman points out, "cannot be conceived as alien."[24] Rather than something imposed on one, it must be conceived as something that expresses the convictions on which we ourselves want to be judged.

This does not mean that a person is free to say he does not like the prohibition against murder and will not give his consent. We saw that for Kant, the moral law is valid a priori and has nothing to do with personal preference. In his view, wrong doing by its nature involves inconsistency: I let myself ignore the sanctity of human life when it comes to dealing with you, but you cannot ignore it when dealing with me. Since reason abhors inconsistency, it demands that we treat others with the same respect with which we want to be treated and make no exceptions. Obviously people make exceptions all the time: "While you have to tell the truth, I have a valid reason for lying." Kant's claim is that we all possess the moral insight needed to see that when this happens, we are being unfair. It is in this sense that he thinks it is impossible not to consent to the moral law.

Though Jewish tradition does not express itself in quite this way, its approach to murder, lying, and stealing is similar. According to the Talmud, these commandments are laws (*mishpatim*) such that if God had not given them to us, we would be justified in giving them to ourselves.[25] The Rabbis also claimed that these laws were part of the covenant with Noah and are therefore binding on all humanity.[26] Some go as far as to say they were known to Adam and Eve.[27] In the words of Yehezkel Kaufmann:

> The cultures which the Israelite tribes had absorbed and out of which they had emerged had highly developed notions of law and morality.... The Bible itself recognizes the existence of a universal moral law from primeval times, to which all men are subject.

Cain, the generation of the Flood, and Sodom are punished for violations of this law. The Sinaitic covenant comes late in the history of man, even according to the Biblical story.[28]

In short, the Sinaitic covenant did not contain anything the people had not heard before. Though honoring one's father and mother is not part of the Noachide covenant, under normal circumstances it would be difficult to think of a more basic principle. Even the institution of a day of rest is alluded to as early as Exodus 5. So there is no question of following God blindly by agreeing to do something before one knows what God is going to ask. On the other hand, if the people had heard this before, or could have figured it out for themselves, why have a covenant at all?

From a Kantian perspective, the answer is that the importance of Sinai is not the fact of its occurrence but the legitimacy of its content.[29] On this reading, Sinai is simply the Torah's way of saying that the commandments were not just given but given *and agreed to*. In theological terms, it was not just a communication that was issued from heaven but a communication that was accepted by people on earth. As Deuteronomy 29:10 tells us, everyone from the leaders of the tribes to women and children, even to hewers of wood and drawers of water, was present to give their consent.

It follows that while the people may not be the source of the commandments in a historical sense, they have made the decision to affirm them as their own. Rather than discussing authorship, the Torah discusses the imposition of law in terms of partnership. If Kant is right, they amount to the same thing. As J. B. Soloveitchik puts it: "Halakhic [observant] man," does not experience any consciousness of compulsion accompanying the norm. Rather, it seems to him as though he discovered the norm in his innermost self . . . "[30] Again we are talking about an ideal. At first blush it may seem that the laws promulgated at Sinai are restrictive and impede self-expression, but on deeper reflection, it will seem otherwise. Whether we account for this by appealing to reason's desire for consistency or halakhic man's love of God, the outcome is the same: divine law is a defining characteristic for what it means to be human. That is what enabled Kant to define religion as the recognition that all duties are divine commands.[31]

5. STATUTORY LAWS

There is an obvious objection to what has been said so far. Suppose we grant that the prohibitions of murder, lying, and stealing are based on moral intuitions that any rational person would have. According to

Jewish tradition, Moses received 613 commandments at Sinai. What do we say about the commandments (*hukkim*) dealing with holidays, dietary requirements, or special clothing? Surely it is fantastic to suppose that they too contain nothing beyond what a rational person would sanction on her own. It is with these commandments that the issue of obedience becomes paramount. If we only obey God when the commandments agree with our sense of right and wrong, then for all intents and purposes, God does not change anything. Again we are inclined to ask: why not simply obey your conscience and forget about God?

Kant was skeptical of ritual and looked forward to the day when everything except the moral core of religion would be discarded.[32] But Maimonides took a different view, arguing that there is a rational justification for every commandment.[33] The only difference between universal laws and ritual laws is that justifications for the former are apparent, while those for the latter may take effort to uncover. Nonetheless it is our job to try to uncover them. In defense of this view, Maimonides cites Deuteronomy 4:5–8:

> Behold, I have taught you statutes (*hukkim*) and laws (*mishpatim*) for you to observe in the land that you are about to enter and occupy. You must observe them diligently, for this will show your wisdom and discernment to the peoples, who, when they hear all these statutes will say: "Surely this great nation is a wise and understanding people." For what other great nation has a god so near to it as the Lord our God is whenever we call to him? And what other great nation has statutes and laws as just as this entire law that I am setting before you today?

The most natural reading of this passage is that no commandment is arbitrary in the sense that it lacks a justification and was promulgated merely as a test of obedience. If so, revelation is not an edict but an attempt at education – hence the reference to a wise and understanding people.

Behind Maimonides' approach is a realistic assessment of human behavior. A religion that limited itself to a small set of moral or metaphysical principles would soon find its ranks depleted.[34] The reason is that people are disposed to trust what they can see, touch, or hear. While it may be possible in principle to eliminate festivals, special clothes, and special foods from religious observance, it is not possible in fact. Note, for example, that even in secular society, governments, corporations, universities, and military regiments have a host of mascots, songs, special clothes, and special ceremonies to represent or reinforce shared commitments. This is another way of saying that human beings do not live by principles alone. In any organized walk of life, there have to be procedures, which, though not strictly deducible from the moral law, help people realize it and console them when they fail. At the very least, there have to be institutions that allow like-minded people to work together.

In addition to symbols and reminders, there also have to be procedures for implementing moral rules. If there is a prohibition against murder, there have to be courts, rules of evidence, guidelines for sentencing, and opportunities for seeking refuge. If there is a law protecting personal property, there have to be rules for how to handle contracts, wills, and rights of inheritance. Though none of these may be universal in Kant's sense, all are necessary if we are to treat people as ends in themselves. In that respect, they have a justification. Clearly there is an element of arbitrariness in any procedure, and we may be able to imagine a society with procedures different from ours. But this does not mean that such procedures are arbitrary and can be disregarded.

Although Maimonides does not speak for all of Jewish philosophy, he does speak for an important part of it. When a law has a reason behind it, a person can appropriate it freely – or, as Kant says, can look upon herself as its author. No act of submission is involved in such acceptance. One can persuade someone to obey the law by appealing to the highest part of her nature rather than issuing threats or insisting on blind obedience. This is the standard the doctrine of autonomy puts forward.

Does acceptance of the standard mean we have abandoned God? The answer is yes if that means we have abandoned the God who asks for obedience above all else, the God who commands without also trying to educate. It is no if that means we have abandoned the God who seeks a partner and wants that partner's consent. With partnership comes accountability. A God who is not accountable to human beings is a God whose covenant means nothing. We can understand the encounters with Abraham and Moses as the Bible's way of making this point. Keep in mind however that the reason the covenant is binding is not that a superior power has enforced it but that each party has agreed to live by it, to be both subject and sovereign.

6. AUTONOMY, AUTHORITY, AND THE RATIONALITY OF CONSENT

There is still a respect in which autonomy poses a threat to traditional religion. In his famous essay "What is Enlightenment?" Kant argues that the motto of enlightenment is to have the courage to use one's own reason or, as he puts it, to think for oneself.[35] Though it could be argued that no serious philosopher of religion ever suggested otherwise, in Kant's hands, "Think for yourself" came to mean a rejection of clerical authority. In the *Religion*, he claims that a true faith would not have the laity dragged around by "the small body of textual scholars" and would accord recognition and respect to "universal human reason as the supremely commanding principle."[36]

It is impossible to overestimate the importance of this remark. Any number of thinkers argued for the autonomy of an intellectual elite who, by mastering the law, would see it as an expression of their own will. These people would become co-authors with God and explain to the laity what the law requires of them.[37] By saying that universal human reason is the supreme commanding principle, Kant meant that the moral law is accessible to everyone and does not require a class of professional interpreters. In principle, each person has the wherewithal to look within his soul for the touchstone of truth. Unless this is so, we could not hold people responsible for their actions and would not have to treat them as ends in themselves.

What is a Jew to make of this? There is no doubt that under the aegis of oral Torah, the Rabbis thought they were speaking for God. In principle, the rulings, interpretations, and specifications they arrive at are as binding on a Jew as the commandments set forth in the written Torah. Indeed, much of the religion as now practiced, including the Prayer Book, the Passover Hagaddah, the celebration of Hanukkah and Purim, the practice of lighting Sabbath candles, and the reading of the Haftarah derives from the Talmud.

From a traditional perspective, the problem with Kant is his naiveté. Can we really believe that lessons intended for a semi-nomadic people living in Asia Minor during the tenth century B.C. can be taken up and applied thousands of years later simply by consulting human reason? Even for commandments intended for the entire human race, do we not need to ask how previous generations understood murder, marriage, or personal property? And what about the statutory portion of the law? Are people not motivated by the fact that the holidays they celebrate and prayers they say have a history that links them to their ancestors?

Again the issues are more complicated than they first appear. Although Rabbinic authority is central to Judaism, the idea of a democratic religion in which each person internalizes the law is not as foreign as some might think. Recall Deuteronomy 29:10, where everyone from the leaders of the tribes to hewers of wood and drawers of water is present to accept God's covenant. Even with respect to Rabbinic law, consent of the laity cannot be ignored. Why should we believe that the ordinances and decrees promulgated by the Rabbis are binding?

In the Introduction to the *Mishneh Torah*, Maimonides argues that they are binding because all Jews agreed to live by them.[38] Later in Book 14, he claims that if enactments and prohibitions designed to safeguard the Torah have been universally accepted, no later court can overturn them.[39] If, for example, a court issues a decree thinking it will meet with general acceptance, but it does not, the decree is void. If a court issues a decree and believes it has met with general acceptance when in fact it has not, a later court is justified in revoking it. In general:[40]

> Before instituting a decree or enacting an ordinance or introducing a custom which it deems necessary, the court should calmly deliberate the matter and make sure the majority of the community can live up to it. At no time is a decree to be imposed upon the public which the majority cannot endure.

To say that a Rabbinical court cannot impose something the majority cannot endure is not to say that it must do whatever the majority wants. Still, consent plays a role in the justification of Rabbinic authority, and that raises the question of how we know when it has been given.

Obviously there was no point when every Jew got together and proclaimed the Talmud authoritative. Even the covenant enacted at Deuteronomy 29 raises questions because according to tradition, it was not just the people listening to Moses' voice who accepted the Torah, but the soul of every Jew who would ever live.[41] According to Hermann Cohen, to interpret this as a purely historical event is to succumb to mythology. What is really going on here is an attempt to transform Sinai from a historical claim to a moral one.[42] Rather than being an agreement between God and a particular generation, it becomes an agreement between God and every generation, an agreement that is justified by the wisdom of its laws and can be renewed in every age.

Instead of saying that consent was achieved because the people nodded their heads with approval, it would be better to say that consent has to do with the fact that any rational person would concur. Those familiar with social contract theory will recognize that what Cohen has done is move from actual consent to virtual consent. Just as it is unnecessary to argue for a historical state of nature to accept the social contract, it is unnecessary to rely on the findings of archaeology to accept the Torah.

Virtual consent offers a better way to understand the idea of a democratic religion. To say that each person should search his soul for the touchstone of truth is not to open the floodgates to anarchy but to uphold an ideal for existing institutions to follow. That ideal is exactly the one articulated by the Torah: each person, from the highest to the lowest, joins together to form a sacred partnership with God. To the degree that Judaism remains faithful to this ideal, there is no distinction between clergy and laity: everyone is a full partner with God in trying to perfect the world. We can say this and still say that a tradition of authoritative interpretation is needed if we are to understand what the partnership requires of us.

Kant spoke for a good deal of Western philosophy when he characterized Judaism as a heteronomous religion that asks people to swear loyalty to a jealous and vengeful God. He also spoke for a tradition of Jewish theologians that sees heteronomy as the only valid form of religion. While there are passages that can be taken in support of this view, I hope I have shown that there is another way to look at them, a way that emphasizes the rationality of divine commands and the responsibilities that go with a moral partnership. If I am right, Judaism has always recognized the importance of human dignity, even when human beings fail to live up to the obligations to which they have pledged themselves. Not only is this *a* theme in Jewish tradition, from my perspective it occupies center stage.

Notes

1. Kant, *Religion within the Limits of Reason Alone*, p. 40. For a book-length study of the the issues discussed in this essay, see my *Autonomy in Jewish Philosophy*, Cambridge: Cambridge University Press, 2001.
2. On this point, see Hermann Cohen's analysis of *Yoma* 85b in *Jüdische Schriften*, Vol. 3, p. 22.
3. Cohen, *Religion of Reason out of the Sources of Judaism*, p. 194.
4. Kant, *Foundations of a Metaphysics of Morals*, Indianapolis, Bobbs-Merrill, 1969, (432–433, p. 51).
5. *Foundations* 431, p. 49.
6. *Foundations* 443, p. 51.
7. *Perek Helek.* For an English translation, see *A Maimonides Reader*, edited by Isadore Twersky, New York: Behrman House, 1976, pp. 402–423. Cf. *Mishneh Torah* 1 Laws of Repentance, 10.1.
8. Cf. Soloveitchik, *Halakhic Man*, p. 78–79, 134–135.
9. Kant, *Critique of Practical Reason*, Chicago: University of Chicago Press, pp. 123, 127.

10. *The Philosophy of Martin Buber*, p. 692. For Borowitz's conception of autonomy, see *Exploring Jewish Ethics*, Detroit: Wayne State University Press, 1990, chapters 14 and 16, as well as *Renewing the Covenant*, pp. 170–181, 221–223.

11. *Foundations* 431, p. 49.

12. Emil Fackenheim, "Abraham and the Kantians," *Encounters Between Judaism and Modern Philosophy*, p. 45.

13. In all likelihood, Kant got the metaphor of a law written on the heart from Romans 2:14–15, where Paul says that when people who do not have the law but do instinctively what it requires, they are "a law to themselves" and show that what the law requires is "written on their hearts." This context differs from Deuteronomy 30, where the people do have the law and have internalized it.

14. See, of example, *Guide for the Perplexed*, 1.65.

15. *Religion* 143, cf. *Foundations* 408, p. 25: "Even the Holy One of the Gospel must be compared with our ideal of moral perfection before He is recognized as such. . ."

16. David Novak, *Jewish Social Ethics*, Oxford: Oxford University Press, 1992 p. 36.

17. For rejection of the idea of natural law in Judaism, see Marvin Fox, "Maimonides and Aquinas on Natural Law," in Fox, *Interpreting Maimonides*, pp. 124–151. The argument (p. 126) that there is no word in Biblical Hebrew corresponding to *physis* or *nature* does not rule out the possibility that there are universal moral standards binding on God as well as humans. For criticism of Fox, see Aharon Lichtenstein, "Does Jewish Tradition Recognize an Ethic Independent of Halakha?" in *Contemporary Jewish Ethics*, edited by Menachem Kellner (ed.), New York: Hebrew Publishing Company, 1978, pp. 102–123, as well as David Novak, "Natural Law, Halakhah, and the Covenant," in Novak, *Jewish Social Ethics*, pp. 25–29, and more recently *Natural Law in Judaism*, Cambridge: Cambridge University Press, 1998.

18. Hartman, *A Living Covenant*, p. 24.

19. *Covenant* covers a wide range of agreements. Sometimes it involves a relation between equals (Genesis 21:32; 31:44), sometimes between unequals (1 Samuel 11:1), sometimes between a king and the council of elders (1 Chronicles 11:30). In other cases, it refers to a marriage vow (Proverbs 2:17) or has the force of an ordinance (Joshua 24:25). There are even cases where it involves non-human participants (Jeremiah 33: 20–25). For a classic account of the history and variety of covenants in the ancient Near East, see George Mendenhall, "Ancient Oriental and Biblical Law," as well as "Covenant Forms in Israelite Tradition," *The Biblical Archaeologist Reader*, vol. 3, pp. 3–53. For a more recent study and partial critique of Mendenhall, see Jon Levenson, *Sinai and Zion*, San Francisco: Harper, 1987. pp. 15–86.

20. Cf. Deuteronomy 29:1.

21. Sarna, *Exploring Exodus*, p. 142.

22. *Shabbat* 88a. According to Rava, the covenant did not become valid until the time of Ahasuerus. For further comment, see Urbach, *The Sages*, pp. 327–329; Soloveitchik, *The Lonely Man of Faith*, p. 45, n. 1; and Novak, *Jewish Social Ethics*, pp. 27–29. For the connection between the freedom to enter the covenant and moral autonomy, see Newman, *Past Imperatives*, Albany, NY: SUNY Press, 1998. p. 74.
23. *Midrash Rabbah* to Psalms 123:1.
24. Goodman, "The Individual and the Community in the Normative Traditions of Judaism," *Autonomy and Judaism*, edited by Daniel Frank, pp. 110–111, n. 48.
25. *Yoma* 67b.
26. *Sanhedrin* 56a. For the details of this interpretation and the implications the Rabbis draw from it, see David Novak, *The Image of the Non-Jew in Judaism*, Lewiston, NY: Edwin Mellen Press, 1983, chapter 9.
27. Maimonides, *Mishneh Torah* 14 Laws of Kings and Wars, 9.1.
28. Yehezkel Kaufmann, *The Religion of Ancient Israel*, Chicago: University of Chicago Press, 1960. p. 233.
29. See *Religion of Reason*, p. 78.
30. Joseph Soloveitchik, *Halakhic Man*, pp. 64–65. In evaluating these remarks, it should be kept in mind that Soloveitchik is speaking from the context of Jewish orthodoxy. Kant would never agree that the details of the ritual law can be discovered from within, and would object that one can see the law as part of his very being only if he first accepts the heteronomy of God's revelation to Moses.
31. Kant, *Religion*, p. 142.
32. Kant, *Religion*, p. 112.
33. Maimonides, *Guide of the Perplexed*, 3.26, 3.31. Cf. *Religion of Reason*, pp. 32-33, 345.
34. Kant comes close to this conclusion in *Religion*, p. 94: "Yet, by reason of a peculiar weakness of human nature, pure faith can never be relied on as much as it deserves, that is, a church cannot be established on it alone."
35. *Foundations*, p. 85.
36. *Religion*, p. 152.
37. For more on this point, see J. B. Schneewind, *The Invention of Autonomy*, Cambridge: Cambridge University Press, 1997, especially chapter 23.
38. Whether this means that the ordinances and decrees were accepted one at a time or together as a whole is unclear. For further comment, see Michael Berger, *Rabbinic Authority*, pp. 101–105, 114–115.
39. *Mishneh Torah* 14, Laws Concerning Rebels, 2.3, 6, 7. For further discussion, see David Novak, "Maimonides and the Science of the Law," *Jewish Law Association Studies* 4 (1990): 104–106.
40. *Mishneh Torah* 14, Laws Concerning Rebels, 2.5.
41. On this point, see Rashi's comment on Deuteronomy 29: 14: "I am making this covenant, sworn by an oath, not only with you who stand here with us today. . ., but also with those who are not here with us today."
42. *Religion of Reason*, pp. 78–79.

11   Joseph Soloveitchik and Halakhic Man

LAWRENCE J. KAPLAN

The modern philosophical critique of revealed religion in general and traditional Judaism in particular has been primarily normative, as opposed
to epistemological, in nature. Take Spinoza, for example. While he contrasted theology and philosophy in epistemological terms – inasmuch
as theology, in his view, does not possess any truth-value as opposed to
philosophy, whose goal is the truth – his primary contrast between the
two was normative – inasmuch as he claimed that theology leads only to
obedience to God, as opposed to philosophy which gives rise to the love
of God. As for the Mosaic Law, for Spinoza it possessed only a purely
political significance and lacked any broader moral or spiritual, much
less any intellectual value.[1]

   Kant adopted Spinoza's critique of Judaism, and in a similar vein
argued that "Strictly speaking Judaism is not religion at all" but "only a
collection of merely statutory laws supporting a political state."[2] Of
course, for both Spinoza and Kant, denying any value to Jewish law
was tantamount to denying any value to Judaism in toto. By contrast,
modern Jewish thinkers who sought to find the significance and value of
Judaism as residing in something other than the study and observance
of the Law could agree with the view of Jewish law taken by Spinoza
and Kant, without believing that they had thereby rejected Judaism as
a whole. Thus the early Martin Buber, for whom the "spiritual process
of Judaism manifests itself in history as the striving for an ever more
perfect realization of three interconnected ideas: the idea of unity, the
idea of the deed, and the idea of the future,"[3] leveled a stinging attack
on the value of Jewish law, equaling if not exceeding anything to be
found in Spinoza and Kant. For Buber, the Law was a degenerate form
of Judaism's emphasis on the "religiosity of the deed,"[4] "a mistaken,
disfigured, distorted, religious tradition...which was alien to reality,
but which accused of heresy and annihilated all that...thirsted after
beauty and was winged, which dislocated feeling and cast thought in
irons."[5]

It is against the background of this philosophical critique of Jewish law, or halakhah, to use the standard Hebrew term, and halakhic man, the type of personality forged by its study and practice, that we must examine the significance of the life and writings of Rabbi Joseph B. Soloveitchik (1903–1993).[6] Soloveitchik's writings on the nature of halakhah and the personality of halakhic man are endowed with a special, almost unique, authority, not shared by any other of the works in the modern era on these subjects. For Soloveitchik, alone among the leading Jewish thinkers in the modern era to have written on the philosophy of halakhah, was both a rabbinic figure of the first rank – indeed, he is considered by many to have been the outstanding traditional rabbinic scholar and jurist of the second half of the twentieth century – and a creative theologian and philosopher who mastered the Western tradition of philosophical and scientific thought and was thus able to write about the halakhah in universal philosophical and phenomenological categories.

Soloveitchik was born in Pruzhna, Belorussia. His father, Rabbi Moses Soloveitchik, was himself a distinguished rabbinic scholar, while his paternal grandfather, Rabbi Hayyim Soloveitchik, communal rabbi of Brisk (Brest-Litovsk), was widely regarded as the outstanding rabbinic scholar of his day. Rabbi Hayyim brought a new method of rigorous, highly abstract, conceptual analysis to the study of the Talmud and the cognate rabbinic literature, which formed the staple of the traditional Jewish curriculum. This method, known as the Brisker method, became the standard method of study in many Eastern European, particularly Lithuanian, Yeshivas (academies for advanced study of the Talmud). As we shall see, his grandfather's method plays a key role in Soloveitchik's philosophy of halakhah.

Soloveitchik, a genuine child prodigy, mastered his grandfather's "Brisker" method under the guidance of his father, who drove him mercilessly in a – successful! – attempt to groom him to become the leading Talmudic scholar of the next generation. At the same time, under the influence of his mother, Pesha, a devotee of both German and Russian literature, he acquired a strong interest in secular education. After attaining the equivalent of a "gymnasium" education from private tutors, he entered the University of Berlin in 1926 to study philosophy, where he received his doctorate in 1932 for a thesis on the epistemology and ontology of Hermann Cohen, the founder of the Marburg school of Neo-Kantianism. Much of Soloveitchik's thinking bears the strong imprint of Cohen's critical idealism, in particular the latter's insistence on the autonomous role of reason in creating out of its own resources, his opposition to the psychologization, sociologization, or historicization of either the natural sciences (theoretical reason) or the moral sciences (practical reason), and his emphasis on the primacy of ethics. Though Cohen himself was a liberal Jew, Soloveitchik made use of Cohenian ideas – suitably modified, of course – in his explication of the nature of the halakhah and defense of its ongoing authority.

During his years in Berlin, Soloveitchik continued his rabbinic studies and was ordained by the eminent authority, Rabbi Abraham Kahana Shapiro. In 1932, the year Soloveitchik received his doctorate, he emigrated to the United States, where he became a rabbi in Boston, and in 1941 he succeeded his father as head of the Talmudic faculty of Yeshiva University in New York, where he also taught Jewish philosophy. In the 1950s, Soloveitchik emerged as the leading figure of American modern Orthodoxy, the stream of Judaism that combines fidelity to the rabbinic tradition with openness to and a positive evaluation of Western culture. Perhaps more than any other single individual, he molded the spiritual profile of the American Orthodox community in the last half of the twentieth century.

While a tireless and indefatigable lecturer, Soloveitchik published relatively little. The sum total of writings that he himself prepared for publication is four major essays – two in English, two in Hebrew – each the size of a small book of some 100–150 pages; and some 15–20 other essays, of varying length and importance, in English, Hebrew, and Yiddish.[7]

Soloveitchik's first major essay, "Ish ha-Halakhah" (*Halakhic Man*), [Henceforth: *HMa*] appeared in 1944.[8] About that time, he was working on two other essays – a companion piece to *HMa*, tentatively entitled "Ish ha-Elohim" ("The Man of God"), and a methodological study, "Is a Philosophy of Halakhah Possible?" For reasons that remain unclear, neither essay appeared at the time. A revised version of "Ish ha-Elohim" appeared in 1978 under the title, "U-Vikashtem mi-Sham" ("But From Thence You Will Seek;" based on Deut. 4:29: "But from thence you will seek the Lord your God and you will find him, if you will seek Him with all your heart and with all your soul") [Henceforth: *BFT*],[9] while "Is a Philosophy of Halakhah Possible?" appeared unchanged in 1986 (!) under the title *The Halakhic Mind* [Henceforth: *HMi*].[10] The fourth of his major essays, *The Lonely Man of Faith* [Henceforth: *LMF*], appeared in 1965.[11] Thus, though the publication dates of *HMa*, *BFT*, and *HMi* are spread out over a period of more than forty years, the three, as we shall see, form a unit and need to be examined together. Another essay deserving of note here is "Mah Dodekh mi-Dod" (1962), which contains an extended analysis of the nature of halakhic creativity, and thereby supplements both *HMa* and *BFT* in significant ways.[12]

This chapter will first discuss Soloveitchik's essay *HMi*, and proceed to use it as a general framework for examining Soloveitchik's conception of the nature of halakhah and the personality of halakhic man. In the course of this examination, I will also present summaries of *HMa* and *BFT*, tracking their main lines of argument. (*LMF* will not be discussed.) The chapter will thus present systematically Soloveitchik's conception of two key moments in the life of halakhic man – that of construction and reconstruction. I trust that at the chapter's end, Soloveitchik's response to the modern philosophical critique of the halakhah and halakhic man will emerge.

HALAKHIC MIND[13]

HMi – Soloveitchik's most abstract and technical philosophical work – begins on a perhaps misleading note. Soloveitchik notes that both medieval and modern philosophy "adopted a scientifically purified world as the subject matter of their studies" (p. 6). However, he goes on to argue, certain developments in both twentieth-century science and philosophy (which we will not discuss here) have led to the emergence of an epistemological pluralism, on the basis of which, for the first time, both the philosopher and humanist have gained "an autonomous access toward reality" (p. 41). Similarly, *homo religiosus* also "may [now] avail [him]self of an autonomous attitude" toward the world (p. 4). For, Soloveitchik argues, basing himself on the modern theory of intentionality, "*homo religiosus* no less than the philosopher . . . is an enthusiastic practitioner of the cognitive act." True, he "comprehends the world from a unique aspect, but this does not devaluate the importance of his cognition" (p. 44). Indeed, since *homo religiosus* "holds fast to temporality and is incapable of tearing himself loose from the moorings of his sensuous environment," he "is not concerned with interpreting God in terms of the world, but world under the aspect of God. . . . He views God from the aspect of His creation. . . . The cognition of this world is of the innermost essence of this religious experience" (pp. 45–46).

Having established to his satisfaction the cognitive character of the religious experience, Soloveitchik raises the question of methodology. Is there a specific methodology that religion ought to adopt in its approach to reality? Here Soloveitchik argues that religion should borrow its methodology not from the modern metaphysician, but from the modern twentieth-century physicist. This seems to go against the principle of cognitive pluralism that Soloveitchik uses to establish religion's right to "an autonomous attitude" toward the world in the first place. But, as Soloveitchik explains: "The heterogeneity of knowledge ... is not based upon a manifold of methods employed by the theoretician, but upon the plurality of the objective orders they encounter" (p. 56). Thus the objective order the *homo religiosus* encounters differs from the one the physicist encounters, but the method they both use for examining their respective objective orders is the same. What is that method?

Soloveitchik argues that the quantum physicist deals with three orders of reality. Like his earlier counterpart, the Newtonian physicist, he begins with the qualitative sense world, which "elude[s] scientific scrutiny" and is not subject to cognition in the strict sense (p. 59). And, again like the Newtonian physicist, he then proceeds to *construct* a parallel objective quantitative order via "atomization and piecemeal summation" (p. 60). However – and this is the critical move – the quantum physicist, *unlike* the Newtonian physicist, in order to understand and account for "the enigmatic behavior of certain 'strings of events,'" proceeds to *reconstruct* out of that objective, quantitative, summative order a structural, subjective whole (p. 60). It is this method of reconstruction, used by the quantum physicist in dealing with the realm of nature, that Soloveitchik urges *homo religiosus* to adopt in dealing with the realm of spirit.[14]

We can now understand why Soloveitchik maintains that religion should borrow its methodology not from the modern metaphysician, but from the modern twentieth-century physicist. The modern metaphysician, rebelling against the objective, quantitative, summative order deemed to be the only scientifically knowable reality by the classical physicist, seeks to intuit the subjective realm of the spirit in all its wholeness and totality. But this intuitive leap into totality is highly objectionable. For, so Soloveitchik contends, such an unscientific, indeed anti-intellectual approach, ends up "reduc[ing] ... religion into some recondite, subjective current ... and frees every dark passion and every animal impulse in man" (p. 55). "It is no mere coincidence," Soloveitchik notes, "that the most celebrated philosophers of the Third Reich were the disciples of Husserl. [His] intuitionism ... was transposed [by them] into emotional approaches to reality.... Reason surrender[ed] its supremacy to dark, equivocal emotions," which brought in their wake "havoc and death" (p. 53).

Homo religiosus, therefore, like the quantum physicist, needs to use the method of reconstruction in the realm of the spirit, a method that, unlike the intuitive method of the modern metaphysician, is both rationally justifiable and ethically responsible. He must move regressively "from objective religious symbols to subjective flux" (p. 90) – that is, he must start from the objective religious order and then proceed to reconstruct out of that order subjective aspects of the religious consciousness without, however, claiming that those subjective aspects in any way generated, caused, or determined that objective order. The Jewish *homo religiosus*, accordingly, should start from the objective order of Judaism – that is, the halakhah – and then "in passing onward from the Halakhah and other objective constructs to a limitless, subjective flux, [he] might possibly penetrate the basic structures of [the Jewish] religious consciousness" (p. 101).

HMi points beyond itself in two ways. First, its emphasis on the method of reconstruction, on the move from the objective religious order to subjective religious experience, appears to imply that the suggested analogy between the methodology employed by the twentieth-century physicist and that employed by *homo religiosus* is incomplete. For the twentieth-century physicist, like the Newtonian physicist, *first* engages in an act of construction, and only *after* that initial act of construction does the twentieth-century physicist, unlike his classical counterpart, proceed to engage in an act of reconstruction. The question arises: Is there anything in the methodology employed by *homo religiosus* that corresponds to this initial constructive stage? Second, towards the essay's end, Soloveitchik argues that the method of reconstruction should be used in carrying out the traditional Jewish enterprise of *taàmei ha-mitzvot*, the rationalization of the commandments (pp. 91–99). We would suggest, however, that the method of reconstruction finds its true application in a series of discourses in which Soloveitchik contends that a halakhic-phenomenological analysis reveals that exteriority of deed and interiority of experience are built into the very fabric of such central commandments as prayer, Torah study, repentance, mourning, and rejoicing on the holidays. This "unfinished business" will provide the framework for the rest of this chapter.

ON HALAKHIC CREATIVITY[15]

If we do not speak of *homo religiosus* in general, but focus on that uniquely Jewish *homo religiosus*, halakhic man, it becomes clear that the initial constructive stage in his religious activity for Soloveitchik is located in his power of *chidush* – that is, his creative interpretation of halakhic texts.

For his model of *hiddush,* Soloveitchik takes the method of conceptual analysis of the Talmud and cognate rabbinic literature developed
by his grandfather, Rabbi Hayyim of Brisk. Soloveitchik argues that his
grandfather introduced a revolution into the study of halakhah comparable to the Galilean-Newtonian revolution in science. Just as the
Galilean-Newtonian scientist, unlike the Aristotelian scientist, does not
seek to explain the world in its own terms – that is, qualitative sense
categories – but rather constructs his own terms and modes of discourse
and explanation – that is – abstract–formal mathematical equations and
functions that parallel the qualitative sense world – so Rabbi Hayyim
was not content to explain halakhic texts in their own terms, but rather
constructed an entire system of abstract concepts and definitions in
order to explain and understand them. Both halakhic and scientific concepts, then, are not *derived* from the data, but are free constructions of
their powerful creative spirits and intellects.

The halakhist of the school of Rabbi Hayyim thus constructs an
ideal, coherent, rational system of law out of the welter of oftentimes
conflicting, perplexing, obscure individual texts, decisions, rules, and
cases, or rather constructs this coherent system and *imposes* it upon that
welter of source material. This abstract–conceptual halakhic system is
(1) systematic in the strict sense; (2) a priori, and (3) ideal. It is systematic
in the strict sense, for the halakhist introduces unified logical structures,
complexes of abstract concepts in order to integrate conglomerations of
diverse, seemingly unrelated laws. It is a priori, for just as the scientist
creates mathematical equations out of his autonomous reason in order
to answer the problems posed by the sense data of empirical reality, so
the halakhist creates abstract concepts out of his autonomous reason to
answer the problems posed by the halakhic data that confront him. (Here
Soloveitchik adopts the contention of Hermann Cohen, who argues that
any attempt to deny the rational, autonomous process of scientific development and to subject it to psychologization, sociologization, or historicization will end up by destroying all genuine mathematical–scientific
thinking, and extends it to halakhic thinking and the process of halakhic
development.) Finally, it is ideal, insofar as the concepts postulated by
the halakhist are always on a higher level of abstraction than those to
be found in the halakhic texts themselves.

Soloveitchik's description of halakhic *hiddush,* as exemplified by
the school of Rabbi Hayyim, thus clearly corresponds to that initial stage
of scientific construction described in *HMi.* But this raises the question
as to who is this halakhic man for whom halakhic *hiddush* plays such

a central and critical role in his intellectual and religious life, and what exactly is the nature of that central and critical role? For answers to these questions we must turn to *HMa* and *BFT*.

HALAKHIC MAN[16]

HMa is divided into two parts: (1) Halakhic Man: His World View and His Life (pp. 3–95), and (2) His Creative Capacity (pp. 97–137). A close analysis reveals, however, that the following division would be truer to its contents: (1) the fundamental problematic of the essay is set up – namely, the conflict between this worldliness and otherworldliness in the consciousness of halakhic man (pp. 3–40); (2) the theme of divine contraction is introduced and employed as a means of enabling halakhic man to resolve this contradiction (pp. 41–79); (3) the theme of halakhic creativity is now introduced, both in the realm of halakhic theory and halakhic practice, creativity which, in turn, is linked with divine contraction (pp. 74–109); and (4) the essay shifts from man as creator of worlds through the actualization of the halakhah in external reality to man as creator of himself (pp. 109–137). Not surprisingly, the man who has completed this process of self-creation turns out to be none other than halakhic man.

The essay sets forth a phenomenology of halakhic man, the rabbinic scholar whose life is devoted to and whose personality is shaped by the practice and, even more so, the study of the halakhah. While in our analysis up to this point we have seen Soloveitchik treating halakhic man as a special type of *homo religiosus*, in *HMa* Soloveitchik sharply contrasts the two. Soloveitchik insists that halakhic man's religious consciousness is unique, insofar as he is both cognitive man and *homo religiosus*. More particularly, halakhic man's consciousness is torn between this-worldliness and other-worldliness.

On the one hand, halakhic man's consciousness is directed toward concrete empirical reality, and this for two reasons: epistemological and moral.

From an epistemological standpoint, halakhic man is a type of cognitive man, and all cognition – Soloveitchik claims in good Kantian fashion – is firmly set within the bounds of space and time. Here Soloveitchik again establishes an analogy between the scientist and halakhic man, focusing on halakhic man's approach to reality.[17] Both halakhic man and the scientist, Soloveitchik argues, use their a priori ideal systems – the halakhic system of laws given to Moses on Mount Sinai and developed

over the centuries and the scientific system, respectively – as comprehensive modes of orienting themselves to and comprehending reality.

This science/world–halakhah/world analogy, drawn by Soloveitchik, with its clear neo-Kantian flavor, is certainly controversial, perhaps
problematic. The point I wish to emphasize, however, is that in terms of
the argument of the essay, the function of the analogy is, as stated earlier, to firmly establish halakhic man as a type of cognitive man, similar
to the cognitive man par excellence, the mathematical-physicist, one
whose consciousness, like that of all cognitive men, is firmly set within
and directed to the comprehension of concrete spatio-temporal reality.

From a moral standpoint, as well, halakhic man's consciousness
is, or perhaps better, ought to be, directed toward our concrete reality. Soloveitchik maintains that those religions that "yearn[ed] to break
through the bounds of concrete reality and escape to the sphere of eternity" were "so intoxicated by their dreams of an exalted supernal existence that they failed to hear... the sighs of orphans, the groans of the
destitute" (p. 41). Ethical seriousness consequently requires that one's
concern should be focused on earthly matters.

On the other hand, halakhic man for Soloveitchik is not just a "secular cognitive type unconcerned with transcendence" (p. 40) Rather,
halakhic man's consciousness, like that of *homo religiosus*, is directed
toward transcendent realms. *Homo religiosus*, Soloveitchik explains,
"intrigued by the mystery of existence" (p. 7) and longing for a "refined
and purified existence" (p. 16), "passes beyond the realm of concrete-
ness and reality set within frame of scientific experience and enters into
a higher realm" (p. 14). In a similar fashion:

> God's Torah has implanted in halakhic man's consciousness both
> the idea for everlasting life and the desire for eternity.... His
> soul... thirsts for the living God, and these streams of yearning
> flow to the sea of transcendence, to "God who conceals himself in
> His dazzling hiddenness." (p. 40)

At this point, Soloveitchik introduces and employs the theme of divine
contraction as a means of enabling halakhic man to resolve this "central antinomy" (p. 39) in his consciousness between this worldliness and
otherworldliness. For the process of divine contraction is a process that
makes possible God's presence in this world via the "lowering of transcendence into the midst of our turbid, coarse, material world" (p.108).

In truth, the process of contraction for Soloveitchik is two-fold. In
the first stage, performed by God Himself, God contracts Himself within
the ideal complex of a priori halakhic concepts, within "the clear and

determinate forms, the precise and authoritative laws, and the determinate principles" (p. 59) of the halakhah that serve as the objects of a person's study. In the second stage, performed by man, when a person actualizes within the concrete world this ideal halakhah that he has studied, he thereby lowers the divine presence, that transcendence which was *already* to be found within the ideal halakhic complex, to that world. It follows, then, that halakhic man is no longer torn by the contradiction in his consciousness, since he is now able, by means of this double contraction, to meet God within the bounds of space and time.

From this theological assumption of double contraction there follow, in Soloveitchik's view, a number of important consequences for the personality and religious world-view of halakhic man. First, halakhic man "is completely suffused with an unqualified ontological optimism and is totally immersed in the cosmos.... As he sees it, the task of man is to bring the divine presence into this lower [material] world" (p. 52). Second, precisely because God's presence is to be found in the ideal complex of a priori halakhic concepts subjected to halakhic man's cognition and in the concrete world sanctified by halakhic man's actualization of this ideal halakhah, halakhic man views this ideal and practical halakhah as "provid[ing] the clearest and strongest testimony to man's importance, his central place in the world" (p. 71). Halakhic man thus not only optimistically affirms the cosmos, but also optimistically affirms himself. More specifically, God's presence in the ideal complex of a priori halakhic concepts subjected to halakhic man's cognition testifies to the importance and religious significance of halakhic man's intellect, while His presence in the concrete world sanctified by halakhic man's actualization of this ideal halakhah testifies to the importance and religious significance of halakhic man's moral will. Halakhic man thereby discovers in the ideal and practical halakhah not only the affirmation of his "importance [and] central place in the world," but, perhaps even more significant, the affirmation of his individuality. Finally, since halakhic man, unlike *homo religiosus*, does not encounter God directly, but only through the mediation of clear and determinate, ideal a priori halakhic concepts and fixed and precise mitzvah performances, which actualize this ideal halakhah, halakhic man rejects any religious subjectivism. His method is that of objectification. Inward religious experience only *follows* upon halakhic cognition and halakhic performance, both of which are objective in nature. And even then, this inner subjective experience itself is structured and ordered by halakhic regulations. In this respect, halakhic man resembles the mathematical physicist, perhaps the cognitive man par excellence, who via "the ordered, illumined, determined world, imprinted with the stamp of creative intellect, of pure reason and clear cognition," arrives at a profound and penetrating experience of the beauty and splendor of the cosmos (pp. 83–84).

In connection with this last point, we should recall that *HMa* appeared in 1944. Thus, perhaps more than philosophical and theological considerations, moral considerations underlie Soloveitchik's critique of religious subjectivism. As Soloveitchik comments, precisely those modern anti-scientific romantic movements, "from the midst of which there arose in various forms the sanctification of vitality and intuition, the veneration of instinct, . . . the glorification of the emotional – affective life, and the flowing, surging stream of subjectivity, . . . have brought complete chaos and human depravity to the world. And let the events of the present era be proof!" (note 4, p. 141). It should be clear that in its emphasis on the importance of the method of objectification in the realm of the spirit and the correlative epistemological and, more important, moral critique of religious subjectivism *HMa* is at one with *HMi*.

At this point, the theme of halakhic man as creator is introduced. Halakhic man is a creator both with respect to halakhic theory and halakhic practice, and this creativity, as already noted, is linked with divine contraction, implicitly in the realm of halakhic theory and explicitly in the realm of halakhic practice. To be more precise, in the realm of halakhic theory, contraction precedes creation. That is, God revealed a priori cognitive-normative halakhic principles in which both His will and wisdom are to be found, and these principles serve as the starting point – provide the raw materials, as it were – for halakhic man's intellectual creativity. "Halakhic man received the Torah from Sinai not as a simple recipient, but as a creator of worlds. . . . The power of creative interpretation (*hiddush*) is the very foundation of the received tradition" (p. 81). Indeed, this power of creative interpretation granted to halakhic man serves as the source of his sense of freedom.

By contrast, in the realm of halakhic practice, creativity precedes and gives rise to contraction. In the realm of practice, creativity is identified, in a Cohenian sense, with actualizing the ideal halakhic in the real world. But, as we have seen, precisely when a person actualizes the ideal halakhah within the concrete world does he thereby lower the divine presence to and contract it within that world. Moreover, Soloveitchik, in a similar vein, understands holiness to "denote . . . the appearance of a mysterious transcendence in the midst of our concrete world" (p. 46). All this leads to the following equation: "the realization of the halakhah = contraction = holiness = creation" (p. 109).

The essay undergoes a fundamental shift as Soloveitchik moves from man as creator of worlds through the actualization of the halakhah in external concrete reality to man as creator of himself. Here Soloveitchik backtracks, for it appears that man at the beginning of this process of self-creation is *not* halakhic man. Rather, as noted, halakhic man is he who has completed this process of self-creation. Soloveitchik's description of this process would appear to be an intriguing, if unstable, blend of Aristotelian and neo-Kantian elements.

> Man, initially, must cause all the potentialities of the species implanted in him to pass into actuality. He must completely realize the form of the species "man." However, once he has actualized this universal form, then instead of having his own specific image obliterated, he acquires particular form, an individual mode of existence, a unique personality, and an active, creative spirit.... The realization of the universal in man's being negates any claim the species has on him. This outlook is truly striking in its paradoxical nature. It is a hybrid of two views: the view of Aristotle with its emphasis on the universal and the view of the Halakhah with its emphasis on the individual. The method is Greek, the purpose halakhic. The goal of self-creation is individuality, autonomy, uniqueness and freedom..... However, the whole process of development unfolds in an ethical-halakhic spirit. (pp. 135, 137).

It must be said that it is difficult see exactly how man, through actualizing this universal form, can acquire a "particular form, an individual mode of existence." And describing this outlook as paradoxical does not make it any clearer. Moreover, if the goal of self-creation is halakhic, it is a halakhah viewed through neo-Kantian lenses, insofar as that goal is "individuality, autonomy, uniqueness, and freedom." Indeed, the very notion of self-creation, of the emergence of an I, derives from the spiritual and intellectual world of Hermann Cohen.

Be this as it may, with the positing of the goals of self-creation as "individuality, autonomy, uniqueness, and freedom," the essay returns to and concludes with halakhic man:

> And halakhic man ... is, indeed, a free man. He creates an ideal world, renews his own being ..., dreams about the complete realization of the Halakhah in the very core of the world, and looks forward to the kingdom of God contracting itself and appearing in the midst of concrete ... reality (p. 137).

If we stand back for a moment from the winding course of the essay's argument, we can see the presence of certain themes that reappear throughout Soloveitchik's work: the cognitive-normative nature of the religious experience; the importance of objectification in the realm of the spirit; an objectification that far from dampening rather gives rise to religious passion; the need for moral seriousness that requires a this-worldly perspective; and an emphasis on freedom and creativity, both personal and intellectual creativity, as the ultimate goals of human development, with the proviso that such freedom and such creativity always be subject to ethical constraints.

BUT FROM THENCE YOU WILL SEEK[18]

Of all of Soloveitchik's essays, *BFT* is the one that deals most directly with that classic theme of religious philosophy, the confrontation between reason and revelation. However, it deals with this issue in a characteristically modern way. Reason and revelation are viewed not so much as two distinct sources of knowledge or two bodies of teaching but rather as two different modes of experience, as two different ways of relating to God, as two different personal stances the individual assumes.

BFT is a highly dialectical description of the stages a religious individual must traverse in his search for God. In the first stage, this search finds its expression in a natural cosmic-ontological encounter with God. Though Soloveitchik describes this initial encounter as a rational religious experience, in truth it derives not so much from man's rationality but from a dynamic, powerful desire to sense the transcendent in the finite, from a quest for the presence of God in the world. To be sure, one cannot rise from finitude to infinity, from the temporal to the eternal, via scientific categories and modes of thought. Soloveitchik agrees entirely with Kant that scientific categories, as categories intended to organize and order finite empirical experience, are operative only within the bounds of time and space. And yet, if the world as understood scientifically cannot lead one from finitude to infinity, the world as experienced in its natural and naive immediacy shines with the light of infinity and eternity (pp. 127–128).

Judaism, Soloveitchik contends, unequivocally approves of this cosmic encounter with God. Indeed, in Soloveitchik's view, following that of Maimonides, every individual is religiously obligated to search for God and seek His traces in every cosmic phenomenon, both natural and spiritual. At the same time, Soloveitchik, unlike Maimonides, claims that this stage of natural, cosmic religiosity reaches a point where it breaks down. Why so?

First, Soloveitchik answers, God oftentimes eludes man, and His presence is not always manifest in His creation. Man, therefore, must not only *experience* God but must *believe* in Him. If experience is a function of God's presence and nearness, belief is a function of His absence and distance.

Moreover, even when the infinite does shine through the finite, the eternal through the temporal, the nature of this transcendent element is indeterminate. The cosmic manifestation of the divine reveals a God who is opaque, obscure, and incomprehensible. He can be defined only in terms of negative attributes, as different from, other-than, our limited, finite, conditioned world. In a word, the transcendent element as it emerges out of man's cosmic encounter with God contains more negativity than positivity (p. 138).

Finally, since this approach to God involves the methods of abstraction and generalization, the God experienced in this manner becomes transformed into a general abstract idea, bordering on emptiness, lacking content, life, and particularity. Such a God tends to be an impersonal God. Thus a wholly rational, cosmic religiosity is always in danger of falling into pantheism (pp. 138–139). In sum, the manifestation of the divine presence through nature, with all its splendor and greatness, will, by itself, not bring man close to God.

But precisely at this moment, a dramatic and unexpected development takes place. Out of the breakdown of the individual's rational religious experience there arises a new, radically different, contradictory religious experience, the revelational religious experience. God assumes the initiative, and appearing, as it were, out of nowhere reaches out to man. "God reveals Himself to His creation above and beyond nature and causes men to prophesy" (p. 142).

Perhaps the best way to grasp how Soloveitchik understands the nature of this revelational religious experience is by examining how he contrasts it with the rational religious experience.

1. In the rational religious experience, man seeks God in the ordered, structured, lawful, illuminated cosmos. In the revelational religious experience, God seeks man from out of the midst of opaque and incomprehensible, torn, evil, crisis-laden existence (pp. 143–144).
2. The God of the cosmic experience, of creation, is the *sekhel ha-neèlam*, the concealed intellect, the object of man's cognitive desire.

The God of the revelational experience, of Sinai, is the *ratzon ha-neèlam*, the concealed will, who imposes upon man a specific mode of life and demands of him unlimited obedience and absolute submission. Revelation is primarily the revelation of the Law.

3. The cosmic experience is the experience of the nearness of God, of divine closeness, of the image of transcendence reflected in creation. In the revelational experience, however, God appears to man from afar, and only the divine commanding voice bridges the gap, the abyss separating God from man (pp. 146–147).

4. The divine attribute that manifests itself to man in the cosmic experience is the attribute of mercy. God is experienced as a source of comfort, meaning, and significance. The divine attribute that reveals itself to man in the revelational experience is the attribute of judgment. God appears as an awesome, frightening, all-demanding Judge, requiring of man absolute obedience, complete self-sacrifice – in a word, the performance of commandments (pp. 156–158).

5. Man responds to God's appearance in the cosmic experience as the merciful God with trust in Him, with a desire to experience His presence, His closeness. Man realizes that his very existence has its source and origin in God. By contrast, man responds to God's appearance in the revelational experience as the God of judgment with fear, terror, and flight from His presence. God is seen as an awesome power that threatens man's very existence (pp. 157–158).

6. The cosmic experience is consequently an experience of freedom, of expansion, testifying to the greatness and reach of man's spirit. The revelational experience is an experience of necessity, of compulsion, of being imposed upon by God (p. 148).

7. Finally, flowing from all of this, the rational religious experience affirms man's identity as a cultural being; indeed it is the highest expression of man's cultural creativity. The revelational experience, however, is "unrelated to the free, creative spirit of man, and is unconcerned with the desires of cultural creativity in all its unfolding" (p. 154).

Despite this series of oppositions, Soloveitchik insists that both experiences are necessary. If a person opts only for the rational religious experience, religion becomes reduced to a cultural epiphenomenon, which, moreover, is unable to discipline the individual with his bodily drives, instincts, and passions. Indeed, since this form of religion is the product of man's own creative spirit, the individual, instead of being subject to the norm, views himself as lord over the norm, insofar as he is its legislator. "Therefore he permits himself to choose this law and reject another..., as if all derived from free human creativity and returned to it. The result of such freedom is moral anarchy" (p. 162). Precisely for this reason one requires a divinely revealed religious norm that clearly derives from a source *other* and *higher* than man, a norm that is *imposed* upon him (pp. 162–163).

On the other hand, it would be wrong to opt only for the revealed religious experience and wholly ignore the rational, natural, cosmic religious experience. God wants man to yearn for Him, desire Him, apprehend Him, reach out to Him in that state of freedom, expansion, elevation that characterizes the rational religious experience. God desires man to experience His presence in the cosmos, in the natural order. Moreover, the halakhah unequivocally approves of man's creative, dynamic activity as a cultural being. It, consequently, bestows its approval on the rational religious experience as the highest form of cultural creativity, as the most exalted level of man's natural-ontological consciousness or, to be more precise, it bestows that approval *so long as* the revealed religious experience is not ignored – that is, so long as the uniqueness of religion is not denied, so long as religion is not translated wholly into cultural categories (pp. 163–164).[19]

But if, according to Soloveitchik, God in the revelational religious experience appears from an infinite distance as sheer otherness, if He reveals Himself in the attribute of judgment, if He inspires in man feelings of fear and terror, of necessity and confusion, of insufficiency and lack, and finally, if He denies man's very identity as a cultural being, how then can man be expected to relate to Him lovingly and wholeheartedly, in a spirit of closeness and warmth? Does it not appear, given Soloveitchik's analysis of the revelational religious experience, that the modern critique leveled against traditional Judaism by such hostile critics as Spinoza, Kant, and the early Buber – namely, the claim that Judaism as a religion of revealed Law gives rise to a spiritual slavishness, grounded in the fear of God and exhausting itself in external obedience – contains a good deal of truth?

Soloveitchik, who throughout his writings displays an acute sensitivity to this critique, answers that the elaborate series of contrasts he has drawn between these two experiences belongs to the preliminary, superficial stage of man's religious consciousness (p. 167). The individual must overcome and transcend this stage of divided consciousness by actively transforming the trans-cosmic divine revelation into a creative experience of freedom in a condition of passionate cleaving love (pp. 167, 234). How is this accomplished?

What happens is the following. The revelational law, which at first appeared to frighten, terrify, and overwhelm man, now, in the final dialectical turn, affirms man's worth and constitutes the deepest source of his creativity and freedom. The revealed contents of the halakhah at first seemed totally other than man. However, man can assimilate those contents and be at one with them. In good Hegelian fashion, then, otherness is posited only to be overcome, and the individual, in becoming one with the halakhah, assimilates it to himself, and thereby both assimilates the thought-will of God to himself and attaches himself to the primordial divine intellect and will.

But exactly how is the otherness of halakhah overcome? How does man assimilate the contents of the halakhah and become one with them? How does the revelational experience acquire those aspects of freedom and creativity that had seemed to be the sole possession of the rational, cosmic, religious experience? In a word, how does the halakhah make *devekut* – cleaving to God – possible?

Soloveitchik answers: "In three ways the desire of Judaism to elevate the religious consciousness to the level of a spiritual consciousness that joins the natural desire of man for God with revelational faith expresses itself: 1) the supremacy of the intellect; 2) the elevation of the body; 3) the perpetuation of the divine word" (p. 204). Let us focus on the first two.

The supremacy of the intellect refers to the halakhah as a systematic corpus of law that is the object of profound study. And again we have a dialectical move. The law, when first revealed, is perceived as other, as a transcendental corpus of texts and rulings that appears to be sealed off from man's intellect. However, in truth, the law as a corpus of study, in the final turn, does not downgrade man's intellect but, on the contrary, exalts it.

Precisely because the halakhah, for Soloveitchik, obligates the sage to engage in original, creative interpretation (*hiddush*), it thereby affirms the supremacy of the intellect in the realm of halakhic study, and by so doing, incorporates the natural-cognitive consciousness within the sphere and domain of the revelational consciousness. Thus the gap between these two modes of consciousness is bridged. We may differentiate here between origin and content. While the Torah originates from heaven, it is no longer in heaven; rather, its contents have been handed over to man to study, analyze, and apply. The revealed law in its *origin* seemed to challenge, overwhelm, and defeat man's intellect, in the systematic and noetic quality of its *content* challenges, affirms, and adorns that intellect. As Soloveitchik states:

> The backdrop is revelational-visionary, but the whirl of colors painted on that background is cognitive – natural.... We have here a blend of opposing principles, a revelational principle and a rational principle.... The postulates [of the Halakhah] themselves, despite their fixed character, become imbued with a content that is vibrant and alive....The revelational consciousness is incorporated into the creative, cognitive consciousness. God gave the Torah to Israel [revelation] and has commanded us to engage in creative interpretation [cognition] (pp. 205–207).

The same type of dialectical process, culminating in the synthesis of the two modes of consciousness, is at work in Soloveitchik's discussion of elevation of the body. Elevation of the body deals with the halakhah as a corpus of practice. As such a corpus, the halakhah, in terms of its *origin*, is imposed on man from on high. In this regard, it would appear, to begin with, to negate man: his body, society, culture and civilization. However, in the final turn, the opposite is true. For if we look at the normative *content and purpose* of the halakhah we see that the halakhah does not negate man, his body, his culture and civilization, but affirms them through elevating and sanctifying them. "The very fact" – Soloveitchik asserts – "that the halakhah has imposed commandments upon man regulating his bodily activities indicates that the halakhah has not abandoned man's body to the realm of blind, mechanical, unredeemed nature but believes that man's biological existence can be infused with meaning, purpose, significance, and spirit" (p. 207).

Similarly, the halakhah takes a positive attitude towards society, culture, and civilization. The broad and profound social concern of the halakhah, its rich variety of social and political institutions, all indicate halakhah's belief that the true religious life is not lived in isolation but among and between people. Moreover, the all-encompassing scope of the halakhah, the fact the halakhah is meant to be realized in the concrete world, requires of man the knowledge of that real, concrete world in all its complexity and particularity (pp. 216–217).

The opposition between the revelational religious consciousness and the creative-rational religious consciousness is thus overcome in the actual study and practice of the halakhah. The halakhah, despite its revealed quality, sheds its "otherness," its threatening nature. The initial impact of revelation constrains man. But the content and purpose of that revelation, both in terms of study and practice, give rise to the sense of freedom, self-affirmation, affirmation of society, culture and civilization, and above all, affirmation of man's creative spirit that had initially characterized the creative-rational religious consciousness. But this dialectical switch can take place only if man accomplishes it, if man in the practice and study of the halakhah himself transforms the experience of necessity into one of freedom.

As the reader has no doubt discerned by now, the individual who has completed the long arduous dialectical religious trek described in *BFT*, who "cleaves to God absolutely and completely, without any recoil or retreat" (p. 234) in passionate love, turns out to be none other than halakhic man himself! Thus most of the major motifs that Soloveitchik uses in *BFT* to describe the final stage of passionate cleaving love appear in *HMa* as part of Soloveitchik's description of that essay's eponymous hero: the halakhah as an intellectual structure similar to mathematical physics; the positive attitude of halakhah toward the body; the halakhah's all-embracing nature; the descent of holiness into the concrete; and, above all, the freedom, autonomy, and creativity of the individual committed to the halakhah, both its practice and study. *BFT* describes the long dialectical journey culminating in the arrival at the final destination; *HMa* is devoted to the portrait of that individual who, via his commitment to the halakhah, has reached that final destination. This fundamental structural difference between the essays results in turn in a critical thematic difference. In *HMa*, the revelational framework within which halakhic man is active is taken for granted, and the essay focuses on halakhic man's freedom and creativity within and, indeed, made possible by that framework. *BFT*, by contrast, places great stress on the initial moment of terror, necessity, and constraint imposed upon man by the revelational framework, and the freedom and creativity within and made possible by that framework are attained by man only after he has completed the long and arduous dialectical trek described by the essay. In this respect, I believe, *BFT* is the more ambitious of the two essays.[20]

OUTWARD DEED AND INWARD FULFILLMENT

If halakhic *hiddush*, which plays such a central role in both *HMa* and *BFT*, corresponds, on Soloveitchik's reading, to the initial constructive stage described in *HMi*, the stage of reconstruction described in that essay is exemplified, again on his reading, in the performance and fulfillment of certain key commandments. This brings us to one of Soloveitchik's best known innovative insights – namely, the distinction he developed in many of his halakhic discourses between the *ma'aseh ha-mitzvah*, the indispensable means whereby one performs a commandment, and the *kiyyum ha-mitzvah*, the actual fulfillment of the commandment. Normally, Soloveitchik points out, *ma'aseh* and *kiyyum* coincide. Thus, for example, one performs the commandment to eat matzah by eating matzah, and that act of eating simultaneously constitutes the fulfillment of the commandment. The same holds true for most commandments. However, he contends, a strictly halakhic analysis reveals that there are central and fundamental "experiential" commandments where performance and fulfillment do not coincide, where the performance is an outward act but the fulfillment consists in an inner experience. Examples of such commandments are prayer, which is performed by the praying individual's verbal recitation of a liturgical text, but fulfilled by his awareness of standing before the divine presence; repentance, which is performed by the returnee's verbal recitation of the confession, but fulfilled by his inner recognition of his sin, regret over the past, and resolve for the future, thereby returning to God, minimally out of fear and maximally out of love; rejoicing on the festivals, which is performed by such acts as the celebrant's eating from the meat of the holiday peace offering (when the Temple was still standing) or (nowadays) by his eating meat and drinking wine, but fulfilled by his inward sense of rejoicing before the Lord; and mourning, which is performed by the mourner's engaging in the rites of mourning, but fulfilled by his undergoing the inner experience of pain and grief, and by his sense that the grisly encounter with death has cut him off from God. (Note how in all four commandments, the inner fulfillment is not just an emotional experience, but involves an awareness of a special, very intimate type of relationship with God.)

It should be clear that, for Soloveitchik, the individual in working his way from *ma'aseh ha-mitzvah*, the outward objective performance of a commandment, to the *kiyyum ha-mitzvah*, the commandment's inward subjective experiential fulfillment, is performing an act of reconstruction. Indeed, in a recently published work, Soloveitchik states that the *ma'aseh ha-mitzvah* is a "piecemeal process of actual execution...denot[ing] a religious technique, a series of concrete media through which the execution of the *mitzvah* is made possible, while the *kiyyum ha-mitzvah* relates to the total effect, to the achievement itself, to the structural wholeness of the norm realization."[21] The striking verbal similarities between this passage and the description of reconstruction in *HMi* speak for themselves.

Of particular significance is Soloveitchik's analysis of the inward experience of repentance, which he generally identifies with repentance out of love. Repentance out of love, for Soloveitchik, is not only an act of self-transformation and self-purification; it is primarily an act of self-creation. As he states: "A person is creative; he was endowed with the power to create at his very inception. When he finds himself in a situation of sin, he takes advantage of his creative capacity, returns to God, and becomes a ... self-creator and self-fashioner. Man through repentance creates himself, his own 'I'" (*HMa*, p. 113). Moreover, this act of self-creation accomplished through repentance out of love is not supernatural but rather wholly psychological in character; it is a rational, comprehensible act that takes place in the depths of the psyche. "Purification is conditional upon drawing near and standing directly before God. ... The act of purification is something each man must perform by himself, each man in his own heart."[22]

In all these respects, Soloveitchik follows the lead of Hermann Cohen. First, for Cohen, "Liberation from sin has to become the goal, and only through the attainment of this will the new I be begotten."[23] Second, this task of liberation from sin is one of self-sanctification and self-purification.[24] Third, this self-sanctification or self-purification must be performed entirely by man. To cite Cohen: "Only man can actualise self-sanctification; no God can help him in this."[25]

It is revealing that, for Soloveitchik, repentance out of fear, in contrast to repentance out of love, is wholly supernatural in character. The absolution or expiation obtained as a result of repentance out of fear is granted by God Himself in a mysterious transcendent act of grace. Here again, by linking the naturalistic, inward, creative act of self-purification with repentance out of love and the mysterious, transcendent act of God's absolution of sin with repentance out of fear, thereby glorifying the former and deprecating the latter, Soloveitchik follows in Cohen's footsteps. That Cohen, the liberal Jewish philosopher, would exalt the creative act of self-purification performed by man over the supernatural expiation granted by God is only to be expected. That Soloveitchik, the leading spokesman for the rabbinic tradition in the second half of the twentieth century, should similarly do so is worthy of note and bears striking witness to his philosophic sensibility.

Of exceptional importance, Soloveitchik links repentance out of fear with the written Torah and repentance out of love with the oral Torah.[26] One way of understanding this is that for Soloveitchik, it is the oral Torah that makes love of God possible and thus makes repentance out of love possible. Here the threads of our analysis come together.

For Soloveitchik, the oral Torah does not so much refer to the oral interpretation of the written Torah revealed to Moses on Mount Sinai and handed down from generation to generation, but rather to the power God granted to the Sages to engage in *hiddush*, creative interpretation, and to determine the meaning of the law thereby. This has two consequences. First, as we have seen, halakhic man, through engaging in creative interpretation, becomes a partner with God in the formation of Torah. Second, as we have also seen, the oral Torah, as opposed to the written Torah, is, in Soloveitchik's view, primarily the product of halakhic man's own creative cognitive act. Consequently, to use Soloveitchik's poetic formulation: the written Torah is written on parchment with ink; the oral Torah is inscribed on man's heart. This partnership between man and God in the formation of Torah and the interior quality of the Torah bring man close to God, serve to bridge the gap between them, and thereby make both love of God possible and repentance out of love possible. We have a move here from creativity to interiority, from construction to reconstruction.

Yet, in general, the stages of construction and reconstruction in the life and activity of halakhic man are not as tightly knit as they are in the scientific activity of the quantum physicist. For the objective, quantitative order out of which the quantum physicist *reconstructs* a structural, subjective whole is the *same* objective, quantitative order that the quantum physicist *constructed* via "atomization and piecemeal summation" to parallel the qualitative sense world. But the objective summative order constructed by the halakhist of the school of Rabbi Hayyim is the system of abstract halakhic concepts and definitions, while the objective religious order out of which the halakhist – indeed all Jews – reconstruct subjective aspects of the religious consciousness is constituted by the outward, objective performance of those special "experiential" commandments whose fulfillment consists in an inner subjective religious experience.[27]

But, as just suggested, perhaps in a more experiential and inward, if technically looser, sense we might link construction and reconstruction in the life of halakhic man as follows. As we saw, the halakhist's act of construction – namely, *hiddush*, creative interpretation – makes him a partner with God in the formation of Torah and inscribes the Torah on his heart, leading to his being close to God and loving Him. But at the same time, as we also saw, the inner subjective religious experience reconstructed out of the outward, objective performance of those special "experiential" commandments is not just an emotional experience, but always involves an awareness of a special, very intimate type of relationship with God. We may say, then, that the acts of construction and reconstruction on the part of halakhic man – though the former gives rise to abstract halakhic principles, while the latter begins with concrete halakhic deeds – together serve to bring him into the presence of God.

To conclude: We may say that Soloveitchik responds to the modern critique of traditional halakhic Judaism with a tacit concession. Had Judaism consisted only of the written Torah, then the accusations leveled against it – its being a slavish religion focused on externalities, concerned only with obedience to God, and leading only to the fear of Him – would be appropriate.[28] But Judaism does not consist only of the written Torah; at its heart stands the oral Torah. And thanks to the oral Torah, in which "the revelational consciousness is incorporated into the creative, cognitive consciousness," in which the halakhist postulates abstract halakhic principles out of his own autonomous reason in order to account for and explain the revealed halakhic data, and, finally, in which the performance of fixed religious deeds results in an inward religious fulfillment, Judaism provides the revealed, objective, covenantal framework so necessary to prevent moral anarchy, while it both calls upon man and enables him to fill that framework with the freedom, intellectual creativity, and religious interiority leading to the knowledge and love of God.

Notes

1. See *Theological-Political Treatise*, Chapters 3–5 and 13–15.
2. *Religion Within the Boundaries of Mere Reason*, translated by George Di Giovanni, in Kant, *Religion and Rational Theology* (Cambridge, U.K: Cambridge University Press, 1996), p. 154.
3. "The Renewal of Judaism," translated by Eva Jospe, in Buber, *On Judaism* (New York: Schocken Books, 1967), p. 40.
4. "Jewish Religiosity," *ibid.*, pp. 91–92.
5. *Der Jude und Sein Judentum*, Cologne, 1963, p. 272, cited in Gershom Scholem, "Martin Buber's Conception of Judaism," *On Jews and Judaism in Crisis: Selected Essays*, edited by Werner Dannhauser (New York: Schocken Books, 1976), p. 134.
6. For a biographical sketch, see Aaron Rakeffet–Rothkoff, "Biography of Rabbi Joseph Dov ha-Levi Soloveitchik" in *The Rav: The World of Rabbi Joseph B. Soloveitchik*, Vol. 1 (Hoboken, NJ: Ktav Publishing, 1999), pp. 21–78.
7. For bibliographical guidance, see Zanvel Klein, "Bnei Yosef Dovrim: Rabbi Joseph B. Soloveitchik: A Bibliography," *The Torah U-Madda Journal* 4 (1993): 84–113.

8. *Talpiyyot* 1:3–4 (1944): 651–735 [= *Halakhic Man*, translated by Lawrence Kaplan, Philadelphia: Jewish Publication Society, 1983.]

9. *Ish ha-Halakhah – Galui ve-Nistar* (Jerusalem: World Zionist Organization, 1979), pp. 115–235.

10. *The Halakhic Mind: An Essay on Jewish Tradition and Modern Thought* (New York: Seth Press), 1986.

11. *Tradition* 7:2 (Summer, 1965): 5–67 (Reprinted: New York: Doubleday, 1992).

12. "Mah Dodekh mi-Dod," Pinhas Peli (ed.), *Be-Sod Ha-Yahid ve-ha-Yahad* (Jerusalem: Orot, 1976), pp. 189–253.

13. The page numbers cited parenthetically in this section are from *HMi*.

14. As Soloveitchik acknowledges (*HMi*, p. 126 n. 75 and p. 128 n. 83), he adopted this method from the Marburg Neo-Kantian, Paul Natorp.

15. The analysis in this section of Soloveitchik's conception of halakhic *hiddush* is based on "Mah Dodekh mi-Dod," pp. 212–235.

16. The page numbers cited parenthetically in this section are from *HMa*.

17. This is to be contrasted with Soloveitchik's scientist/halakhic man analogy in his discussion of halakhic creativity in "Mah Dodekh mi-Dod," which, as we saw, focuses on the halakhist's approach to the halakhic texts that serve as his source material.

18. The page numbers cited parenthetically in this section are from *BFT*.

19. See *LMF* 1965, pp. 60–65, for a similar point about "the untranslatability of the complete faith experience" (p. 62).

20. Indeed, Soloveitchik once stated, "In my opinion it [*BFT*] surpasses it [*HMa*], in content and form." See "On a Draft of U-Vikkashtem mi-Sham," in Joseph Soloveitchik, *Community, Covenant, and Commitment: Selected Letters and Communications*, Nathaniel Helfgot (ed.) (Jersey City, NJ: Ktav Publishing, 2005), p. 321.

21. Joseph Soloveitchik, "Prayer, Petition, and Crisis," in *Worship of the Heart*, Shalom Carmy (ed.) (Jersey City, NJ: Ktav Publishing, 2003), pp. 17–18.

22. "Absolution and Purification," Pinhas Peli, *On Repentance: From the Oral Discourses of Rabbi Joseph Soloveitchik* [in Hebrew] (Jerusalem: World Zionist Organization, 1975), p. 19.

23. Hermann Cohen, *Religion of Reason out of the Sources of Judaism*, translated by Simon Kaplan, 2nd edition (Atlanta: Scholars Press, 1995), p. 187. Cf. p. 193.

24. Cohen, pp. 204–205.

25. Cohen, p. 205.

26. In an as yet unpublished discourse delivered in 1969.

27. But note how in *HMa*, pp. 83–85, there is a move in the case of both halakhic man and cognitive man from cognition, be it halakhic or scientific, to a "powerful exalted experience … possessed of a profound depth and a clear penetrating vision," again be that experience halakhic or scientific. It would also appear that in Soloveitchik's discussion of the perpetuation of the prophetic word in *BFT*, pp. 217–222, we have a similar move from the objective study and practice of the Torah to inward experience.

28. Perhaps more than tacit. For in *HMa*, p. 114, Soloveitchik states that "Spinoza and Nietzsche...did well to deride the idea of repentance" held by *homo religiosus*. But though he does not say so explicitly, it is quite clear that, for him, the idea of repentance held by *homo religiosus* is in all essentials identical to repentance out of fear, for in both repentance is viewed from the perspective of atonement. Thus, if "Spinoza and Nietzsche...did well to deride the idea of repentance" held by *homo religiosus*, they also would have done well to deride repentance out of fear, which, as noted, is linked with the written Torah.

12 Emmanuel Levinas: Judaism and the Primacy of the Ethical

RICHARD A. COHEN

> God tells us to be holy, not meaning that we ought to imitate Him, but that we ought to strive to approximate to the unattainable ideal of holiness.
>
> Immanuel Kant, Lectures on Ethics (1775–1781)

> To every judge who judges truly, even for an hour, the Scripture reckons it as if he had been a partner with God in the work of creation.
>
> B. Talmud, Tractate Shabbat, 10a.

LEVINAS' ITINERARY

Emmanuel Levinas was born on January 12, 1906,[1] in the Lithuanian city of Kaunas, known as "Kovno" to both Poles and Jews. In 1923, at the age of sixteen, Levinas left Kovno to study philosophy at the University of Strasbourg in France. During the 1928–29 academic year, he studied in Freiburg under Edmund Husserl and Martin Heidegger. In 1930, he moved to Paris; married Raisa Levy, who as a child lived on the same block in Kovno as Levinas; became a French citizen; found employment at the *École Normale Israelite Orientale*; published academic articles on Husserlian phenomenology, his Strasbourg thesis, the prize-winning book *The Theory of Intuition in Husserl's Phenomenology* (1930), and short pieces in Jewish journals on Jewish topics; and otherwise entered into the vibrant intellectual life of Paris. Conscripted into the French army in 1939, Levinas spent the war years in a German prisoner-of-war camp. After the war, he became Director of the *École Normale Israelite Orientale*, and in 1947 published his first two original philosophical books: *Time and the Other*[2] and *Existence and Existents*.[3] After the war, Levinas also began his Talmudic studies under the hidden Talmudic master known only as "Monsieur Shoshoni" or "Professor Shoshoni," who was also at the same time teaching Elie Wiesel, amongst others.[4] In 1959, Levinas delivered the first of his many "Talmudic Readings" at the annual colloquia of French Jewish Intellectuals, a group that had been formed two years earlier.

In 1961, Levinas published his magnum opus, an ethics, *Totality and Infinity*,[5] which served as his thesis for the French Doctorate in Letters. With the support of Jean Wahl, Levinas obtained his first academic post at the University of Poitiers in 1963. In 1967, he moved to the University of Paris-Nanterre, to join Paul Ricoeur there; and finally, from 1973 to his retirement in 1976, Levinas finished his academic career at the University of Paris-Sorbonne where, as an Emeritus Professor of Philosophy, he taught courses until 1979.

In 1974, Levinas published his second magnum opus, *Otherwise than Being or Beyond Essence*.[6] In addition to the four philosophical books named earlier, from the 1930s to the 1990s Levinas published many articles both in philosophy and Judaism, almost all of which have by now been collected into various volumes, most of them assembled and prefaced by Levinas, but some also edited by others and published posthumously.

Levinas died at the age of eighty-nine on December 25, 1995 (the eighth day of Chanukah), after a few debilitating years suffering from Alzheimer's disease.

The central message of Emmanuel Levinas's philosophy is in fact quite simple, well-known, and ancient, though at the same time notoriously difficult in execution: "Love your neighbor as yourself." Nevertheless, despite the straightforwardness and the near-universal consent to this essential moral teaching, the language Levinas utilizes to set his philosophy in motion and the context to which his philosophy responds, are rather complex and at least initially quite daunting. Many neophyte readers of Levinas complain of the density of his texts, and it is true that Levinas makes little concession to mass opinion or taste. He is writing on the basis of the entirety of Western civilization, from Athens to Jerusalem to Rome, and writing with all of its greatest contributors and interlocutors in mind.

Levinas's thought is not only engaged in philosophy and committed to modernity, fully open to the discoveries of the modern sciences and the phenomenological extensions of science; it is also faithful to a long tradition of Jewish monotheist spirituality and wisdom. Levinas is at once and without compromise both a philosopher and a Jewish thinker. "There is," he once said in an interview, "a communication between faith and philosophy and not the notorious conflict."[7] In the following, we shall have to see more precisely how Levinas harmonizes, or rather begins in the continuity of, the thought of Judaism and philosophy, but we can say right away that because he avoids the tempting simplicity of certain all too obvious dichotomies, entrance into his thought is for this reason, too, made more difficult.

It is time to enter into Levinas's thought, which we will do by first grasping the meaning of *monotheism*. Judaism, whatever its specific character, is a monotheism. What then is the essence of monotheism? Furthermore, how does *modernity*, the shift from the ancient and medieval standards of intellection, permanence, and eternity, to those of will, change, and time, mark a difference for monotheism? How is the ethical metaphysics of Emmanuel Levinas to be thought in relation to monotheism in general, to the ethical monotheism of Judaism in particular, and, with regard to both, to the intellectual and spiritual shift from a classical to a modern sensibility? These are the questions that guide this chapter.

Levinas's thought is at once philosophical and Jewish, and Judaism is a monotheist religion. "The God of Abraham, the God of Isaac, and the God of Jacob" – the God of the Jewish people, of Judaism – is a monotheistic God. Nevertheless, beyond Bible stories, rituals, dietary restrictions, holy places and times, beyond everything that constitutes the particularities of the particular monotheist religions (Judaism, Christianity, Islam), to *comprehend* monotheism is impossible because monotheism, by its very nature, *exceeds* human understanding. But how exactly does *monotheism* exceed human understanding? Let me explore this question by examining what I call the "paradox of monotheism."

THE PARADOX OF MONOTHEISM

The paradox unravels in three steps. All three are necessary, and all three together lie at the core of all monotheist religions. First, the monotheistic God is *perfect* – by definition. It is the basic irrevocable premise of monotheism. If one worships an imperfect God, one is not worshipping the God of monotheism. Moreover, the perfection of God's perfection is absolute. No attributes, qualities, or adjectives can be applied to God's perfection insofar as they all are taken from *our* finite world and can therefore only be applied to God by analogy or negation. God's absolute perfection, what Levinas, citing from Rabbi Hayyim of Volozhyn's *Nefesh HaChayim* (*The Soul of Life*), refers to as "God *on his own side*,"[8] is perfection without duality, multiplicity or contrast. Here the "oneness" (*echud*) of God is not numerical, one among other ones, but unique, incomparable. Levinas invokes a phrase from *Deuteronomy* 4:39: "there is nothing outside him."[9] Here is God prior to or without Creation. It is what kabbalists have called *ayin*, literally "nothingness," or "pure spirituality" (if we leave the term "spirit" undefined and indeterminate), in contrast to *yesh*, "existence" or "palpable reality," literally "there is."

Second, the perfect God of monotheism[10] *creates* an *imperfect* universe. The process of creation – which is one of the central topics of the Kabbalah, or so, at least, are the opening verses of *Genesis* – is a mystery unto itself. What is important for the paradox, however, is the imperfection of creation (possible, so say certain kabbalists, only through the "withdrawal" of God, whatever this means). It includes, *in some sense*, ignorance as well as knowledge, evil as well as good, ignoble feelings as well as noble feelings, the profane as well as the holy. Here, then, in "this world," instead of a unique and absolutely perfect One with no other, there is *hierarchy*, the above and the below, the better and the worse. In contrast to absolute perfection, here one has "God *on our side*," to again invoke the language Levinas takes from Rabbi Hayyim of Volozhyn's master work. In Judaism, the term "holy" (*kadosh*), according to the classic interpretation given by Rabbi Solomon ben Isaac (Rashi), refers to "separation": of the holy from the profane, the pure from the impure, the noble from the vulgar. Separation refers, on the one hand, to the fundamental difference between Creator and creation and, on the other hand, to the differences within creation, between beings. "Before you could feast your eyes" directly on God, the rabbis have taught in the Midrash, "you fell to earth."[11]

Regarding the differences within and between the three great monotheistic religions, each determines in what primary sense creation is a diminution, an imperfection of God's original perfection. Each answers the question about the meaning and nature of creation in relation to God. What follows from the answers to this basic question is the very legitimacy and the hierarchy of the religiously sanctioned countermeasures – such as wisdom, faith, prayer, charity, repentance, good works, sacrament, sentiment, righteousness, asceticism, and so on – of which creatures are thought to be capable in order to rectify the imperfection of creation. That is to say, determining the meaning of creation's imperfection specifies the meaning and function of the actual monotheistic religion, Judaism, Christianity or Islam.

So, step one: the perfection of God. Step two: the imperfection of creation.

Third, however, because God is perfect, everything that follows from God is also perfect, completely perfect like its source – including creation! Only the perfect follows from perfection, otherwise perfection would not be perfection. Because all is perfect, nothing is required, no countermeasures are called for, and no legitimation or rectification is needed. From the point of view of this third element, even for a creature to be grateful for perfection is essentially an ungrateful attitude, since grateful or not, all remains perfect. Nothing is required. Perfection cannot require anything without diminishing itself. And perfection, because it is perfection, is undiminished. Here, then, latent in this third element, *taken by itself*, lies the seduction of *nihilism*, a *holy nihilism*, the temptation of *excess*, let us call it, in contrast to *surplus*. "The spiritualism beyond all difference that would come from the creature," Levinas has written of this excess originating in creation, "means, for man, the indifference of nihilism. All is equal in the omnipresence of God. All is divine. All is permitted."[12] But so too nothing is permitted because nothing is forbidden . . . whatever is, is – without hierarchy, without orientation, without motivation. *Nihil obstat* [nothing stands in the way], but also *nil admirari* [to admire nothing]. But no less, or, more accurately from the monotheistic perspective, far more: this perfection is nothing less than the pure splendorous glory of God's perfect holiness. All is God and God is all.

The paradox of monotheism derives from the simultaneous truth of all three elements: God is perfect, and creation is at once both imperfect and completely perfect.[13] It is precisely *the surplus opened up by this paradox that lies at the root of all monotheism*. It is upon this paradox (metaphorically called a "foundation stone" or "rock") *and because of this paradox* that actual monotheistic *religions* – not "religion in general" but Judaism, Christianity and Islam – are built, and which they reflect in all their concrete particularity from liturgy to daily activity to theology. It is precisely *this paradox* that cannot be grasped or known, for it exceeds human understanding. This is the specific incomprehension that lies at the root of monotheism.

THE PARADOX BENEATH OR ABOVE

Like any paradox, the paradox of monotheism is fundamentally *non-rational*. It oversteps the two constitutional principles of propositional logic – namely, the principles of non-contradiction and excluded middle. According to the strictures of such logic, nothing can be, and no coherent statement can affirm, both "A" and "not A" at the same time.

Everything, in order to be, and in order to be coherently stated, must be either "A" or "not A." In the case of monotheism, however, as we have just seen, these conditions of logic are not only unmet, they *must* be broken. Hence monotheism "is" *beyond* the logic of being and the "sense" it makes (if it makes sense at all) is *beyond* the logic of rationality. The very language of *being*, as understood by philosophers, is thus inadequate to the paradox of monotheism. Being adheres to itself, subsists in itself, develops from itself, while the God of monotheism is both being (God as the im-perfection of creation) and beyond being (God prior to or without creation) at once – "otherwise than being," to use Levinas's formula. One cannot "think," "feel," or "obey" the God of monotheism without invoking an absolute *transcendence* – God's perfection, with or without the world – whose "content" overflows its "container," whether the latter, the container, is conceived as thought, felt as emotion, or enacted via action. It is not by accident, then, but by necessity that paradox lies at the core of monotheistic religion.

This otherwise-than-rationality does not mean, however, that monotheism is *irrational*. Indeed, the key to the *sense* of monotheism – whether in thought, feeling or action, or somehow otherwise – depends on seeing as precisely as possible how the monotheist religions concretely *express* the extra-logical "relation" between God and creation. While a genuinely atheist nihilism might claim that "because there is no God, everything is permitted," it is nonetheless never the case that for monotheistic religion, everything is permitted. And everything is not permitted precisely *because* there is God. The entire effort of the monotheistic religions – Judaism, Christianity, Islam – is to highlight the significance of, without utterly confining, what cannot be contained, to reveal without reducing that which ruptures manifestation. Revelation is thus never *only* a particular "content" – for instance, the specific texts, rituals, declarations, services, saints and sages revered by the three monotheisms. Revelation is also closer to the true essence of monotheistic religion, a *more* in the *less* – the *surplus* of the paradox. It is often pointed out that a sacred text, in contrast to a profane text, is inexhaustible, indeed infinite. This does not mean that it has one "literal" meaning, allegedly God's meaning. Rather this implies that the sacred text has an infinite number of readings, equal only to the infinity, the perfection of the God whose Will it is said to reveal. To determine and make concrete the explosive *sense* of the surplus of the paradox of monotheism, whether primarily it is love, compassion, intellection, command, grace, action, meditation, or something else – this is the task of religion, of the concrete religions, in contrast to philosophy.

There have been two broad and fundamentally opposed responses to the paradox of religion. For those figures such as Spinoza and Western philosophers generally, those who adhere consistently to the logic of rationality, the paradox indicates that monotheistic religious mentality is *less* than rational, is *sub-rational*. The real, as Parmenides first insisted and as Hegel later elaborated, conforms to the rational: "The real is rational and the rational is real." The actuality of Jewish, Christian, and Muslim monotheistic beliefs and practices, based as they are in paradox, would thus be explained away as the psychological-sociological products of ignorance, primitivism, pathology, herd instinct, grand politics, mass delusion, class consciousness, and the like. For all forms of rationalism, the non-rationality of monotheism is merely sub-rational, merely the symptom of a deeper unacknowledged failure.

In contrast, for those persons who adhere to monotheism, the non-rationality of the paradox indicates that religious mentality is *more* than rational, is *supra-rational*. All that is not rational is not therefore illusory, superstitious, mere appearance. Unlike the "either/or" dualism of the rationalist, the monotheist makes a tri-part distinction: irrationality, which one opposes; rationality, which one exceeds; and religion, to which one adheres. *Religion is the making sense of paradox.* The monotheistic religions account for their superior significance as the gift of divine revelation, holy spirit, prophetic inspiration, celestial grace, or other-like elevated sources. The critical objections of the rationalists are met by characterizing rationality, contrary to its own self-serving claims, as narrow, blind to the transcendence of the divine. The basic effort of monotheistic religions is to point towards and approach a "dimension" (what *is* the proper way to speak of this? – *that* is the question) of the *holy* unknown to and unattainable by rationality alone.

REFERENCE, INTENTIONALITY, AND CONSCIENCE

It has often been said that between science and religion there can be no middle ground or term, and hence only conflict without quarter, because they are mutually exclusive. One side exalts the paradox at the expense of rationality, while the other exalts rationality at the expense of the paradox.[14] Leo Strauss, who has done much to propagate this raw dichotomy, has also shown that when it is posed in such an opposition, neither side can convince the other of its errors because each is based on different grounds entirely.[15] But we must take more seriously the notion that science and religion are not mirror images of one another: neither accepts the other's contextualization. In contrast to the distinction between the rational and the irrational recognized by rationality, religion would offer a third alternative, one based on a positive appreciation of the paradox of monotheism. "This human impossibility of conceiving the Infinite," Levinas writes, "is also a new possibility of signifying."[16]

We know that and how rationality rejects religion as a species of the *sub-rational*. The intelligibility of religious persons would be rejected for being stubborn, infantile, deluded, and the like. But our question and Levinas's is neither how rationality rejects religion nor how religion rejects rationality. Rather, the question is how monotheism admits its fundamental paradox without producing the chaos of irrationality. The real may not be rational, but for all that it is not irrational. The answer of religion is that the *sense* of the paradox finds expression in the *symbol*, not the symbol as a corruption of thought, nor the symbol as a mystification of matter, but rather the symbol as the unstable unity – the "singularity," to use the current term – of the proximate and the distant, being and the otherwise than being. Oriented upward, diagonally, it functions as a pointing, a disruption, a challenge. The great originality of Levinas is to argue that the *symbol* – the *sense* of monotheism as a surplus – is at bottom neither an ontological-epistemological structure nor an aesthetic structure, but an ethical one. In *Totality and Infinity* (1961), he had already written: "God rises to his supreme and ultimate presence as correlative to the justice rendered unto men."[17] and: "Everything that cannot be brought back to [*se ramener à*] an [ethical] inter-human relation represents not the superior form but the forever primitive form of religion."[18]

The problem, then, is one of establishing a level of sense independent of the rationalist dyadic worldview, and yet generative of rationality. It is a question, beyond the paradox of religion, that has troubled, and whose effort to answer it, has determined most of modern thought. In general, these various "middle term" alternatives to sense and nonsense have relied on what we can call an *aesthetic ontology* – that is to say, an attentiveness to the manifestation of manifestation in its own right taken as a new form of epistemology. One sees this quite clearly in the poetry of Heidegger's "ontological difference," where the source of the significance of beings is not their rational or irrational inter-relations, whether scientific or historical, but their upsurge from the opening of an openness, a "giving" (which is simultaneously a withdrawal) that is the very "be-ing" (verb) of their being. Such would be the pre-rational, but not irrational, structure of the revelation of being. Until Levinas, however, no one had thought this new sense of origination in terms of ethics, and even less had it been thought in terms of an ethics based in inter-subjectivity. Furthermore, and this is most important, Levinas thinks ethics *ethically*. That is to say, Levinas thinks ethics as the "metaphysics" of the paradox of monotheism, such that its non-coincidence concretely "is" the self morally "put into question" by the other person, in contrast to all the philosophical accounts, which remain based in one form or another of self-positing, self-consciousness, or aesthetic upsurge.

THE SIGNIFICANCE OF SIGNIFYING

One of the best avenues into Levinas's thought is to follow his account of the intimate link between the semantic and communicative functions of language. Levinas's careful study of signification led him to discover a dimension of meaning whose true significance was overlooked by the "intentional" or "noetic-noematic" analyses of meaning laid out by his teacher Husserl as well as by the "revelatory" hermeneutics of Heidegger.

We must remember, first, that Husserl's great discovery was a turn to consciousness as the source of meaning – as the source of meaning for the true, that is to say, for *science*, the "hard" objective sciences. Hitherto, natural science, in contrast to philosophical idealism, had wrested truth out of meaning by correlating signs to their referents. This was its realism, based on a simple correspondence model of truth. Here is the model:

Correspondence Theory of Truth

Sign/symbol → refers to – Signified/thing itself

What Husserl saw was that a complete understanding of meaning would also require an elucidation of the production of signs by consciousness, a turn to "meaning-bestowing" or constitutive acts. Thus Husserl supplemented the realist sign-referent structure with its "origin" in the signifying acts of consciousness. Here is the model:

Intentional (or "Transcendental") Analysis of Signification

Signifier/consciousness ⇒ (Sign/symbol → refers to – Signified/thing itself)

Of course this "transcendental" approach opened the door not only to a clarification of the origin in consciousness of scientific or representational significations, but also to a clarification of the origin in consciousness, broadly interpreted as "intentional" meaning-bestowal, of many more regions of meaning besides those of representational consciousness, such as the significations opened up by perceptual, imaginative, practical, and emotive signifying. Heidegger, for instance, early in *Being and Time* (1927), analyzed the ground of theoretical significations in instrumental significations, in the "worldliness" of the subject's primordial "being-in-the-world.[19]

What Levinas saw, however, was that in his legitimate concern to provide a broader ground for signification by turning to consciousness, Husserl still favored a representational model of meaning, a model that he had unwittingly borrowed from the objective sciences he aimed to supplement. What struck Levinas's attention, beyond Husserl's broader signifying-sign-signified structure ("intentional" consciousness), was the *communicative* dimension of meaning. Not only is realist meaning, the sign-signified correlation, intended or meant through an act of consciousness; meaning is also that which is said *by* someone *to* someone – it has an *accusative* dimension.[20] There is not only what is *said*, even adding that what is said is produced by consciousness and thus has an "intentional" structure, there is also the *saying* of the *said to someone*. As I have done before, I will write "Here is the model," but in a moment we shall see why there can be no model, no outside perspective with which to thematize what it is that Levinas is pointing to in highlighting the accusative dimension of signification. Here is the model:

Inter-Subjective Event of Meaning

Someone/Other

(Sign/symbol→ refers to – signified/thing itself) – to
⇑
Signifier/Subject

What Levinas saw was not only that the *accusative* dimension of meaning could not be recuperated within the signifying-sign-signified structure of intentionality that Husserl had advanced. What he saw, and here lies one aspect of his originality, was that the recognition of the irreducible accusative dimension of signification meant that signification was a function ultimately neither of correspondence with things nor of an intentional origination in consciousness (which, thinking so, led Husserl back to idealism), but rather it is a function of the inter-subjective relation.

But this is not all. Second, and even more significant, is what comes into play with this recognition of the role of inter-subjectivity. It is precisely because the inter-subjective relation is fundamental to signification that it is an error to understand and interpret the inter-subjective relation in terms of signifying structures that are themselves derivative and not constitutive of it. Rather, then, signification must be interpreted based on the structures of inter-subjectivity. And inter-subjectivity, to say it again, cannot be interpreted in terms of signifying-sign-signified – that is to say, in terms of language as a system of signs (coherent, revealed, deferred, or otherwise) or as a product of consciousness. The proper interpretation of inter-subjectivity, the very essence of inter-subjectivity – such is the second aspect of Levinas's claim and his most profound and original insight – is an *ethical* structure: the moral priority of the other person over the self, the self responsible for the other person. The asymmetrical priority of the other person, the other as infinite moral obligation and the self as moral responsibility in the face of ("accused" by) the other's transcendence – this ethical orientation of the "I" and "You" is what cannot be contained within the signifier-sign-signified structure of language. It is what cannot be "viewed from the outside," cannot be represented, but nevertheless makes language significant, meaningful, important in the first place.

Unlike for the later structuralists, for Levinas this surplus does not indicate the impact of a larger web of historical-cultural signs. Unlike for the later deconstructionists, for Levinas this surplus does not indicate the impact of a semiotic slippage, which would again occur at the level of signs deferring to signs. Rather, for Levinas, the irrecoverable *accusative* dimension of signification must be "understood" beyond signs, beyond the *said* (*dit*). What it brings to bear is the impact of an inter-subjective or inter-human dimension, a *saying* (*dire*) that is from the first an ethical exigency. The impact of the communicative situation of a self brought in its first person singularity into proximity with another self across discourse cannot properly speaking be "understood," because as exterior, transcendent, other, it also cannot be captured in a theme or represented. Beyond the structure of signifier-sign-signified, discourse, speaking, expression – what in another context J. L. Austin conceived in terms of "performance" – do not indicate some failure of signifying to be sufficiently precise or the intrusion of larger cultural or semiotic determinations (which would undermine the subject's freedom) relative to the sign. Rather, the necessity of discourse, of communication, is not neutral, and points to an irreducible *priority* deriving from the inter-subjective relation, a priority that gives meaning to the entire signifying-sign-signified structure without undermining its validity. This *priority* of the inter-subjective dimension can only be accounted for in *ethical* rather than epistemological, ontological, or aesthetic terms. The alterity of the other person to whom one speaks and, even more importantly, the alterity of the other person who speaks and to whom the I responds, even in listening, would have the *moral significance* of an *obligation*. *Responsibility*, then, the responsibility to respond to the other person as other, would be the non-intentional root of the intentional construction of signification. The entirety of Levinas's intellectual career is the effort to articulate as precisely as possible this *overriding social and moral surplus* of meaning and its consequences and ramifications for all the dimensions of human life.

INTER-SUBJECTIVE ETHICS AND MONOTHEISM

Our guiding questions have to do with Levinas and Judaism. Perhaps the connection is now not so difficult to see. The paradox of monotheism can be construed as the irruption of transcendence within immanence, without that transcendence either absorbing immanence into itself or itself being absorbed by immanence. The paradox, in other words, mimics the structure of *saying-said* that for Levinas is the root structure of ethics. But does monotheism only mimic the structure of ethics, or is ethics rather its best articulation, its closest most faithful realization, monotheism's highest and most holy dispensation? Levinas will say yes. "Ethics is not the corollary of the vision of God, it is that very vision" – at least for a "religion of adults" such as Judaism.[21] Let us consider the parallels.

Monotheism characterizes transcendence as perfection and immanence as imperfection (and perfection), neither divorcing the two nor identifying them, but holding them in paradoxical relation. What Levinas understood was that the paradox of monotheism could be neither an ontological nor an aesthetic structure, for both of these dimensions of sense, which ultimately reduce away the independence or separation of selfhood, are essentially incapable of maintaining the extraordinary "relation without relation" (*relation sans relation*)[22] – transcendence in immanence – characteristic of the monotheistic paradox. Ethics, however, maintains the self in relation to absolute alterity in virtue of responsibilities and obligations. It is the very structure of transcendence in immanence. *Monotheism is an ethical structure.* "Religion," Levinas writes in *Totality and Infinity*, "where relationship subsists between the same and the other, despite the impossibility of the Whole – the idea of Infinity – is the ultimate structure."[23] "To know God is to know what must be done."[24]

Thus it is not the abstract philosophical omniscience of God, but his concrete personal *benevolence* that is the key to understanding creation. Creation in its relation to God, in the paradoxical conjunction of imperfection and perfection, is constituted by the work of *sanctification as the responsibility of morality* and *redemption as the striving for justice*.[25] The paradox of monotheism is ethics as *tikkun olam*, "repairing the world" through a justice tempered by mercy. One could cite many elucidating texts by Levinas to support this claim, and I invite readers to examine the entire subsection entitled "The Metaphysical and the Human," of Section One of *Totality and Infinity*, from which the following *philosophically* oriented citations are taken.

> The proximity of the Other, the proximity of the neighbor, is in being an ineluctable moment of the revelation of an absolute presence (that is, disengaged from every relation), which expresses itself.... God rises to his supreme and ultimate presence as correlative to the justice rendered unto men.... The work of justice – the uprightness of the face to face – is necessary in order that the breach that leads to God be produced....
>
> The establishing of this primacy of the ethical, that is, of the relationship of man to man – signification, teaching and justice – a primacy of an irreducible structure upon which all the other structures rest (and in particular all those which, in an original way, seem to put us in contact with an impersonal sublime, aesthetic or ontological), is one of the objectives of the present work.[26]

Morality and justice are not only "like" religion; they are religion. The path to God is not beneath, around or above morality and justice but through them. "The harmony between so much goodness and so much legalism constitutes the original note of Judaism."[27]

I have cited from *Totality and Infinity* as much as from Levinas's so-called "confessional" writings (for my part, the only difference between these two sorts of writings is not in what Levinas says, but in who he says it to). We cannot indulge in the misleading notion that Levinas interprets monotheism *ethically* in his philosophical works alone, as if this manner of speaking were merely the public and acceptable face of what otherwise and more authentically derives from a tribal field of significance from which non-Jews are forever excluded. This is incorrect. There is nothing exclusionary about Judaism (except that it struggles to exclude and eliminate evil and injustice), and nothing supra-ethical, no faith or blind faith (in the manner of Kierkegaard's Knight of Faith) undergirding Levinas's conception of Judaism. For Levinas, the "highest moment" in Abraham's near sacrifice of Isaac, to take the apparently most difficult "religious" counter-instance, is not any rejection of morality on Abraham's part, but precisely Abraham's submission to the moral imperative, the "no" of the Angel of God who will not allow murder.[28] Murder is not evil because the Angel or because God forbids it; it is evil, and thus God forbids it and we find this affirmed, so Levinas argues against Kierkegaard, shortly after the near-sacrifice story when we learn that Abraham, who has obviously learned the lesson well, argued with God about saving the cities of Sodom and Gomorrah *in the name of the justice that both humans and God must obey*. Such is "covenant" religion, for covenant – "in the name of justice" – is the *political* expression of the paradox of monotheism. Already in 1937, in an article on "The Meaning of Religious Practice,"[29] Levinas understood Jewish ritual practices not by reducing them like Aesopian fable to moral lessons, or to a hygiene or symbolism, but by seeing in them an interruption, a pause, a check before the passions of the natural attitude and its absorption in the gathering of things (that so impressed Heidegger), hence a distance-taking from any purely natural or naturalist reality. In his mature thought, this hesitation – taught by religious ritual – will be understood in its deepest sense as shame before the evil of which our vital powers are capable, ultimately the recognition, in the face of the other person, that "Thou shall not murder."

In his philosophical writings, Levinas focuses a great deal of attention, some of which I have tried to indicate, on the disruptive trace of morality as a non-intentional surplus giving meaning to the signifying functions of intentional consciousness.[30] In his Jewish writings, too – without in the least reverting to an abstract universalism, hence faithful to the concrete spiritual world of the normative rabbinic tradition – Levinas will no less articulate the "breach" of the absolute in the relative, the disruption of the *said* by *saying*, in terms of morality and justice. The primacy of ethics is articulated and defended throughout Levinas's writings, both philosophical and Jewish.[31] Insofar as the aim of philosophy is *wisdom* rather than *knowledge*, there is no need and there can be no justification, from the point of view of philosophy itself, for separating philosophical writings from confessional writings. Not surprisingly, however, since the very topic of "monotheism" is a

religious topic, the most explicitly monotheistic readings of the primacy
of ethics are found in Levinas's "Jewish" writings. There are several, but
I refer now to the concluding pages of two essays published in 1977 (six
years after the publication of *Otherwise than Being or Beyond Essence*,
hence in the fullest maturity of his thought): "Revelation in the Jewish Tradition" and "*In the Image of God*, according to Rabbi Hayyim
Volozhiner."[32]

In "*In the Image of God*, according to Rabbi Hayyim Volozhiner,"
for instance, Levinas recognizes that when Rabbi Hayyim finds the paradox of monotheism in the very syntax of Jewish blessings, which begin
by addressing God in the second person and conclude by referring to God
in the third person, the coordination of "God *on our side*," the immanent God who acts in history, and "God *on his own side*," the transcendent God in his pure perfection, it is *also and no less* a reference to the
moral imperative placed upon the I facing a You, on the one hand, *and*
to the demand for a "dis-interested-ness" that, striving for perfection,
aims at *justice* for all,[33] on the other hand. "In this radical contradiction
[between *God on our side* and *God on his own side*], neither of the two
notions could efface itself before the other. . . . And yet this *modality* of
the divine is also the perfection of the moral intention that animates
religious life as it is lived from the world and its differences, from the
top and the bottom, from the pure and the impure."[34] In the conjunction
of proximity ("You") and distance ("He") enunciated in Jewish prayers,
Levinas finds *in a certain sense* precisely what so many previous Jewish
commentators had found before him – the conjunction of this world and
another, the conjunction of the human and the divine, the conjunction
of the God's deeds and His Essence. But in Levinas's hands, these con-
junctions rest not on an impossible "knowledge" (or mystification) but
on the imperatives of a morality obligated to infinity – a "glory" that
"does not belong to the language of contemplation" – yet rectified by
justice, a justice serving morality.[35]

The imperfection-hierarchy of creation is precisely a moral imperative, from and to perfection. When Levinas, continuing in the article
on Rabbi Hayyim of Volozhin, writes of this as "[a] spiritualization that
dismisses the forms whose elevation it perfects, but which it transcends
as being incompatible with the Absolute," he means precisely religious
life as ethical self-overcoming. Religion, in this holy-ethical sense, is
no longer a miraculous or predetermined escape from nothingness, a
flight from the utter worthlessness of creation, from its "husks," but
rather the perfecting of a creation whose highest sense would be precisely

this movement – not necessary or impossible, but *best* – toward moral perfection. In the order of the face-to-face, this means acts of kindness and compassion. At the social level, this – what Levinas calls "political monotheism"[36] – means the struggle for justice, just laws, just courts, just institutions, not only enforcing but promoting and improving fairness in access and distribution of basic goods and services.[37] Ethics as the ground of the real, Levinas writes, is "a new possibility: the possibility of thinking of the Infinite and the Law together, the very possibility of their conjunction. Man would not simply be the admission of an antinomy of reason. Beyond the antinomy, he would signify a new image of the Absolute."[38] Man in the "image and likeness of God" would be ethical man. "*His compassion,*" says the Psalmist, "*is upon all His creations.*"[39]

The concluding pages of Levinas's article entitled "Revelation in the Jewish Tradition" are even more explicit regarding the height of ethics as the ultimate and irreducible *sense* of the paradox of monotheistic Judaism. Levinas writes:

> The path I would be inclined to take in order to solve the paradox of the Revelation is one which claims that this relation, at first glance a paradoxical one, may find a model in the non-indifference toward the other, in a responsibility toward him, and that it is precisely within this relation that man becomes his self: designated without any possibility of escape, chosen, unique, non-interchangeable and, in this sense, free. Ethics is the model worthy of transcendence, and it is as an ethical *kerygma* that the Bible is Revelation.[40]

In another essay, Levinas adds: "the Bible...is a book that leads us not toward the mystery of God, but toward the human tasks of man. Monotheism is a humanism. Only simpletons made it into a theological arithmetic."[41] The paradox of monotheism cannot be thought, but it can be enacted as righteousness. Such, indeed, was the demand of the prophets and the refinement of the rabbis.

In this way, through ethical readings – what I have elsewhere called "ethical exegesis,"[42] the hollowing out of selfhood as *sacrifice*, as *circumcision of the heart*, as *prayer* – is "brought back" to its sense as infinite obligation to the other person, as "hostage" – "the opposite of repose – anxiety, questioning, seeking, Desire."[43] Such is a selfhood "more awake than the psyche of intentionality and the knowledge adequate to its object" – "a relation with an Other which would be *better* than self-possession" – "where the ethical relation with the other is a modality of the relation with God."[44] Levinas continues in the same article: "Rather than being seen in terms of received knowledge, should not the Revelation be thought of as this awakening?"[45] Levinas is not merely serving up homiletics for what in truth are ontological or aesthetic structures: the real is itself determined by the "messianic" ideality of morality and justice. It is perhaps this more than anything else that monotheism "understands" better than philosophy.

Judaism is based in the paradox of monotheism; it is not a Manichaeism. God transcends the world but "is" also within it. God transcends the world without having separated Himself from it: he has given His Torah, His instructions. For many Jews, the most direct path to God is through Torah study. Levinas gives his assent to this emphasis, but with a twist. Torah study does not mean pure erudition or knowledge for the sake of knowledge. Nor is it the province of the intellectual elite alone. Rather, for Levinas, Torah study means learning to be ethical, and not just "learning" to be ethical. It is the teaching of ethics, a goad to moral behavior and a call to justice. Torah study is thus an ethical activism for Levinas.

Levinas's originality, his interpretation of the paradox of monotheism in ethical rather than epistemological terms, opens up the possibility of a new way to resolve certain conflicts that continue to haunt Jews, Christians, Muslims, and the religious of the world more generally. What Levinas has to contribute is an escape from the hardened and hence inevitable and irresolvable clash of *theologies* for the sake of the shared values of inter-human kindness, the morality of putting the other first, and inter-human fairness, the call for justice for all.

This is not to say that a shift from epistemological grounds, from the clash of theologies and ideologies to an ethical ground, to love of the neighbor and the call to justice, will automatically solve or resolve all human problems. Not at all. But by opening lines of communication between people, rather than simply between ideas, by placing *saying before the said*, Levinas's thought opens up opportunities for discourse, communication, exchange, and inter-human understanding that are lost from the start when one begins with the *said as said*. Levinas took the title of one of his articles from a phrase in a fictional newspaper feature on which he had been asked to comment: "Loving the Torah More than God." What he means, of course, is not that one loves the Torah *more* than God, but that "loving the Torah," – that is, loving your neighbor – is precisely the way, and the only way, one loves God. To love God before or above or without loving one's neighbor is to turn away from God. Such is the meaning contained in the Hebrew word *shalom*, "peace," which refers not to the peace of conquest, the peace that is really the victor's continual suppression of rebellion, an order Levinas calls "totality," but to the peace of harmony, the peace of respect for and learning from the otherness of the other.

The *sense* of Judaism, as of all genuine humanism (the two are in no way in conflict – Levinas writes of a "biblical humanism" and a "Jewish humanism"), would be to preserve the surplus of the more in the less, the perfect in the imperfect, via the demands of an imperative voice from beyond: the voice of the other person, commanding the self to "its unfulfilable obligation"[46] to one and all. The perfection of a personal God would be the perfecting of the world. And the perfecting of the world would be to care for the other before oneself, for "the orphan, the widow, the stranger," and from there to care for humanity, for animals, for all sentient life, and finally for all of creation. Not sentimentality but morality, morality requiring justice. "And with justice, judge in your gates" (*Zechariah* 8:16) – upon which Rabbi Simeon ben Gamliel comments: "Where justice is wrought, peace and truth are wrought also."[47]

Notes

1. Levinas was born on December 30, 1905, according to the Julian calendar then in effect in Lithuania.
2. Emmanuel Levinas, *Time and the Other [and Additional Essays]*, trans. Richard A. Cohen (Pittsburgh: Duquesne University Press, 1987).
3. Levinas, *Existence and Existents*, trans. Alphonso Lingis (The Hague: Martinus Nijhoff, 1978).
4. See Salomon Malka, *Monsieur Chouchani: L'enigme d'un maître du XXe siècle* (Paris: Jean-Claude Lattes, 1994).
5. Levinas, *Totality and Infinity: An Essay on Exteriority*, trans. Alphonso Lingis (Pittsburgh: Duquesne University Press, 1969).
6. Levinas, *Otherwise than Being or Beyond Essence*, trans. Alphonso Lingis (Pittsburgh: Duquesne University Press, 1998).
7. Levinas, "On Jewish Philosophy" (1985), in Emmanuel Levinas, *In the Time of the Nations*, trans. Michael B. Smith (Bloomington: Indiana University Press, 1994), p. 170.
8. Levinas, "'In the Image of God' According to Rabbi Hayyim Volozhiner" (1978), in Emmanuel Levinas, *Beyond the Verse*, trans. Gary D. Mole (Bloomington : Indiana University Press, 1994), p. 162 and passim.
9. Ibid., p. 164.
10. Monotheism must be contrasted with monism. Monism, expressed by both Hinduism and Buddhism, represents a form of spirituality fundamentally distinct from monotheism. For monism, the Godhead is the real in its totality; for Hinduism, this ultimate reality is Brahman; for

Buddhism, it is the absolute Void. For monotheism, in contrast, one must distinguish God from His creation.

11. *Sifre Deuteronomy, Berachah*, no. 355, 17.

12. Levinas, "In the Image of God," *Beyond the Verse*, 166.

13. I am deliberately using the dyad "perfect/imperfect" rather than such alternatives as "infinite/finite," "unconditioned/conditioned," or "absolute/relative" because the former *begins* with God while the latter begin with *creation*.

14. Nonetheless, there is a third alternative: to affirm a non-religious irrationality, a sub-rationality that denies rationality, but at the same time also denies the perfection, that is to say, the existence of God. This is the position of sophism, skepticism, or what Levinas calls a "pure humanism" (in contrast to "biblical humanism") that denies truth in the name of *extra-rational* power relations such as habit, good manners, force, equanimity, will, libido, the "nomadic," and the like. Influential and destructive though this third posture has been, and continues to be, it is essentially *pagan* and – except for a few allusions to Heidegger – is not the concern of the present paper.

15. See, for example, Leo Strauss, *Jewish Philosophy and the Crisis of Modernity: Essays and Lectures in Modern Jewish Thought*, ed. Kenneth Hart Green (Albany: State University of New York Press, 1997).

16. Levinas, "In the Image of God," *Beyond the Verse*, 165.

17. Levinas, *Totality and Infinity*, 78.

18. Ibid., p. 79 (my translation). Lingis translates *"se ramener à"* as "be reduced to." In this context, this is both wrong and misleading. It is made all the worse because in this sentence, Levinas is articulating one of his most important thoughts. A religious signification can have several meanings and does not need to be *reduced* to only one meaning, even if that one meaning invokes an "inter-subjective relation." Nevertheless, all religious significations, so Levinas teaches, can be and should be *brought back* to their inter-subjective significance, for at this level one discovers their "superior" or highest significance: their ethical sense. This "bringing back" is similar to the way a phenomenologist peels away a term to its most extreme or irreducible sense, from whence all its other related senses borrow their meaning. For instance, in *From Existence to Existents, Time and the Other*, and *Totality and Infinity*, Levinas shows that the term "transcendence," while in a certain sense applicable to death, only gains its full meaning from the absolute alterity of the other person, which is more other, more transcendent than death. Thus, Levinas is saying of religious significations that they gain their full (or "superior" or "adult") sense from the ethical inter-subjective relations they express, and that other levels of meaning are, wittingly or not, derived from or dependent upon these. Other levels of meaning are therefore not to be reduced away in the sense of eliminated, but are (or can be) intensified and infused with transcendence through their ethical sense. (Perhaps they can be eliminated, however, in cases where they cannot be brought to an ethical inter-subjective sense and are therefore purely mythological.) This return of sense is, given

the limitations Levinas discovered in the phenomenological method's commitment to "intentional analysis," the ultimate function of *ethical exegesis*, as one sees practiced most clearly in all of Levinas's "Talmudic Readings." Many rabbis, in a different context to be sure, have said something quite similar, if not the same. Rabbi Samson Raphael Hirsch, for instance, has written (and not in a reductive sense): "The Sanctuary of the Law in particular, and the Law of God in general, strive solely for moral objectives." Samson Raphael Hirsch, *Jewish Symbolism: The Collected Writings, Vol. III*, Paul Forchheimer (Nanuet, NY: Feldheim Publishers, 1995), 60.

19. Martin Heidegger, *Being and Time*, trans. John Macquarrie and Edward Robinson (New York: Harper & Row, 1962); see especially Part One, Division One, sections II and III (78–148).
20. While one usually associates the "to" of "to someone" with the dative, which refers to an indirect object, it is not always so easily distinguishable from the accusative, which refers to an immediate object. Beyond grammatical niceties, however, what Levinas is emphasizing is that signification originates in communicative speaking, and hence arises from a dimension of provocation or "accusation," of being accused or charged with a responsibility to and for the other person.
21. Levinas, "A Religion for Adults," in Emmanuel Levinas, *Difficult Freedom: Essays in Judaism*, trans. Seán Hand (Baltimore: Johns Hopkins University Press, 1990), 17.
22. Levinas, *Totality and Infinity*, 80.
23. Levinas, *Totality and Infinity*, 80.
24. Levinas, "Religion for Adults," *Difficult Freedom*, 17.
25. In a chapter entitled "Monotheism and Ethics" (74–119), from his book *Monotheism: A Philosophic Inquiry into the Foundations of Theology and Ethics* (Totawa, NJ: Allanheld, Osmun & Co., 1981), Professor Lenn Goodman writes (86): "The emulation called for by the very contemplation of the concept of divine perfection – expressed Biblically as the human pursuit of holiness (*Leviticus* 19) and in Plato as the striving to become as like to God as lies in human capacity (*Theaetetus* 176) – means simply the pursuit of the highest conceivable moral standards." See also a later revised version of this chapter in Lenn Goodman, *God of Abraham* (New York: Oxford University Press, 1996), 79–114.
26. Levinas, *Totality and Infinity*, 78–79 (with some minor revisions of the Lingis translation).
27. Levinas, "Religion for Adults," *Difficult Freedom*, p. 19.
28. Levinas, *Proper Names*, trans. Michael B. Smith (Stanford: Stanford University Press, 1996), 74.
29. Levinas, "The Meaning of Religious Practice," trans. Peter Atterton, Matthew Calarco, and Joelle Hansel, in *Modern Judaism*, Vol. 25, no. 3 (2005), 285–289 (with a translators' Introduction).
30. See, for example, his close analyses of Husserlian phenomenology in Emmanuel Levinas, *Discovering Existence with Husserl*, ed. and trans. Richard A. Cohen and Michael B. Smith (Evanston: Indiana University Press, 1998).

31. The unity of Levinas's philosophical and confessional writings can hardly be better recognized than on the pages of his extraordinary essay of 1973, "God and Philosophy" (trans. Richard A. Cohen), found in *Collected Philosophical Papers*, ed. and trans. Alphonso Lingis (Dordrecht: Martinus Nijhoff, 1987), 153–186; found in a second English translation in Emmanuel Levinas, *Of God Who Comes to Mind*, trans. Bettina Bergo (Stanford: Stanford University Press, 1998), 55–78.

32. These two essays were both reprinted in the 1982 collection entitled *Beyond the Verse*.

33. Levinas, *Beyond the Verse*, 163.

34. Ibid., 165.

35. In *Ethics and Infinity*, Levinas says the following: "In certain very old prayers, fixed by ancient authorities, the faithful one begins by saying to God "Thou" and finishes the proposition thus begun by saying "He," as if, in the course of this approach of the "Thou" its transcendence into a "He" supervened. It is what in my descriptions I have called the "illeity" of the Infinite. Thus, in the "Here I am!" of the approach of the Other [person], the Infinite does not show itself. How then does it take on meaning? I will say that the subject who says "Here I am!" *testifies* to the Infinite. It is through this testimony, whose truth is not the truth of representation or perception, that the revelation of the Infinite occurs. It is through this testimony that the very glory of the Infinite glorified *itself*. The term "glory" does not belong to the language of contemplation." Emmanuel Levinas, *Ethics and Infinity*, trans. Richard A. Cohen (Pittsburgh: Duquesne University Press, 1985), 106–107. For a better understanding of what Levinas might mean by "a 'He' supervened" in the passage just cited, by means of a concise review of several classic Jewish commentators (Talmud, Abudraham, Riva, Rashba, Ramban, et al.) on the "You" – "He" syntax of Jewish blessings, see B. S. Jacobson, *Meditations on the Siddur*, trans. Leonard Oschry (Tel-Aviv: Mtzuda Press, 1966), 61–64.

36. Levinas, "The State of Caesar and the State of David," in *Beyond the Verse*, 186.

37. That justice, *for Levinas* – which operates otherwise than morality – that is, in terms of equality rather than inequality – is required to rectify morality and is also regulated by morality has escaped critics of his politics, including Howard Caygill, Robert Bernasconi, and Asher Horowitz. See, for example, Asher Horowitz, "Beyond Rational Peace," in *Difficult Justice: Commentaries on Levinas and Politics*, ed. Asher Horowitz and Gad Horowitz (Toronto: University of Toronto Press, 2006), 27–47.

38. Levinas, "The State of Caesar and the State of David," in *Beyond the Verse*, 166–167. For a more extended discussion of Levinas's appropriation of Rabbi Hayyim of Volozhyn, see Chapter 11, "The Face of Truth and Jewish Mysticism," in Cohen, *Elevations*, 241–273 (especially, 261–273).

39. *Psalm* 145.

40. Levinas, *Beyond the Verse*, 148.

41. Levinas, "For a Jewish Humanism," *Difficult Freedom*, 275.
42. See Richard A. Cohen, *Ethics, Philosophy and Exegesis* (Cambridge: Cambridge University Press, 2001).
43. Levinas, *Beyond the Verse*, 149.
44. Ibid., 149.
45. Ibid., 150.
46. Levinas, *Beyond the Verse*, 150.
47. *Pesikta D'Rav Kahana*, 140a.

13 Emil Fackenheim, the Holocaust, and Philosophy

MICHAEL L. MORGAN

Emil Fackenheim's intellectual career, if we date its origin with his entrance into the Hochschule in Berlin in 1935, spanned sixty-eight years (b. 1917–d. 2003). Looking back over his career, it is probably not inaccurate to take the Holocaust to be its core and to assess his post-Holocaust writings as his most important contribution and legacy. But for Fackenheim, the Holocaust was not solely a rupture in Jewish history and Jewish thought; it was also a rupture in world history and philosophical thought. Yet too little attention has been paid to the way in which for Fackenheim the Holocaust can be understood as a rupture in the philosophical tradition itself.

During Purim 1967, March 26, Steven Schwarzschild, then editor of *Judaism*, convened a symposium in New York at the annual meeting of the board of the journal and under the auspices of the American Jewish Committee, on the theme "Jewish Values in the Post-Holocaust Future." Schwarzschild chaired a panel of four speakers, each of whom was invited to make a short statement; discussion followed. The four participants were George Steiner, Richard Popkin, Elie Wiesel, and Emil Fackenheim.[1] This was the first public occasion on which Fackenheim presented his formulation of the 614th commandment. It was an invitation, Fackenheim later said, that he could not refuse, although it took an extreme emotional and moral toll on him.[2]

By March of 1967, then, Fackenheim had begun to turn his thinking centrally to Auschwitz and how to confront it as a Jew. During that same year, he published in *Deadalus* a long essay entitled "On the Self-Exposure of Faith to the Modern-Secular World: *Philosophical Reflections in the Light of Jewish Experience.*"[3] The essay is framed as a response to various critical trends in Christian theology, from Dietrich Bonhoeffer to Harvey Cox, to the "death of God" theologians then in vogue (Thomas Altizer, William Hamilton, Paul Van Buren), ending with a discussion of Buber's "eclipse of God" and some final, tentative reflections on the Holocaust. The thrust of those remarks is that a genuine

Jewish response may not be known to theologians or philosophers, but perhaps one might find something in the work of a novelist. Fackenheim cites, with little comment, passages from three novels by Wiesel – *Night*, *The Accident*, and *The Gates of the Forest*. Moreover, he registers a caution, that a facing up to Auschwitz that is a commitment to "survival for survival's sake is an inadequate stand."[4] In the symposium piece of March 1967 and then later in the essay "Jewish Faith and the Holocaust" and in the introduction to *Quest for Past and Future*, Fackenheim would say: "I confess I used to be highly critical of Jewish philosophies which seemed to advocate no more than survival for survival's sake. I have changed my mind. I now believe that, in this present, unbelievable age, even a mere collective commitment to Jewish group-survival for its own sake is a momentous response, with the greatest implications."[5] This evidence recommends the conclusion that in the summer of 1966, at the I. Meier Segals Center for the Study and Advancement of Judaism meetings in Quebec, Fackenheim's paper was gave a version of the long paper on faith, secularity, and the "death of God" phenomenon.

Some time, then, during the fall and winter of 1966–67, Fackenheim had changed his mind about the importance of a commitment to Jewish survival.[6] Between that summer and the next spring, he had immersed himself in thinking about the issue of Auschwitz and genuine or "authentic" Jewish response; the symposium statement was the outcome – or part of the outcome, the larger version of which appeared the next year in *Commentary* and in the introduction to *Quest for Past and Future*.[7] The invitation from Schwarzschild had presented him with a moral imperative and had put him in the position of making a public statement on an issue that he had, for years, suppressed or even repressed. What made it necessary and possible to do so?

One development was philosophical. During the years before the fall of 1966, Fackenheim the philosopher had been preoccupied with Hegel.[8] Since the mid-1950s, and indeed even earlier, he had been at work on a project concerning faith and reason in German philosophy, from Kant to Kierkegaard.[9] But, as Fackenheim would later note, the project reached an obstacle when he turned to Hegel and he began to immerse himself in Hegel's philosophy and the Hegelian system. On the one hand, he sought to understand the role of religion and faith in Hegel's system and hence in their relation to philosophical thought. On the other hand, he was interested in the Hegelian system itself, its claim to an encompassing reason, and its relation to historical actuality. By 1966–67, he had come to understand the Hegelian system, its inner workings, and its coherence, and he had come also to grasp the relation in Hegel between historical reality and philosophical thought. He had also come increasingly to believe that Hegel himself, if he had lived during and after the Nazi destruction, the death camps, and the atrocities, would have seen in them an unprecedented and radical form of evil that would have defied Hegelian synthesis, that is, the assimilation of history into the philosophical thought that Hegelian philosophy represented as its highest form. He wrote about this claim, that the evils of Auschwitz could not be assimilated into the Hegelian system and hence by implication by any philosophical thought and indeed by any thought at all, briefly in his book *The Religious Dimension of Hegel's Thought*, published in 1968, and then again in an essay, "Would Hegel Today Be a Hegelian?" in the Canadian philosophical journal *Dialogue* in 1970.[10] His study of Hegel had shown him that not only was Hegelian philosophy, and hence thought itself, vulnerable to critique from the point of view of the particular flesh and blood person, and the concrete encounter between that individual and God – the Kierkegaardian critique – but it was also vulnerable to a new critique, that of an evil that defied assimilation into the Hegelian system and hence defied all thought – an evil that was unexplainable, without any meaning or purpose, an absolute and unqualified rupture of Western thought and life.[11] This he called "the scandal of the particularity of Auschwitz."

But if the threat to philosophy and thought in general was radical, could there still be hope for the future? Could one go on after Auschwitz without capitulating wholly to its evil, to its negativity, to its destruction of our categories and principles? For Jews, what could remain of the ideas of salvation and redemption? Did integrity require complete despair?

Fackenheim often said, in later years, that what made possible the responsible and serious exposure to Auschwitz for Jews and for Jewish theologians like himself was the example of Elie Wiesel.[12] Fackenheim already hints at this at the end of the secularity essay and then again in the essay "Jewish Faith and the Holocaust" when he cites Wiesel's testimony in *Night, The Accident,* and *The Gates of the Forest.* Wiesel represented for Fackenheim, and for many of those who assembled for discussion in Quebec at the Segals meetings, the fact that faith had in fact exposed itself to the horrors of the death camps, been shattered, even virtually destroyed, and then recovered, if in revolutionary and surprising forms. The role that Wiesel played for Fackenheim was not as a novelist per se but rather as a survivor and a reflective one who expressed his experiences of descent and of recovery fictionally. But the central point is that Wiesel embodied the idea that resistance to the evil of Nazism, total as it was, was necessary and possible. In "Jewish Faith and the Holocaust" and in the third chapter of *God's Presence in History*, this conviction becomes articulate as Fackenheim's claims that Auschwitz is "the rock on which throughout eternity all rational explanations will crash and break apart"; that "seeking a purpose is one thing, but seeking a response is another"; and finally that after twenty years, he had come to what he calls a "momentous discovery: that while religious thinkers were vainly struggling for a response to Auschwitz, Jews throughout the world.... had to some degree been responding all along."[13] This "discovery" was what the example of Elie Wiesel had taught Fackenheim. If response as resistance and recovery was actual, then it could be possible, and if possible, then we could "read off of existing responses" a set of norms or imperatives for how authentic response ought to be conducted. This is the source – for those who now recognize it – of Fackenheim's 614th commandment, of its origin and its content.

This intellectual situation gave rise to a complex and poorly under-stood reflection on the role of the Holocaust for Jews, Christians, histo-rians, Germans, and others, a reflection articulated most fully in those years in the third chapter of *God's Presence in History*, but prefigured in the writings I have already cited. Fackenheim's reasoning proceeds this way. The task that faced him was manifold: to show how Auschwitz challenged all thought – how it was meaningless and without purpose and unexplainable; to show how the turn from thought to life – as he often put it "thought must go to school with life" – pointed to the actu-ality of resistance; to derive from this actual resistance a conception of why continued resistance is necessary; to give some content to the norms or imperatives that might be used to express that necessity; to explain what the ground of that necessity is – what the force of the obli-gation is – for believing and for secular Jews; and to say something about the possibility of our performing such obligations or imperatives. The formulation of the 614th commandment occurs within this line of think-ing and incorporates several of its steps, which is part of what makes it so challenging and difficult to understand.[14] In it, Fackenheim is not doing one thing but rather many things at once. The commandment not to give Hitler any posthumous victories, that is, expresses the resistance of continued acts of faithfulness to Judaism and the Jewish people and to human dignity; it expresses the idea that a believing Jew would take such acts to be responses to a commandment and that the source of the commandment's authority would be Divine. Moreover, the command-ment as it is formulated and then interpretively expanded into its four parts is the outcome of how Fackenheim now – and those who would see things his way – would interpret the content of that resistance, that is, the shape that such resistance and continued fidelity to Judaism and humanity would take. Even in those years, and this is very explicit in the symposium piece and in the third chapter of *God's Presence in History*, Fackenheim never held that all Jews must take the imperative to be a commandment, strictly speaking, or that all Jews must take it to be a Divine commandment. Secular Jews would not. For them, there would be a sense of acting under an obligation even without an understanding of where it came from or what stood behind it, so to speak. This would be a sense of receiving an imperative without asking what gives it its authority.

This is the position that Fackenheim had come to by 1970. By 1974, a new project began to take shape, an extension of this line of thinking and the demands that it expressed – to take Auschwitz seriously and to take God and Judaism seriously. In 1976, Fackenheim was awarded a prestigious Killam Fellowship from the Canadian government to spend two uninterrupted years working on this new, expanded project on post-Holocaust Jewish thought and more, but, as so often happens, what had been planned as one book with six chapters became transformed in unforeseen ways.[15] As Fackenheim began to think through more deeply what the first chapter would contain, the challenges that faced him became more and more imposing.[16] The first chapter became a book on its own. It was completed in 1981, virtually on the eve of the family's departure to Israel on aliyah, as what we now know as *To Mend the World: Foundations of Future Jewish Thought*, published in 1982.[17]

The central chapter of the book is Chapter IV, where Fackenheim enters the thought of Martin Heidegger to show how it fails to face up to Nazism and how neither Heidegger's early nor late thinking can prevent his failure of authenticity. Heidegger's account of the historicity of human existence called for standards of authenticity but could not provide them in a way that could block his commitment to Nazism and his failure to recant. From Heidegger, Fackenheim turns to other forms of inauthentic response to the Holocaust, including ones by Jewish thinkers, and then asks whether the result is not a total paralysis of thought, an impasse. It is here that thought must go to school with life. Fackenheim's inquiry becomes empirical, as he winds his way through an examination of the perpetrators, at all levels, and the victims, in order to descend to the depth of the horror and to recoil at it, to find a moment of self-reflective resistance, that is, at once a moment of horror, of surprise, and of resistance, all at once. Here what emerges is an imperative of resistance and the ground for its possible accomplishment. At this point, however, when the rupture is as radical as it can be, philosophy offers no hope of articulating such an imperative, but Judaism does, in the form of a concept that acknowledges at once both an unconditional rupture and a post-rupture recovery, the concept of *tikkun olam*. It is under the umbrella of such a notion that philosophy, Christianity, and Judaism can take shape as post-Holocaust responses. The book ends with a further chapter on Judaism as a religion of *teshuvah*, in which Yom Kippur is recovered from its centrality in Rosenzweig, but with a new sense.

For our purposes, as we try to understand the stages in Fackenheim's appreciation of the role of the Holocaust for Jewish life and thought, for philosophy, and for much else, the main issues are raised by the central chapter, and specifically what he accomplishes once he locates the failure of Heidegger's philosophy to cope with Nazism and Auschwitz, and turns to an exploration of what he calls "resistance during the Holocaust" and then "resistance as an ontological category." What we have here is the deepest account Fackenheim gives of the evil of Auschwitz and the failure of all thought to understand or encompass it and, following that, his most sustained argument for the role and ground of resistance to that evil. The result of these two sections, sections 8 and 9 of Chapter IV, is that resistance to Auschwitz and all it stands for was actual, necessary, possible. But, I think, whereas *earlier*, in *God's Presence in History* and the essays that preceded it, Fackenheim was taken up *with understanding the ground of the necessity or normative force of the imperative to resist or oppose Nazi purposes and with its articulation* – which here occurs later as the filling in of the idea of *tikkun*, *here* his focus is on *the possibility of performing the obligation, of in fact continuing to live our lives as resisting actions*. To put it simply, resistance cannot be so easy for us today that it belittles those who did not exercise it in those days, nor can it be so hard today that it makes the resistance of those who performed it pointless, so that Hitler has indeed won his posthumous victories.[18]

Fackenheim is very explicit about the chief problem he felt in writing these sections of Chapter IV. In the Introduction to *To Mend the World*, he discusses how he had handled it earlier and why that treatment was inadequate, and he outlines how he will deal with it here, in sections 8 and 9.[19] What he says is this: it is his most profound example of "thought going to school with life." Earlier he had used two strategies to understand how the imperative of resistance – or what he then called the 614th commandment – could be performed, that is, how it was possible to follow it. One strategy was to follow Kant, who argued that *ought* implies *can*, that morality requires freedom. To say that the command to oppose Nazi purposes existed was to say that those for whom it existed were free to act on it. Another, more theological, strategy was to follow Rosenzweig, who had argued that God, in giving the commandments, also gave us the freedom to follow them. This neo-orthodox strategy could be seen, I think, to be a religious version of the Kantian strategy, and the point of both was that the issue of possibility was, in a sense, treated as automatic. Fackenheim, however, came to see it in very concrete terms, that by calling upon either strategy, one was demeaning all those victims who did not resist and belittling all those who did. Most of all, as he came to see, such responses are "glib" and reveal how inadequately he had immersed himself in the dark world called Auschwitz.[20] He calls attention to the Musselmanner (a term used in the camps to describe those who had lost all hope), whom he had come to see – following Primo Levi – were the characteristic products of the death camps, and asks, "Who dares assert that, had he been then and there rather than here and now, he would not have been reduced to a Musselmann?" In other words, no account of how it is *possible* to accept the burden of an imperative of resistance today is genuine and responsible if it rules out the possibility that one could be overwhelmed, dehumanized, and annihilated.

This might seem to lead to a dead end. If we look hard enough at Auschwitz, we see only a "midnight of dark despair." But at the time of writing *To Mend the World*, Fackenheim believed that he could see, as he put it, a "shining light" in that dark night. That is, he felt that in the event itself, even if it was "irresistible," it was being resisted, and by locating that resistance, analyzing it, and clarifying it, he could find a ground for the possibility of our responding today to that horror then (and to our own horrors today). What he was looking for were lucid, transparent, acts of resistance, and he found them in several cases, especially in the life and then the writings of Pelagia Lewinska, a Polish noblewoman, whose acts of resistance and whose struggles for dignity were illuminated by a clear and focused understanding of the purposes of those who assaulted her and of the entire world of which that assault was a part.[21]

Fackenheim came to this answer to his central question: it is possible for us to resist Nazi purposes now because resistance was actual then in a way that understood itself as the target of radical evil and yet as acts of resistance against it. This result, coupled with the unique role of *tikkun* as the concept that facilitates our understanding of the modes of resistance that follow, is the central teaching of Fackenheim's magnum opus, or at least its central teaching with regard to the Holocaust.

The core argument of *To Mend the World* has important implications. Among them is what it teaches about the very character of post-Holocaust philosophical thought. But it is a teaching that is hard to appreciate.

In Chapter I of *To Mend the World*, after contrasting the book's contents with that of *Encounters Between Judaism and Modern Philosophy*, Emil Fackenheim points out:

> In the grim but ineluctable task of a direct confrontation with the Holocaust, our thought receives much help from historians, novelists, poets. It receives more help still – indispensable help – from witnesses that survived the ordeal and told the tale. But so far as thought (philosophical or theological) is concerned, one still is, except for a few comrades-in-arms, alone. (TMW, 22)

Let me draw attention to Fackenheim's acknowledgment of the central importance to his inquiry of what he here calls the "indispensable help" of the testimony of survivors and witnesses. A page later, having identified the central task of the work, to show how Jewish thought "can both expose itself to the Holocaust and survive," Fackenheim refers to the most important "help" that this testimony provides, "a shining light," he calls it, "in this midnight of dark despair"(25). What he is referring to is the "resistance in thought and the resistance in life" that grounds the possibility of Jewish thought's endurance, *"To hear and obey the commanding voice of Auschwitz is an 'ontological' possibility, here and now, because the hearing and obeying was* already an 'ontic' reality, *then and there"* (25). The crucial testimony, then, discloses "the shining light" of a resistance that is in some way paradigmatic. For those familiar with the work, it is no surprise that the testimony includes that of Pelagia Lewinska, from her memoir *Twenty Months in Auschwitz*, when she describes her first awareness of the Nazi intent and remarked that she "felt under orders to live" (Lewinska, 41ff., 50). From the first moment that Fackenheim learned of those remarks, reading about them in Terence Des Pres's *The Survivor*, when it was first published in 1976 (Des Pres, 62–63), their significance increased for him, culminating in their role in *To Mend the World*.

Lewinska's testimony Fackenheim later calls "a historic statement," and says that it is "pivotal" to the book. In section 8 of Chapter IV, he engages in a descriptive account of various types of resistance during the Holocaust, but in the "critical analysis" of "resistance as an ontological category" in section 9, it is Lewinska's testimony that has pride of place. The thought that has tried in every way to confront and comprehend the evil of the death camps arrives at a "horrified surprise, or a surprised horror" (247), and this is a philosophical thought that is itself possible only because it was already exemplified in the Holocaust by resisting victims, preeminently by Pelagia Lewinska, whose grasp of the evil and her situation is "epistemologically ultimate" (249). At this pivotal moment in *To Mend the World*, Fackenheim draws the conclusion that "Resistance in extremity was a way of being," which he calls the end of a necessary excursus, clearly a philosophical one, in which the impasse of thought trying to comprehend and cope with Auschwitz is now seen to be neither absolute nor permanent. Post-Holocaust thought is possible now because resistance in thought was actual then, and because then it led to actual acts of resistance, whereas now it also must lead not just to thought but to life.

All of this deserves careful, critical examination, much more than it has thus far received, but the problem we want to uncover lies in a different direction. Pelagia Lewinska's testimony is not the only testimony Fackenheim appropriates and explores. Various witnesses are considered in his descriptive account of resistance, including Hasidim in Buchenwald and the Warsaw Ghetto fighers. But the role of these cases is to lead us to Lewinska's culminating testimony, with its self-awareness and its self-conscious commitment to life. Later, in sections 12–14, however, Fackenheim calls attention to cases of resistance for different purposes, as part of his articulation of post-Holocaust philosophy, Christianity, and Judaism. Post-Holocaust philosophical thought can occur today because there was already a resisting philosophical moment – what he calls a *tikkun* [mending] – during that event, by Kurt Huber and the "White Rose" in Munich (the German-Catholic resistance group). Post-Holocaust Christianity is possible now because of the resistance of one such Christian as Bernhard Lichtenberg, who responded to Kristallnacht with a public prayer in behalf of Jews. And post-Holocaust Jewish life is possible for Jews because of the resistance of the Warsaw Ghetto fighters, the Buchenwald Hasidim, and honorary Jews such as Pelagia Lewinska.

All this is to say that the testimony by witnesses of acts of resistance, and in particular the "indispensable testimony" of Pelagia Lewinska, occur at different moments in Fackenheim's central chapter in *To Mend the World*. First, they occur in the course of a philosophical analysis of exposure to the evil of Auschwitz and an attempt to grasp what the exposure leads to. Second, they occur in particular articulations of post-Holocaust life and thought. What separates these two stages of Fackenheim's thinking may help us to understand the different roles that these citations play and more importantly to understand something important about Fackenheim's entire enterprise in *To Mend the World*.

The philosophical excursus, as he calls it, and the inquiries into post-Holocaust existence are separated by two important points. The first is the introduction of the notion of *tikkun*; the second is the formulation of what he calls a contemporary "hermeneutical teaching" that begins with historical situatedness. Let me say a word about each of these points.

First, *tikkun*. Fackenheim's recovery of this Jewish concept is not a matter of scholarly inquiry but is itself an interpretive appropriation of a Jewish idea through a brief reflection on its liturgical and Kabbalistic settings as well as its use in the work of a Budapest Hasid during the Holocaust. It is, then, itself an act of hermeneutical recovery of an element of the Jewish past via an encounter with its invocation during the Holocaust. In this case, however, this hermeneutical act of recovery is not conducted in order to articulate something about Jewish life exclusively. Rather it is intended to serve a philosophical purpose. Having argued that resistance during the Holocaust is ontologically ultimate, and the ground of the possibility of all subsequent existence, Fackenheim returns to ask how thought – philosophical thought – does not meet an impasse but can go on. But thought is constituted by concepts, categories, and principles. Once thought reacts with surprised horror to the evil itself, it still seeks to think. If there is a sense of imperative or obligation about going on as thought, then how does thought understand its going on? That is, Fackenheim sees philosophy as having reached a point where its own conceptual resources, the resources of the Western philosophical tradition, are inadequate. This point is not about having the conceptual resources to grasp the evil of Auschwitz. It is about having the conceptual resources to articulate grasping the evil with horrified surprise and reacting by going on and responding in opposition to it. What is needed, as Fackenheim sees it, is a "new departure and a new category" (249, 250). This new category must incorporate, with respect to the past and the present, a sense of total rupture or discontinuity and yet also, in some way, a sense of continuity and continuation, and it is Fackenheim's contention that there is no such concept available within the philosophical tradition. Rather, for it, one must turn to Judaism, and it is the idea of *tikkun* that he believes and seeks to show incorporates these almost paradoxical components, absolute rupture and fragmentary mending.[22] What the new category does is to provide a term, a concept, for articulating post-Holocaust life: if such life is an attempt to obey the imperative of going on exposed to Auschwitz, then it is a *tikkun*, and in fact it is this term, rather than "resistance" that Fackenheim now proceeds to use – for philosophy and Christianity, as well as for Judaism. This concept or category of *tikkun*, then, is the bridge between a philosophical analysis of resistance that seeks to ground the possibility of post-Holocaust life in an actual resistance to radical evil during that event and a hermeneutical articulation of what that post-Holocaust life ought to be.[23]

The second point that separates the uses of the testimony of resistance and especially that of Pelagia Lewinska is the contemporary hermeneutic. In a note, Fackenheim explicitly refers to Heidegger, Gadamer, Bultmann, Ricoeur, Buber, and Rosenzweig as the figures he has in mind as the sources for this hermeneutical conception of human existence. For the moment, the crucial element of the hermeneutic is that it takes all human existence as historically situated, with all that implies about encountering one's situation with presuppositions of all kinds, not being able to escape one's embeddedness in traditions, practices, and so forth. And what this means is that what follows are examples of post-Holocaust existence – philosophy, Christianity, and Judaism – and that they are just that, examples, of a myriad of such cases, indeed of all the cases of post-Holocaust life that are responsible and serious. Moreover, all post-Holocaust existence, like all human existence, is hermeneutical and historically situated. To understand itself, each example must understand its situation, its prejudices, and presuppositions, and seek to recover the past for the present and future, if only fragmentarily, by returning to the past.

The appropriation of the testimony about resistance during the Holocaust, or what Fackenheim now calls *tikkun* during the Holocaust, is thoroughly hermeneutical. It is engaged in from our situated point of view, and, if Fackenheim is right, since that situation is a post-Holocaust situation, the appropriation is shaped – fundamentally but not exclusively – by Auschwitz. Who, then, are the agents of such *tikkun*? The answer of course is that we are, all of us, all who live now and seek to go on with our lives – as philosophers, historians, Americans, Jews, Christians, Germans, and so forth.

But now we draw near to the second point we have been seeking to articulate: who, then, was the agent of the earlier excursus, of the philosophical inquiry and analysis of resistance that yielded the account of thought's encounter with the evil as horrified surprise and a surprised horror and utilized, so centrally, the testimony of Pelagia Lewinska?

Clearly that agent was Emil Fackenheim. The thought is his; the description of types of resistance and the philosophical analysis of resistance as an ontological category is his. But here, then, is the question we have been seeking: what is the status of the excursus? What kind of philosophical analysis is it? Is it a mode of the old thinking or the new? Does it too take place within the hermeneutical standpoint of the "authentic" post-Holocaust philosopher? And if it does, what does that mean for its results, for its conclusions? What is their status? How can it be both a philosophical grounding of the necessity and possibility of post-Holocaust philosophical thought and also a hermeneutical expression of it?

In one sense, of course, Emil Fackenheim, as philosopher and as the author of *To Mend the World* and its philosophical excursus on resistance as ontological ground, is historically situated; his thinking and his life are set in North America (in those years), in Toronto, Canada, during the sixties and seventies and early eighties. He teaches at the University of Toronto, is immersed in the study of Kant, Hegel, and German Idealism, and is one among a circle of Jewish thinkers involved in exploring and clarifying a kind of Jewish existential theology. He is also, of course, motivated to confront the memories of Nazism and the Nazi atrocities and to rethink Judaism and Jewish life in its aftermath. And, in works from about 1966 to the writing of *To Mend the World*, he has been engaged in that project, while speaking widely of its significance and challenging others – often Christians – who attack the Jewish people, Israel, and Zionism.

But in another sense, Emil Fackenheim as philosopher takes himself, in these central sections of Chapter IV of *To Mend the World*, to be engaging in a philosophical reflection of ultimate significance, from a point of view that hovers back and forth from particular points of view to a detached, objective point of view, the perspective of reason, with the aim of arriving at secure and unconditional philosophical conclusions about the necessity and possibility of post-Holocaust life – all life, as he says, not only some one mode of life, of a *tikkun* that is *olam* (of the world or total) and not limited or parochial. That is, the author of the philosophical excursus wants to achieve philosophical detachment and objectivity. He will not be satisfied by a hermeneutically restricted or conditional set of conclusions. But how can Fackenheim think that he himself has accomplished this point of view? Does the later hermeneutical teaching, which Fackenheim accepts and endorses, not hold that *all human existence* is *historically situated* and hence qualified or conditioned by the specific presuppositions, traditions, communities, and more that always define our particular points of view? Does the truth of such a hermeneutic not compromise the objectivity of the earlier excursus and its conclusions about the ultimacy of resistance and about the special status of the case of Pelagia Lewinska?

In different terms, does the hermeneutical nature of all human existence and hence of all post-Holocaust life, including that of the philosopher, in any way qualify the status of the earlier reflection as philosophy? Does it make it in some way less philosophical? Or does it make it differently philosophical? That earlier reflection was Hegelian in character, akin to that of the thought in Hegel's *Phenomenology* that moves from the stance of natural consciousness to that of absolute knowledge and back, hovering back and forth, moving from one mode of natural consciousness to another, yet at each stage rising above that natural consciousness to ask what is false and what is true in it, what is left behind and what is recovered at the next stage of the dialectic. In *To Mend the World*, the modes of existence or consciousness that Emil considers are modes of Nazi agency and then modes of resistance, at each stage thought trying to follow the agent's self-understanding and yet reflecting on it, seeking to grasp what is experienced more and more fully, until thought goes as far as it can – by confronting the evil as a whole of horror with a horrified surprise and a surprised horror, with an apprehension that is at the same time a resistance, an act of opposition. But for Hegel, the perspective of the philosopher is rooted in its being absolute knowledge that can move from the perspective of various agents to its own absolute standpoint, back and forth. Does Fackenheim's commitment to a historically situated hermeneutic of existence not exclude such an absolute standpoint? Does it not rule out the possibility of philosophical objectivity altogether? Does it do away with philosophy or alter it completely? And what is the relationship between the historically situated hermeneutic and the Holocaust? Does Fackenheim accept the hermeneutic for philosophical reasons or because of the radical nature of the evil of the Holocaust as a rupture?

These are important and central questions regarding Fackenheim's entire enterprise, in *To Mend the World*, and beyond. Moreover, he himself was aware of the issues. He knew that in a sense, *To Mend the World* would require a kind of "hovering" between perspectives or points of view, from engaged interpretation (which is my term, not his) to philosophical reflection, back and forth, although the hovering he had in mind was between the perspective of the perpetrators and the victims, on the one hand, and that of the philosopher, on the other. But recognizing that there is a problem about his own status as a philosopher and about the status of the core of *To Mend the World* as philosophy and dealing with the problem are not one and the same. If Fackenheim did recognize the problem, how did he respond to it?

Here is one proposal. Fackenheim was persuaded by the historical situatedness of human existence and its hermeneutical character by 1966 or so. This commitment is already reflected in his account of textual interpretation in Chapter 1 of *God's Presence in History*, an account based on Collingwood's notion of reenactment but one that is also based on his reading of Heidegger. But what convinced him of the hermeneutic was the study of Hegel (and Heidegger and Gadamer, but later). Because the historical character of the Hegelian system exposed philosophical knowledge to history, the Holocaust refuted the very idea of such absolute knowledge, leaving behind philosophical reflection in situated human experience but nothing beyond it. This realization did not depend upon the outcome of the later analysis in *To Mend the World*, that the necessary and possible thought directed at the Holocaust must incorporate action in opposition to it. What it did depend upon were the assumptions that there is no more complete case of philosophical thinking than the Hegelian system, and that the evil of Auschwitz was such that even that system could not comprehend it. In principle, then, for Fackenheim by 1966 or so, and certainly in the years through 1970, a philosophically framed understanding of Jewish existence after the Holocaust was immersed in history, and no feature of it was in principle immune to historical or empirical refutation.

Nonetheless, insofar as he, Fackenheim, was a Jew and a philosopher, his own reflections always began with certain presuppositions, beliefs, conceptual resources, practical commitments, and so forth; what he did with them was then a hermeneutical matter. (There is no better overall account of this process than the one we find in *What Is Judaism?* published in 1987.) But this means that whatever "objectivity" arises from these kinds of philosophical reflections, say the ones in *To Mend the World* about epoch-making events and about resistance as an ontological category, is an objectivity within this hermeneutical framework. The accounts may be persuasive, compelling, and arrived at by a process of reasoning and analysis that one finds convincing. For example, one might treat the analysis as a kind of best explanation of how to understand the testimony of Pelagia Lewinska; Fackenheim himself argues that other types of explanations of resistance are inadequate. And since we do have that testimony and hence have reason to believe that she did in fact experience what she says she did, we might feel satisfied with Fackenheim's dialectical examination that shows why thought should lead to a horrified surprise, and a surprised horror gives us an account of what it was that was going on in Lewinska's experience. We might judge it to be a better analysis than others that might be offered; in fact, we might agree with Fackenheim that no other could do equal justice to that experience. And since the experience was actual, it must have been possible, and we might take Fackenheim's dialectical account as a kind of best explanation of how it was possible. We might, that is, read it as a sort of transcendental argument for the possibility of a comprehending thought that was necessarily integrated with a resisting action, all at once. Hence, even if we realize that Fackenheim's account is based on his own situation, with his own presuppositions, we might take it to be persuasive and compelling, because it satisfies our concerns and convinces us. And that might be all the objectivity we get and all we can hope for. This insight of ours – and his – would be grounded in the thought that since there is no such thing as a point of view completely detached from historical situatedness, there are no absolute or unconditional truths or principles or doctrines or concepts. Fackenheim uses the Rosenzweigian vocabulary of old and new thinking at times, and we can appropriate it here as well. That there is a philosophical view of things that is utterly detached from history and the personal point of view is a construction of philosophy and a hallmark of the "old thinking," but in fact, as the "new thinking" realizes, all thinking, even philosophical thinking (and scientific and religious as well), is personal and historically situated. Hence, when we give up the "old" notion of objectivity, we need not have given up on objectivity altogether. What we mean by objectivity, however, is the kind of firmness, stability, and persuasiveness that we seek for our understanding of things and sometimes achieve, in our lives. And we can expect such virtues from Fackenheim's analysis of resistance as an ontological category, and even think that his account has achieved them.

If this way of reading Fackenheim's thinking in *To Mend the World* is plausible, is there evidence in that work that he himself holds it? Does he himself say anything about the status of his own philosophical reflection in that work? In the introductory chapter (pp. 19–28), as Fackenheim sketches the itinerary of the book, he does not directly answer our questions, but he does show very clearly that his stance as a philosopher is an issue for the work and how that stance influences the thinking in the excursus and prior to it.

First, after outlining his original plan for the project "Radical Responses to Epoch-Making Events in Contemporary Jewish History," Fackenheim remarks that the "neatness of the systematic project was soon to dissolve in the process of execution." In the original plan, the first chapter was to deal with philosophical foundations and not until Chapters IV and V was he to arrive at the encounter with the Holocaust and the attempt to confront its utter uniqueness from various historically situated points of view. But, as he notes, in order to avoid losing the Holocaust in a priori conceptual reflections, it became necessary to place thought, "as it were, *beween* the concept 'epoch-making event' and *this* epoch-making event, prepared to be pulled in both directions... there had to be what may be called a selective anticipation of the 'empirical'... in the 'a priori'" (TMW, 20). Fackenheim calls this a change "at the empirical extreme"; it was a necessity grounded in the empirical uniqueness of the evils of Auschwitz. At the "a priori extreme," he notes a change as well, so that instead of beginning the project with bare philosophical speculation, he chose to engage "thinkers of the first rank" and use a more "goal-directed... historical-dialectical approach" by confronting "their thought with the events to which self-exposure is necessary" (20) – namely, the Holocaust.

These comments, of course, do not speak directly to the status of the philosophical excursus on resistance but rather to the attempt to understand the very concept of an epoch-making event. But these points, when taken together, are relevant to the questions we just raised. They concern the problems of anticipation and perspective. In general terms, these comments show that Fackenheim was aware that the philosophical preparations for the hermeneutical applications could not be completely severed from the introduction of the Holocaust and from the historical situatedness of post-Holocaust agents, nor could the philosophical preparations be carried out without attention to the way the Holocaust might shape those preparations. He admits that "such a method" of somehow thinking together the philosophical foundations and the hermeneutical articulations in terms of the Holocaust is "circular," but, he says, "provided this circle is recognized, and the recognition of it permeates the whole discourse, it merely illustrates... that a philosophical writer with a systematic purpose cannot say everything that needs to be said" (21).

But the question I have been asking is, in these terms, "recognized" by whom? By the philosopher as detached and neutral, or by the historically situated philosopher? And what does this imply about the objectivity of the outcome? Later in *To Mend the World*, Fackenheim presents and then challenges Heidegger's way of formulating and then coping with the ontic-ontological circle. Without examining Fackenheim's account in detail (pp. 162–166), we can distill from it, in the terms I have been using, the judgment that something is amiss with a historical situatedness that is either guided by vacuous standards or wholly historicized. In terms of the problem of the status of the philosophical excursus on resistance, then, and the role of Pelagia Lewinska's testimony, presumably Fackenheim would not be happy with saying that they are integral to either a merely hermeneutical exercise or an utterly disengaged, detached one. Where, if anywhere, does objectivity lie?

In a discussion of language in the introduction to *To Mend the World*, Fackenheim addresses directly the questions of communicating the incommunicable and of objectivity (pp. 26–28). How, he asks, can the philosopher write about the Holocaust *"in its totality,"* about the world of the victims and of the criminals? This question is not ours, but since he is asking precisely about how the philosopher can conduct the analysis into the whole of horror and resistance to it, his answer may help us to see what he thinks about the point of view or stance of the philosopher who carries out that analysis. "One may wish to reply," he says, "by resorting to a thought and a language that *enter into* that world and also seek a *transcending comprehension* of it" (27). This was Hegel's strategy, but, he argues, it cannot be his. Why not? Because Hegel's "ultimate Whole of wholes is one of wonder" whereas "the Holocaust . . . is a whole of horror. A transcending comprehension of it is impossible, for it would rest on the prior dissolution of a horror that is indissoluble. This horror leaves our thought and our language with but two choices. One is surrender. . . . The other is the 'no' of an ever-new, ever-again-surprised outrage . . . that would be lost by a 'clinical' tone of 'objective' detachment" (28) or by an expression of the writer's own feelings. What is necessary is a language and a thought "of sober, restrained, but at the same time unyielding outrage" (28). This is the perspective of the survivors, and it is one neither novelist nor historians, philosophers nor theologians should try to "transcend."

Can we apply this outcome to our question? Is the philosopher who engages in the analysis of resistance as an ontological category involved and engaged, hermeneutically situated in a post-Holocaust world? Is that analysis, in its own way, a response to that event? Is its objectivity compromised by its situatedness? Fackenheim seems to be saying that no philosophical analysis of the criminals or the victims should be disengaged and detached. If it enters into that world, it cannot simply then seek to transcend it. Rather it must follow the survivors themselves, thinking the event and yet with a "restrained and unyielding outrage." Even the analysis of the survivor's resistance itself must be an expression of such outrage; what philosophical thought does is to recast or rearticulate that outrage, that 'no,' in a different language, in different words, but its outcome is, in a sense, self-confirming.

Is this a circle? And if it is, is it vicious? Do such philosophical conclusions have any objectivity at all? With these questions, we come to the conclusion both of the second point I mentioned earlier and of this chapter. Clearly, there is some kind of circle here, but for Fackenheim it certainly is not vicious. Philosophy may have once had the luxury, if one wants to call it that, of being purely cognitive, exploratory, or even descriptive. Today, after Auschwitz, it cannot be that. Thinking about the Holocaust and then about suffering and atrocity in today's world, philosophy must think as resistance, with a "restrained but unyielding outrage" – it must think with a moral edge. Such a conception of philosophy may require some serious revision and difficult recasting of the philosophical enterprise. But in a post-Holocaust world, it is unavoidable, and that is one of the central teachings of *To Mend the World*.

Notes

1. I have been told that the idea for the theme of the symposium that year – the year before, the theme had been about Jewish unity – came out of discussions at the Segal Institute the summer before – in 1966 – when it had been agreed that Wiesel represented something very important for the participants, the fact that Jewish faith could confront the horrors of the death camps and still survive, albeit in an embattled and conflicted form. Popkin, a historian of philosophy famous for his work on skepticism, was a colleague of Schwarzschild's at Washington University in St. Louis; Steiner, a literary critic from Cambridge and Switzerland, had published a powerful review of Wiesel called "The Language of Silence" and a collection of essays *Language and Silence*. He was also at work on a book, *In Bluebeard's Castle*, that dealt with such themes. He was a secularist and a strong advocate of German and modernist culture and literature. Wiesel had just published *The Jews of Silence* and was increasingly an emblem of memory about the Nazi atrocities.
2. Fackenheim discusses the event, the emotional toll it took, and his preparation for it, in the Preface to the Second Edition of *To Mend the World*, xvi–xx. Also in Emil Fackenheim, *An Epitaph for German Judaism* (University of Wisconsin Press, forthcoming), 158–159.
3. *Daedalus* 96 (1967), 193–219; also in *Religion in America*, edited by Wm. G. McLoughlin and R. N. Bellah (Boston: Houghton Mifflin, 1968), 203–229; and in Fackenheim's collection, *Quest for Past and Future* (Bloomington: Indiana, 1968), Ch. 18, 278–305.
4. "On the Self-Exposure....," in QPF, 303.
5. "The 614th Commandment," reprinted in Michael L. Morgan (ed.), *The Jewish Thought of Emil Fackenheim*, 158.

6. In Fackenheim, *An Epitaph for German Judaism* (forthcoming), Emil recalls that at one of the Quebec meetings, Milton Himmelfarb, responding to someone who said that "mere survival" cannot be the "purpose" of either the Jewish people or Judaism, exploded: "After the Holocaust, let no one call Jewish survival 'mere'" (151). Over the years, he cited this remark regularly; it is likely that Himmelfarb had made it at the meeting during the summer of 1966 or possibly at the next meeting in 1967.

7. In discussing the chronology of these years with me on many occasions, especially in the early 1990s, during the time he was working on his memoirs, Emil contended that the earliest public occasion at which he spoke about the Holocaust seriously was at a conference on "The Future of Hope," convened by the department of religion at the University of California at Santa Barbara; other participants were Jurgen Moltmann and Johann Baptist Metz, and the proceedings were published as *The Future of Hope* by Fortress Press in 1970, edited by W. H. Capps. Emil's contribution was "The Commandment to Hope: A Response to Contemporary Jewish Experience," 68–91, 93, 99–101, 131–133. Emil remembered the conference as occurring in 1966, but Capps, in the introduction to the volume, dates it to 1968. The content of Emil's presentation suggests the later date, since the formulation of a commandment for the future occurred, I think, during the fall and winter before the 1967 symposium. There is no other evidence of it prior to that date. In a recent conversation, however, Eugene Borowitz told me that late in the summer of 1965, after Fackenheim had attended the first of the Segals conferences earlier that summer, and had talked especially with Irving Greenberg about the death camps and Nazi assault, Fackenheim had said that he could no longer ignore the central importance of the Holocaust.

8. For brief comments, see Fackenheim, *An Epitaph for German Judaism*, 156–157.

9. The earliest prospectus for the project dates from the late 1940s. Essays on Kant and Schelling in the early 1950s are parts of it. His successful proposal for the Guggenheim Foundation, for 1956–57, outlines it.

10. Fackenheim shows how prominent Hegel was in his thinking during this period when he discusses the existentialist critique of Hegel's thinking and the "limits of the essence-approach," as he calls it, and asks how a Jew today must respond to the "here-and-now" that includes "the events associated with the dread name of Auschwitz." The discussion occurs in Chapter 1 of *Quest for Past and Future*, "These Twenty Years: A Reappraisal," published in 1968, pp. 15–17. The Preface of the book is dated October 4, 1967; one can date the writing of this previously unpublished chapter during the summer and early fall of 1967, just after the Six Day War, to which it refers. For an excellent discussion of the relation between history and philosophical thought in Hegel, see Fred Beiser, *Hegel* (Routledge, 2005).

11. This was something already signaled for Fackenheim by Schelling's treatment of radical evil in *Of Human Freedom*. See *An Epitaph for German Judaism*, 179–182.

12. Fackenheim says this explicitly in the Preface to the Second Edition of *To Mend the World*, xvi: "One participant would be Elie Wiesel, the one writer then known to me who genuinely confronted Judaism with the Holocaust – and the Holocaust with Judaism."

13. These quotations are from "Jewish Faith and the Holocaust," in *The Jewish Thought of Emil Fackenheim*, 163–164.

14. Fackenheim discusses some of the problems raised by his formulation, problems he tried to deal with earlier in the writings of 1967–1970 but which had plagued discussions of him, in the Preface to the Second Edition of *To Mend the World*, xix–xx.

15. An outline of the chapters of the book appears on p. 19 of *To Mend the World*. The book was to have a chapter on reading the Bible. It never materialized, although Fackenheim did give a set of lectures in Manchester and elsewhere that became *The Jewish Bible after the Holocaust*, published in 1993. Another chapter was to be on reading *midrash* after the Holocaust, a development beyond Chapter 1 of *God's Presence in History*, but this was never written. The chapter on Israel might be said to have emerged, in bits and pieces, over the years after 1983 and Fackenheim's aliyah to Israel. One might claim, that is, that the project as formulated in 1976 did become in one way or another the framework for Fackenheim's work during the remaining twenty years of his life, after the first publication of *To Mend the World*. Fackenheim discusses the book and the project, but not in any detail, in *An Epitaph for German Judaism*, 173–178.

16. In Chapter 1 of *To Mend the World*, he explains precisely how the first chapter came to be a book on its own. The original project was to have begun with a chapter on the concept of an epoch-making event, to be followed later in the book by empirical accounts of actual resistance during the Holocaust and philosophical reflection on them. But, as he explains, he came to realize that neither the a priori or conceptual discussion nor the empirical accounts could be carried out separately; in the end, one required the other or, perhaps better, the conceptual account of epoch-making events could not be carried out without some anticipation of the absolute rupture that was Auschwitz. The first chapter required thought to "hover" between the poles, and it required too much expansion and articulation.

17. Fackenheim discusses briefly the plan and its execution on pages 19–30 of the Introduction to the original edition of the book. It was subsequently reprinted in new editions, the second and the third, without changes but each time adding an additional preface or prologue, in 1989 and 1994.

18. I believe that Fackenheim's basic problem is akin to what Eliezer Berkovits calls the situation of "Job's brothers," all of us today who seek to respond to Auschwitz and to our Jewish situation. Our faith cannot be so easy to maintain that it demeans those who lost it in the death camps, nor can it be so hard to maintain that it degrades the simple faith who kept it. There are tremendous differences between the two, Fackenheim and Berkovits, concerning their outcomes and also the character of their systematic thinking, but still the dialectical way that

Berkovits characterizes authentic post-Holocaust faith does bear a similarity to what Fackenheim requires of a genuine post-Holocaust resistance. Fackenheim himself emphasizes the problem of the possibility of performing the imperative in his Preface to the Second Edition of *To Mend the World*, xx–xxii.

19. *To Mend the World*, 24–28.

20. *To Mend the World*, 24–25.

21. Lewinska is one of three examples he describes; the others are of Jewish mothers at Auschwitz and Rabbi Zvi Hirsch Meisels and his Hasidim in Buchenwald; see *To Mend the World*, 216–219.

22. It is worth noting two points concerning this new category. (1): As long ago as the introduction to *Quest for Past and Future* and the first chapter of *God's Presence in History*, Fackenheim had claimed that *midrash* expresses fundamental contradictions in human existence that philosophy seeks to dissolve or resolve; this view of religion as acknowledging and seeking to live with the contradictory or paradoxical character of human existence is something that Fackenheim derives, I believe, from his reading of Kierkegaard. (2) The theme that Western philosophy has something important to learn from Judaism is one central theme of *Encounters Between Judaism and Modern Philosophy* and goes back to Fackenheim's essays on Kant in the 1960s. It is tempting to think that in this regard, Fackenheim has some affinity with Hermann Cohen and his claims about Messianism and Kantian ethics.

23. In essence, all of this fills out the gap left in *God's Presence in History* between the identification of the imperative to respond to Auschwitz and the formulation of it as a 614th commandment, with its ramified content.

14 Evil, Suffering, and the Holocaust

BEREL LANG

> As far as human eyes can judge, the degree of evil might have been less
> without any impediment to good.
>
> Samuel Johnson

The need to account for the appearance of evil in a world assumed to be
ruled by goodness and justice provoked Jewish religious and philosophical reflection long before the Holocaust. The 'problem' of evil, pointed
most sharply in the phenomenon of human suffering and loss, figured
in the very origins of Jewish philosophy (as in Saadya's commentary
on *Job*[1] [c. 935 C.E.]), and *Genesis* itself provided an earlier view of the
knowledge of good and evil in its synthesis of cosmology and genealogy –
the entry into human nature of moral conscience, which ensured that
man would then make his own way across the grain of historical contingency *and* face divine judgment for his actions. That *second* nature
would then impel the Biblical narrative and subsequent Jewish ethical
reflection.

Motivation for philosophical and religious reflections on evil is
ample in Jewish thought. On the one hand, the world was found 'good'
at each stage of the Biblical creation, and except for scattered moments
of mystical enthusiasm, subsequent Jewish commentary never disputed
that judgment. On the other hand, a profusion of evidence attests to
individual and group suffering in people who appear to deserve that condition no more (often much less) than contemporaries who fare better –
often, *much* better. At least from the time of Rabbinic Judaism, in any
event, the issue thus stated would recur in Jewish theological and philosophical discussion: how to reconcile misfortune, suffering or persecution – and exile – with the goodness of creation and the authority of
an all-powerful and beneficent creator. And if modern pre-Holocaust
Jewish thinkers, from Spinoza to Hermann Cohen, seem less troubled
than their predecessors by the phenomenon of evil as a historical and
then religious or metaphysical factor, this reflected new anxieties about

primarily epistemological themes more than any diminished significance in ethical issues themselves.

History, however, has a way of undoing the most conscientious expec-
tations, and the Holocaust has had just that unsettling effect on moral
history and theory. Evidence of this appears in the assembly of claims
representing the Holocaust as unique or as a 'novum,' a breach or turning
point in moral history generally and in Jewish history specifically.[2] Such
characterizations start out from the systematic cruelty inflicted in the
Holocaust – with that enormity also expressed in a related set of terms
that call the Holocaust – "indescribable," "beyond words," "ineffable."[3]
Often, to be sure, such terms are figurative, hyperbolic; but even allowing for this rhetorical element, their literal core remains: the *fact* of the
Holocaust, involving systematic cruelty on a scale that portends a rupture or paradigm shift in moral understanding generally and an issue
for Jewish thought and consciousness in particular. The meta-historical
implications thus noted evidently presuppose the historical ground –
a dependence of moral or religious conclusions on historical premises
that, although not unique to accounts of the Holocaust, requires closer
than usual scrutiny because of the scale of the issues.

This requirement is not without its own difficulties, however, as
even common references to the phenomenon of evil make clear. On the
one hand, if evil were not apparent, there would be no moral 'problem' at
all to discuss. On the other hand, to speak of evil as real – for example,
without scare-quotes – turns out, on inspection, to be tendentious –
since a significant philosophical tradition has argued that evil is *only*
apparent. Any assumption that it is more than that shows only a lack
of understanding – since whatever else evil is, it is *not* real. In this way,
the 'problem' of evil proves itself to be a problem.

Even this deflationary conclusion, however, cannot obscure the
occurrence of human suffering and loss – and it is these, after all, that
on the scale of the Holocaust impel the claim of a breach or transformation in moral history, necessitating the revision and possible abandonment of traditional moral categories. Again, the prima facie grounds
are clear for both the historical and the 'meta'-historical sides of this
thesis: the undoubted and distinctive cruelty in the agents and the suffering in the victims impel the finding of a meta-historical breach in
moral and religious history. Against that background, 'Where was God
in Auschwitz?' has become a formulaic question, recurring in Jewish
and other religious reflections on the Holocaust (slightly altered, in secular accounts as well). With Auschwitz itself a metonym for Nazism,

furthermore, *'after* Auschwitz' also now designates a metonymic line of (chronological) demarcation – a transformative moment in moral and social and religious history.[4]

This line of reasoning underscores the need to assess the historical basis for the meta-historical conclusion that regards the Holocaust as having broken the traditional instruments of moral measurement. I can here only sketch this comparative historical critique thus assumed (recognizing also that comparisons among such instances of suffering are necessarily invidious – and themselves cruel). But the conception of the Holocaust as a moral turning point is (also necessarily) comparative – requiring that the event itself be scrutinized in the same terms, whether in relation to Jewish history or to world history. Surprisingly, the former – the Holocaust viewed in the context of Jewish history – has been less often attempted than study of the Holocaust on a global scale. Common to both views, however, has been the finding of rupture in the post-Holocaust moral universe – a transformation in moral conscience and consciousness. Thus, the need for testing the historical ground – for unless that ground is substantiated, the *contrary* view would hold, of continuity between pre- and post-Holocaust consciousness in Jewish and/or world history, with the Holocaust making no essential difference to the philosophical or theological analysis of evil. That, too, remains a possibility.

The turning points in Jewish history that suggest likely comparison to the Holocaust are both few and evident: the destruction of the two Temples (586 B.C.E and 70 C.E.); the destruction and disruption accompanying the Crusades beginning in 1096 C.E.; the natural disaster of the Black Death (1348–1350 C.E.) and the related massacres of Jews who were blamed for it; the expulsion of the Jews from Spain and Portugal (1492 and 1497); the Chmielnicki 'massacres' (1648–1649). The numbers or percentages of Jews killed in these catastrophes are not the only measure of their significance, but they provide a starting place for the comparison required. So, for example, the sweep of the First Crusade through Central Europe, which began in 1096, caused the deaths of an estimated 5,000 Jews and corresponding communal disruption. But the communities evidently overcame the shock of those events: with "no substantial discontinuity in Franco-German [Jewish] society as a whole. . . . The towns were quickly resettled, commerce and trade were reconstructed."[5] The Jewish suicides in Mainz at this time (choosing death rather than capture) made an enduring impression within and beyond the local communities, and some contemporary accounts of the persecution understood it as a "trial of the righteous" rather than (as others did) a form of collective punishment. But both these explanations had precedents in Jewish history, and cruel as the pressures were, there seems no basis for regarding the events themselves as a caesura or turning point in the collective moral consciousness.[6] Similarly, the expulsions from Spain and Portugal involved the dislocation of a Jewish populace numbering in various estimates between 100,000 and 300,000, with deaths caused by the expulsion or otherwise by the Inquisition at the time (at most) in the thousands. The communal upheaval and the crisis in the flourishing 'Golden Age' of Sephardic Jewry were evident; but again, the survival through emigration of most of that group allowed for continuity among those expelled, and even enrichment for the Jewish communities that absorbed them.

For its proportion of victims, the Black Death of 1348–1350 arguably looms larger than any other recorded natural catastrophe – having killed between a quarter and half the populace of Europe and approximately the same proportion of Jews (250,000 of 500,000). To the latter figure must be added Jewish victims of related massacres – as Jews were variously held responsible for the Plague itself (for example, through the libel of well-poisoning). The number of victims in this related persecution was certainly in the thousands, possibly in the tens of thousands, and the period of recovery required by the Jewish communities was proportionately large. But in part because the plague affected *all* groups in its path, its impact, in terms of moral or religious upheaval, seems to have been relatively subdued; the Polish and Lithuanian Jewish communities, not very far off, were themselves relatively unaffected by the plague or the associated persecution. Estimates of the Chmielnicki massacres of 1648–1649 refer to victims in the tens of thousands, with a round figure of 100,000 sometimes cited (and up to 300 communities destroyed). The period was spoken of at the time by Rabbi Shabbetai Sheftel Horowitz as the 'Third Destruction' (after the First and Second Temples); but if the Massacres seemed from within to warrant that label, it was also apparent, to some extent at the time, that the Jewish communities in Western and other parts of Eastern Europe were relatively unaffected.

Even the vague numbers in these instances are unavailable for the conflicts that ensued in the destruction of the First and Second Temples and the exiles that followed them. What evidence there is suggests a minimal number of deaths – but it is also clear that in their communal and religious (and conceptual) consequences, the destruction of the Temples was at least equal to and probably greater than any of the later events mentioned. The religious prophecies prior to the first destruction and the ensuing exile that apparently validated them, effecting a revolution in religious thought and practice – the confluence threatening a breach in God's covenant with Israel – loom larger in their impact than any of the later events. This would include the Holocaust itself, which in a number of ways allowed for regeneration and communal continuity (more about this later).

Doubts about the breach caused by the Holocaust in *Jewish* history leave untouched, however, the analogous claim in world-historical terms. Here the argument has a sharper edge as the Holocaust represents a paradigm instance of genocide (whether or not the first): the intentional, state-sponsored, and systematic attempt to erase "that" people "from the face of the earth" (Heinrich Himmler's wording in a 1943 speech to the S.S. in Poznan). To be sure, 'uniqueness' claims for the Holocaust build to some extent on subordinate rather than on essential features of the Holocaust. That the Nazi genocide against the Jews was initiated by a nation closely tied to both the Christian tradition and the Enlightenment; that it was carried on often in view of other countries with the same traditions; that it implemented a process of industrialized killing 'invented' for the occasion; that aside from its principal purpose of annihilation, it constantly applied what Primo Levi chillingly calls 'Useless Violence' – these remarkable features do not alter the basic structure of the genocidal act itself.[7]

The same claim applies to the extreme consequences of the Holocaust *within* the Jewish community. The murder of two-thirds of the European Jews ended the role of Eastern Europe as a primary source of Jewish communal existence; it was also a death sentence for Yiddish as a language and cultural means. Most basically, of course, it cut off the lives and futures of six million people. That the Nazis did not succeed in fully implementing their 'Final Solution' is, furthermore, also 'accidental'; they advanced sufficiently far on that goal, in any event, to mark that act as genocide (a conceptual feature of genocide – in contrast to homicide – is that it need not be 'complete'). And it remains the phenomenon of genocide itself that ultimately distinguishes what the Nazis intended and did – and which also may render it more significant in moral history as such than specifically in Jewish history. It does not diminish the enormity of the Holocaust to acknowledge that it left certain centers of Jewish life physically untouched (in North and South America, to some extent in Great Britain, in Palestine, in the Islamic countries of Asia and in North Africa), and that it thus allowed both for communal continuity there and for their valuable – arguably, decisive – contributions to Israel's founding. Certain commentators who emphasize the continuity of Jewish history as a whole view that continuity as also a primary 'lesson' of the Holocaust: another threat to Jewish existence as added to earlier ones that were *also* thwarted. Only on this basis could as measured a post-Holocaust writer as Eliezer Berkovits conclude that "We [Jews] have had innumerable Auschwitzes ... Each generation had its Auschwitz problem."[8] Continuity indeed.

On the one hand, then, post-Holocaust Jewish ethical reflection faces the large-scale and systematic destruction caused by the Holocaust; on the other hand, the evidence remains of comparable or larger breaches in the moral and religious fabric of Jewish history and consciousness. In this sense, the claim for the Holocaust as indicating or demanding a moral transformation applies more clearly to world-history; that the Jews were the principal victims of the Holocaust only intensifies the irony here. But this does not mean that post-Holocaust Jewish thinkers have not *claimed* that the Holocaust requires a transformative moral and religious response in Judaism itself; many such claims have been made, and with emphasis. These turn out, however, to represent a minority view that overstates its implications even in its own terms. It does not follow, of course, that formulations that place the Holocaust on a continuum with prior events of Jewish history are by that fact adequate, but even the possibility that the enormity of the Holocaust might nonetheless leave the status of evil in Jewish thought unaltered is significant.[9] Admittedly, the question would then arise of how far the meta-historical claim of continuity extends. But also a limited claim of continuity would bear directly on post-Holocaust Jewish thought – among other things, also providing a baseline for assessing accounts that emphasize *dis*continuity.

Thus, the conceptualization of the Holocaust 'within the bounds of Jewish history' appears in various formulations, with several versions of the most common formulation revolving around a single thesis: that since whatever occurs in history reflects divine intention (at least, concurrence), all such events are also justified or good – and that this holds whether the rationale for such events is humanly intelligible or not. This 'theodicy' (in Leibniz's coinage of 1710)[10] – 'God-justice' – has itself appeared in philosophical and theological variants, but also with a constant basis: that God, himself outside history, nonetheless governs it through his qualities of goodness and omnipotence. *Apparent* evil is, in these terms, only that; in fact, whatever occurs is not evil, but justified, good – perhaps in direct response to previous events, but always, in any event, as part of a larger framework. Anything not so justified would, quite simply, not have occurred.

The most urgent application of this principle is to actions or events that ensue in suffering or loss and thus invite interpretation as punishment. Traditional claims in Judaism for such divine supervision have been widespread and substantial. So, for example, Maimonides writes in the *Guide* about "our" [the central Jewish] view: "It is in no way possible that He [God] should be unjust... All the calamities that befall men and all the good things that come to men, be it a single individual or a group, are all of them determined according to the deserts of the men concerned through equitable judgment which is no injustice whatsoever."[11] An earlier, more specific formulation (cited by Maimonides in the same context) is Rabbi Ammi's: "There is no death without sin and no suffering without transgression."[12] A prayer recited in the Jewish 'new month' and Holiday service points to the same principle in collective form: "Mip'ne Chata'enu, Ga-linu Me'artzenu" ("Because of our sins, we have been exiled from our land").[13]

The implications of this 'punishment-reward' model are evident. And for the Holocaust, it implies that victims suffer only for a reason – because of their own wrongdoing or because of someone else's for which they were responsible or because, on balance, the whole of which a particular event was part warranted its occurrence. This conclusion applies equally, furthermore, to the children and the aged among the victims, to the pious and the unbelievers, the criminal and the righteous – as for every other type of religious or moral practice in the afflicted Jewish communities of Europe: all of them, now, justly punished.

The evident harshness of this judgment as applied to the Holocaust has provoked numerous objections, some of which extend the argument beyond that event; thus, for example, Berkovits's sharp dissent: "That all suffering is due to [sin] is simply not true. The idea that the Jewish martyrology through the ages can be explained as divine judgment is obscene."[14] Yet, 'obscene' as the interpretation may appear, it has recurred – and if its formulations seem marginal philosophically, their cultural and religious significance is undeniable. So, for example, Rabbi Yoel Teitelbaum, then Satmar Rebi, finds Zionism the wrong that precipitated and therefore warranted the Holocaust: due punishment for its effort to preempt the Messiah's role in initiating the return to Zion. An analogous rendering is Rabbi Elhanan Wasserman's rhetorical tour de force: "In those [pre-Holocaust] days, the Jews chose for themselves two forms of idolatry... socialism and nationalism.... A miraculous event occurred: in Heaven the two idolatries were combined into one – National Socialism. A terrible staff of ire was created which extends harm to all the ends of the earth."[15] A more recent expression of the punishment-and-reward view was Rabbi Ovadiah Yosef's, in 2001, who finds in the Jewish victims of the Holocaust "reincarnations of earlier souls, who sinned and caused others to sin."[16] (The logic here is swift: the appeal to reincarnation anticipates the objection that apparent innocents – children and pious elders – were among the Holocaust victims; there could be due cause from their prior existence also for *their* suffering.)[17]

Again, the severity of this position is clear: the cruelty and suffering inflicted in the Holocaust seem disproportionate to any possible wrongdoing by its victims. A further problematic implication is this view's representation of the perpetrators of this suffering (indeed, Hitler himself) as instruments of divine justice, in effect doing God's work. That consequence is unavoidable: if the punishment is just, whoever administers it must also, ultimately, be acting justly.[18] Yet, despite these implications, the view's persistence is in its own terms not arbitrary or groundless – as becomes evident in more nuanced explanations that hope to avoid the notion of suffering as divine justice by shifting responsibility for it from God to man, but are in the end forced to revert to the same source: God's sanction for the events of world history.

The principal argument in this second variant of the punishment-reward model emphasizes man's free moral agency. Acting on his own, man rather than God becomes responsible for whatever evil occurs in human history, even on the scale of the Holocaust. It is not that the victims always bring their fate on themselves, but that *some* human agents act in such a way as to produce the harm to them. Again, the logic here is straightforward: Man has the freedom to do good or evil – a (arguably, *the*) distinctive human attribute. Given God's benevolence and omnipotence, evil, when it does occur – inflicting suffering and loss on the innocent – expresses human, not divine, character and choice. God *could* not have a role here if man's freedom is to be preserved – and the result of human agency and decision is what one would expect: human responsibility. So Berkovits writes, "[Human] freedom must be respected by God himself. God cannot as a rule intervene whenever man's use of freedom displeases him. It is true, if he did so, the perpetration of evil would be rendered impossible, but so would the possibility for good."[19]

The reason for this effort to shift responsibility from God to man is evident; but the move also invites the charge of question-begging on the issue of whether man's freedom is worth the price of a world that includes the Holocaust – and of how to settle *that* question. The response of theodicy here would be certain: "Yes, of course: human freedom, whatever its consequences." And more generally: "Better the world as it is, including the Holocaust, than otherwise, or any other world." This version of the 'Continuum' argument avoids finding fault in the specific victims, but the omission counts for little because of the argument's insistence that *on the whole* whatever happens is justified. The question of who specifically provoked a certain punishment thus becomes irrelevant – in deference to the interest of justice 'on the whole.' All this, again, on the principle that whatever happens in history is just.

A third variant of the punishment-reward account of evil situates the Holocaust on a continuum of Jewish history within the framework of redemptive Jewish history – citing the 1948 founding of Israel as a central item of evidence. This assertion of the good that may come out of evil is often set within a religious framework, but it also occurs in secular terms (for the founding of Israel, on the principles of nationalism and self-determination). Both interpretations, however, find the Holocaust an important, arguably necessary stage on the way to Israel's statehood, itself viewed as a consummatory moment in Jewish history. Thus, the Holocaust is redeemed, whether partly or in full, by the creation of Israel, which *would not* have occurred (this, as either a tacit or explicit assumption) had there been no Holocaust. The latter claim is itself a straightforward historical assertion, albeit with the problems of any counterfactual conditional. In strictly historical terms, the claim has often been disputed. But those objections do not, of course, address the 'meta'-historical elements in the redemptive theory of Jewish history, which finds hardship and suffering ultimately, and necessarily, transfigured. The significance claimed for the connection between the Holocaust and the founding of the State of Israel is an especially dramatic application of this theory.

The fourth and last variation on the punishment-reward model invokes the concept of *hester panim* – [God's] 'hiding of the face' – as a means of preserving God's justice and power and yet leaving room for (localized) injustice. The metaphor of 'hiding' describes a divine withdrawal from history that allows events to occur that God would otherwise have prevented – the withdrawal occurring not because God wills the events but because he wills man's freedom more. So Norman Lamm writes: "[In a period of *hester panim*] ... we are given over to the uncertainties of nature and history where we can be raised ... to the crest of the world's waves – or herded pitilessly into the fierce troughs of life."[20] And Berkovits, with further emphasis on the role of human freedom, adds: " ... If man alone is the creator of value ... then he must have freedom of choice and freedom of decision.... That man may be, God must absent himself.... He hides his presence."[21] This view has the (temporary) advantage of dividing history into divine and human parts: the former, where God is active, the latter, which moves by human decision. To be sure, God *could* control the human part if he chose to – but he chooses not to, in order to ensure man's freedom. *Hester panim* thus intensifies the shift of evil-doing (and suffering) to man as initiator; also here (as in the second version earlier of the punishment-reward argument), the privileging of human freedom above other, possibly conflicting values is unquestioned. But once again, since also *hester panim* must acknowledge that God *chooses* to hide when he does (he could not, after all, be forced to do that), this 'choice,' too, emerges as a version of theodicy: whatever happens – including God's withdrawal – reflects a decision to do so: an *intention*. Thus, too, the claim, even for the prospect of the Holocaust, that what occurs must be "for the best."[22]

The 'punishment-reward' interpretation of the Holocaust in these four versions is one of three formulations of the Continuum view, which finds the Holocaust unexceptional in terms of traditional Jewish thought and texts – *and* justifications. The second formulation, also with a lengthy past, interprets apparently unwarranted suffering not as punishment, but as something quite different; thus, a 'Reductive' account. One version of this conceives of suffering as a test, with its 'proof-text' in the Biblical 'Akedah' – the 'binding' of Isaac – where God commands Abraham to sacrifice his son *as* a test. Other 'tests' also appear in the Bible (for example, in *Job*), and indeed, conceptually, treating suffering or harm as a test has a dialectical advantage, since even a just ruler might reasonably test a blameless subject – in contrast to punishing him. But this conceptual looseness comes at a price – since unless there are limits to what counts as a test, what could be said about victims of the Holocaust who died in the 'test' (in contrast to the survivors) would remain unclear.

A second variant of this 'Reductive' interpretation views suffering as having positive value in itself. At times echoing Rabbi Akiba's statement that "suffering is precious,"[23] suffering is accorded a justified place in the world – as it anticipates future reward, or as the price to be paid in the present for the goodness of the whole, or as proof of faith in the present, or (most basically), for the experience of suffering itself. Versions of this view range from a flat denial of the experience (so, Reb Zusya of Anipol: 'I don't understand why you ask me this question [about *my* suffering]. Ask it of someone who has known such evil. As for me, this does not apply, for nothing ill has ever happened to me")[24] to the near-utilitarian justification that Joseph Soloveitchik offers even in reference to the Holocaust: " . . . Suffering occurs in the world in order to contribute something to man, in order that atonement be made for him, in order to redeem him from corruption, vulgarity, and depravity."[25]

The third formulation of the Continuum position, overarching the others, accounts for evil by *refusing* to account for it – that is, by falling back on the limits of human comprehension: for certain 'difficult' events, human understanding finds *no* adequate ground – not because there is none, but because of its own incapacity. Such limits, if invoked for an event such as the Holocaust, would, of course, apply more generally as well, and the arguments to this effect have a lengthy tradition both within and outside Judaism. Thus we hear that God's ways are not man's ways, that the difference between finite and infinite understanding makes access impossible from the one to the other – in short, that there *is* no way of comprehending the rationale for human history, whatever its turns, since that would require, per impossibile, a human grasp of God's reasons.[26]

Superficially, this account might seem to replace theodicy with agnosticism – the view, for example, that 'A certain event *appears* to have produced terrible injustice – but this is because our limited understanding cannot fathom the reasons.' The implied directive here, however, is not agnostic at all – since its claim of incomprehensibility invariably surfaces as a means of justifying catastrophes, *not* of raising doubts about them: 'There *are* reasons – if only we could grasp them.' Otherwise, as Hugh Rice argues, consistency would require the tag of incomprehensibility also for occasions of rejoicing – indeed, for all God's actions, whatever their consequences.[27] The unstated assumption of the Argument from Incomprehensibility, then, is that there are reasons, and *good* ones, even for suffering and loss that seems senseless and unjustifiable to man's limited understanding. Far from putting God's supervision of history in question, this argument advocates its acceptance as just – attesting to human limits, not God's. Thus, again, theodicy survives.

Despite their recognition of cruelty and suffering in the Holocaust, none of the accounts of evil noted so far finds in that a basis for reconceptualizing moral principle or religious commitment within the context of Judaism. Whatever the Continuum view finds demanded 'after Auschwitz,' the traditional principles and texts of Jewish thought remain adequate, in both explanation and justification. That the principal sources for this view come from religious 'Orthodoxy' may not be surprising, but neither should it discount the response itself. Indeed, the Continuum position appears also in secular writers and in others who, although religiously committed, address the Holocaust in the context of ethical judgment as such. So, for example, Emmanuel Levinas acknowledges the Holocaust as a 'paradigm' of suffering, but also finds it parallel to "the Gulag and all other places of suffering in our political century" – in other words, part of a broader, and in that sense, non-specific, historical tendency.[28] Certain commentators, apart from offering any judgment on the character of evil in the Holocaust, call attention to the psychological or social grounds that, within the context of Jewish thought, influence responses to that aspect of the Holocaust. Thus, David Hartman writes, "For some, suffering is bearable if it results from the limitations of finite human beings, but it becomes terrifying and demonic if it is seen as part of the scheme of their all-powerful creator. Others would find life unbearably chaotic if they did *not* believe that suffering, tragedy, and death were part of God's plan for the world."[29] Undoubtedly, these ad hominem considerations affect responses to the Holocaust, and it would be valuable to have them systematically analyzed – but even if the difficulty of doing this were overcome, we would still have to analyze the reasoning in the responses themselves.

The Continuum position reflects a conception of evil in which distinctions among its instances (in their explanation or justification) are finally irrelevant. And, indeed, it seems to follow logically that the slightest occurrence of evil is as much a test of theodicy as any larger one, since for a just and all-powerful God, *no* evil or injustice should have a place. The Continuum position, drawing mainly on variations of theodicy, readily accommodates this implication – as in Berkovits's summing-up: "As far as our faith in an absolutely just and merciful God is concerned, the suffering of a single innocent child poses no less a problem to faith than the undeserved suffering of millions."[30] That conclusion by itself is non-committal on whether evil *does* occur – but this point is then addressed in the several versions of the Continuum argument that displace or simply deny all such occurrence.

The claim of a rupture caused by the Holocaust in Jewish history must then argue against the Continuum position on grounds not of logic but of substance – asserting in both historical and moral terms that events are *not* all of a kind, that their differences may be qualitative as well as quantitative, and that the scope and scale of murder in the Holocaust marks a quantum jump from 'ordinary' wrongdoing. On this account, the Holocaust is sufficiently distinctive to require new categories of moral understanding – in the context of Jewish history and, arguably, for world history as well. On this view, too, variant accounts emerge concerning the nature and consequences of the breach alleged in moral consciousness. Thus the dramatic thesis that even the extremity of the Holocaust makes no essential difference to moral understanding in the context of Jewish thought shifts to the drama of its opposite – which then faces the problem of showing how the Holocaust makes just such an essential difference, but without either severing post-Holocaust Jewish thought from its religious and philosophical past or asserting connections to that past that are arbitrary or vacuous.

The most extreme example of this response was as clear in anticipation as it has proved difficult to sustain. If the traditional view of evil in Jewish thought had to confront God's role as omnipotent and benevolent, an obvious break with the tradition would be to argue *against* that role – and this indeed is the direction taken by Richard Rubenstein, first in *After Auschwitz* and then in later writings.[31] *After Auschwitz* itself appeared in a setting not specifically related to the Holocaust – through the 'death of God' theme, which, echoing Nietzsche's Zarathustra, had been circulating among non-Jewish theologians such as Thomas Altizer, Harvey Cox, and William Hamilton.[32] Indeed, Rubenstein's own earlier 'Reconstructionist' leanings laid the ground for this move in its Deweyan (by way of Mordechai Kaplan) denial of God's transcendence. But Rubenstein, arguing 'after Auschwitz,' believed he had a still stronger case against Judaism's traditional conception of God – one that extended to what he regarded as the cultural and social liabilities to which that belief had contributed.

This meant also that there was (and in the event, would remain) a question about what Rubenstein could *affirm* in Jewish principle or thought, and his subsequent writings seem at once to have sought and to have avoided such affirmation. Their dominant theme has combined a view of truth and knowledge as functions of power (after Nietzsche and Foucault) with a social or cultural definition of Judaism centered on the entry into history (and power) of the State of Israel. This emphasis on political rather than moral or religious factors offers a prescription for Jewish survival *given* the stripped-down world articulated in the Holocaust; it says little about any specifically Jewish religious or even social link to the past as an essential element. The lesson of the Holocaust disclosed for Rubenstein through the lens of powerlessness affords little positive basis for Jewish – indeed, for any religious or even ethnic – particularism, and little more for the institution of religion as such. The metaphor of 'triage' to which Rubenstein later turns as a basis for political theory seems at once to epitomize the break he sees in Jewish history as caused by the Holocaust and the difficulty of finding a source of continuity – other than force itself – that can overcome it.[33]

A less radical reaction against the traditional view of transcendence appears in Hans Jonas, who finds in a limitation, not the denial, of God's power a means of accounting for the breach caused by the Holocaust. For Jonas, the Holocaust serves not as disproof of God's existence or of his justice but as evidence of certain constraints on him. It is not, on this view, that God could have acted in that history and chose not to – but that he could not act, however much he wished to. Jonas thus argues for a conception of God as limited by his own earlier choices – if not to the same extent as man in *his* history, analogously. Admittedly, the logical limitations of omnipotence (as in the puzzle of whether God could create a rock so heavy that he could not pick it up) had been long discussed, but for Jonas, they have a very specific point. It is not the priority of human freedom that motivates the shift of moral responsibility for the Holocaust away from God (although Jonas affirms such freedom), but that, given his own earlier decisions, "[God] *could* not intervene."[34] In these terms, evil becomes an ingredient in existence, with the responsibility for its occurrence neither God's nor man's (exclusively), but shared between them and including the constraints of history that are beyond either of them. This view does not exonerate God any more than it does man – nor does it depict evil as an impersonal and independent force. Evil appears rather as friction that can be mitigated or redirected, at times even stopped – but never entirely avoided, since its occurrence does not depend only on acts of will, human or divine.

Neither Rubenstein's nor Jonas's response to the Holocaust is rooted specifically in that event. Like other 'death of God' pronouncements, Rubenstein's would apply retroactively: implying not that Judaism's transcendent God had suddenly died but that he had never actually lived. And for Jonas as well: the limits on God's power did not *originate* with the Holocaust. For both writers, however, it was the breach they find in the Holocaust that provoked the turn in their thinking about the status of evil.

A second version of the Holocaust viewed as transformative in Jewish thought and practice uses law or halakhah as a bridge to the past, which now, post-Holocaust, is elaborated or changed *because* of the Holocaust. The reason for considering this an example of 'discontinuity' is its reference to the law, which, immutable for subtraction *or* addition in Orthodox terms, retains a privileged position also for others who would now add to it. The most notable advocate of this view is Emil Fackenheim, who proposed a 614th commandment – "not to give Hitler posthumous victories" – as a literal commandment, not a figurative expression.[35] The ground for Fackenheim's proposal was two-fold: first, the extraordinary – for him, unique – evil that found expression in the Holocaust; and second, his understanding of halakhah as involving a historical or contextual dimension throughout its past. In other words, all the mitzvot, in Fackenheim's view, respond to historical conditions, which then also shape them; given this general feature, the extraordinary character of the Holocaust ought also to be reflected in the law. This principle would not by itself determine what the 614th commandment would be; for that, Fackenheim draws on the distinctive goal of the Nazi genocide to destroy the Jewish people: the fitting response to that, as he analyzes it, should then be a corresponding affirmation of commitment by its members to that people. Sometimes charged with basing such commitment exclusively on negative grounds – as reactive or ressentiment, part of the tradition holding anti-Semitism to be at once cause and reason for Jewish survival[36] – Fackenheim's basis is broader than that, encompassing also other commandments and sources.

The basis of Fackenheim's account, again, is the "rupture in history" he finds in the Holocaust as an unparalleled example of evil committed for the sake of doing evil – unparalleled, as he sees it, either in Jewish or in world history.[37] As argued here earlier, the historical claim that thus serves as the basis for the meta-historical claim would have to stand on its own historical evidence – as compared with other events in Jewish and world history. Fackenheim's contention that the evil in Nazism is unparalleled stands on the border between the historical and meta-historical – and is no easier either to demonstrate or disprove because of that. Most notable about Fackenheim's account is the correspondence he affirms between the distinctive historical 'moment' of the Holocaust and the addition he infers from that for Jewish law as serving at once as marking a breach and a bridge. The general question of who has the authority, and on what grounds, to add 'laws' remains a question in Fackenheim's account.[38] His suggestion that the absolute evil represented in the Holocaust can only be shown, not explained, adds to the difficulty of assessing the premise itself.

A third position in the view of the Holocaust as a rupture – both historical *and* meta-historical – resembles the last position mentioned in connection with the Continuum model in its reference to the Holocaust's 'incomprehensibility.' By contrast to the Continuum model reference, however, this one offers no assurance of a positive outcome even in its conclusion. A compelling statement of this view appears in the work of Arthur A. Cohen, who, imposing Rudolf Otto's conception of the 'tremendum' on the Holocaust, finds the latter "beyond the discourse of morality and rational condemnation."[39] This stance might seem to bring Cohen back (full circle) to Rubenstein's skepticism about the possibility of a religious covenant – to say nothing of a living God. But Cohen rejects that rejection, although acknowledging at least some of what it asserts. Thus, evil, as Cohen finds it in the Holocaust, *is* real – "no less than good." Yet God is also present and active – almost in partnership with man: "...God describes the limits but man sets them...God engenders possibilities but...man enacts them" (p. 93). One problem, of course, for any claim of incomprehensibility is that it must itself be articulated and explained – and Cohen seems at times to make the Holocaust less incomprehensible than he otherwise would have it (for example, in the comparison he defends between the impact of the Holocaust and that of the Jewish expulsion from Spain, or when he suggests that what the Jews find unique in the Holocaust is a feature of every group's response to *its* genocide). There is, then, a question of consistency here, together with a question of what the substance of Cohen's affirmation is. The stark terms of the opposition with which Cohen both begins and concludes radically dramatize the issue posed by the Holocaust: on the one hand, the 'tremendum' – in effect, an atrocity that is outside history; on the other hand, the affirmation nonetheless not only of the Jewish people but of the God who did not prevent it and yet who, in Cohen's view, remains as a "source of hope."

The schematism of the moral analysis presented here has been divided between responses in which issues raised by the occurrence of the Holocaust are seen as continuous with issues raised by other occurrences or instances of evil, and responses that have regarded the Holocaust as a genuine 'novum': first, historically, and then, because of that, in its moral consequences. Undoubtedly the single most widely discussed analysis of evil in relation to the Holocaust remains that by Hannah Arendt in *Eichmann in Jerusalem: A Report on the Banality of Evil*.[40] There, Arendt also views the Holocaust as in some sense a novum – yet, in the conclusions she draws about the nature of its evil (through Eichmann himself), she also endorses a 'Continuing' view that links up with elements of theodicy from which the present discussion set out. Arendt is rarely counted a 'Jewish' philosopher (she rejected the designation of philosopher tout court), but the relevance of her work to both those characterizations can certainly be argued.[41] Her book on Eichmann analyzes the trial in Jerusalem of an important agent of the Holocaust – and her conclusions on Eichmann's 'evil' would thus be significant for reflections on the Holocaust even if it did not (as I would claim it does) bring out in sharp relief a basic crux in the understanding of evil that impinges both on Jewish thought and on moral conceptualization more generally. On the one hand, Arendt's view of Eichmann echoes in a shadowy way the aspect of the Continuum view, which, in agreement with theodicy, disputes the depth and even the reality of evil. On the other hand, Arendt has no doubt, despite her procedural misgivings about the Eichmann trial itself, that Eichmann was criminally responsible and that he should have been, as he was, executed. If the tension between these claims is puzzling, that says as much about the issues as it does about her specific account.

The meaning of the phrase "banality of evil" has been often misrepresented, partly because of its confusion with other issues in her account, partly because of Arendt's own unsystematic development of the theme. What is clear in her usage and her subsequent reflections on it, however, is that the phrase opens a question that goes to the heart of the analysis of evil. The first step in this progression is Arendt's rejection of the view of Eichmann as demonic or as an agent of "radical" evil. Compared with such sterotypic evil-doers as Iago or Richard III, she insists, Eichmann does not come close; he is, by contrast, "thoughtless," "a clown" – dependent on clichés in his speaking and, still more fundamentally, in his thinking. This is, in fact, the source of his evil-doing even in the monstrousness of the 'Final Solution'; the source or agent himself was and remained "banal" – his actions not so much unintentional as "non-intentional"; he did not, in Arendt's depiction, *think* about what he was doing and its consequences.

This view of Eichmann was quickly contested by critics who did not accept the disproportion alleged between source and effect in such an event. In the course of what then became a heated aftermath, Arendt realized that a general theory of evil-doing was at issue in the contrast she had at first only assumed between "radical" evil (as in Kant's rendering) and evil as banal. Perhaps in part as she noticed that her own examples of radical evil were drawn from literary, not historical sources, Arendt began to question whether historical (human) evil was *ever* "radical" in the sense of being intended or committed "thoughtfully" – that is, with true reflection or full knowledge of its character. The outcome of this deliberation was anti-climactic, and perhaps because of that was not much attended to in the critical response to it. But the outcome is also clear, and reveals itself as standing in a lengthy philosophical tradition – one initiated by Plato (then also in Platonism) and reappearing in modern rationalism (as in Spinoza and Leibniz). On this view, evil, whatever its scale, is not positive but a privation; those who commit it act not out of deliberation and choice – thoughtfully, knowledgeably – but precisely because they have *not* adequately considered or understood what they were doing. Certainly Eichmann, in Arendt's terms, did not know better; indeed, he hardly thought at all about what he was doing – with the crucial implication following from this description, that if he *had* been more thoughtful, had understood more or more adequately, he would not, or perhaps even could not, have done what he did.

The latter conclusion – itself "radical" – has precedent in the Platonic doctrine that "To know the good is to do the good" (in its contra-positive, "Not to do the good means not to know the good"). Evil-doing in this view reflects a failure of understanding – or, in Arendt's term, "banality." And this, it seems, would for her characterize not only the trivial wrongs commonly cited as "thoughtless" but extreme wrongs as well; it marks off what evil *is*. Thus, in a letter to Gershom Scholem (shortly before he stopped all communication with her *because* of the Eichmann book), Arendt wrote: "It is indeed my opinion now that evil is never radical, that it is only extreme, and that it possesses neither depth nor any demonic dimension. It can overgrow and lay waste the whole world precisely because it spreads like a fungus. . . . It is 'thought-defying' . . . because thought tries to reach some depth, to go to the roots, and the moment it concerns itself with evil, it is frustrated because there is nothing. That is its banality. Only the Good has depth and can be radical."[42]

Arendt adds certain nuances to this position in her subsequent writings, but the view thus unfolded in the discussion around Eichmann remains essentially unchanged – as do its grave implications for the account of evil in or after the Holocaust. For if the charge against Eichmann – and, as it might be extrapolated, Nazism more generally – is one of "thoughtlessness," of such terrible wrongdoing as having been committed mindlessly and without deliberation (and committed *because* of this), then the character of Holocaust-evil, together with related questions of moral responsibility for it, become quite different from what they would be for evil as the outcome of meditated or deliberate intention and act. At issue here is not Nazi 'pseudo-science' (as in their biological rationale for racism); it is a question of a failure to 'think' in the face of atrocity. Arendt's analysis in these terms had begun more than twenty years earlier in her conception of totalitarianism as rendering the individual person "superfluous," as depriving him of all agency.[43] Compelling as that account is in political terms, however – arguably more dramatic even than Socrates' individual encounter with Protagoras in Plato's dialogue by that name – neither in that early work nor in her analysis of Eichmann does she provide an explanation of what happens to moral agency or responsibility under what now turn out to be the near-universal conditions of evil as "banal." Eichmann, she concludes, *should* have been hanged, as he was, and the implication of this is that banality does not preclude that verdict; but the basis of that verdict is not explained in the verdict itself.

The first phase of the circle traced in the present discussion of evil in the post-Holocaust – a beginning that also denied the possibility of radical or 'real' evil – offered by contrast a solution to what, at the closing of the circle in Arendt, seems to become, and to remain, a problem. In those first discussions, human agency and responsibility were asserted as constant even in a divinely ordered world – and irrespective of the social conditions under which any particular individual person or agent lives. The 'Yetzer Ha'rah' introduced in *Genesis* had the function of asserting the lure of evil (not necessarily its triumph, but its presence) even in the presence of understanding and thinking, which would *always* be options. The problem for this juxtaposition, we saw, concerned the imposed resolution of theodicy – that whatever happened in history, up to and including the Holocaust, was ultimately for the best, with God and man in some sense collaborative agents. Arendt would certainly reject this verdict on history – on world history, on Jewish history, *and* on Eichmann's history. But the terms that she herself sets for the problem of Holocaust-evil by insisting at once on its banality and its extraordinary criminality afford her no ready way of reconciling the two sides of that tension. She is, of course, not alone in facing this difficulty, and no doubt Jewish thought in the post-Holocaust will continue to wrestle with it.

Notes

1. *The Book of Theodicy*, translated and with a commentary by L. E. Goodman (New Haven: Yale University Press), 1988.
2. See, for a variety of examples, Arthur A. Cohen, *The Tremendum: A Theological Intepretation of the Holocaust* (New York: Crossroads, 1981), p. 21; Emil Fackenheim, "Leo Baeck and Other Jewish Thinkers in Dark Times," *Judaism*, 51 (2002), p. 288; Irving Greenberg, *Living in the Image of God* (Northvale, NJ: Jason Aronson, 1998), p. 234. In his 2002 Nobel Prize speech, Imre Kertesz speaks of the "break" caused by the Holocaust, with Auschwitz "the end point of a great adventure" (*PMLA*, 118 (2003), p. 607.
3. As, for example, in such books (and titles) as Sara Horowitz, *Voicing the Void* (Albany: SUNY Press, 1997); Andy Leak and George Paizis, eds., *The Holocaust and the Text: Speaking the Unspeakable* (London: Macmillan,

1999); George Steiner, *Language and Silence* (New York: Atheneum, 1967).

4. Consider, as one of many possible examples, the statement by Werner Hamacher: "We do not just write 'after Auschwitz.' " There is no historical or experiential 'after' to an absolute trauma. The continuum being disrupted, any attempt to restore it would be a vain act of denegation ... This 'history' cannot enter into history. It deranges all dates and destroys the ways to understand them." Werner Hamacher, Neil Hertz, and Thomas Keenan, eds., *On Paul deMan's Wartime Journalism* (Lincoln: University of Nebraska Press, 1989), pp. 458–459. Cf. also John Rawls, on 'after Auschwitz': *The Law of Peoples* (Cambridge: Harvard University Press, 1999), p. 20.

5. Alan Mintz, *Hurban: Responses to Jewish Catastrophe in Hebrew Literature* (New York: Columbia University Press, 1984), p. 98. See also Jacob Katz, *Tradition and Crisis*, trans. Dov Bernard Cooperman. (New York: New York University Press, 1993): " ... The essential attitude toward tradition did not change." (p. 184)

6. In the range of possible 'moral' consequences, see, for example, Yisroel Yuval's controversial suggestion, as part of that aftermath, of a possible causal connection between suicidal martyrdom (including the killing of their children by Jewish parents) and the medieval emergence of the blood libel ["Ha'Nakam v'Haklalah" (Hebrew), *Zion*, 58 (1993)], pp. 33–90.

7. Cf. Primo Levi, *The Drowned and the Saved*, trans. Raymond Rosenthal (New York: Summit, 1988). On the claim of Holocaust-uniqueness, cf. especially Steven T. Katz, *The Holocaust in Historical Perspective* (New York: Oxford University Press, 1994), vol. 1. Katz's arguments for the *historical* uniqueness of the Holocaust leaves unaddressed the question of what, if any, moral or philosophical implications would follow if that *were* the case.

8. Eliezer Berkovits, *Faith after the Holocaust* (New York: Ktav, 1973), pp. 90, 98.

9. I would relate this to a question that seems to me indicated for 'uniqueness' claims for the Holocaust quite apart from the issue of their historical basis; that question would ask what difference it makes if the Holocaust *is* unique – or more bluntly, "So what?" Cf. Berel Lang, *The Future of the Holocaust* (Ithaca: Cornell University Press, 1999), pp. 77–91.

10. G.W. Leibniz, *Theodicy: Essays on the Goodness of God, the Freedom of Man, and the Origin of Evil*, trans. E.M. Huggard. (New Haven: Yale University Press, 1952).

11. Maimonides, *Guide of the Perplexed*, 3:17. Trans. S. Pines. (Chicago: University of Chicago Press, 1963, p. 469.) Maimonides distinguishes his *own* position from this communal and traditional one – although *how much* difference his own formulation entails is arguable (cf. *Guide*, III, 51 (p. 625).

12. Shabbath 55a. Cited by Maimonides, ibid., p. 470.

13. The Art Scroll prayer book says of this statement: "This is a cardinal principle of Jewish faith. History is not haphazard. Israel's exile and

centuries-long distress is a result of its sins." *The Art Scroll Siddur*, trans. Nosson Scherman (Brooklyn: Mesorah, 1984), p. 678.

14. Eliezer Berkovits, ibid., p. 94. See also, for example, Amos Funkenstein, "Theological Responses to the Holocaust," in *Perceptions of Jewish History* (Berkeley: University of California Press), 1993, p. 311.

15. Taitlebaum and Wasserman as cited in Yosef Roth, "The Jewish Fate and the Holocaust," in *I Will be Sanctified: Religious Responses to the Holocaust*, edited by Yehezkel Fogel. (Northvale, N.J.: Jason Aronson, 1952), pp. 58–59.

16. Reported in *The New York Times*, August 7, 2001.

17. For other examples (and analysis) of the 'punishment-reward' view in Orthodox and Haredi sources, cf. especially the writings of Gershon Greenberg (for example, "Orthodox Jewish Thought in the Wake of the Holocaust," in *In God's Name: Genocide and Religion in the Twentieth Century*, edited by Omer Bartov and Phyliss Mack (New York: Berghahn, 2001) and "Jewish Religious Thought in the Wake of the Catastrophe," in *Thinking in the Shadow of Hell*, edited by Jacques B. Doukhan (Berrien Springs, MI: Andrews University Press, 2002).

18. Ignaz Maybaum openly affirms this (admittedly, as a rhetorical question): "Would it shock you if I were to imitate...[Isaiah's] prophetic style and formulate the phrase 'Hitler, my [God's] servant'?" (Cf. *Ignaz Maybaum: A Reader*, ed. Nicholas De Lange (New York: Berghahn Books, 2001), p. 165.

19. Berkovits, ibid., p 105

20. "The Face of God: Thoughts on the Holocaust" in B. H. Rosenberg and F. Heuman, eds., *Theological and Halakhic Reflections on the Holocaust* (Hoboken, NJ: Ktav, 1999), pp. 191–192.

21. Berkovits, ibid., pp. 105, 107.

22. Maimonides preempts this explanatory effort in favor of the literalist view of punishment and reward: "It is clear that *we* [emphasis added] are the cause of this '*hiding of the face*', and we are the agents of this separation...If, however, his God is within him, no evil at all will befall him." Maimonides, idem, p. 626.

23. *Sanhedrin*, 101a.

24. Cited in Arthur Green, *The Tormented Master* (Tuscaloosa, AL: University of Alabama Press, 1977), p. 175.

25. "Kol Dodi Dofek," trans. L. Kaplan, in B.H. Rosenberg and F. Heuman, eds., idem, p. 56. The value posited would presumably hold also for people who did not survive their suffering; in any event, the statement is presumably not a prediction about human behavior, since no evidence (here or elsewhere) suggests that suffering typically *has* the effects described.

26. David Weiss Halivni offers an intriguing variation on this thesis in his application of the concept of 'Tsimtsum' ['contraction'] to the question of God's presence. [See "Prayer in the Shoah," *Judaism*, 50 (2001), pp. 268–291.] There are differences that Halivni emphasizes between *tsimtsum* and *hester panim* – but a common element in their logical structures holds that at some historical moments, divine non-intervention, no

matter how severe the context, is preferable to intervention. Eliezer Schweid argues that since free choice does not *require hester panim*, this line of explanation as a whole seems either redundant or beside the point. Cf. *Wrestling until Daybreak: Searching for Meaning in Thinking about the Holocaust* (Latham, MD: University Press of America, 1994), p. 390.

27. Hugh Rice, *God and Goodness* (New York: Oxford University Press, 2000), p. 92.

28. Emmanuel Levinas, *Entre Nous: Thinking-of-the-Other*, trans. Michael B. Smith and Barbara Harshav (New York: Columbia University Press, 1998), p. 241.

29. Arthur A. Cohen and Paul Mendes-Flohr, eds., *Contemporary Jewish Religious Thought* (New York: Scribners, 1987), p. 945.

30. Berkovits, ibid., p. 128.

31. Richard Rubenstein, *After Auschwitz* (Indianapolis: Bobbs-Merrill, 1966); cf. also *The Cunning of History: The Holocaust and the American Future* (New York: Harper, 1978). For a fuller account of Rubenstein and especially of Emil Fackenheim, see Michael Morgan, *Beyond Auschwitz: Post-Holocaust Jewish Thought in America* (New York: Oxford University Press, 2001).

32. For example, Thomas J.J. Altizer and William Hamilton, *Radical Theology and the Death of God* (Indianapolis: Bobbs-Merrill, 1966); Harvey Cox, *The Secular City* (New York: Macmillan, 1965); William Hamilton, *The New Essence of Christianity* (New York: Associated Books, 1965).

33. Richard Rubenstein, *The Age of Triage: Fear and Hope in an Overcrowded World* (Boston: Beacon Press, 1983).

34. Hans Jonas, "The Concept of God after Auschwitz: A Jewish Voice," in *Mortality and Morality: A Search for God after Auschwitz* (Evanston: Northwestern University Press, 1996), p. 140.

35. See, for example, Emil Fackenheim, *Quest for Past and Future* (Bloomington: Indiana University Press, 1968), ch. 1.

36. See, for example, Michael Wyschogrod, "Faith and the Holocaust," *Judaism*, 20 (1971), p. 250.

37. Emil Fackenheim, "Leo Baeck and Other Jewish Thinkers in Dark Times," *Judaism*, 51 (2002), p. 288. For earlier and fuller accounts of the Commandment, see *God's Presence in History: Jewish Affirmations and Philosophical Reflections* (New York: New York University Press, 1970), p. 70 ff; and *The Jewish Return into History* (New York: Schocken, 1978), pp. 27–29.

38. Irving Greenberg, who speaks of the Holocaust as a breach in the Covenant – to be repaired thereafter only by a new, 'Voluntary Covenant' – articulates a 'principle' (not, as he defines it, a law) with some of the force of Fackenheim's commandment: " ... No statement, theological or otherwise, should be made that would not be credible in the presence of burning children," in Eva Fleischner, ed., *Auschwitz: Beginning of a New Era* (New York: Ktav, 1977), p. 22. See also "Voluntary Covenant" in *Perspectives*. National Jewish Resource Center, 1982.

39. Arthur A. Cohen, *The Tremendum: A Theological Interpretation of the Holocaust* (New York: Crossroads, 1981), p. 8.

40. *Eichmann in Jerusalem: A Report on the Banality of Evil* (New York: Viking, 1963).

41. See on Arendt's relation to Jewish sources, Richard Bernstein, *Hannah Arendt and the Jewish Question* (Cambridge: MIT Press, 1994), pp. 6–13.

42. Letter dated 7/24/63, in *The Jew as Pariah*, ed. Ron H. Feldman (New York: Grove, 1978), p. 251. Arendt elaborates on this view in the opening pages of *The Life of the Mind* (New York: Harcourt, Brace, and Jovanovich, 1978). Richard Bernstein (idem.) emphasizes the vagary in Arendt's distinction between "judgment" and "thinking." An arguably more basic issue is justification for the power that Arendt ascribes to thinking – apart from the question of its relation to judging.

43. *The Origins of Totalitarianism* (New York: Harcourt, Brace, and Jovanovich, 1951).

15 Revelation, Language, and Commentary: From Buber to Derrida

LEORA BATNITZKY

The turn to language in twentieth-century philosophy is well-known. Despite the profound methodological differences and ultimate philosophical disagreements between them, many if not most Anglo-American and Continental-European philosophers continue to emphasize philosophical reason's intimate relation to, if not dependence on, language.[1] But there is of course an enormous difference between the more minimalist thesis that reason is expressed in language and the more maximalist statement that reason depends on language. This difference goes to the heart of the question of what "philosophy" actually is and does. Can and should philosophy stand above our particular language games and articulate some deeper truth behind the cultural and historical contexts in which all human life is embedded? And what are the scientific, ethical, and indeed the theological implications of how we might answer this question?

While suggesting that these questions are philosophically and historically tied to modern philosophical discussions about the relations between reason and revelation, this chapter explores twentieth-century Jewish philosophical approaches to language. For a number of Jewish philosophers, the turn to language is a turn away from the historically implicit Christian assumptions of much of Western philosophy. As many have observed, the linguistic turn brought philosophy much closer to some of the central concerns of the Jewish historical tradition, and Jewish thinkers were quick to pursue their work in this new area of overlap. To appreciate these Jewish philosophical arguments, and their similarities to and differences from each other as well as to twentieth-century philosophies of language generally, this chapter has been laid out in four parts. Part I describes briefly how the linguistic turn in philosophy redefines the notions of both "philosophy" and "revelation." Part II focuses on the specific treatments of language, revelation, and commentary in twentieth-century Jewish philosophies rooted in the pre-Holocaust German philosophical tradition. Part III turns to the rethinking of these themes in post-Holocaust Jewish philosophy. Finally, Part IV turns more specifically to the question of the meaning of "philosophy" and indeed of "Jewish philosophy," after "the linguistic turn" in philosophy.

I

Immanuel Kant's transcendental idealism set the parameters for the modern discussion of the possible relation between philosophy and religion. Arguing that in and of itself, reason could not obtain knowledge of the divine (or the soul or the world), Kant nevertheless left the door open to the possibility of what he called "religion within the limits of reason alone."[2] Kant's bracketing of the question of religious faith from knowledge had two decisive consequences. First, it affirmed a particularly modern separation between reason and revelation, which would define much of Western religious-philosophical thought after him. Kant's philosophy came to define the framework for asking and answering the question of whether revelation can or should aspire to the status of scientific reasoning. Second, it encouraged the translation of all prior faiths into universalistic moral practice, a "reduction" he urged on the grounds that only in this form could they survive in the modern world.

In the nineteenth century, Friedrich Nietzsche inverted the modern dichotomy between reason and revelation by claiming that there was in fact no epistemological distinction between the two. As he put it in *Beyond Good and Evil*:

> [Philosophers] pose as if they had discovered and reached their real opinions through the self-development of a cold, pure, divinely unconcerned dialectic (as opposed to the mystics of every rank, who are more honest and more stupid than they are – and talk of 'inspiration'); while at bottom it is an assumption, a hunch, indeed a kind of 'inspiration' – most often a desire of the heart that has been filtered and made abstract.[3]

Nietzsche's insight was arguably as decisive for twentieth-century Jewish philosophy as Kant's was for nineteenth-century Jewish philosophy. While many Christian thinkers after Kant affirmed the distinction between reason and revelation in order to affirm a notion of Christian faith,[4] most, if not all, modern Jewish philosophers resisted describing Jewish revelation as the antithesis of philosophical reason. Modern Jewish philosophers after Nietzsche would all grapple one way or another with the Kantian claim that revelation should be understood in moral terms and the Nietzschean claim that there was in fact no distinction, from an epistemological perspective, between reason and revelation.

While Kant's claim gave modern Jewish philosophers the possibility of providing a particularly modern rationale for Jewish revelation, Nietzsche's contention presented twentieth-century Jewish philosophers with the opportunity to reformulate a notion of Jewish revelation that wasn't intrinsically irrational. The project of much of twentieth-century Jewish philosophy can in fact be understood as an attempt to reconcile these two competing philosophical positions of Kant and Nietzsche, respectively. The first notion, following Kant, is that Jewish revelation must have a modern, moral meaning. The second notion, after Nietzsche, is that Jewish revelation contributes to understandings of philosophy. From a Nietzschean perspective, these claims together would of course be contradictory. This is because, for Nietzsche, the similar forms of reason and revelation point to their ultimate difference, which concerns the ways in which both philosophy and religion legislate – that is, will to power, their respective ideas of the good. Here, twentieth-century Jewish philosophers do not agree with Nietzsche's conclusion that philosophy is the will to power. In rejecting Nietzsche's conclusion, but while affirming with Nietzsche that revelation is no less rational than reason, the project of modern Jewish philosophy is not alone. And it is in this context that language would become central for the attempt of twentieth-century Jewish philosophers to understand revelation.

Drawing on and yet criticizing Nietzsche, Martin Heidegger would come to claim that Being *reveals* itself in language. As he famously put it, "language is the house of Being."[5] Heidegger's notion that language is the revelation of Being stems from his attempt to move beyond what he called "metaphysics." By "metaphysics," Heidegger referred to what he maintained were the false and harmful philosophical claims that "reason," "cognition," or, even in the case of Nietzsche, "will" defines reality. "Metaphysics," however, is not simply rejected by Heidegger. Instead, Heidegger attempts in his well-known essay "What is Metaphysics?" to define a more viable form of metaphysics.[6] In his later lectures on Nietzsche, Heidegger claimed that Nietzsche's philosophy had thus far been the greatest achievement of metaphysics but that Nietzsche, while declaring an end to metaphysics, was nonetheless the last metaphysical philosopher because he was unwittingly embedded in the metaphysics he sought to overcome.[7] According to Heidegger, Nietzsche's transvaluation of all values, including his claim that truth is a matter of will to power, remains rooted in a subject-object dichotomy that defines Western metaphysics. Nietzsche, Heidegger argues, like the tradition of Western metaphysics he seeks to overcome, still understands truth and falsehood as attributes applying to discursive judgments insofar as the judgments are adequate to the objects disclosed.

In *Being and Time,* Heidegger famously sought to move beyond what he regarded as this false dichotomy between subject and object. To do so, he drew on his teacher Husserl's phenomenological contention that consciousness is always consciousness of something, and that this something is something shared. Reversing Husserl, however, Heidegger refigured the transcendental question of how cognition makes our experience of the world possible into the question of how our experience of what is shared makes cognition possible. Language, for Heidegger, is the shared experience of Being, which even Plato, he suggests, could not help recognize, if unwittingly. As he put it in a set of lectures on Plato's *Sophist* presented two years before the publication of *Being and Time,*

> The *onoma* [name] in which the *eidos* becomes visible is itself made up of *grammata* [letters]... The multiplicity of forms... stand in an inner factual *koinonia*: things, visibility of things, words, word sound-being, world, distinctiveness of beings, talk, announcement. This is no other than the universal connection of phenomena... It is finally in Being-in, the preceding uncoveredness of the world.[8]

The emphases in Heidegger's philosophy would change over time, but the notion that language is the space in which Being is revealed remained central to his thought. It is this insight that twentieth-century Jewish philosophers interested in language would share with Heidegger, an insight however that, we will see later, Jewish philosophers would define as fundamentally "Jewish."

Before turning to specific accounts of language and revelation in twentieth-century Jewish philosophy, it is important to recognize that in significant ways, twentieth-century Jewish philosophers interested in language are post-Nietzschean and post-Heideggerian. They share Nietzsche's view that philosophy itself can be understood as a kind of revelation as well as Heidegger's view that revelation happens in and through language. This isn't to suggest, however, that these thinkers are themselves Nietzschean or Heideggerian in terms of historical influence or philosophical conclusion. But it is to suggest that they share in a philosophical discourse that from the start allows for the possibility of considering philosophically the meanings of revelation as a linguistic phenomenon (regardless of the philosophical intentions or conclusions of the best-known philosophical proponents of these positions, such as Nietzsche and Heidegger). A number of twentieth-century Jewish philosophers in fact argue that it is the Jewish tradition that best understands the philosophical meanings of both revelation and language. Far from assimilating Judaism to abstract concepts foreign to it, twentieth-century Jewish thinkers interested in language maintain that philosophy can best understand itself by way of Jewish revelation and language. To appreciate these arguments, as well as some of their differences and tensions, we turn to a variety of Jewish philosophical accounts of language.

II

In his magnum opus, *The Star of Redemption*, Franz Rosenzweig (1886–1929) affirmed a Nietzschean view of philosophy that could provide, at most, access to particular points of view. Based on this definition, Rosenzweig prescribed revelation as an antidote to philosophy's inability to ground universal truth. Revelation could, Rosenzweig maintained, provide philosophy with a much-needed objective basis, while philosophy, again understood in a Nietzschean sense, could provide revelation with a much needed sense of subjectivity, which Rosenzweig also described as a sense of creatureliness. Rosenzweig argued that Nietzsche's position, while ultimately limited, was superior to German idealist thought in its inadvertent recognition that human creatures are created beings. A "sibling-like" relationship between philosophy and religion could, Rosenzweig suggested, restore a notion of creation to modern people. And once twentieth-century cultured-despisers of religion recognized this *philosophical* truth about creation, the twentieth-century person might again have access to God's revelation.[9]

Describing his approach to philosophy as, alternatively, "the new thinking," "speech-thinking," and "absolute empiricism," Rosenzweig sought to turn away from the abstractions of philosophy and move toward "common sense." As for his German-speaking contemporary Ludwig Wittgenstein, whom Rosenzweig did not know, language was the key to this turn to "healthy" thinking.[10] And like his contemporary Heidegger, Rosenzweig claimed that language rather than abstract reason appropriately reflected and defined the finitude intrinsic to human existence.[11] And as for both Wittgenstein and Heidegger, the meaning in local language games is for Rosenzweig communally constituted.[12] Rosenzweig's particularly *Jewish* philosophical claim, as opposed to Heidegger's agnostic[13] one, is that God reveals himself to human beings in and through language – and the language of the Bible more particularly. While Heidegger claimed that it is "language that speaks,"[14] Rosenzweig asserted that "we seek the word of man in the word of God."[15] And the Jewish people, as the original and true receivers of God's word embody, Rosenzweig maintained, God's revelation to human kind, from which all peoples may learn.

Drawing largely on his friend Eugen Rosenstock's philosophy of language, Rosenzweig described the three moments of divine interaction with human beings – creation, revelation, and redemption – as grammatical moods, the indicative, imperative, and cohortative, respectively.[16] In understanding revelation as grammar, Rosenzweig also emphasized the temporal dimension of language, claiming that the grammatical moods of creation, revelation, and redemption correspond to the past, present, and future, respectively. For Rosenzweig, revelation, as speech, demands a response from those who receive God's word. In the central, and indeed middle, section of the *Star*, Rosenzweig describes revelation as the disruption of the individual's self-enclosed existence. Like the Protestant theologian Karl Barth (1886–1968), Rosenzweig maintained that God's revelation breaks open the purely human realm. Other types of modern Jewish and Christian thought whose concern is solely the human realm remained, Rosenzweig contended, "atheistic theology."[17]

However, Rosenzweig also insisted that God, of necessity, speaks to the human being in the language of humans. Rosenzweig begins his discussion of revelation in the *Star of Redemption* by quoting the Song of Songs. He writes:

> Love is strong as death. Strong in the same way as death? But against whom does death display its strength? Again him whom it seizes. And love, of course, seizes both, the lover as well as the beloved, but the beloved otherwise than the lover. It originates in the lover. The beloved is seized, his love is already a response to being seized.[18]

The power of death is that it is the end of being oneself. This is what it means to die: to no longer be who one is in life. For Rosenzweig, love is as strong as death because love is as transforming as death is.[19] But love, Rosenzweig suggests, is more complicated than death. Love seizes both the lover as well as the beloved. For this reason, love breaks open the notion of the self-contained existence of the individual even more profoundly than death does because love concerns the relation between two subjectivities, while death concerns only one subject. The experience of revelation, Rosenzweig claims, is a two-stage process that consists of two statements made by the beloved to the lover (who again is the initiator of love). These two statements are "I have sinned" and "I am a sinner." Drawing again on the Song of Songs, Rosenzweig suggests that in response to the beloved's acknowledgment of sin, the lover says to the beloved, "You are mine."[20] As Rosenzweig continues, this "is a sentence which does not have 'I' for a subject."[21] Purposefully emphasizing the ambiguity of the language of the Song of Songs, Rosenzweig maintains that language is more than allegory (*Gleichnis*). Before the nineteenth century, he avers, "One knew that the distinction between immanence and transcendence disappears in language."[22]

Rosenzweig's declarations about immanence and transcendence in language reflect the post-Nietzschean as well as the post-Kantian context of his thought. Abandoning an academic career after writing the *Star*, Rosenzweig gave up any pretension to academic philosophy, concentrating instead on a number of adult Jewish education projects. Describing his reasons for leaving academia in order to pursue Jewish adult education, Rosenzweig wrote to his academic mentor Friedrich Meinecke that the abstract questions of philosophy "are meaningless to me. On the other hand, the questions asked by human beings have become increasingly important to me. This is precisely what I meant by 'cognition and knowledge as service'...."[23] Yet while Rosenzweig's philosophy of revelation and language bring to focus the particularity of Jewish language and revelation, his thought nevertheless remains a piece with much of post-Kantian German-Jewish philosophy in insisting on a unique moral role for the Jewish people in providing the nations of the world insight into God's revelation. For Rosenzweig, Judaism's language of revelation, while defined by its particularity, paradoxically serves as a unique yet universal model of relating to the divine, for all humankind.[24] Rosenzweig's specific work in Jewish adult education attempted to give his fellow German Jews the tools with which to become conversation partners with the divine as well as the Jewish textual tradition. For Rosenzweig, textual commentary and the translation of texts replaces both philosophy and theology as the proper means to truth.[25] Judaism, as a fundamentally textual tradition, Rosenzweig suggests, is a model for modern philosophers and theologians to emulate, just as the existence of the literal embodiment of God's revelation in the Jewish people is the unique model for the nations of the world to emulate in their quest for God's revelation.[26]

Martin Buber (1878–1965), Rosenzweig's friend and collaborator on the translation of the Hebrew Bible into German, was deeply influenced by Rosenzweig's approach to language. Buber's dialogical philosophy holds that in encountering one another in basic "word pairs," the human being and God, as well as individual human beings, come into relation with each other.[27] The linguistic turn in Buber's mature philosophy was largely indebted to his ongoing engagement with Rosenzweig's thought.[28] Nonetheless, important differences remained between Buber and Rosenzweig, especially concerning their respective views of Jewish law and Zionism. These differences were also reflected in their views of language. Rosenzweig's understanding of the divine nature of speech extended for him to an affirmation of the authority of Jewish law. Buber's more humanistic thought, in contrast, rejected the ultimate authority of Jewish law.[29] For Buber, "Man, he alone, speaks."[30] Their different views of divine authority led Rosenzweig to warn against the Zionist profanation of the Hebrew language, while Buber's cultural Zionism included first and foremost an attempt at the renewal of Hebrew as a living language.[31] Despite their differences, Buber and Rosenzweig both emphasized the centrality of revelation, language, and commentary for the modern Jew from the perspective of the modern Jew alienated from the Jewish tradition. Therefore, to varying degrees, each worked through Western philosophy, and German philosophy more specifically, in coming to their claims about Jewish language, revelation, and commentary.

While educated in German philosophy, the European-born American-Jewish philosopher Abraham Joshua Heschel (1907–1972) provides both an interesting overlap with and contrast to Buber and Rosenzweig. Rather than beginning with the question of the relation between philosophy and Judaism, Heschel attempts to articulate a philosophy of Judaism.[32] The question for Heschel is not about how an understanding of language transforms our understanding of philosophy, but rather about the meaning of a Jewish philosophy of language. In his most comprehensive attempt to develop his rabbinic theology, *Torah min ha-shamayim*, Heschel distinguishes between two modes of rabbinic exegesis – that of Rabbi Akiva and that of Rabbi Yishmael.[33] The former understands the Torah as the embodiment of God, while the latter understands the Torah as God's means of intelligible communication. Sympathetic to Akiva's stance, Heschel emphasizes the infinite meanings of the language of the Torah and hence the ultimate religious value for Jews of the study of Torah.[34] While the Torah consists of written texts, the study of Torah is always oral. This is because the meaning of the Torah's language of revelation can never be fully captured, Heschel contends. As Heschel puts it elsewhere, "the Oral Torah was never written down. The meaning of the Torah has never been contained by books."[35]

Heschel's articulation of a Jewish philosophy of language allows us to appreciate a particular point of tension in Rosenzweig's and Buber's (as well as, for instance, Heidegger's) philosophies of language. Like Rosenzweig and Buber, Heschel not only implicitly rejects the idea that Judaism should be subservient to modern philosophy, but in fact suggests that a particularly Jewish account of revelation, language, and commentary defines the parameters of philosophical thinking. The question is then: what good is philosophy in and of itself?

In this context, it is perhaps significant to note the definition of Jewish revelation offered by Gershom Scholem (1914–1982), who writes: "Revelation needs commentary in order to be rightly understood and applied – this is the far from self-evident religious doctrine out of which grew both the phenomenon of biblical exegesis and the Jewish tradition it created."[36] While different from each other, Rosenzweig, Buber, and Heschel would concur with Scholem's definition. Yet Scholem, the founder of the modern academic study of Jewish mysticism, associates this notion of revelation with the Jewish mystical tradition, while emphasizing the difference between this dynamic view of revelation and what he considers to be the deadening and static enterprise of "philosophy." Within the context of medieval Jewish philosophy and mysticism, Scholem is surely correct that the medieval Jewish philosophers would certainly reject the view of Jewish revelation presented by Rosenzweig, Buber, and Heschel. This is because, for the medieval Jewish philosophers, the emphasis on language would come at the unfortunate cost of any kind of rationality that could stand above an account of revelation, language, and commentary.[37]

Two main philosophical concerns emerge in response to the kind of philosophy of language offered by Rosenzweig, Buber, and Heschel. First, has such a philosophy of language really gone beyond the metaphysical claims it purports to transcend?[38] Second, is anything left to the notion of "philosophy" (and "Jewish philosophy" more particularly) after this early twentieth-century turn to language?

Much of late twentieth-century Continental philosophy occupies itself with the question of how to acknowledge the centrality and particularity of language while somehow giving an account of philosophy's universal aspirations. This concern to account for particularity and universality in both Jewish and Continental philosophy is not merely academic but stems also from the existential question of how to respond philosophically to the Nazi genocide, which challenges contemporary philosophers not only to account for the particularity of a particular people's suffering but also for the possibility of some kind of universal, moral discourse. For this reason, much of late twentieth-century Continental philosophy (and not only philosophy concerned with Judaism qua Judaism) addresses the issue of the relation between particularity and universality with reference to claims about "Judaism's" relation to Western philosophy.[39] Particularly in post-war French philosophy, discussion of the philosophical meanings of revelation, language, and commentary takes what might be called a "Jewish" turn.

III

Jacques Derrida (1930–2004) is perhaps best known in the English-speaking world for his radical claims about philosophy and language. Derrida's often-quoted dictum, "There is no outside the text,"[40] has become a rallying cry for both his critics and defenders. Derrida's interest is in putting an end to what he calls Western metaphysical conceptions of "presence." Just as Heidegger drew on Nietzsche's thought, but also discerned in it precisely what Nietzsche sought to reject, so too Derrida draws on Heidegger's insights while contending that Heidegger was not ultimately able to follow through on the premises of his own thought. In the end, Derrida claims, Heidegger's notion of language is saturated with a notion of "presence," by which Derrida means the unspoken premise that there is a direct correspondence between language and meaning (even if, according to Heidegger, that meaning is never complete). While Heidegger, for Derrida, had attempted to overcome "metaphysical" thinking, his thought remains predicated on nostalgia for an original, authentic moment that has been forgotten. Central to Derrida's endeavor to move beyond "metaphysics" is his reversal of what he contends is the priority of speech over writing in Western metaphysics (including Heidegger).[41] Derrida gives priority to writing over speech, and in this makes a connection between his notions of "Judaism" and post-metaphysical philosophy. The Jewish textual tradition, for Derrida, embodies the very sense of textuality of which twentieth-century European philosophy, long clouded by its Christian inheritance, is only just becoming aware. While Rosenzweig attributes the orality of speech to the Jewish tradition, Derrida suggests that it is just the "logocentrism" of *speech* that "Judaism" as a tradition *rejects*.[42]

An Algerian Jew by birth, Derrida makes much of the significance of his Jewish origins for his claims about writing. As he puts it in an essay about the French-Jewish poet Edmond Jabès: "Between the fragments of the Broken Tablets the poem grows and the right to speech takes root. Once more begins the adventure of text as week, as outlaw far from the 'fatherland of the Jews,' which is a 'sacred text surrounded by commentaries.'"[43] Any claim to speech, Derrida contends, is derivative of writing, which is always already fragmented, broken, and contaminated by other claims to meaning. The intertextuality of the rabbinic tradition for Derrida points to the way in which it is not possible to get back to an originary meaning that is somehow present in the text. While denying that his thought is a continuation of any traditional conception of Jewish thought, Derrida nevertheless makes repeated reference to the importance, philosophically and not merely historically, of Judaism for his thinking.[44]

Derrida's interest in Judaism is enhanced and complicated by his relation to Emmanuel Levinas (1906–1995), with whom Derrida began a long dialogue, beginning with his well-known 1967 essay "Violence and Metaphysics,"[45] which focuses on Levinas' *Totality and Infinity*. Levinas, a Lithuanian Jew by birth, studied philosophy in Germany with Husserl and Heidegger and then settled in France, where he was one of the first French translators of Husserl's work. Held as a French soldier in a German prisoner of war camp during the Second World War, while his wife and daughter were in hiding, the question of ethics and philosophy, as well as Judaism's relation to this question, became central to Levinas. After the war, Levinas devoted himself to adult Jewish education and eventually secured a university position teaching philosophy.

In the preface to *Totality and Infinity*, Levinas credits what he calls Rosenzweig's "opposition to totality" for the claims that he (Levinas) will make about philosophy and ethics.[46] But while Levinas and Rosenzweig share some broad themes – such as the rupture of what both understand as modern philosophy's overreaching claims about reason – Levinas' appropriation of Rosenzweig is ironic for two, interrelated reasons. First, while in his account of language Rosenzweig deliberately attempts to blur the distinction between the human and divine in order to suggest the divine origin of language, his claims about revelation and language are rooted in his conviction that, even as God affects humanity, the divine exists wholly outside of the human realm.[47] Levinas, in contrast, claims in *Totality and Infinity* that any notion we may have of God can only have an ethical, or inter-human, meaning. Second, and perhaps more importantly, although Levinas sees himself as Rosenzweig's philosophical heir, his thought is a return to what he himself calls "Platonism," by which he advocates a return to talking philosophically about trans-historical or trans-contextual meaning.[48] While *Totality and Infinity* is an attempt to reinvigorate philosophy by showing that ethics is first philosophy, Rosenzweig, we have seen in our brief portrait of him, left the critical task of philosophy behind for the "speech-thinking" of common sense. Rosenzweig rejects what he takes as Western philosophy's premise that there is something above or below what he calls "speech-thinking." As he put it, "All philosophy has asked about essence [*Wesen*]. This is the question by means of which it differentiates itself from the *unphilosophical* thinking of common sense, which does not ask what a thing 'actually' is."[49]

So, too, while Levinas has been associated in the English-speaking world with Derrida, his philosophy is in many ways a rejection of the premises of Derrida's thought, and his philosophy of language in particular. For Levinas, there is something outside of the text of experience, meaning, and indeed one's own phenomenological horizon: *This is the face of the other person, which signifies my infinite responsibility for this person.* In *Totality and Infinity*, Levinas links the possibility of language with the face-to-face relation of ethics:

> For significations do not present themselves to theory, that is, to the constitutive freedom of a transcendental consciousness; *the being of signification consists in putting into question in an ethical relation constitutive freedom itself.* Meaning is the face of the Other, and all recourse to words takes place already within the primordial face to face of language.[50]

Similar to Rosenzweig's contention that the difference between immanence and transcendence disappears in language, Levinas describes language as the voice from the other shore that provides a link to the face of the other person. But unlike Rosenzweig, Levinas gives this account of language a decidedly moral emphasis.

Levinas in fact begins *Totality and Infinity* by asking, "whether we are not duped by morality"? Presenting a view of ethics as each individual's infinite obligation toward another, Levinas' answer is that we are not. In "Violence and Metaphysics," Derrida criticizes Levinas not so much for his view of language but for the metaphysical (a term Levinas affirms) underpinning of his thought. Derrida argues that Levinas' error lies precisely in his attempt to posit a notion of pure violence (what Levinas, trans-valuing Heidegger's "es gibt," calls the "there is" the "il y à") and pure peace (Levinas' concept of "infinity"). In "Violence and Metaphysics," Derrida evokes Heidegger's "ontological difference" in order to suggest to Levinas that, simply put, there is no getting past oppositionality. In Derrida's words, "A Being without violence would be a Being that would occur outside the existent; nothing, non-history; nonoccurance; nonphenomenality."[51] "Oppositionality," for Derrida,

constitutes writing and all meaning. It is important to note that while
Derrida considers Heidegger's "ontological difference" a vestige of metaphysical thinking because it continues to be predicated on a crypto-
metaphysical distinction between the original and derivative, Derrida
nonetheless remains indebted to Heidegger's ontological difference in
reconsidering the priority of speech and writing.

Derrida's and Levinas' philosophical exchanges affect each of their
subsequent philosophies. Levinas, in his essay "Transcendence and
Evil," published eleven years after Derrida's critique of *Totality and
Infinity*, seems to respond explicitly to Derrida's charge in "Violence
and Metaphysics" when he states, "The ontological difference is preceded by the difference between good and evil. Difference itself is this
latter; it is the origin of the meaningful."[52] In his second major work,
Otherwise than Being or Beyond Essence, Levinas develops his view of
language further, claiming that his assigning priority to speech (what
Levinas calls "the saying") does not fall prey to notions of presence. As
Levinas puts it:

> Saying signifies otherwise than as an apparitor presenting essence
> and entities . . . Our task is to establish its articulation and
> signifyingness antecedent to ontology . . . The plot of the saying
> that is absorbed in the said is not exhausted in this manifestation.
> It imprints its trace on the thematization itself, which hesitates
> between, on the one hand, structuration, order of a configuration
> of entities, world and history for historiographers and, on the other
> hand, the order of non-nominalized apophansis of the other, in
> which the said remains a *proposition*, a proposition made to a
> neighbor, 'a signifying dealt' (*significance baillée*) to the other.[53]

For Levinas, revelation is this remaining trace. While making a distinction between his philosophical and apologetic work, Levinas nevertheless equates this trace with what he contends is a particularly Jewish
notion of revelation. Jewish revelation, for Levinas, affirms the material
world of thought and calculation (what Levinas calls alternatively "totality" and the "said") while also signifying something that cannot entirely
be captured by thought, which is the unique ethical responsibility each
individual bears. In his Jewish writings, Levinas calls Judaism "religion
for adults" because of its sober affirmation of both human finitude and
human responsibility.[54]

In much of his later work, Derrida came to reiterate many Levinasian
themes, beginning perhaps with his 1980 essay "At this very moment"
and his 1983 analysis of apocalyptic thought.[55] But as significantly,

Derrida does not affirm the fullness of Levinas' view of a peace prior
to war but only suggests the necessity of thinking about the possibility of a non-oppositional peace in order to rethink democracy. Derrida's
questioning about good and evil (about peace and war, friend and enemy)
points to the radical instability of systems of meaning (including views
of good and evil). Levinas' writings on the other hand (as Derrida himself remarks, again particularly in "Violence and Metaphysics") do not
attempt to consider the *possibility* of good and evil beyond oppositionality (beyond the ontological difference) but to *affirm* their reality and
argue in fact that oppositionality itself is made possible by their reality.

This difference between Derrida and Levinas is ramified in their different understandings of commentary. We have already mentioned that
the intertextuality of the Jewish tradition confirms for Derrida his view
that all systems of meaning are unstable. Levinas, in contrast, while
emphasizing multiple voices in rabbinic texts, does not view the intertextuality of the Jewish tradition as pointing to the fundamental instability of meaning. Rather, for Levinas, who more than Derrida views
himself as perpetuating a kind of *Jewish* thought, instability of meaning
comes only in the context of the ethical relation. Ethics, for Levinas,
is the destabilization of meaning but this destabilization points to the
event of the ethical relation. As Levinas defines Jewish revelation in its
relation to commentary:

> The revelation has a particular way of producing meaning, which
> lies in its calling upon the unique in me. It is as if a multiplicity of
> persons . . . as if each person by virtue of his own uniqueness, were
> able to guarantee the revelation of one unique aspect of truth, so
> that some of its facets would never have been revealed if certain
> people had been absent from mankind . . . I am suggesting that the
> totality of truth is made out of the contributions of a multiplicity
> of people: the uniqueness of each act carries the secret of the
> text; the voice of Revelation, in precisely the inflection lent by
> each person's ear, is necessary to produce all the dimensions of
> meaning; the multiplicity of meaning is due to the multiplicity of
> people.[56]

Any affirmation of the instability of meaning in Levinas' philosophy
comes in the context of his claim that to be human is to be ethically
responsible. Indeed, Levinas ends *Otherwise than Being* by affirming
yet revaluing philosophical skepticism so as to claim that the truth of
skepticism is predicated on the ethical relation.[57] Levinas and Derrida
both emphasize the instability of meaning, but in the former case this

instability points to a radically stable truth about what it means to be human, while for the latter the articulation of such a truth is always itself fundamentally unstable.

Levinas' and Derrida's differences emerge in the end from what is another profound similarity between them. While both of their philosophies are technically complex and reflect a deep engagement with the German phenomenological tradition, the impetus for their respective philosophies is a shared claim about philosophy and ethics. Both believe that Western philosophy is complicit with the horrors of the twentieth-century and both seek to remedy this complicity. Derrida, in the end, claims that violence stems from gestures of totalization, of which "thought" and "philosophy" are formal representations. While agreeing with this, and while for Levinas difference belongs to the very structure of goodness, Levinas nonetheless affirms a notion of goodness beyond the differences that constitute any possibility of meaning. For Levinas, the reality of evil points to the truth of ethics. For Derrida, the reality of evil points to the possibility of thinking about the possible truth of ethics.[58] Deconstruction for Derrida undoes what he claims is the violent totalizing of thought. In contrast, for Levinas, a turn to metaphysics after Heidegger reminds philosophy of its grounding in ethics.

Despite the important differences between them, both Derrida and Levinas share a claim that "Judaism" contributes to the task of philosophy. In their shared philosophical emphasis on language and commentary, both suggest that philosophy has made and should continue to make a "Jewish" turn. In this way, their meditations on the meaning of language for philosophy allow us an opportunity to think about what the notion of "Jewish philosophy" could mean. We turn now to consider how philosophical conceptions of revelation, language, and commentary determine and are determined by the question of the definition of "Jewish philosophy."

IV

In part one of this chapter, we explored briefly some of the ways in which twentieth-century philosophical considerations of language are tied historically and philosophically to accounts of the relation between reason and revelation. After exploring in detail various claims of different twentieth-century Jewish thinkers about language, I would like to suggest that the basic question underlying these inquiries concerns what philosophy is, and more particularly whether philosophy is or should be something useful. Put differently, the question of whether philosophy can and should transcend language is simultaneously the question of whether there is some particular purpose to philosophy, beyond an articulation of the rules and grammars of particular languages. By way of conclusion, I would like to suggest that although twentieth-century Jewish philosophers did a lot to follow Nietzsche in putting revelation and reason on a par and in seeing both as linguistically constituted, they nevertheless only did so within the "moral" framework set up by Kant. I suggest that this tension between Jewish philosophical appropriations of Nietzsche and Kant not only defines twentieth-century Jewish philosophical views of language but the attempts at, and stakes in, thinking about "Jewish philosophy" in the twentieth century as well.

But before turning to the specific issues involved in thinking about "Jewish philosophy," it is necessary to turn once again to the broadly Kantian premises about the scope of philosophical inquiry. Kant's bracketing of religious faith from knowledge is predicated on a claim about philosophy's appropriate aims. One may understand Kant's project as the attempt to define not only the proper parameters of faith, but also more broadly the proper parameters of what he calls "pure reason" and "practical reason." Kant famously maintained that while pure reason in and of itself cannot give us knowledge of the world as it really is, pure reason has a regulative function that guides the pursuits of both theoretical and practical knowledge.[59] Pure reason on its own cannot obtain knowledge, but by providing practical reason with proper postulates, philosophy can and does account for both the truths of everyday experience and of scientific knowledge. The bad news for Kant is that we cannot say anything about the world of objects in and of themselves. But the good news is that philosophy, and Kant's transcendental idealism more specifically, can show that the objective world does in fact exist outside of necessarily subjective perceptions.[60] In this way, Kant's philosophy simultaneously acknowledges and accounts for our inability to transcend our subjectivity while nonetheless retaining and affirming the critical use and need for philosophy.

The turn to language in twentieth-century philosophy is intimately related to a qualification, if not a rejection, of the Kantian view that philosophy has a critical function to play in the constitution of human knowledge as well as in moral and political matters. Nietzsche denied that philosophy has critical aims either for the theoretical constitution of knowledge or for the practical ordering of the good society, but his philosophy nevertheless held on to a distinction between theoretical and practical knowledge and, perhaps more broadly, between that which is

useful and that which is not useful. As we have seen, Heidegger attempts
to reject this very premise in contending that philosophy, or what he calls
"thinking," is neither theoretical nor practical. As Heidegger puts it:

> This thinking is neither theoretical nor practical. It takes place
> before this differentiation. This thinking, in so far as it is, is the
> remembrance of Being and nothing else . . . Such thinking has no
> result. It has no effect. It satisfies its nature simply by being.[61]

The context of these remarks is Heidegger's 1946 "Letter on Humanism" in which he maintains that "thinking," which replaces "philosophy," must move beyond humanism. Heidegger's famous contention
that "language is the house of being" leads him to attempt a kind of
thinking beyond the humanism intrinsic to philosophy toward, in his
later work, an engagement with poetry.[62]

Much of the philosophical criticism of the linguistic turn in philosophy is directed at this Heideggerian attempt to move beyond a notion
of philosophical instrumentality. Significantly, this criticism is often
linked to claims about the specifically moral, if not humanistic, function of philosophy and critical thinking. While not denying the importance and indeed centrality of language for philosophy, Jürgen Habermas
nevertheless insists that there is a critical and indeed rational function immanent to linguistified social interaction. As he puts it, "*In
the final analysis, the speaker can illocutionarily influence the hearer
and vice versa, because speech-act-typical commitments are connected
with cognitively testable validity claims* – that is, because the reciprocal bonds have a rational basis."[63] While there is much to be said about
Habermas' contention, the central point for our purposes is that Habermas connects an affirmation of the philosophical centrality of language
to the claim for philosophy's critical and indeed ethical and political
function. And in so doing, Habermas affirms important aspects of the
modern Kantian attempt to retain philosophy's theoretical and practical
aims.

In this regard, Rosenzweig's complex relationship to the neo-Kantian
Jewish philosopher Hermann Cohen is particularly relevant. Rosenzweig famously claimed that in his *Religion of Reason*, Cohen made
not only an existential turn but also a linguistic one.[64] Much of recent
Cohen scholarship has put this extremely questionable reading of Cohen
to rest, suggesting that Cohen's *Religion* is a piece with his neo-Kantian
system of philosophy.[65] Rosenzweig was right, however, that Cohen does
give an account of language in *Religion*, as well as in his earlier *Aesthetic
of Pure Feeling*. But this account of language, from which Rosenzweig

drew much for his understanding of revelation, remains within Cohen's critical idealist framework. In this sense, Cohen's treatment of language is not unlike Habermas' attempt to acknowledge the importance of language while also advocating for the critical function of philosophy. Just as Habermas urges philosophers at the beginning of the twenty-first century to reconsider the critical function of philosophy for ethical and political purposes, so Cohen might challenge twentieth-century Jewish philosophers to do the same.

This said, the accounts of language and Jewish revelation in the thoughts of Rosenzweig, Buber, Levinas, and Derrida nonetheless share a broad premise of Cohen's that, however different from each other, affirms the *philosophical usefulness* of an account of Jewish revelation, language, and commentary. I suggested in Part I of this chapter that much of twentieth-century Jewish philosophy grapples with the Kantian claim that revelation has a moral meaning and the Nietzschean claim that revelation is no less rational than philosophy. Significantly, despite the important differences between them, when twentieth-century Jewish philosophers turn to language, they do not give up entirely on the Kantian claim that revelation has a particularly moral meaning. This is clearly the case for Levinas who, despite all of his criticisms of modern philosophy, nevertheless returns to Kant, albeit a transformed Kant, in making his claims about the morality of religion and the moral purposes of philosophy. But Derrida also retains a critical, if not moral, purpose for philosophy after Heidegger. Despite his insistence on the instability of meaning and truth, deconstruction, for Derrida, as a post-metaphysical philosophical project, moves beyond assumptions of presence in order to return a critical, if ultimately undecidable, function to philosophical thinking.

Perhaps even more telling is the ambivalent relationship that Buber's and Rosenzweig's philosophies of language have to claims about philosophical purposefulness. Despite Buber's attempt to give priority to the non-instrumental I-thou relation over the instrumental I-it relation, he nevertheless continually and emphatically affirms the humanistic, and indeed ethical, impulse behind his dialogical philosophy.[66] So, too, while Rosenzweig's more theologically oriented thought continually affirms the particularity of the language of Jewish revelation, this particularity, for Rosenzweig, serves to propel the nations of the world toward redemption. The Jewish people perform their role through their existence, and the Jewish people do not do more than exist. Yet this existence, and the particular language of Jewish revelation, is for the sake of all of humanity.[67]

In conclusion, twentieth-century Jewish philosophical approaches to language pose the very problem of much of twentieth-century Continental philosophy, which is how to account philosophically for particularity. While the notion of "Jewish philosophy" is difficult to define, one minimal definition might be "the attempt to ask and answer the question of whether 'Judaism' offers any particular insights about philosophy." Any sort of Jewish philosophical thinking has to account for the very question of the relation between the particular and the universal, as this relation is at the very heart of any attempt to understand "Judaism." God's promise to Abraham encapsulates the complex dialectic between particular and universal that is found throughout the Jewish textual tradition: "I will make of you a great nation, and I will bless you, and make your name great, and you will be a blessing" (Genesis 12:2). As Rosenzweig put it, "the devout and the wise among the peoples will participate in the eternal life of the coming of the world, which but a short time ago seemed reserved for Israel. Those who were blessed will themselves be a blessing."[68] Because it is by definition situated between the particular and the universal, "Jewish philosophy" may seem then especially suited to grapple with the linguistic turn in twentieth-century philosophy, for all of its promises and limitations.

Notes

1. In the Anglo-American context, Ludwig Wittgenstein, J. L. Austin, and Gilbert Ryle are most often credited for the linguistic turn in the interwar period, while in the German context, the interest in language grew more directly from work in biblical hermeneutics, beginning with Schleiermacher. For a broad overview of the very different issues informing this common turn to language in the twentieth-century, see Ian Hacking, *Why Does Language Matter to Philosophy?* (Cambridge: Cambridge University Press, 1975); Ernst Cassirer, *The Philosophy of Symbolic Forms*, trans. Ralph Manheim, Vol. 1 (New Haven: Yale University Press, 1953), especially pp. 117–176; and Richard Palmer, *Hermeneutics: Interpretation Theory in Schleiermacher, Dilthey, Heidegger, and Gadamer* (Evanston: Northwestern University Press, 1969). See also Cristina Lafont, trans. José Medina, *The Linguistic Turn in Philosophy* (Cambridge: MIT Press, 1999). I suggest implicitly in this essay that Jewish philosophical approaches to language, even as they move into the French context, are tied closely to German philosophical debates about language, and especially to the implications of Nietzsche's philosophy (with which Cassirer does not deal in his survey).
2. *Critique of Pure Reason*, trans. Norman Kemp Smith (New York: St. Martin's Press, 1965); *Religion within the Limits of Reason Alone*, trans.

Theodore M. Greene and Hoyt H. Hudson (New York: Harper Collins, 1960).
3. Friedrich Nietzsche, *Beyond Good and Evil*, trans. R. J. Hollingdale (New York: Penguin, 1986), p. 18, translation modified; German original at *Jenseits von Gut und Böse*, in *Werke in Drei Bänden*, ed. Karl Schlechta (Munich: Carl Hanser Verlag, 1963), II, p. 805.
4. See for example Søren Kierkegaard, *Philosophical Fragments*, ed. and trans. Edna H. Hong and Howard V. Hong (Princeton: Princeton University Press, 1985).
5. "Letter on Humanism," *Basic Writings*, trans. David Farrell Krell (New York: Harper & Row, 1977), p. 193.
6. For Heidegger's broad argument, see "What is Metaphysics," *Basic Writings*.
7. For Heidegger's lectures on Nietzsche, see *Nietzsche*, in *Gesamtausgabe*. Vol. 50 (Frankfurt am Main: Vittorio Klostermann 1990), p.6, trans. in David Farrell Krell, *Nietzsche: Volumes One and Two* (San Francisco: Harper & Row, 1991), p.3.
8. Heidegger, *Platon: Sophistes*, in *Gesamtausgabe*, bd. 19 (Frankfurt: Vittorio Klostermann, 1992), pp. 580–581.
9. See, in particular, Rosenzweig's introduction to Part 2 of *The Star of Redemption*, "On the Possibility of Experiencing Miracle," trans. William W. Hallo (New York: University of Notre Dame Press, 1985).
10. For a comparison with Wittgenstein, see Hilary Putnam's introduction to Rosenzweig's *Understanding the Sick and the Healthy: A View of World, Man, and God*, edited, translated, and with an introduction by Nahum Glatzer (Cambridge: Harvard University Press, 1999).
11. For a comparison of Rosenzweig and Heidegger, see Peter Eli Gordon, *Rosenzweig and Heidegger: Between Judaism and German Philosophy* (Berkeley: University of California Press, 2003).
12. For the argument that meaning is communally constituted for Rosenzweig, see Leora Batnitzky, *Idolatry and Representation: The Philosophy of Franz Rosenzweig Reconsidered* (Princeton: Princeton University Press, 2000), Chapter 3, "The Philosophical Import of Carnal Israel."
13. By "agnostic" I am merely referring to Heidegger's rejection of both theism and atheism in his "Letter on Humanism" in *Basic Writings*, especially pp. 226–230.
14. Martin Heidegger, *Poetry, Language, and Thought*, trans. A. Hofstadter (San Francisco: Harper and Row, 1971), p. 190.
15. *Star*, p. 198.
16. Eugen Rosenstock-Huessy, *Angewandte Seelenkunde* in *Die Sprache des Menschengeschlects* (Heidelberg: Lambert Schneider, 1968), pp. 739–810.
17. "Atheistic Theology," in *Philosophical and Theological Writings*, ed. and trans. Paul W. Franks and Michael L. Morgan (Indianapolis: Hackett, 2000).
18. *Star*, p. 156.
19. Peter Eli Gordon rightfully argues in his chapter on Rosenzweig in this volume that revelation for Rosenzweig does not transform the person but permits the human being to be. Nevertheless, Rosenzweig's account

of the human being's acknowledgment of sin in response to revelation, indeed as part and parcel of the experience of love, suggests strongly that the human being, in the experience of love, is profoundly transformed. I discuss this transformation briefly later. See especially *Star*, p. 183.

20. *Star*, p. 183.
21. Ibid.
22. *Star*, p. 199.
23. Letter dated August 30, 1920, in *Franz Rosenzweig: His Life and Thought*, ed. Nahum Glatzer (New York: Schocken, 1953), p. 97.
24. As Rosenzweig puts it, "By being an individual people, a nation becomes a people among others . . . But this does not hold when a people refuses to be merely an individual people and wants to be 'the one people.' Under these circumstances it must not close itself off within borders, but include within itself such borders as would, through their double function, tend to make it one individual among others." *Star*, p. 305.
25. Rosenzweig's commitment to the centrality and specificity of the language of Jewish revelation extended to his efforts at translating various Jewish texts, including the poetry of the medieval philosopher Judah Halevi and also the Hebrew Bible itself. "Translation" in fact became the model of all language and speaking, for Rosenzweig, because it captured the simultaneous particular and universal (or immanent and transcendent) features of language. See especially his comments about translation in *Scripture and Translation*, trans. Lawrence Rosenwald with Everett Fox (Bloomington: Indiana University Press, 1994), p. 47.
26. Rosenzweig argues that Christianity is the way in which the nations of the world will come to know Jewish revelation. See Part 3, Book 2 of the *Star* for Rosenzweig's discussion of Christianity as well as Chapter 6 of *Idolatry and Representation* for further explication of the role of Christianity in Rosenzweig's thought.
27. *I and Thou*, trans. Ronald Gregor Smith (New York: Charles Scribner's Sons, 1958).
28. See Rivka Horwitz, *Buber's Way to I and Thou* (Heidelberg: Lambert Schneider, 1978) and Steven Kepnes, *The Text as Thou: Martin Buber's Dialogical Hermeneutics and Narrative Theology* (Bloomington: Indiana University Press, 1992).
29. See Buber and Rosenzweig's exchange on the status of Jewish law in "The Builders," in *On Jewish Learning*, ed. Nahum Glatzer (New York: Schocken Books, 1965).
30. Martin Buber, "The Word That Is Spoken," trans. M. Friedman, *The Knowledge of Man*, p. 117.
31. Buber's work for a Jewish national renewal in Palestine and then Israel also has broad affinities with some of his German philosophical contemporaries' interests in a German national renewal. In a theme present, if initially underdeveloped, in his early work to his mature work, Buber suggested that the language of Jewish texts, biblical and hasidic especially, could provide humankind with a renewed access to being itself. In his later work, Buber defined existence itself as the ontological condition of what he called "the between." Dialogical speech, for Buber,

is this "between." In this work, Buber's continued poetic engagement with Hasidism parallels and in some ways even anticipates historically Heidegger's engagement with the pre-Socratics. For more on the relationship between Buber and Heidegger, see Leora Batnitzky, "Renewing the Jewish Past: Buber on History and Truth," *Jewish Studies Quarterly* 10:4 (2003), pp. 336–350.

32. This is expressed most clearly in the subtitle of Heschel's *God in Search of Man: A Philosophy of Judaism* (New York: Farrar, Straus, & Cudahy, 1955).

33. *Torah min ha-shamayim be-aspaklaryah shel ha-dorot* (London, NY: Defus Shontsin: 1962–1990), three volumes (Hebrew). Literally translated as "Torah from Heaven" or "Revelation from Heaven." The broader context of the work is Heschel's argument that the narrative (aggadic) aspect of rabbinic literature is as important as its legal (halakhic) component; see especially Vol. 1, p. iii.

34. *Torah min ha-shamayim*, Vol. 1, pp. 170–179.

35. *God in Search of Man*, p. 276.

36. "Revelation and Tradition as Religious Categories," *The Messianic Idea in Judaism* (New York: Schocken), p. 287.

37. For instance, rather than trying to describe God in language, Maimonides asserts that "Silence and limiting oneself to the apprehensions of the intellect are more appropriate" (*Guide of the Perplexed*, trans. S. Pines (Chicago: University of Chicago Press, 1963, I: 59, p. 140)).

38. Yudit Kornberg-Greenberg contends that Rosenzweig is logocentric but also anticipates postmodernism. Greenberg suggests we should focus on the latter. See *Better than Wine: Love, Poetry, and Prayer in the Thought of Franz Rosenzweig* (Atlanta: Scholars Press, 1996).

39. See, for instance, Jean-François Lyotard, *Heidegger and "the jews"* (Minneapolis: University of Minnesota Press, 1990).

40. *Of Grammatology*, trans. Gayatri Chakravorty Spivak (Baltimore: Johns Hopkins University Press, 1976), p. 158.

41. As Derrida writes in *Of Grammatology*: "Nietzsche...has written that writing – and first of all his own – is not originarily subordinate to the logos and to truth. And that this subordination has come into being during an epoch whose meaning we must deconstruct. Now in this direction...Heideggerian thought would reinstate rather than destroy the instance of logos and of the truth of being as "primum signatum:" the "transcendental" signified...implied by all categories or all determined significations, by all lexicons and all syntax, and therefore by all linguistic signifiers, allowing itself to be precomprehended through each of them, remaining irreducible to all the epochal determinations that it nonetheless makes possible, thus opening the history of the logos, yet itself being only through the logos; that is, being nothing before the logos and outside of it" (pp. 19–20).

42. For this distinction between Judaism and Christianity, see Jacques Derrida, "Faith and Knowledge: The Two Sources of 'Religion' at the Limits of Reason Alone," in *Religion*, ed. Jacques Derrida and Gianni Vattimo (Stanford: Stanford University Press, 1996), p. 55.

43. "Edmond Jabès and the Question of the Book," in *Writing and Difference*, trans. with an introduction by Alan Bass (Chicago: The University of Chicago Press, 1978), p. 67.

44. For an enlightening discussion of Derrida and Judaism, see Susan Handelman, *The Slayers of Moses: The Emergence of Rabbinic Interpretation in Modern Literary Theory* (Albany: State University of New York Press, 1982).

45. "Violence and Metaphysics: An Essay on the Thought of Emmanuel Levinas," in *Writing and Difference*, pp. 79–153.

46. For extensive analyses of the relation between Rosenzweig and Levinas, see Robert Gibbs, *Correlations in Rosenzweig and Levinas* (Princeton: Princeton University Press, 1992) and Richard Cohen, *Elevations: The Height of the Good in Rosenzweig and Levinas* (Chicago: University of Chicago Press, 1994).

47. I thank Samuel Moyn for making this point clearer to me.

48. "Totalité et infini," *Annales de l'Université de Paris* 31 (1961): p. 386.

49. "The New Thinking," in *Franz Rosenzweig's "The New Thinking,"* ed. and trans. Alan Udoff and Barbara Galli (Syracuse: Syracuse University Press, 1999), p. 73.

50. *Totality and Infinity*, trans. Alphonso Lingis (Pittsburgh: Duquesne University Press, 1969), p. 206.

51. Derrida, "Violence and Metaphysics," p. 147.

52. "Transcendence and Evil," in *Collected Philosophical Papers*, trans. Alphonso Lingis (Dordrecht: Martinus Nijhoff, 1987), p. 182.

53. *Otherwise than Being or Beyond Essence*, trans. Alphonso Lingis (The Hague: Martinus Nijhoff, 1981), pp. 46–47.

54. *Difficult Freedom: Essays on Judaism*, trans. Seán Hand (Baltimore: Johns Hopkins University Press, 1990).

55. "At This Very Moment in This Work Here I Am," in *Re-Reading Levinas*, ed. Robert Bernasconi and Simon Critchley, trans. Ruben Berezdivin (Bloomington: Indiana University Press, 1991), pp. 11–48. *D'un ton apocalyptique adopté naguère en philosophie. Collection Débats* (Paris: Galilée, 1983). For an English translation of "On a Newly Risen Apocalyptic Tone in Philosophy," see *Raising the Tone of Philosophy : Late Essays by Immanuel Kant, Transformative Critique by Jacques Derrida*, trans. John Leavey, in Peter Fenves, (Baltimore: Johns Hopkins University Press, 1998).

56. "Revelation in the Jewish Tradition," *The Levinas Reader*, ed. Seán Hand (New York: Blackwell, 1989), p. 195.

57. As Levinas puts it, "The periodic rebirth of skepticism...recalls the breakup of the unity of the transcendental apperception, without which one could not *otherwise than be*" (*Otherwise than Being*, p. 171).

58. This question of possibility is also the common denominator in Derrida's writings on religion. For a particularly representative essay on this theme, see "Faith and Knowledge," in *Religion*.

59. See, in particular, Kant's discussion of the antinomies of pure reason in *Critique of Pure Reason*.

60. For this argument, see, in particular, "The Transcendental Unity of Apperception" in *Critique of Pure Reason*.

61. "Letter on Humanism," *Basic Writings*, p. 236, translation modified; German original, *Über den Humanismus* (Frankfurt: V. Klostermann, 1981), p. 48.

62. See, in particular, Heidegger's *Erläuterungen zu Hölderlins Dichtung* in *Gesamtausgabe*, Vol. 4 (Frankfurt: Vittorio Klostermann, 1981), translated as *Elucidations of Hölderlin's Poetry*, by Keith Hoeller (Amherst, New York: Humanity Books, 2000).

63. "What is Universal Pragmatics," in *Communication and the Evolution of Society*, trans. Thomas McCarthy (Boston: Beacon Press, 1979), p. 63.

64. See Rosenzweig's "The New Thinking" and his *Einleitung*, in Hermann Cohen, *Jüdische Schriften* (Berlin: C.A. Schwetschke & Sohn, 1924), Vol. 1.

65. For the most comprehensive studies in English, see Andrea Poma, *The Critical Philosophy of Hermann Cohen*, trans. John Denton (Albany: State University Press of New York, 1997) and Michael Zank, *The Idea of Atonement in the Philosophy of Hermann Cohen* (Providence, R.I: Brown Judaic Studies, 2000).

66. See, in particular, Buber's essay "Biblical Humanism," in *The Martin Buber Reader*, ed. Asher Biemann (New York: Palgrave Macmillan, 2002) and Grete Schaeder's comprehensive *The Hebrew Humanism of Martin Buber*, trans. Noah J. Jacobs (Detroit: Wayne State University Press, 1973). Although less systematic, Heschel's thought, and his philosophy of language in particular, also share this ambivalent relation to an affirmation of humanism. Here, Heschel's social activism in the United States is particularly relevant. For an overview of Heschel's relation to the civil rights movement, see *Cross Currents* (Fall 1996), Vol. 46:3.

67. For a broad argument about Rosenzweig's "mission" argument, see Leora Batnitzky, *Idolatry and Representation*.

68. *Star*, p. 308.

16 Feminism and Modern Jewish Philosophy

TAMAR RUDAVSKY

I. INTRODUCTION: FEMINISM, PHILOSOPHY, AND JEWISH PHILOSOPHY

The interactions between feminism and philosophy, and feminism and Judaism, have undergone serious development in recent decades. Starting with the former, many feminists have argued that Western philosophy has systematically excluded women. More specifically, feminists have argued that what Western male philosophers have presented as "essentially human" is in fact rooted in the male experience and does not reflect women's experiences; that because the (male) ideals of reason were formed completely without female input, the Western philosophical tradition is thus biased; and that many philosophical works, written by men, contain numerous misogynist statements. In a similar vein, feminist theologians have maintained that Western religious traditions have systematically excluded women's voices; that religious institutions have been predominantly male-oriented and reflect male concerns and priorities; and that many canonical religious texts, written almost exclusively by men, contain misogynist statements.

That feminist philosophers and theologians have risen to the challenges raised by an androcentric philosophical and theological canon has been well-documented.[1] Jewish feminists as well, influenced by their feminist peers, have begun to level significant attacks against what they see as a Judaism entrenched in patriarchal institutionalism. This patriarchy is perhaps best expressed by Judith Plaskow in her seminal work *Standing Again at Sinai*: "Underlying specific halakhot ... is an assumption of women's Otherness far more basic than the laws in which it finds expression ... men – and not women with them – define Jewish humanity. Men are the actors in religious and communal life because they are the normative Jews. Women are 'other' than the norm; we are less than fully human. This otherness of women as a presupposition of Jewish law is its most central formulation."[2] Nevertheless, despite the challenges raised by Plaskow and others, Jewish feminist engagement of issues in Jewish philosophy is in its infancy.

While scholars of religion, Talmudists, and Jewish cultural historians have explored feminist concerns in the corpus of Jewish law,[3] philosophers have been conspicuously absent from this endeavor. With the exception of one recent anthology, Jewish philosophers (both male and female) have for the most part not taken up the challenges posed by their non-Jewish feminist peers.[4] And so the topic 'feminism and Jewish philosophy' must, in part, explore the reasons why Jewish philosophers have been loathe to participate in the feminist conversation. In this chapter, I shall examine the main lines of attack leveled by feminist theorists against the Western philosophical tradition in general, and Jewish philosophy in particular. I shall develop the implications of this attack first for epistemology and metaphysics, both of which are rooted in our conceptions of reason, and then for ethics and philosophy of religion. Each of these areas is reflected in the works of Jewish philosophers, and I shall concentrate on the works of Spinoza, Soloveitchik and Levinas. I shall end the chapter with what I take to be a motif essential to understanding entrenched attitudes toward the feminine in Judaism – namely, the notion of temporality as a metaphysical category.

2. ATHENS AND JERUSALEM REVISITED BY FEMINIST PHILOSOPHERS

2.1. The Rejection of Reason: Athens under Attack

For many feminists, the proper enemy is the faculty of reason itself. As Genevieve Lloyd has argued in a now classic work, maleness has been associated throughout the history of philosophy with reason, while the female is associated with what rational knowledge transcends.[5] The domain of reason, which involves minimally the method of giving arguments and subjecting them to tests of logical validity, took on special associations with the realm of pure thought, a realm from which women were excluded. Enlightenment philosophers reinforced the importance of a self rooted in rationality, with its connections to individualism and political liberalism. The privileging of reason by philosophers assumes what feminists call the "nonsituated distanced standpoint" – namely, the view that things in the world are independent of us, and their behavior is constrained by their natures. We can best discover these natures by looking for their regularities, which are exhibited under "normal circumstances." This position assumes "direction of fit," according to which ones beliefs about the world conform to the world.

Feminists see the entire epistemological program, including rationalism, empiricism, and naturalized epistemology, as both philosophically and politically uncritical in that it is presented as a "value-
neutral" enterprise. According to feminist theorists, no mode of thought
is value-neutral; theories of knowledge have ethical and political implications. Feminist standpoint theory was introduced by Sandra Harding,
who argued that gender relations necessarily affect our epistemic standpoint and that in fact women may often occupy a privileged epistemic
standpoint.[6] Feminists emphasize that the identity of the knower, who
is socially situated, *must* enter into the production of knowledge. Feelings and emotions are valid sources of knowledge, and knowledge
becomes distorted when feelings and emotions are not acknowledged.
Feelings must be recognized as a valid "route to truth."

Now the rationalist strain of both metaphysics and epistemology
had already been subjected to critique from within the history of philosophy: Kant developed the view that reason and knowledge are limited
by the intellectual and perceptual attributes of humans; Hegel argued
further that knowledge and reason are marked by history in that they
are temporally located or indexed; Nietzsche and Freud rejected the
rigid demarcation between abstract reason and body; recent Continental philosophers have attempted to render the view otiose. In this sense,
the feminist critique of reason sits squarely within a long philosophical
tradition. But feminists have sharpened this historical and contextual
critique by arguing that concepts of reason themselves represent reflections of gendered practices passing as universal practices, thus carrying
political implications that far surpass the intentions of epistemologists
and metaphysicians.[7]

It should be noted further that the very relation between working philosophers and feminists is tenuous at best. Not surprisingly, the
majority of feminist philosophers (with some notable exceptions) have
tended to be women, but these women often bring to bear a certain
ambivalence to their project. How can women reconcile their commitment to feminism with a scholarly life devoted to the study of philosophers (for example, Aristotle, Kant, Hume, and so on) who explicitly
describe women as inferior to men, as unfit for the best life available
to human beings? On the one hand, many female philosophers agree
that the revealed misogyny of Western philosophy and theology cannot simply be dismissed as accidental; on the other hand, they too are
committed to reason and objectivity and hence want to pursue the one
discipline that purports to value these modes of thought. The tension is
underscored by Plaskow's exclamation, "I am not a Jew in the synagogue

and a feminist in the world. I am a Jewish feminist and a feminist Jew in every moment of my life."[8]

2.2. A Return to Jerusalem?

So far we have noted two main areas in which feminists have argued that Western philosophy has denigrated or marginalized women's experiences. The first has to do with the primacy of reason – which is upheld as a predominantly male feature – at the expense of emotions and bodily reality. The second has to do with the false espousal of objectivity, which ignores the "point of view" of the knower. In fact, even a cursory glance at relevant texts and discussions within the history of Jewish philosophy reveals an affinity between contemporary feminist positions and those of Jewish philosophers, past and present, on a number of issues.

Let me turn first to the area that most interests both feminists and Jewish philosophers – namely, the area of method. Feminist theorists have rejected the primacy of reason and its attendant "dispassionate objectivity" on the grounds that both reflect a male, patriarchal bias. I suggest that a similar distrust of reason can be found within Jewish philosophical writings. Many Jewish philosophers, both medieval and modern, have moved away from using reason as a criterion for achieving religious truth, arguing that religious truth derives its veridical nature from divine revelation and not from rational argument. This is not to say that all Jewish philosophers have rejected reason as the ultimate grounding of human cognitive activity. But as we peruse the pages of both medieval and modern Jewish texts, we find among many Jewish philosophers a tendency to posit a religious model of truth based on faith. I refer in particular to the traditional Jewish notion of faith that is associated with a non-cognitivist "trust in God" rather than as a propositional affirmation or denial.

Nowhere is this gravitation better reflected than in Soloveitchik's celebrated distinction between cognitive man, *homo religiosus*, and halakhic man, a distinction elaborated in his two works *The Lonely Man of Faith* and *Halakhic Man*. In *The Lonely Man of Faith*, Soloveitchik starts out with his rejection of the Cartesian *cogito*, a rejection that is shared by feminists: "I am lonely because, in my humble, inadequate way, I am a man of faith for whom to be means to believe, and who substituted *"credo"* for *"cogito"* in the time-honored Cartesian maxim."[9] Halakhic man represents for Soloveitchik an epistemic synthesis of two poles, cognitive man and *homo religiosus*, represented by Adam the first and Adam the second, respectively. Adam the first is paradigmatic of the contemporary individual involved in subduing nature, focused upon scientific advances, asking "How does the cosmos function?"[10] His is a practical, not a metaphysical, concern, and his telos incorporates a utilitarian understanding of the nature of the universe. His motto is "success, triumph over the cosmic forces,"[11] and he is best exemplified by the mathematical scientist. In contradistinction to Adam the first, Adam the second is described in language very often characterized as stereotypically "female." Adam the second realizes that he is existentially alone, alienated from the natural world, "experiencing ontological incompleteness and casualness, because there is no one who exists like the 'I' and because the *modus existentiae* of the 'I' cannot be repeated, imitated, or experienced by others."[12]

Soloveitchik notes that Adam the first was created simultaneously with Eve, reinforcing the metaphysical fact that Adam the first from his inception lives in society, with the other: "Adam the first is never alone . . . Adam the first was not left alone even on the day of creation. He emerged into the world together with Eve and God addressed himself to both of them as inseparable members of one community."[13] Eve represents "a functional partner to whom it would be assigned to collaborate with and assist Adam the first in his undertakings, schemes, and projects."[14] Adam the second, on the other hand, is created without a mate, and must sacrifice a part of himself in order to attain an equal companion.[15] He must be introduced to Eve by God. Adam the second and Eve "participate in the existential experience of being, not merely working, together."[16] Soloveitchik argues that the prayer community is what redeems the relationship between Adam the second and Eve. Only when God revealed himself from the transcendent darkness do Adam and Eve "reveal themselves to each other in sympathy and love on the one hand and in common action on the other."[17] True existential friendship, according to Soloveitchik, can be realized "only within the covenantal community, where in-depth personalities relate themselves to each other ontologically and total commitment to God and fellow man is the order of the day."[18] This last motif is further developed in Soloveitchik's work *Halakhic Man*. Like Adam the first, cognitive man is a natural scientist, bent upon mastering and subduing the environment, and like Adam the second, *homo religiosus* is more attuned to the miraculousness in nature, to a transcendent reality, resembling a "Romantic type of individual."[19] The ontological duality of cognitive man and *homo religiosus* finds its synthesis in halakhic man.[20]

We shall examine in greater detail later the importance of time itself as a metaphysical construct. Let me point out here, though, that Soloveitchik is much aware of the differing temporal models recognized and utilized by his two paradigmatic individuals. Adam the second is constantly aware of the passing of time. He is immersed in the flow of temporal time: he recognizes there was an endless past, is aware of an endless future, and, with a nod to Aristotle's definition of the "now," he recognizes the ephemeral nature of the present instant, "which vanishes before it is experienced."[21] Whereas Adam the second experiences both the transcendence and evanescence of the "now," Adam the first is completely unaware of the passage of time. For Adam the first "lives in micro-units of clock time, moving with ease from "now" to "now," completely unaware of a "before" or an "after.""[22] But unlike the Aristotelian, for whom the "now" is ephemeral and defies capture, Adam the second experiences redemption by means of cyclic time, according to which every temporal experience both reconstructs and recalls the past, while anticipating the future. Within the covenantal community, "each single experience of time is three-dimensional, manifesting itself in memory, actuality, and anticipatory tension."[23] This awareness cuts through linear time and unites generations of practitioners. Unlike Adam the first, Adam the second thus "feels rooted in the past and related to the future."[24]

How then, can a feminist reader approach the metaphysical landscape inhabited by Soloveitchik's protagonists? On the one hand, feminists must struggle both with Soloveitchik's apparent exaltation of a halakhic world that itself is male-dominated and oriented, and with an orientation that construes the female, at best, as an existential partner. And yet it is important to note that Soloveitchik's attitude toward that halakhic world is ambivalent. Remember, as I claimed earlier, that the very language used to describe Adam the first (or cognitive man) is what we normally associate as "male," whereas the passive, meek, self-demeaning nature of Adam the second is stereotypically regarded as "female" in nature. Soloveitchik, however, clearly rejects the life-project of Adam the first, worshipper of reason, proponent of scientific detachment and objectivity, joiner of organized religion, as representative of a life that is alienating and ultimately devoid of meaning. It is halakhic man, who necessarily incorporates the insights and temperament of Adam the second, who achieves the spiritual and epistemological goals laid out by Soloveitchik.

I maintain that Soloveitchik (and his followers) thus share with feminists a distrust of reason, of rational objectivity, as the ultimate method for achieving knowledge of reality. Both Soloveitchik and feminist epistemologists postulate an alternative basis for coming to know the world, an epistemology that emphasizes the primacy of emotions and human interaction. Furthermore, just as feminists have emphasized the primacy

of emotions, of bodies, as modes of knowing, so too Soloveitchik emphasizes non-cognitivist modes of knowing as exemplified by the relation
between Adam the second and Eve.

3. THE IMPLICATIONS OF DUALISM FOR JEWISH PHILOSOPHY

3.1. The Enemy is Descartes

We have seen that the denigration of reason is itself double-edged,
and carries with it enormous implications with respect to philosophers'
attitudes towards women. Given the feminist characterization of Western philosophy as both phallocentric and anti-female, one might expect
Jewish philosophers to equal, if not surpass, their misogynist peers in
their denigration of women. When, however, we turn to the mind-body
distinction, which plays such a crucial role in Western thought, matters
become more complex. Feminists have criticized Cartesian dualism on
the grounds that it privileges reason over emotion. Because emotions
are traditionally associated with the female, the very elevation of reason over emotions is seen as male-biased.[25]

The metaphysical basis for gender associations in dualism can be
traced back to Pythagoras' *Table of Opposition*, in which the female
principle is aligned with negative characteristics: unlimit, plurality, left,
moving, darkness and evil, thus emphasizing the overall unsavoriness of
the female principle.[26] This male/female dichotomy, reiterated throughout medieval philosophy, reappears in the Cartesian notion of the solitary ego, a concept that not only underlies much of modern philosophy,
but carries with it the privileging of the mental over the physical.

In response to Cartesian dualism, feminist philosophers have argued
that a preferable starting point for understanding the content of human
consciousness is the relational self, "the self presented as involved in and
importantly constituted by its connectedness to others."[27] Husserl had
already dealt a blow to Cartesian solipsism by emphasizing the intentionality of consciousness. According to Husserl's phenomenological
platform, there can be no subject (*noesis*) without a corresponding object
(*noema*); consciousness is always consciousness *of*. But feminists assert
that the very model of intentionality must be expanded. On this latter
view, each of us is connected by invisible threads to an indefinite number
of specific other human beings.[28] The Cartesian problem of other minds
simply does not exist when we adopt a feminist standpoint. Reflecting Soloveitchik's analysis of Adam the second who is ontologically
dependent upon Eve, feminists reiterate Aristotle's claim that "[hu]man

is a social animal," and argue that we are essentially societal, and not solitary.

One feminist response to Descartes has been to postulate the human self as intrinsically embodied, emphasizing the centrality of the physical in human psychology and cognition. Early ("first wave") feminists like Simone de Beauvoir argued that in order to avoid the inevitable identification of body with the female that results when reason is associated with the male, women should refuse marriage and motherhood, thus regaining ownership of the rational realm. The "second wave" of feminists have argued that the radical feminist project to re-appropriate mind will never work, and that feminists must "reconfigure the role of bodily experience in the development of knowledge."[29] French feminists such as Hélène Cixous, Luce Irigaray, and Julia Kristeva claim that inasmuch as thinking takes place within a human body, "embodied thinking" must be adopted in contradistinction to the male phallocentric thinking models. To complicate matters even further, while some feminists have attacked Cartesianism as a hindrance to feminist concerns, other Descartes scholars have challenged this attack, arguing that Descartes' intellectual heritage contains a variety of critical resources helpful to feminist concerns. Sara Heinamaa for example has recently argued that Descartes' concept of equal reason should be central to feminist arguments for women's education and scholarship and that his arguments against dogmatic philosophy should be paradigmatic of any philosophical enterprise emphasizing self-inquiry.[30]

3.2. Spinoza's Response to Cartesianism

Tempting as it may be to argue that Jewish philosophy has perpetuated this androcentric rejection of the physical, along with the coupling of the physical with sexuality, evil and the feminine, let me temper this temptation by maintaining that the attitude of Jewish texts towards the body is itself ambiguous. Peter Brown has noted a divide between Jewish and Christian notions of sexuality.[31] Similarly, Daniel Boyarin has argued that rabbinic Judaism invested significance in the body which in the other formations was invested in the soul: "for rabbinic Jews, the human being was defined as a body... while for Hellenistic Jews and Christians, the essence of a human being is a soul housed in a body."[32]

Notwithstanding Spinoza's excommunication and subsequent dissociation from organized Jewish life, let me suggest that Spinoza's conception of body shares a marked similarity to that of the rabbis. In recent years, Spinoza has been reappropriated by a number of feminists as a philosopher much more congenial to the feminist project than were many of his peers. According to Heidi Ravven, Spinoza collapses the time-honored distinction between theoretical and practical intellect: she argues that according to Spinoza, there is no thinking that is not practical, embodied and impassioned.[33] On her feminist reading, Spinoza does not fall into the trap of reifying the body and dichotomizing it as male or female.[34] Unlike Descartes, for whom body is passive and mind active, for Spinoza body and mind are one entity; mind is the consciousness of the body, and both can be regarded as either active or passive depending on the intellectual level achieved. Descartes' substance dualism and Spinoza's monistic materialism represent the radical alternatives represented by Platonism and Aristotelianism.[35]

Let me further strengthen the feminist appropriation of Spinoza by focusing upon Spinoza's theory of personal identity. On Spinoza's theory of individuation, part of what makes me who I am is that I am affected by other individuals; individuation on this model turns out to be relational, incorporating both material and formal elements. It is bodies that are the source of identification of persons: the ideas that make up an individual mind acquire their identity by being ideas of a particular body. This identification with body remains embedded in the mind after the death of the body. The crucial point overlooked by many commentators is that for Spinoza there exists a difference of degree, not of kind, between persons and other objects. To admit that the eternity of mind incorporates the idea of the body, as expressed in E2p7 (*Ethics*, Part 2, Proposition 7), and that therefore the corresponding body is eternal as well as the mind, reinforces Spinoza's rigorous monist ontology.

Perhaps Spinoza's most important statement is his claim that "the mind is nothing but the idea of the body." What Spinoza means here is that the mind does not have ideas, but mind *is* the ideas. For Spinoza, mind and body are extensionally identical. And so the free person who lives according to the dictates of reason alone (E4p67) must of necessity incorporate the dictates of body as well. The very concept of reason undergoes a revolutionary shift, one that is applauded by feminists. Since good and evil are the result of inadequate ideas, the free person is not ruled by this conventional type of morality (E4p68). In fact, I would maintain that this is precisely what the isomorphism of God/nature amounts to, and should not be regarded as an inconsistency in Spinoza's ontology. That Spinoza emphasizes the eternity of part of the mind, which incorporates the body *qua* idea of the mind, is undeniable in the sense that mind has an idea of the "essence of body under the form of eternity."[36] The knowledge I have of my body differs in kind from the knowledge I have of anybody else's body, or that anybody else has of my or another body, in large part because of the isomorphism between *my* mind and body. Hence the worry that if two minds have eternal and adequate ideas of another body (not their own), there is no way to distinguish their token ideas, simply does not apply for Spinoza. If my analysis is correct, then I have shown that matter (and hence body) is integral to the individuation of the person; by incorporating both temporality and the concomitant materiality expressed in a hylomorphic ontology, the individual, male or female, retains its individuality while becoming one with God.[37] It is precisely this ontologically grounded moral theory that is so appealing to feminists.

4. "THE FEMININE" AS AN ONTOLOGICAL/ETHICAL CATEGORY

4.1. Feminist Critiques of Kantian Moral Theory

The metaphysical and epistemological principles adduced in Section 3 carry with them implications for both ethics and religious thought. Feminists have developed a moral theory that, following Carol Gilligan's ethics of care and responsibility, is contrasted with more "masculine" theories based on justice and universalizable values. Many feminists seek to elucidate a notion of the self that is not wholly autonomous but that is responsive to the vulnerability of others.[38] They suggest that ethics and responsibility emerge from human dependence and vulnerability, and they describe this dependence and vulnerability as "feminine" in character.

The feminist ethics of care is often contrasted to biblical models that emphasize obedience and law in contradistinction to care and responsibility. Sabina Lovibond, for example, argues that we ought not be so quick to reject our ancient Greek heritage in favor of a biblical theory of morality. Relying upon Matthew Arnold's distinction between "Hellenic" and "Hebraic" conceptions of morality, she contrasts the Hellenic emphasis upon "spontaneity of consciousness" as opposed to the Hebraic emphasis upon "strictness of consciousness" or obedience and argues that "we can see the opposition of 'justice' and 'care' . . . as a reworking of that between Hellenism (with its ideal of order and balance) and "Hebraism" (with its ideal of submission)."[39] Lovibond's point is that a counterweight to the Judaeo-Christian theme of unconditional obedience, which, for all its grandeur, is (in worldly terms) full of danger for women,"[40] can be found in Hellenism. The Judaeo-Christian moral code in general, and the Judaic insistence upon law and authority in particular, are regarded as failing to acknowledge women's full moral equality with men as moral agents.[41]

Kant's ethical system has for some feminist critics seemed to represent one of the least appealing theories in both Hellenism and Hebraism, and hence has come under particular attack.[42] On the Kantian view, generalized maxims are matters of morality only if they take on the form of universal and categorically necessary laws; the morally autonomous individual is one who grasps the categorical necessity of universal moral law and attempts to act accordingly. Emotion, desire, and inclination are contingent, and so do not enter into moral behavior. Inasmuch as the Kantian ethical norm privileges concerns of justice and rights over matters of care, emotions, close relationships, and so on, it is rejected by feminists as unduly masculinist and not sensitive to feminist realities. Just as feminists have rejected the "Hebraic" emphasis on obligation, so too, argues Marilyn Friedman, must feminists rethink their attitude toward the Kantian notion of moral autonomy. Rather than rejecting Kant altogether in favor of a "social conception of moral understanding" that in itself can neglect the moral competence of women, Friedman urges that a focus on individual moral capacity, as in the Kantian tradition, is required by any ethical perspective that aims to "challenge the conception of morality as obedience or the application of such a conception to women."[43]

4.2. Levinas and "the Feminine": Friend or Foe?

The feminist concern with ethics thus gives rise to two questions: first, does the move from a model of justice to one of care reinsert feminine concerns into a system that has focused upon male values and paradigms? Second, how do relational models replace more traditional ethical models based on notions of obedience and obligation? It is in this context that the works of Buber and Levinas are instructive. Leora Batnitzky has maintained that both Buber and Levinas have much to offer feminist thought in their respective emphases upon the vulnerability of human existence. "These Jewish philosophers and contemporary feminist philosophers of care agree that the fundamental experience of relationality grounds existence."[44] The receptivity of the human gives meaning not only to ethics but also to the relationship between God and the Jewish people.[45]

According to Levinas, the dialogical relation is both non-cognitive and non-reciprocal. Levinas uses the notion of "the feminine" to characterize this relation. This notion is developed both in his phenomenological works (*Time and the Other; Totality and Infinity*) and in his more expressly Jewish essays (for example, "And God Created Woman" and "Judaism and the Feminine"). In these latter pieces, Levinas explicitly equates Judaism – the "other" within a Christian, male-dominated Western milieu – with "the feminine" – itself "the other" within a male-construed ontology. Both Judaism and "the feminine" thus come to represent for Levinas moral spheres that have been silenced by philosophy's concern with Kantian universalizability and utilitarian theories of calculable justice.[46]

But Levinas's appropriation of "the feminine" as both an ontological and ethical category is itself controversial. His critics (Derrida, Irigaray, Sandford, et al.) have argued that "the feminine" in Levinas's works is linked with qualities belonging to the most conventional gender stereotypes: a gentle, self-effacing, intimate, familiar presence in the home that reinforces notions of weakness, tenderness, and frailty.[47] Stella Sandford, for example, maintains that the frank and unselfconscious account of the nature and the place of "the feminine" in *Totality and Infinity* is "gratingly patriarchal . . . the feminist case for Levinas does not look good."[48] But other feminist scholars have championed Levinas as an important supporter of feminist concerns.[49] Let us turn briefly, then, to those discussions in *Totality and Infinity* that are most relevant to this controversy.

In *Totality and Infinity*, Levinas states his project as one of reviving the notion of the subject: "this book does present itself as a defense of subjectivity . . . as founded in the idea of infinity."[50] The self for Levinas is totally at home in the world, totally alone. But, Levinas argues, the apparent independence of the self is possible only because the existence of the Other defines my awareness of my own existence.[51] In order to avoid the reduction of the Other to a mere phenomenological object, Levinas carefully describes the relationship with the Other as "a relation without relation,"[52] one in which the Other remains Other and is not reduced to another "same." The relation between self and other can occur through desire, and what Levinas calls "the face." Desire is seen as "desire for the absolutely Other"[53] and is founded in an erotic relation in which the loved one is caressed but not possessed. The term "*le visage*" (the face) reinforces the fact that the Other is simply there, present to me in an irreducible relation that Levinas calls *le face à face*, a relation that does not reduce the Other to an intentional object. In the context of ethics, the Other confers upon me my freedom, inasmuch as I am confronted with real choices with respect to behavior towards the Other.

We have seen that for Levinas, the Other comes to be understood as the ontological "feminine," outside the domain inhabited by the self, but necessary to its self-definition. Much of Levinas's discussion centers on the relationship, both ontological and moral, between self and Other, personified as "the feminine." Levinas describes the world of the separate ego as one of "enjoyment" (*jouissance*); the ego derives from the intimacy of home and dwelling an ability to recollect and represent. The intimacy of the home is revealed through the welcome of the other as "feminine." In *Time and the Other*, "the feminine" functions as the condition for the recollections of another. She herself does not recollect; she (passively) allows for the possibility of ethical relation, but she is not herself part of it.

It is here that feminist critics have found Levinas's ontology and subsequent moral theory problematic. When Same and Other come together and produce a child,[54] the metaphor of fecundity appears to dissolve into conventional gendered discourse: the feminine-Other allows for the possibility of the child with a male-Same. The self in Levinas's work is always a male self-described in relation with a feminine-other; it is the relation between father and son that results in the "redemption" that is so important in Levinas's ethical system. Weakness and passivity thus appear as manifestations of the feminine: in the words of Edith Wyschogrod, the helplessness of the beloved is "what makes the beloved to be what she is. To be the beloved is to be fragile and vulnerable. The world is always too gross and too cruel for the beloved."[55] The paternalism inherent in these passages is palpable.

And so it would appear that the very heart of Levinasian ethics, which domain feminists have wanted to reclaim as supportive of an "ethics of care," turns out at best to denigrate the feminine. Feminist reactions to Levinas's conception of "the feminine" have been varied. In a famous footnote in her work *The Second Sex*, Simone de Beauvoir castigated Levinas for those passages that marginalized "the feminine" as other.[56] Luce Irigaray leveled an even more trenchant critique, arguing that "the feminine" is apprehended from the point of view of man, through a purely erotic strategy that is dictated by male pleasure.[57] On Irigaray's reading, "the feminine" appears to Levinas as the "underside or reverse side of man's aspiration toward the light, as its negative."[58] In a similar vein, Tina Chanter argues that Levinas continues in the long-standing tradition of male-authored texts that figure "the feminine" as unknowable, mysterious, ineffable, unrepresentable, and intractable. Levinas repeats the "same exclusionary gesture that denies women language, and confines them to a gestural, corporeal asocial psychosis."[59]

And Catherine Chalier, while acknowledging that "the feminine" gives birth to a space that allows the masculine to move from ontology to ethics, without which the ethical stance would be impossible, nevertheless claims that Levinas has excluded "the feminine" from the ethical domain: the highest destiny (ethics) is "reserved for the masculine once it has been converted to ethics thanks to the feminine."[60] Could a woman have written these passages? Clearly not, argue Levinas's detractors.

Might it not be responded in Levinas's defense that "the feminine" does not apply to actual empirical women, and hence that such feminist worries are unfounded? Levinas himself, sensitive to the charges of de Beauvoir, Derrida, and others, tried to defend himself by arguing that "the feminine" does not designate a being, or empirical woman, but rather represents a *"façon de parler,"* a tendency, a way. Levinas's protestations notwithstanding, his ontology and subsequent moral theory remain problematic. In a carefully argued paper, Batnitzky, noting that Levinas (as well as Rosenzweig) were both Jewish men trying to articulate an alternate conception of philosophy and ethics from within the Western philosophical tradition that was historically largely Christian and hence in important ways anti-Jewish,[61] nevertheless maintains that their use of the feminine is uncritical. In using this type of language, they ultimately relegate women to the roles of mother and keeper of the home, the very roles that feminists have wanted to overcome. It is not a coincidence, she maintains, "that these two philosophers are considered more theologically 'Jewish' than some of their more rationalistic predecessors."[62] In fact, Buber's stress on reciprocity and on consciousness as an essential mode of relation turns out to be a welcome antidote to Levinas's and Rosenzweig's "more Heideggerian emphasis on the primacy of non-cognitive praxis."[63]

Levinas's feminine is thus left without a face. Levinas has appropriated the patriarchalism of monotheism, and once again "the feminine" has been removed from canonical philosophical discourse. His philosophy falls "radically short of ethics."[64] In this regard, Levinas is not alone; as Batnitzky and others have argued, Levinas's very use of the "feminine" was itself influenced by Rosenzweig's *Star of Redemption*, in which "the feminine" was utilized as an important theoretical category but was devoid of feminist concerns. Levinas has confined women to the private domain and to the hearth, adding legitimacy to such halakhic claims that because women are "private" individuals, they cannot count in a "public" prayer quorum.[65] The implications of this exclusion become all the more palpable when we turn to the area of Jewish liturgy and ritual.

5. FEMINISM AND PHILOSOPHY OF RELIGION

5.1. A Philosophy of Ritual?

Some of the most exciting and innovating recent work in feminist thought has occurred in the area of feminist theology. Feminist theologians have taken the reconstruction of gender paradigms into the theological realm, questioning patterns of theology that justify male dominance and female subordination, such as exclusive male language for God, the view that males are more like God than females, that only males can represent God as leaders in Church and society, or that women are created by God to be subordinate to males. Jewish feminists have followed suit, questioning the rituals and patterns of exclusion that have been so endemic to rabbinic Judaism.

The intercession of feminist theology has once again forced the question, "What has Athens to do with Jerusalem?" In one of the first attempts to articulate a feminist philosophy of religion, Pamela Anderson describes the typical philosophy of religion anthologies as utilizing both privileged-male history and masculine symbols: "If philosophy of religion is equated with rationally justifying belief in the existence of a God who is both male and patriarchal, then what role can feminists play except as a subject for radical critique and feminist subversion."[66] We tend to forget, she claims, that the theistic frame of reference accepts a very strange conception of God – a personal being without a body who is omniscient, omnipotent, omnibenevolent, eternal, and so on. If this conception of deity is not shared by feminists, or if it represents a male corruption of who we are, then why seek to either defend or challenge it? Instead, she suggests, "let us consider a shift away from philosophy's privileged Western point of view which has been identified as the God's-eye point of view or the view from nowhere."[67] Anderson urges feminist theologians to create an alternative sketch of philosophical conceptions of reason and belief that are not based on patriarchal assumptions of the Deity. She argues that gender considerations must be taken into account when discussing epistemological justification for religious beliefs; further, that arguments grounded in feminist concerns must evaluate belief and its constitution.

The majority of contemporary Jewish feminist theologians, while sharing Anderson's concerns about a male-biased philosophical theology, have nevertheless focused upon the more practical aspects of Judaism. They echo the pragmatic view of Amy Hollywood that "attention to the role of practice and ritual in religion will force feminist philosophers to understand religious beliefs and its objects in new ways."[68] Given the bodily nature of ritual and other forms of religious practice, any philosophy of religion that focuses upon them must take into account the nature of corporeality itself with respect to religious practice. Religion cannot be identified solely with belief; for many religious people, practice takes precedence over articles and statements of belief. It is here that feminist examination of ritual and practice can be of benefit to Jewish philosophers.

Despite the caveat expressed earlier by Boyarin, most Jewish feminist scholars agree that the halakhah is a document written by men for men, one in which women are conceived as "other."[69] Not only have women been marginalized from the text itself, but until the present century, traditional Jewish women have not been permitted to study the Law. Only in the late nineteenth and twentieth centuries have we been witness to a groundswell of Talmudic study among women. In light of this traditional exclusion, Jewish feminists have focused on the role played by halakhah in defining the constraints upon women in Jewish life. It is not the purpose of this chapter to examine the details of exclusion; they have been provided by many scholars.[70] Rather, in the final section of this chapter, I should like to generalize the exclusivity of halakhah by framing it in the context of an ontological theory rooted in time and temporality.

5.2. Ritual, Temporality, and Exclusion

That many of the commandments are subject to rigorous time conditions that affect the moment and nature of their performance has resulted in a well-ordered structure in the flux of time, a comprehensible pattern in the cycle of the seasons. I have argued elsewhere that the concept of time plays an important role in Jewish thought.[71] My final question in this study, however, is the extent to which notions of temporality have affected the status of women in Judaism. I shall argue that images of the "feminine" in Jewish thought can be traced to attitudes towards temporality itself, and the role played by time in Jewish practice.

We must fight the temptation to postulate a metaphysics of time upon pronouncements in the rabbinic corpus. For the Rabbis were not philosophers and were not interested in elucidating a philosophical theory of time *per se*. With the exception, perhaps, of *Ecclesiastes*, there is very little speculation of a specifically metaphysical nature in Biblical texts, little awareness of time as a metaphysical construct. Nevertheless, let me suggest that the historicity of the Bible associated with linear temporality does in fact exist; it can be underscored through three defining moments and represents a linearity that lies at the heart of the systematic exclusion of women. The first is represented by the moment of creation, the very (beginning) instant in which God gave momentum to temporality. Second, the people of Israel are marked by a covenant with God. This covenant, articulated first with Abraham, and culminated during the revelation at Sinai, defines the ongoing, linear relationship between a Deity and its people. Finally, the eschatological tenor of the prophets reinforces those moments in which the covenant is in jeopardy. Religious eschatology culminates in the kingdom of heaven, which represents the final consummation of past and present into the future.[72] In each of these three defining moments, temporality is juxtaposed against eternity, linearity against cyclicity, temporal flow against a static timelessness. And yet in all three cases, what marks the Jewish relationship with a Deity is the ongoing, temporal nature of these events.[73]

But these three defining moments – creation, covenant and revelation – which reflect temporal slices through which the Israelites experience their journey as the "chosen" people of God, function to marginalize women from the core of Jewish experience. Creation is construed as a linear event, an event rooted in the non-materiality of the Deity. The material, physical event of creation associated with women is absent from the Genesis account of creation. As Carole Ochs has so eloquently argued, "God's own nonphysicality makes the physical suspect, if not absolutely evil. If God, the perfect Creator, creates in a nonphysical way (by word alone), then our nonphysical creations are more divine than our physical creations . . . procreation is certainly not viewed as a central spiritual experience."[74] Furthermore, the covenant between God and Abraham, reiterated in the "brit milah," is characterized as an instant in a linear temporal model, an instant from which women are excluded by virtue of their sex. And as Plaskow has so strikingly reminded us, women were conspicuously absent from the moment of revelation: "At the central moment of Jewish history, women are invisible . . . the Otherness of women finds its way into the very center of Jewish experience."[75] The continual cyclic re-enactment of this Sinaitic event serves as a yearly reminder to women that temporal linearity has excluded them from the drama.

The contrast between the linear flow of events, associated with the human domain, and an eternal timeless domain associated with divinity, is reflected in feminist writing as well. Julia Kristeva suggests that "phallo-logocentric thought is founded on a repression of the semiotic and maternal body . . . whereas the semiotic order is cyclical and eternal, the symbolic order represents linear and sequential time."[76] The two orders lead to two kinds of writing. Masculine writing, which is linear, rational and objective, is governed by the rules of normal syntax, whereas feminine writing, which emphasizes rhythm, sound, and color, permits breaks in syntax to express what horrifies and disgusts us.[77] Both monumental and symbolic modes of temporality, associated with the female, "are found to be the fundamental, if not the sole, conceptions of time in numerous civilizations and experiences, particularly mystical ones."[78] They are contrasted by Kristeva with linear time, associated with the temporality of history. This conception of linear temporality is "readily labeled masculine and is at once both civilizational and obsessional."[79]

Nowhere is the identification of gender with time manifested more clearly than in the rabbinic discussion of women's exemption from positive time-bound ritual commandments, a discussion in which Maimonides the legalist plays an important role. In the following well-known mishnah, women's and men's obligations are compared with respect to ritual observance. "And all positive mitzvot that are time-bound (*mitzvot aseh she-ha-zeman gerama*), men are obligated but women are exempt. And all positive *mitzvot* that are not time-bound, the same holds for men and for women, they are [both] obligated. And all negative *mitzvot*, whether or not time-bound, the same holds for men and for women, they are obligated."[80] In this text, both women and men are obligated to performance of three out of four categories: negative time-bound commandments, negative non-time-bound commandments, and positive non-time-bound commandments. Only in the area of positive time-bound commandments are women exempt from obligation. Examples of positive time-bound commandments are given in the Tosefta: "What is an example of a positive time-bound commandment? *Succah, lulav, shofar, tzitzit,* and *tefillin.*"[81]

In articulating these examples, the rabbis were apparently exempting women from observances that were to be performed at a particular time of day. But the rabbis do not explain *why* it is that women are exempt from these positive time-bound commandments. Why is it, in other words, that the category of time-bound commandments was chosen to delineate women's exemption? Judith Hauptmann examines some of the reasons commonly given for this exemption – for example, that performance of these commandments might interfere with women's domestic responsibilities, and she finds these apologetic reasons inadequate.[82] Her own suggestion is that these exemptions reflect the fact that a woman is owned by another and therefore "cannot be independently obligated to perform them [positive time-bound rituals]."[83] Pointing out that the phrase "positive time-bound" is mentioned only in connection with women, Hauptmann argues further that the very taxonomy exists only to distinguish between a women's ritual obligations and her exemptions; therefore the essence of the distinction must reside in the meaning of the phrase itself – namely in that these are the "key mitzvot of marking Jewish time."[84] By exempting women from those very ritual acts that mark Jewish time, women are cut off from the temporal patterns that define a religious community. If the positive time-bound commandments represent the key commandments involved in marking time, and if the Children of Israel are commanded to sanctify time, then clearly women are excluded from this enterprise. Activities such as reciting the *Shema* three times a day and putting on phylacteries are central public duties that mark the passage of time. By exempting women from these duties, temporality itself has been utilized to erode the relation between women and the Deity.[85]

6. CONCLUDING REMARKS

In this Chapter, I have attempted to unravel the interweaving of several strands within feminist thought and Jewish philosophy: strands connected to philosophical methodology having to do with the role of reason; implications of this methodology with respect to issues in metaphysics, epistemology, and ethics; and the reverberations of both matter and time pertaining to gender and sexuality. The identification of materiality itself with the female carries with it implications with respect to ontology, epistemology, ethics, and theodicy; these implications reappear throughout modern Jewish philosophy. The very existence of evil can be associated with the material substratum, accounting for how an omnipotent, omniscient, benevolent Deity can permit an imperfect world. I ultimately explored the relevance of materiality to the ontology of time, arguing that temporality has been used as a marginalizing device to exclude women from essential roles within normative Judaism.

If in fact the Torah itself, *pace* divine revelation, relegates women to a position of ontological inequality, then to paraphrase Susannah Heschel, either the God who has revealed the Torah is a malevolent deity or the Torah is not God's revelation, but merely the projection of a patriarchal society intent on preserving its status quo.[86] Many feminists have tried to suggest that the Torah must contain the basis within itself for eliminating the subservience of women by invoking 'justice' as an absolute criterion. Consider Cynthia Ozick's rallying cry: "if, in the most fundamental text and texture of Torah, the lesser status of women is not worthy of a great "thou shalt not," then perhaps there is nothing inherently offensive in it, then perhaps there is no essential injustice, then perhaps the common status of women is not only sanctioned, but, in fact, divinely ordained?"[87] More recently, arguing from the perspective of Jewish orthodoxy, Tamar Ross has taken up Ozick's challenge, and presents a compelling argument that halakhah contains within itself the wherewithal to counteract the centuries of patriarchy. In a daring work, she begins from Yeshayahu Leibowitz's statement that "the question of Women and Judaism is more crucial than all the political problems of the state."[88] Ross claims that this question goes far beyond practical considerations, and addresses "moral sensibilities that are pivotal to human experience, touching upon religious attitudes and principles that define our total vision of ourselves, the nature of human sexuality, the family, and society at large."[89] Recognizing that feminist concerns tear at the heart of Judaism, Ross argues that "Jewish tradition itself provides ways and means of dealing with the challenges."[90]

In a final note, however, I must point out the irony involved in using the criterion of "justice," the very value rejected by feminist philosophers of care, in an attempt to redress the wrongs done to women. Ozick's query, articulated in 1983, and reiterated by Heschel, remains unanswered: "what constitutes the revealed, immutable essence of Judaism and what should be viewed as merely a temporal, human invention?"[91] If Jewish philosophers are willing to engage this issue dialectically, perhaps they can start by responding to Ozick's query, a query that ultimately forces a rethinking of Judaism, by determining whether "justice" is even a category applicable to Jewish thought and practice.

Notes

1. For an excellent introduction to the state of the field in feminist philosophy, see the collection of articles in *The Cambridge Companion to Feminism in Philosophy*, edited by Miranda Fricker and Jennifer Hornsby (Cambridge: Cambridge University Press, 2000). This work covers recent scholarship in metaphysics, epistemology, ethics, history of philosophy, and philosophy of language and mind.
2. Plaskow, *Standing Again at Sinai*, p. 63.
3. For an introduction to this vast literature, see, for example, Rachel Biale, *Women and Jewish Law: An Exploration of Women's Issues in Halakhic*

Sources (New York: Schocken, 1984); Judith Plaskow, *Standing Again at Sinai: Judaism from a Feminist Perspective* (New York: Harper & Row, 1990); Tamar Ross, *Expanding the Palace of Torah: Orthodoxy and Feminism.* (Waltham: Brandeis University Press, 2004).

4. Hava Tirosh-Rothschild, ed., *Women and Gender in Jewish Philosophy* (Bloomington: Indiana University Press, 2004).

5. See Genevieve Lloyd, *The Man of Reason: "Male" and "Female" in Western Philosophy* (Minneapolis: University of Minnesota Press, 1984).

6. See, for example, Sandra Harding and Merrill B. Hintikka, ed., *Discovering Reality: Feminist Perspectives on Epistemology, Metaphysics, Methodology, and Philosophy of Science* (Dordrecht: Reidel, 1983); and Sandra Harding, *Whose Science? Whose Knowledge?* (Milton Keynes, Buckinghamshire, UK: Open University Press, 1991).

7. See Linda Martin Alcoff, "Is the Feminist Critique of Reason Rational?" in *Philosophical Topics* 23 (1995) p. 8.

8. Plaskow, *Standing Again at Sinai*, p. xi.

9. Joseph Soloveitchik, *The Lonely Man of Faith.* (New York: Doubleday, 1992), p. 13.

10. Ibid. p. 13.

11. Ibid. p. 18.

12. Ibid. p. 41.

13. Ibid. p. 27.

14. Ibid. p. 32.

15. Ibid. p. 39.

16. Ibid. p. 53.

17. Ibid. p. 68.

18. Ibid. p. 69.

19. Joseph B. Soloveitchik, *Halakhic Man*, translated by Lawrence Kaplan (Philadelphia: Jewish Publication Society, 1983), pp. 43–4.

20. Reinier Munk, *The Rationale of Halakhic Man: Joseph B. Soloveitchik's Conception of Jewish Thought* (Amsterdam: J. C. Gieben, 1996), p. 82.

21. Soloveitchik, *Lonely Man of Faith*, p. 69.

22. Ibid. p. 70.

23. Ibid. p. 71.

24. Ibid. p. 72.

25. Ibid. p. 104.

26. Aristotle, *Metaphysics*, 1.5 986a 22-b2. For a penetrating discussion of the implications of Pythagoreanism in Western culture, see Margaret Wertheim, *Pythagoras' Trousers: God, Physics and the Gender Wars* (New York: W. W. Norton & Co., 1995).

27. Eve Browning Cole, *Philosophy and Feminist Criticism* (New York: Paragon House, 1993), p. 61.

28. Cole, *Philosophy and Feminist Criticism*, p. 62.

29. Ibid. p. 9.

30. Sara Heinamaa, "The Soul-Body Union and Sexual Difference from Descartes to Merleau-Ponty and Beauvoir," in *Feminist Reflections on the History of Philosophy*, edited by Lilli Alanen and Charlotte Witt (Dordrecht: Kluwer Academic Publishers, 2004), p. 137.

31. See Peter Brown, *The Body and Society: Men, Women, and Sexual Renunciation in Early Christianity* (New York: Random House, 1989), p. 266–7.

32. Daniel Boyarin, *Carnal Israel: Reading Sex and Talmudic Culture* (Berkeley: University of California Press, 1993), p. 5.

33. Heidi Miriam Ravven, "Spinoza's Ethics of the Liberation of Desire," in *Feminism and Jewish Philosophy*, edited by Hava Tirosh-Samuelson (Bloomington: Indiana University Press, 2004), p. 82.

34. See Ravven, "Spinoza's Ethics," p. 86.

35. Ibid.

36. For a depiction of the three levels of knowledge, see Spinoza, *Ethics*, 2p40s2 ff.

37. It is only fair to mention Spinoza's notorious statement in *Tractatus Politicus* ch xi, where he calls into question women's full humanity. I acknowledge this to be a problem, but consider it to be a minor chord in an otherwise dominant feminist-friendly ontology. In most contexts, Spinoza presumes women's full humanity, for example in recommending marriage at its best as a friendship between equals devoted to mutual independence. (E468S on Eve)

38. Leora Batnitzky, "Dependency and Vulnerability: Jewish and Feminist Existentialist Constructions of the Human," in *Women and Gender in Jewish Philosophy*, ed. by Hava Tirosh-Samuelson (Bloomington: Indiana University Press, 2004), p. 128.

39. Sabina Lovibond, "Feminism in Ancient Philosophy," in *The Cambridge Companion to Feminism in Philosophy*, edited by Miranda Fricker and Jennifer Hornsby (Cambridge: Cambridge University Press, 2000), p. 21.

40. Ibid, p. 23.

41. Marilyn Friedman, "Feminism in Ethics: Concepts of Autonomy," in *The Cambridge Companion to Feminism in Philosophy*, edited by Miranda Fricker and Jennifer Hornsby (Cambridge: Cambridge University Press, 2000), p. 215.

42. Ibid. p. 214.

43. Ibid. p. 215.

44. Batnitzky, "Dependency and Vulnerability," p. 129.

45. Ibid. p. 130.

46. Ibid. p. 137.

47. Levinas, *Totality and Infinity*, pp. 165–6; See Davis, Colin. *Levinas: An Introduction* (Notre Dame: University of Notre Dame Press), 1996.

48. Stella Sandford, "Levinas, Feminism and the Feminine," in *The Cambridge Companion to Levinas*, edited by Simon Critchley and Robert Bernasconi (Cambridge: Cambridge University Press, 2002), p. 147.

49. See, for example, Claire Elise Katz, who maintains that "Levinas's characterization of 'the feminine' can be viewed as positively inflected. Claire Elise Katz, "From Eros to Modernity: Love, Death, and "the Feminine" in the Philosophy of Emmanuel Levinas," in *Women and Gender in Jewish Philosophy*, edited by Hava Tirosh-Samuelson (Bloomington: Indiana University Press, 2004), p. 155.

50. Emmanuel Levinas, *Totality and Infinity: An Essay on Exteriority*, trans. Alphonso Lingis (Pittsburgh: Duquesne University Press, 1969), p. 26.
51. Compare Levinas's description of the interaction of the self and the Other with that of Heidegger in *Being and Time*. Whereas Heidegger's ontological locus is *Dasein*, that of Levinas is always self-Other.
52. Levinas, *Totality and Infinity*, p. 79–80.
53. Ibid. p. 34.
54. Ibid. p. 266.
55. Edith Wyschogrod, *Emmanuel Levinas: The Problem of Ethical Metaphysics* (New York: Fordham University Press, 2000), p. 127.
56. See Simone de Beauvoir's comments in *The Second Sex* translated and edited by H.M. Paishley (New York: Random House, 1974), pp. xxxiii–xxxiv.
57. Luce Irigaray, "Questions to Emmanuel Levinas: On the Divinity of Love," in *Re-Reading Levinas*, edited by Robert Bernasconi and Simon Critchley (Bloomington: Indiana University Press, 1991), p. 109.
58. Ibid. p. 109. The description of pleasure given by Levinas is unacceptable to Irigaray in that it presents man as the sole subject exercising his desire and his appetite upon the woman, who is deprived of subjectivity except to seduce him. So the woman's pleasure is alienated to that of the man, according to the most traditional of scenarios of temptation and fall. In Irigaray's opinion, "if there is a fall, it is located in the reduction of the feminine to the passive, to the past tense, and to the object of man's pleasure ... " See Irigaray, "Questions," p. 115.
59. Tina Chanter, *Time, Death and the Feminine: Levinas with Heidegger* (Stanford: Stanford University Press, 2001), p. 258.
60. Catherine Chalier, "Ethics and the Feminine," in *Re-reading Levinas* (Bloomington: Indiana University Press, 1991), p. 123.
61. Batnitzky, "Dependency and Vulnerability," p. 144.
62. Ibid. p. 147.
63. Ibid. p. 147.
64. Irigaray, "Questions," p. 113.
65. Consider, for example, the arguments made by Moshe Meiselman in *Jewish Women in Jewish Law* (New York: Ktav Publishing, 1978). Meiselman argues halakhically that because women are "private" by nature, they cannot engage in "public" activities, and so even ten women do not constitute a prayer quorum. On these grounds, he rules out women's prayer groups.
66. Pamela Sue Anderson, "Feminist Theology as Philosophy of Religion," in *The Cambridge Companion to Feminist Theology*, edited by Susan Frank Parsons (Cambridge: Cambridge University Press, 2002), p. 43. See also P. S. Anderson, *A Feminist Philosophy of Religion: The Rationality and Myths of Religious Belief* (Oxford: Blackwell, 1998).
67. Anderson, "Feminist Theology," p. 54.
68. Amy Hollywood, "Practice, Belief and Feminist Philosophy of Religion," in *Feminist Philosophy of Religion*, edited by Pamela Sue Anderson and Beverly Clark (London: Routledge, 2004), p. 226.

69. Rochelle Millen argues that the textual tradition, while presented as if it were gender-neutral, nevertheless derives from men and a masculine framework. It is not possible to eliminate the patriarchal perspective from the Talmud. See Rochelle Millen, *Women, Birth and Death in Jewish Law and Practice* (Waltham: Brandeis University Press, 2004), p. 4. See also Judith Hauptmann, *Rereading the Rabbis: A Woman's Voice* (Boulder: Westview Press), 1998.

70. For a particularly careful examination, see the recent work by Tamar Ross, *Expanding the Palace of Torah: Orthodoxy and Feminism* (Waltham: Brandeis University Press, 2004). We shall return to her work later.

71. See T. M. Rudavsky, *Time Matters: Creation, Time and Cosmology in Medieval Jewish Philosophy* (Albany: SUNY Press, 2000).

72. See P. Steensgaard, "Time in Judaism," in *Religion and Time*, ed. A. N. Balslav and J. N. Mohanty (Leiden: Brill, 1993), pp. 77ff, for a discussion of the importance of religious eschatology.

73. The modern Jewish philosopher perhaps most attuned to the importance of time in defining the relationship between God and Israel is Franz Rosenzweig, whose work *Star of Redemption*, steeped as it is in a Heideggerian analysis of time, plays temporality and eternality against each another. For a sensitive examination of the role of time played in Rosenzweig, see Peter Gordon, *Rosenzweig and Heidegger: Between Judaism and German Philosophy* (Berkeley: University of California Press, 2003).

74. Carole R. Ochs, *Women and Spirituality* (London: Rowman and Littlefield, 1997), p. 21.

75. See Judith Plaskow, *Standing Again at Sinai: Judaism from a Feminist Perspective* (New York: Harper Collins, 1990), p. 25.

76. Julia Kristeva, "Womens Time," *Signs: Journal of Women in Culture and Society* (Autumn 1981), pp. 13–35.

77. Tirosh-Rothschild, "Dare to Know," p. 93.

78. Kristeva, "Womens Time," p. 17.

79. Ibid. p. 18.

80. *Mishnah Kiddushin* 1:7b, Hauptmann, *Rereading the Rabbis*, p. 224.

81. *Kiddushin* 1:10, quoted in Hauptmann, *Rereading the Rabbis*, p. 224.

82. Hauptmann, *Rereading the Rabbis*, p. 225. See also Ross, *Expanding the Palace of Torah*, pp. 33ff, where a similar dismissal of apologetics is presented.

83. Hauptmann, *Rereading the Rabbis*, p. 226.

84. Ibid. p. 227.

85. See Rochelle L. Millen, *Women, Birth, and Death in Jewish Law and Practice* (Hanover and London: University Press of New England, 2004).

86. Susanna Heschel, "Feminism," in *Contemporary Jewish Religious Thought: Original Essays on Critical Concepts, Movements, and Beliefs*, ed. Arthur A. Cohen and Paul Mendes-Flohr (New York: Scribner, 1987), p. 255.

87. Cynthia Ozick, "Notes toward Finding the Right Question," in *On Being a Jewish Feminist: A Reader*, edited by Susannah Heschel (New York: Schocken, 1983), 120–51.
88. Ross, *Expanding the Palace of Torah*, p. xiii.
89. Ibid, p. xv.
90. Ibid., p. xvii
91. Heschel, "Feminism," p. 256.

Bibliography

GENERAL SURVEYS ON MODERN JEWISH THOUGHT

Altmann, A. *Essays in Jewish Intellectual History*. Hanover, New Hampshire and London: University Press of New England, 1981.

Bouretz, Pierre. *Témoins du futur. Philosophie et messianisme*. Paris: Gallimard, 2003.

Brenner, Michael. *The Renaissance of Jewish Culture in Weimar Germany*. New Haven: Yale University Press, 1996.

Cohen, Arthur A., and Mendes-Flohr, Paul, editors. *Contemporary Jewish Religious Thought*. New York: Scribners, 1987.

Davidowicz, Lucy S., editor. *The Golden Tradition: Jewish Life and Thought in Eastern Europe*. Boston: Beacon Press, 1967.

Eisen, Arnold M. *Rethinking Modern Judaism*. Chicago: University of Chicago Press, 1998.

Fackenheim, Emil L. *Encounters between Judaism and Modern Philosophy*. New York, NY: Basic Books, 1973.

Fackenheim, Emil L. *Jewish Philosophers and Jewish Philosophy*, edited by Michael L. Morgan. Bloomington: Indiana University Press, 1996.

Frank, Daniel H. and Oliver Leaman, eds. *History of Jewish Philosophy*. London: Routledge, 1997.

Funkenstein, Amos. *Perceptions of Jewish History*. Berkeley and Los Angeles: University of California Press, 1993.

Guttmann, Julius. *Philosophies of Judaism*. New York: Schocken, 1964.

Mendes-Flohr, Paul, and Reinharz, Jehuda. *The Jew in the Modern World*. Oxford and New York: Oxford University Press, 1995.

Morgan, Michael. *Dilemmas in Modern Jewish Thought: The Dialectics of Revelation and History*. Bloomington and Indianapolis: Indiana University Press, 1992.

Mosès, Stéphane. *L'Ange de l'Histoire. Rosenzweig, Benjamin, Scholem*. Paris: Éditions du Seuil, 1992.

Myers, David N. *Resisting History: Historicism and its Discontents in German-Jewish Thought*. Princeton: Princeton University Press, 2003.

Ravitzky, Aviezer. *Messianism, Zionism, and Jewish Religious Radicalism*, translated by Michael Swirsky and Jonathan Chipman. Chicago: University of Chicago Press, 1996.

Rynhold, Daniel. *Two Models of Jewish Philosophy: Justifying One's Practices*. Oxford: Oxford University Press, 2005.

Seeskin, Kenneth. *Autonomy in Jewish Philosophy*. Cambridge and New York: Cambridge University Press, 2001.

THE SIXTEENTH AND SEVENTEENTH CENTURIES: SPINOZA AND OTHERS

Primary Texts by Spinoza

Spinoza, Baruch. *Complete Works*, translated by Samuel Shirley, edited by Michael L. Morgan. Indianapolis: Hackett Publishing, 2002.

Spinoza, Baruch. *Spinoza Opera*, 5 volumes, edited by Carl Gebhardt. Heidelberg: Carl Winters Verlag, 1972.

Spinoza, Baruch. *The Collected Works of Spinoza*, vol. 1, translated by Edwin Curley. Princeton: Princeton University Press, 1984.

Spinoza, Baruch. *Theologico-Political Treatise*, translated by Samuel Shirley. Indianapolis: Hackett, 1998.

Secondary Literature

Cooperman, Bernard, ed. *Jewish Thought in the Sixteenth Century*. Cambridge: Harvard University Press, 1983.

Garrett, Don, ed. *The Cambridge Companion to Spinoza*. Cambridge: Cambridge University Press, 1996.

Harvey, Warren Zev. "A Portrait of Spinoza as a Maimonidean." In *Journal of the History of Philosophy*, 19 (1981): 151–172.

Levy, Ze'ev. *Baruch or Benedict: On Some Jewish Aspects of Spinoza's Philosophy*. New York: Peter Lang, 1989.

Mason, Richard. *The God of Spinoza*. Cambridge: Cambridge University Press, 1997.

Nadler, Steven. *Spinoza: A Life*. Cambridge: Cambridge University Press, 1999.

Nadler, Steven. *Spinoza's Heresy: Immortality and the Jewish Mind*. Oxford: Oxford University Press, 2004.

Popkin, Richard. "Some New Light on Spinoza's Science of Bible Study." In *Spinoza and the Sciences*, edited by Marjorie Grene and Deborah Nails. Dordrecht: Reidel, 1980.

Smith, Steven B. *Spinoza, Liberalism, and the Question of Jewish Identity*. New Haven: Yale University Press, 1997.

Twersky, Isadore, and Bernard Septimus, editors. *Jewish Thought in the Seventeenth Century*. Cambridge, MA: Harvard University Press, 1987.

Walther, Manfred. "Was/Is Spinoza a Jewish Philosopher? Spinoza in the Struggle for a Modern Jewish Identity in Germany: A Meta-Reflection." In *Studia Spinozana*, 13 (1997): 207–237.

Wolfson, Harry Austryn. *The Philosophy of Spinoza*, 2 vols. Cambridge: Harvard University Press, 1934.

Yovel, Yirmiyahu. *Spinoza and Other Heretics: The Marrano of Reason*. Princeton: Princeton University Press, 1989.

Yovel, Yirmiyahu. "Biblical Interpretation as Philosophical Praxis: A Study of Spinoza and Kant." In *Journal of the History of Philosophy*, XI (1973): 189–212.

THE ENLIGHTENMENT: MOSES MENDELSSOHN, SOLOMON MAIMON, AND OTHERS

Primary Texts in English Translation

Friedländer, David. *A Debate on Jewish Emancipation and Christian Theology in Old Berlin*, translated and edited by Richard Crouter and Julie Klassen. Indianapolis: Hackett Publishing, 2004.

Maimon, Salomon. *Salomon Maimon: an Autobiography*, translated by J. Clark Murray. Urbana: University of Illinois Press, 2001.

Mendelssohn, Moses. *Jerusalem, or on Religious Power and Judaism*, translated by Allan Arkush and edited by Alexander Altmann. Hanover and London: University Press of New England, 1983.

Mendelssohn, Moses. *Philosophical Writings*, translated and edited by Daniel O. Dahlstrom. Cambridge: Cambridge University Press, 1997.

Secondary Literature

Altmann, A. *Moses Mendelssohn: A Biographical Study*. Tuscaloosa: University of Alabama Press, 1973.

Arkush, Allan. *Moses Mendelssohn and the Enlightenment*. Albany: State University of New York Press, 1994.

Feiner, Shmuel. "Mendelssohn and Mendelssohn's Disciples: A Reexamination." In *The Year Book of the Leo Baeck Institute*, XL (1995): 133–167.

Feiner, Shmuel. *Moshe Mendelssohn*. Jerusalem: Zalman Shazar Center, 2005.

Feiner, Shmuel. *The Jewish Enlightenment*. Philadelphia: University of Pennsylvania Press, 2002.

Gideon Freudenthal, ed. *Salomon Maimon: Rational Dogmatist, Empirical Skeptic: Critical Assessments*. Dordrecht: Kluwer, 2004.

Harvey, Warren Zev. "Mendelssohn's Heavenly Politics." In *Perspectives on Jewish Thought and Mysticism*, edited by Alfred L. Ivry, Elliot R. Wolfson, and Allan Arkush. Amsterdam: Harwood, 1998.

Katz, Jacob. "To Whom was Mendelssohn Replying in his *Jerusalem*?" In *Zion*, 36, nos. 1–2 (1971): 116f.

Katz, Jacob. *Tradition and Crisis*, translated by Dov Bernard Cooperman. New York: New York University Press, 1993.

Melamed, Yitzhak. "Salomon Maimon and the Rise of Spinozism in Germany." In *Journal of the History of Philosophy*, 42:1 (2004): 57–96.

Sorkin, David. *Moses Mendelssohn and the Religious Enlightenment*. Berkeley and Los Angeles: University of California Press, 1996.

THE NINETEENTH CENTURY

Primary Texts

Gans, Eduard. *Eduard Gans (1797–1839): Hegelianer-Jude-Europäer. Texte und Dokumente*, edited by Norbert Waszek. Frankfurt am Main: Peter Lang Verlag, 1991.

Hirsch, Samson Raphael. *The Collected Writings*. Nanuet, NY: Feldheim Publishers, 1995.

Krochmal, Nachman. *Kitve Rabbi Nachman Krochmal*, edited by Simon Raw-idowicz, 2nd edition. Waltham, MA: Ararat Press, 1961.

Secondary Literature

Habermas, Jürgen. "The German Idealism of the Jewish Philosophers," translated by Frederick G. Lawrence. In Habermas, *Religion and Rationality: Essays on Reason, God, and Modernity*, edited by Eduardo Mendieta. Cambridge: MIT Press, 2002.

Harris, Jay. *Krochmal: Guiding the Perplexed of the Age*. New York, NY: New York University Press, 1993.

Yovel, Yirmiyahu. *Dark Riddle: Hegel, Nietzsche and the Jews*. University Park: Pennsylvania State University Press, 1998.

HERMANN COHEN

Primary Texts

Cohen, Hermann. *Jüdische Schriften*, edited by Bruno Strauß. Berlin: Schwetschke Verlag, 1924.

Cohen, Hermann. *Religion of Reason out of the Sources of Judaism*, translated and with an introduction by Simon Kaplan, 2nd edition. Atlanta: Scholars Press, 1995.

Secondary Literature

Poma, Andrea. *The Critical Philosophy of Hermann Cohen*, translated by John Denton. Albany: SUNY Press, 1997.

Zank, Michael. *The Idea of Atonement in the Philosophy of Hermann Cohen*. Providence: Brown Judaic Studies, 2000.

FRANZ ROSENZWEIG

Primary Texts

Rosenzweig, Franz. *Franz Rosenzweig: Der Mensch und sein Werk*. Volumes I–II: *Briefe und Tagebucher*; Volume III: *Zweistromland*. Dordrecht: Martinus Nijhoff, 1984.

Rosenzweig, Franz. *Die "Gritli"-Briefe: Briefe an Margrit Rosenstock-Huessy*, edited by Inken Rühle and Reinhold Mayer. Tübingen: Bilam, 2002.

Rosenzweig, Franz. *Franz Rosenzweig, Philosophical and Theological Writings*, translated and edited with notes and commentary by Paul W. Franks and Michael L. Morgan. Indianapolis and Cambridge: Hackett Publishing, 2000.

Rosenzweig, Franz. *God, Man, and the World*, edited and translated by Barbara Galli. Syracuse, NY: University Press, 1998.

Rosenzweig, Franz. *Hegel und der Staat*. München and Berlin: Verlag R. Oldenbourg, 1920.

Rosenzweig, Franz. *On Jewish Learning*, edited by Nahum Glatzer. New York: Schocken Books, 1965.
Rosenzweig, Franz. *The Star of Redemption*, translated by William W. Hallo. New York: Holt, Rinehart and Winston, 1971. Reprinted, Notre Dame: University of Notre Dame Press, 1985. (In German) *Der Stern der Erlösung*, 4th edition. Frankfurt am Main: Suhrkamp, 1993.
Rosenzweig, Franz. *Understanding the Sick and the Healthy: A View of World, Man, and God*, translated and edited by Nahum Glatzer. Cambridge: Harvard University Press, 1999.

Secondary Literature

Batnitzky, Leora. *Idolatry and Representation: The Philosophy of Franz Rosenzweig Reconsidered*. Princeton: Princeton University Press, 2000.
Bieberich, Ulrich. *Wenn die Geschichte göttlich wäre: Rosenzweig's Auseinandersetzung mit Hegel*. St. Ottilien, Germany: Verlag Erzabtei St. Ottilien, 1989.
Freund, Else. *Die Existenzphilosophie Franz Rosenzweigs*. Hamburg: Felix Meiner, 1959.
Gibbs, Robert. *Correlations in Rosenzweig and Levinas*. Princeton: Princeton University Press, 1992.
Glatzer, Nahum. *Franz Rosenzweig: His Life and Thought*. New York: Schocken, 1953.
Gordon, Peter Eli. *Rosenzweig and Heidegger: Between Judaism and German Philosophy*. Berkeley, Los Angeles, and London: University of California Press, 2003.
Gordon, Peter Eli. "Rosenzweig Redux: The Reception of German-Jewish Thought." In *Jewish Social Studies*, Vol. 8, No. 1, Fall (2001): 1–57.
Löwith, Karl. "M. Heidegger and F. Rosenzweig, or, Temporality and Eternity." In *Philosophy and Phenomenological Research*, Volume III, No. 1, September (1942): 53–77.
Mendes-Flohr Paul, ed. *The Philosophy of Franz Rosenzweig*. Hanover: University Press of New England for Brandeis University Press, 1988.
Santner, Eric. *On the Psychotheology of Everyday Life: Reflections on Freud and Rosenzweig*. Chicago: University of Chicago Press, 2001.

ISAAC BREUER

Primary Texts

Breuer, Isaac. *Concepts of Judaism*, edited by Jacob S. Levinger. Jerusalem: Israel Universities Press, 1974.
Breuer, Isaac. *Mein Weg*. Jerusalem and Zürich: Morascha Verlag, 1988.

Secondary Literature

Mittleman, Alan. *Between Kant and Kabbalah: An Introduction to Isaac Breuer's Philosophy of Judaism*. Albany: SUNY Press, 1990.

MARTIN BUBER

Primary Texts

Buber, Martin. The *Martin Buber Reader*, edited by Asher Biemann. New York: Palgrave Macmillan, 2002.

Buber, Martin. *Between Man and Man*. New York: Macmillan, 1965.

Buber, Martin. *Daniel, Dialogues on Realization*, translated with an introductory essay by Maurice Friedman. New York: Holt, Rinehart and Winston, 1965.

Buber, Martin. *Eclipse of God*, translated by Maurice Friedman et al. Atlantic Highlands, NJ: Humanities Press, 1988.

Buber, Martin. *Hasidism and Modern Man*, translated by Maurice Friedman. New York: Harper, 1966.

Buber, Martin. *I and Thou*, translated by Ronald Gregor Smith. New York: Charles Scribner's Sons, 1958. Also translated by Walter Kaufmann, New York: Scribner's, 1970.

Buber, Martin. *On Judaism*, translated by Eva Jospe and edited by Nahum Glatzer. New York: Schocken Books, 1967.

Buber, Martin. *On the Bible*, edited by Nahum Glatzer. New York: Schocken, 1982.

Buber, Martin. *Scripture and Translation*, translated by Lawrence Rosenwald and Everett Fox. Bloomington: Indiana University Press, 1994.

Buber, Martin. *The Prophetic Faith*. New York: Harper and Row, 1949.

Buber, Martin. *The Knowledge of Man*, edited by Maurice Friedman and translated by Maurice Friedman and Ronald Gregor Smith. New York: Harper & Row, 1965.

Secondary Literature

Diamond, Malcolm. *Martin Buber: Jewish Existentialist*. Oxford: Oxford University Press, 1960.

Friedman, Maurice. *Martin Buber's Life and Work*. 3 volumes. New York: Dutton, 1981–1985.

Horowitz, Rivka. *Buber's Way to 'I and Thou'*. Heidelberg: Lambert Schneider, 1978. Reprinted New York: The Jewish Publication Society, 1988.

Kepnes, Steven. *The Text as Thou: Martin Buber's Dialogical Hermeneutics and Narrative Theology*. Bloomington: Indiana Universiy Press, 1992.

Kohanski, Alexander. *Martin Buber's Philosophy of Interhuman Relation*. London: Associated University Presses, 1982.

Mendes-Flohr, Paul. *From Mysticism to Dialogue: Martin Buber's Transformation of German Social Thought*. Detroit: Wayne State University Press, 1989.

Schaeder, Grete. *The Hebrew Humanism of Martin Buber*, translated by Noah J. Jacobs. Detroit: Wayne State University Press, 1973.

Schilpp, Paul A., and Freidman, Maurice S., eds. *The Philosophy of Martin Buber*. LaSalle, IL: Open Court, 1967.

Scholem, Gershom. "Martin Buber's Conception of Judaism," in *On Jews and Judaism in Crisis: Selected Essays*, edited by Werner Dannhauser.

Vermes, Pamela. *Buber on God and the Perfect Man*. London: Littman Library, 1994.

WALTER BENJAMIN

Primary Texts in English Translation

Benjamin, Walter. *Illuminations*, translated by H. Zohn. New York: Harcourt, Brace & World, 1955.

Benjamin, Walter. *The Correspondence of Gershom Scholem and Walter Benjamin, 1932–1940*, translated by Gary Smith and André Lefèvre. New York: Schocken, 1989.

Benjamin, Walter. *Selected Writings*, edited by Michael W. Jennings. 4 vols. Cambridge: Harvard University Press, 1996–2003.

Secondary Literature

Alter, Robert. *Necessary Angels*. Cambridge: Harvard University Press, 1991.

Brodersen, Momme. *Walter Benjamin, A Biography*, translated by Malcom R. Green and Ingrida Ligers. London: Verso, 1996.

Rabinbach, Anson. "Between Enlightenment and Apocalypse: Benjamin, Bloch and Modern Jewish Messianism." In *New German Critique*, 34 (1985): 78–124. Reprinted in *In the Shadow of Catastrophe*. Berkeley: University of California Press, 1997.

Scholem, Gershom. *Walter Benjamin: Story of a Friendship*, translated by H. Zohn. Philadelphia: The Jewish Publication Society, 1981.

Witte, Bernd. *Walter Benjamin: An Intellectual Biography*. Detroit: Wayne State University Press, 1985.

GERSHOM SCHOLEM

Primary Texts in English

Scholem, Gershom. *From Berlin to Jerusalem: Memories of My Youth*, translated by H. Zohn. New York: Schocken Books, 1980.

Scholem, Gershom. *Major Trends in Jewish Mysticism*. New York: Schocken Books, 1954.

Scholem, Gershom. *The Messianic Idea in Judaism and Other Essays on Jewish Spirituality*, translated by M. A. Meyer. New York: Schocken Books, 1971.

Scholem, Gershom. *On Jews and Judaism in Crisis*, edited by W. J. Dannhauser. New York: Schocken Books, 1976.

Scholem, Gershom. *Sabbatai Sevi. The Mystical Messiah*, translated by R. J. Werblosky. Princeton: Princeton University Press, 1973.

Secondary Literature

Biale, David. *Gershom Scholem: Kabbalah and Counter-History*. Cambridge: Harvard University Press, 1979.

356 Bibliography

Bibliography

ndt, Hannah. *Eichmann in Jerusalem: A Report on the Banality of Evil.* New York: Viking, 1963.
Arendt, Hannah. *Men in Dark Times.* New York: Harcourt, Brace & World, 1968.
Arendt, Hannah. *The Jew as Pariah,* edited by Ron H. Feldman. New York: Grove, 1978.
Arendt, Hannah. *The Life of the Mind.* New York: Harcourt, Brace, and Jovanovich, 1978.
Arendt, Hannah. *The Origins of Totalitarianism.* New York: Harcourt, Brace, and Jovanovich, 1951.
Arendt, Hannah. *Rahel Varnhagen: The Life of a Jewess.* Edited by Liliane Weissberg, translated by Richard Winston and Clare Winston, Baltimore: Johns Hopkins University Press, 1997.

Secondary Literature in English

Bernstein, Richard. *Hannah Arendt and the Jewish Question.* Cambridge: MIT Press, 1994.
Villa, Dana. *Arendt and Heidegger: The Fate of the Political.* Princeton: Princeton University Press, 1995.

POST-WAR AMERICAN JEWISH THEOLOGY

Greenberg, Irving. *Living in the Image of God.* Northvale, N.J.: Jason Aronson, 1998.
Greenberg, Irving. "Voluntary Covenant." In *Perspectives.* National Jewish Resource Center, New York, 1982.
Herberg, Will. *Judaism and Modern Man.* New York: Harper & Row, 1951.
Heschel, Abraham Joshua. *God in Search of Man: A Philosophy of Judaism.* New York: Farrar, Straus & Cudahy, 1955.
Heschel, Abraham Joshua. *Man Is Not Alone.* New York: Farrar, Straus & Cudahy, 1951.
Heschel, Abraham Joshua. *Torah min ha-shamayim be-aspaklaryah shel ha-dorot,* 3 vols. London, NY: Defus Shontsin: 1962–1990. English translation, *Heavenly Torah.* New York: Continuum, 2005.
Kellner, Menachem, ed. *Contemporary Jewish Ethics,* New York: Sanhedrin Press, 1978.

Kellner, Menachem, ed. *The Pursuit of the Ideal: Jewish Writings of Steven Schwarzschild*. Albany: SUNY Press, 1990.

Konvitz, Milton. *Torah and Constitution: Essays in American Jewish Thought*. Syracuse, NY: Syracuse University Press, 1998.

Levenson, Jon. *Sinai and Zion*. Minneapolis: Winston Press, 1985.

Novak, David. *Covenantal Rights: A Study in Jewish Political Theory*. Princeton: Princeton University Press, 2000.

Novak, David. *Jewish Social Ethics*. New York: Oxford University Press, 1992.

Novak, David. *Natural Law in Judaism*. New York: Cambridge University Press, 1998.

Novak, David. *The Image of the Non-Jew in Judaism: An Historical and Constructive Study of the Noahide Laws*. New York: E. Mellen Press, 1983.

Novak, David. *The Election of Israel*. Cambridge: Cambridge University Press, 1995.

Novak, David. *The Jewish Social Contract: An Essay in Political Theology*. Princeton: Princeton University Press, 2005.

Sarna, Jonathan. "The Cult of Synthesis in American Jewish Culture." *Jewish Social Studies*, 5, no. 1–2 (Fall 1998/Winter 1999): 52–79.

Schwarzschild, Steven. "An Agenda for Jewish Philosophy in the 1980s." In *Studies in Jewish Philosophy: Collected Essays of the Academy for Jewish Philosophy (1980–1985)*, edited by Norbert Samuelson. Lanham, MD: University Press of America, 1987.

Schweid, Eliezer. *Democracy and Halakhah*. Lanham, MD, New York, and London: University Press of America, 1994.

Wyschogrod, Michael. *The Body of Faith*. Minneapolis, MN: The Seabury Press, 1983.

PHILOSOPHY AND THEOLOGY AFTER THE HOLOCAUST

Adorno, Theodor. *Minima Moralia, Reflections from a Damaged Life*, translated by E. F. N. Jephcott. London: Verso, 1978.

Altizer, Thomas J. J., and Hamilton, William. *Radical Theology and the Death of God*. Indianapolis: Bobbs-Merrill, 1966.

Berkovits, Eliezer. *Faith after the Holocaust*. New York: Ktav, 1973.

Bernstein, Michael André. *Foregone Conclusions*. Berkeley: University of California Press, 1994.

Braiterman, Zachary. *(God) After Auschwitz*. Princeton: Princeton University Press, 1998.

Cohen, Arthur A. *The Tremendum: A Theological Interpretation of the Holocaust*. New York: Crossroads, 1981.

Jonas, Hans. "The Concept of God after Auschwitz: A Jewish Voice." In *Mortality and Morality: A Search for God after Auschwitz*. Evanston: Northwestern University Press, 1996.

Lang, Berel. *Act and Idea in the Nazi Genocide*. Chicago: University of Chicago Press, 1990.

Lang, Berel. *The Future of the Holocaust*. Ithaca: Cornell University Press, 1999.

Leak, Andy, and Paizis, George, editors. *The Holocaust and the Text: Speaking the Unspeakable*. London: Macmillan, 1999.

Levi, Primo. *The Drowned and the Saved*, translated by Raymond Rosenthal. New York: Summit, 1988. Reprinted, New York: Vintage International, 1989.

Mintz, Alan. *Hurban: Responses to Jewish Catastrophe in Hebrew Literature*. New York: Columbia University Press, 1984.

Morgan, Michael L., ed. *A Holocaust Reader*. New York: Oxford, 2001.

Morgan, Michael L. *Beyond Auschwitz: Post-Holocaust Jewish Thought in America*. New York: Oxford University Press, 2001.

Rubenstein, Richard. *After Auschwitz*. Indianapolis: Bobbs-Merrill, 1966. 2nd edition, London: The Johns Hopkins University Press, 1992.

Rubenstein, Richard. *The Cunning of History: The Holocaust and the American Future*. New York: Harper, 1978.

Schweid, Eliezer. *Wrestling until Daybreak: Searching for Meaning in Thinking about the Holocaust*. Lanham, MD: University Press of America, 1994.

Wyschogrod, Michael. "Faith and the Holocaust." In *Judaism*, 20 (1971): 286–294. Reprinted in *A Holocaust Reader*, edited by Michael L. Morgan, 164–171. Oxford: Oxford University Press, 2001.

EMIL FACKENHEIM

Primary Texts

Fackenheim, Emil. *An Epitaph for German Judaism*. Madison: University of Wisconsin Press, forthcoming.

Fackenheim, Emil. *God's Presence in History: Jewish Affirmations and Philosophical Reflections*. New York: New York University Press, 1970.

Fackenheim, Emil. *The Jewish Bible after the Holocaust: A Re-reading*. Bloomington: Indiana University Press, 1990.

Fackenheim, Emil. *The Jewish Return into History*. New York: Schocken, 1978.

Fackenheim, Emil. *The Jewish Thought of Emil Fackenheim: A Reader*, edited with introductions by Michael L. Morgan. Detroit: Wayne State University Press, 1987.

Fackenheim, Emil. *The Religious Dimension in Hegel's Thought*. Bloomington: Indiana University Press, 1967.

Fackenheim, Emil. *To Mend the World*. Bloomington: Indiana University Press, 1994.

Fackenheim, Emil. *Quest for Past and Future*. Bloomington: Indiana University Press, 1968.

Fackenheim, Emil. *What Is Judaism?: An Interpretation for the Present Age*. New York: Summit, 1987.

EUGENE BOROWITZ

Primary Texts

Borowitz, Eugene B. *Exploring Jewish Ethics*. Detroit: Wayne State University Press, 1989.

Borowitz, Eugene B. *Renewing the Covenant*. Philadelphia: Jewish Publication Society, 1991.

LEO STRAUSS
Primary Texts

Strauss, Leo. *Jewish Philosophy and the Crisis of Modernity*, edited with an introduction by Kenneth Hart Green. Albany: SUNY Press, 1997.

Strauss, Leo. "Introductory Essay to Hermann Cohen's 'Religion of Reason out of the Sources of Judaism.'" In *Studies in Platonic Political Philosophy*, edited by Thomas Pangle. Chicago: University of Chicago Press, 1984.

Strauss, Leo. "Jerusalem and Athens: Some Preliminary Reflections." In *Studies in Platonic Political Philosophy*, edited by Thomas Pangle. Chicago: University of Chicago Press, 1983.

Strauss, Leo. *Jewish Philosophy and the Crisis of Modernity*, edited with an introduction by Kenneth Hart Green. Albany: State University of New York Press, 1997.

Strauss, Leo. *Leo Strauss: The Early Writings (1921–1932)*, translated with an introduction by Michael Zank. Albany: SUNY Press, 2002.

Strauss, Leo. *Natural Right and History*. Chicago: University of Chicago Press, 1953.

Strauss, Leo. *Persecution and the Art of Writing*. New York: Free Press, 1952. Reprinted, Chicago: University of Chicago Press, 1988.

Strauss, Leo. *Philosophy and Law: Essays Toward the Understanding of Maimonides and his Predecessors*, translated by Fred Baumann. Philadelphia: Jewish Publication Society, 1987.

Strauss, Leo. "Preface to Spinoza's Critique of Religion." In *Liberalism Ancient and Modern*, 224–259. New York: Basic Books, 1968.

Strauss, Leo. *Spinoza's Critique of Religion*, translated by E. M. Sinclair. New York: Schocken Books, 1965.

Secondary Literature

Batnitzky, Leora. *Leo Strauss and Emmanuel Levinas. Philosophy and the Politics of Revelation*. Cambridge: Cambridge University Press, 2006.

Deutsch, Kenneth L., and Nicgorski, Walter, editors. *Leo Strauss: Political Philosopher and Jewish Thinker*. Lanham, MD: Rowman & Littlefield, 1994.

Green, Kenneth Hart. *Jew and Philosopher: The Return to Maimonides in the Jewish Thought of Leo Strauss*. Albany: SUNY Press, 1993.

Janssens, David. "Questions and Caves: Philosophy, Politics, and History in Leo Strauss's Early Work." In *The Journal of Jewish Thought and Philosophy*, 10 (2000): 111–144.

Lampert, Laurence. *Leo Strauss and Nietzsche*. Chicago: University of Chicago Press, 1996.

Meier, Heinrich. *Carl Schmitt and Leo Strauss: The Hidden Dialogue*, translated by Harvey Lomax. Chicago: University of Chicago Press, 1995.

Schweid, Eliezer. "Religion and Philosophy: The Scholarly-Theological Debate Between Julius Guttmann and Leo Strauss." In *Maimonidean Studies*, edited by Arthur Hyman, vol. 1, 163–95. New York: Yeshiva University Press, 1990.

Smith, Steven B. *Reading Leo Strauss: Politics, Philosophy, Judaism*. Chicago: University of Chicago Press, 2006.

Udoff, Alan, editor. *Leo Strauss's Thought: Towards a Critical Engagement*. Boulder: Lynne Rienner, 1991.

FEMINISM

Anderson, Pamela Sue, and Clark, Beverly , eds. *Feminist Philosophy of Religion*. London: Routledge, 2004.

Biale, Rachel. *Women and Jewish Law: An Exploration of Women's Issues in Halakhic Sources*. New York: Schocken, 1984.

Davidman, L., and Tenenbaum S., eds. *Feminist Perspectives on Jewish Studies*, New Haven: Yale University Press, 1994.

Fricker, Miranda, and Hornsby, Jennifer, editors. *The Cambridge Campanion to Feminism in Philosophy*. Cambridge: Cambridge University Press, 2000.

Hauptmann, Judith. *Rereading the Rabbis: A Woman's Voice*. Boulder: Westview Press, 1998.

Heschel, Susannah, ed. *On Being a Jewish Feminist: A Reader*. New York: Schocken, 1983.

Meiselman, Moshe. *Jewish Women in Jewish Law*. New York: Ktav Publishing, 1978.

Parsons, Susan Frank, ed. *The Cambridge Companion to Feminist Theology*. Cambridge: Cambridge University Press, 2002.

Plaskow, Judith. *Standing Again at Sinai: Judaism from a Feminist Perspective*. New York: Harper Collins, 1990.

Ross, Tamar. *Expanding the Palace of Torah: Orthodoxy and Feminism*. Waltham: Brandeis University Press, 2004.

Tirosh-Samuelson, Hava, ed., *Women and Gender in Jewish Philosophy*, Bloomington: Indiana University Press, 2004.

J. B. SOLOVEITCHIK

Primary Texts in English

Soloveitchik, Joseph. *Fate and Destiny*. Hoboken, NJ: Ktav Publishing, 2000.

Soloveitchik, Joseph. *Halakhic Man*, translated by Lawrence Kaplan. Philadelphia: Jewish Publication Society, 1983.

Soloveitchik, Joseph. *Look, My Beloved Knocks*. New York: Yeshiva University Press, 2006.

Soloveitchik, Joseph. "Prayer, Petition, and Crisis." In *Worship of the Heart*, edited by Shalom Carmy, 17–18. Jersey City, NJ: Ktav Publishing, 2003.

Soloveitchik, Joseph. *The Halakhic Mind: An Essay on Jewish Tradition and Modern Thought*. New York: Seth Press, 1986.

Soloveitchik, Joseph. *The Lonely Man of Faith*. New York: Doubleday, 1992.

Secondary Literature

Angel, Marc, ed. *Exploring the Thought of Rabbi Joseph B. Soloveitchik*. Hoboken, NJ: Ktav Publishing, 1997.

Goldman, Eliezer. "Repentance and Time in the Thought of R. Soloveitchik." In *Emunah bi-Zemanim Mishtanim*, edited by Avi Sagi, 175–189. Jerusalem: World Zionist Organization, 1996.

Hartman, David. "*Halakhic Man*: Soloveitchik's Synthesis." In *A Living Covenant: The Innovative Spirit in Traditional Judaism*, 60–89. New York: Free Press, 1985.

Hartman, David. *Love and Terror in the God Encounter: The Theological Legacy of Rabbi Joseph B. Soloveitchik*. Woodstock, VT: Jewish Lights Publishing, 2001.

Kaplan, Lawrence. "Rabbi Joseph B. Soloveitchik's Philosophy of Halakha." In *The Jewish Law Annual*, 7 (1987): 139–197.

Kaplan, Lawrence. "Hermann Cohen and Rabbi Joseph Soloveitchik on Repentance." In *Journal of Jewish Thought and Philosophy*, forthcoming.

Kaplan, Lawrence. "The Multi-Faceted Legacy of the Rav: A Critical Analysis of Rabbi Hershel Schachter's *Nefesh Ha-Rav*." In *Bekhol Derakhekha Daehu: Journal of Torah and Scholarship*, 7 (1998): 63–65.

Klein, Zanvel. "Bnei Yosef Dovrim: Rabbi Joseph B. Soloveitchik: A Bibliography." In *The Torah U-Madda Journal*, 4 (1993): 84–113.

Munk, Reinier. *The Rationale of Halakhic Man: Joseph B. Soloveitchik's Conception of Jewish Thought*. Amsterdam: J. C. Gieben, 1996.

Peli, Pinhas, editor. *Soloveitchik on Repentance: The Thought and Oral Discourses of Rabbi Joseph B. Soloveitchik*. Ramsey, NJ: Paulist Press, 1984.

Ravitzky, Aviezer. "Rabbi J. B. Soloveitchik on Human Knowledge: Between Maimonidean and Neo-Kantian Philosophy." In *Modern Judaism*, 6 (1986): 157–188.

Singer, David, and Moshe Sokol. "Joseph Soloveitchik: Lonely Man of Faith." *Modern Judaism* 2, 3 (1982), 227–272.

EMMANUEL LEVINAS

Primary Texts in English Translation

Levinas, Emmanuel. *Beyond the Verse*, translated by Gary D. Mole. Bloomington: Indiana University Press, 1994.

Levinas, Emmanuel. *Difficult Freedom: Essays on Judaism*, translated by Seán Hand. Baltimore: Johns Hopkins University Press, 1990.

Levinas, Emmanuel. *Entre Nous: Thinking-of-the-Other*, translated by Michael B. Smith and Barbara Harshav. New York: Columbia University Press, 1998.

Levinas, Emmanuel. *Ethics and Infinity*, translated by Richard A. Cohen. Pittsburgh: Duquesne University Press, 1985.

Levinas, Emmanuel. *In the Time of the Nations*, translated by Michael B. Smith. Bloomington: Indiana University Press, 1994.

Levinas, Emmanuel. *Of God Who Comes to Mind*, translated by Bettina Bergo. Stanford: Stanford University Press, 1998.

Levinas, Emmanuel. Seán Hand, ed. *The Levinas Reader*. New York: Blackwell, 1989.

Levinas, Emmanuel. *Otherwise than Being or Beyond Essence*, translated by Alphonso Lingis. Pittsburgh: Duquesne University Press, 1998.

Levinas, Emmanuel. *Proper Names*, translated by Michael B. Smith. Stanford: Stanford University Press, 1996.

Levinas, Emmanuel. *Time and the Other [and Additional Essays]*, translated by Richard A. Cohen. Pittsburgh: Duquesne University Press, 1987.

Levinas, Emmanuel. *Totality and Infinity: An Essay on Exteriority*, translated by Alphonso Lingis. Pittsburgh: Duquesne University Press, 1969.

Secondary Literature

Atterton, Peter, Calarco, Matthew, and Friedman, Maurice, eds. *Levinas and Buber: Dialogue and Difference*. Pittsburgh: Duquesne University Press, 2004.

Bernasconi, Robert, and Critchley, Simon, eds. *Rereading Levinas*. Bloomington: Indiana University Press, 1991.

Chanter, Tina. *Time, Death and the Feminine: Levinas with Heidegger*. Stanford: Stanford University Press, 2001.

Cohen, Richard. *Elevations: The Height of the Good in Rosenzweig and Levinas*. Chicago: University of Chicago Press, 1994.

Cohen, Richard. *Ethics, Exegesis and Philosophy: Interpretation After Levinas*. Cambridge: Cambridge University Press, 2001.

Critchley, Simon, and Bernasconi, Robert, eds. *The Cambridge Companion to Levinas*. Cambridge: Cambridge University Press, 2002.

Davis, Colin. *Levinas: An Introduction*. Notre Dame: University of Notre Dame Press, 1996.

Handelman, Susan. *Fragments of Redemption*. Bloomington, IN: Indiana University Press, 1991.

Horowitz, Asher, and Horowitz, Gad, eds. *Difficult Justice: Commentaries on Levinas and Politics*. Toronto: University of Toronto Press, 2006.

Lescourret, Marie-Anne. *Emmanuel Levinas*. Paris: Flammarion, 1994.

Malka, Salomon. *Emmanuel Levinas: La vie et la trace*. Paris: Jean-Claude Lattes, 2002. Forthcoming in an English translation, *Emmanuel Levinas: His Life and Legacy*. Pittsburgh: Duquesne University Press.

Morgan, Michael L. *Discovering Levinas*. Cambridge: Cambridge University Press, 2007.

Moyn, Samuel. *Origins of the Other: Emmanuel Levinas between Revelation and Ethics*. Ithaca: Cornell University Press, 2005.

Robbins, Jill, editor. *Is It Righteous to Be? Interviews with Emmanuel Levinas*. Stanford: Stanford University Press, 2001.

Wyschogrod, Edith. *Emmanuel Levinas: The Problem of Ethical Metaphysics*. New York: Fordham University Press, 2000.

JACQUES DERRIDA

Primary Texts

Derrida, Jacques. "Faith and Knowledge: The Two Sources of 'Religion' at the Limits of Reason Alone." In *Religion*, edited by Jacques Derrida and Gianni Vattimo. Stanford: Stanford University Press, 1996.

Derrida, Jacques. "Edmond Jabès and the Question of the Book." In *Writing and Difference*, translated with an introduction by Alan Bass. Chicago: University of Chicago Press, 1978.

Derrida, Jacques. *Acts of Religion*. Gil Anidjar, ed. London: Routledge, 2001.

Derrida, Jacques. "Interpretations at War: Kant, the Jew, the German." In *New Literary History*, 22 (1991): 39–95.

Derrida, Jacques. *Of Grammatology*, translated by Gayatri Chakravorty Spivak. Baltimore: Johns Hopkins University Press, 1976.

Derrida, Jacques. "Violence and Metaphysics: An Essay on the Thought of Emmanuel Levinas." In *Writing and Difference*, translated with an introduction by Alan Bass. Chicago: University of Chicago Press, 1978.

Derrida, Jacques. *Adieu à Emmanuel Lévinas*. Paris: Galilé, 1997. English translation by Pascale-Anne Brault and Michael Naas. Stanford: Stanford University Press, 1999.

Secondary Literature

Caputo, John. *The Prayers and Tears of Jacques Derrida: Religion Without Religion*. Bloomington: Indiana University Press, 1997.

Cixous, Hélène. *Portrait of Jacques Derrida as a Young Jewish Saint*, translated by Beverley Bie Brahic. New York: Columbia University Press, 2004.

Weber, Elizabeth, ed. *Questioning Judaism*. Stanford: Stanford University Press, 2004.

MISCELLANEOUS TEXTS

Bloch, E. *The Spirit of Utopia*, translated by A. Nassar. Stanford: Stanford University Press, 2000.

Green, Arthur. *The Tormented Master*. Tuscaloosa: University of Alabama Press, 1977.

Lyotard, Jean-François. *Heidegger and "the jews."* Minneapolis: University of Minnesota Press, 1990.

Malka, Salomon. *Monsieur Chouchani: L'enigme d'un maître du XXe siècle*. Paris: Jean-Claude Lattes, 1994.

Maybaum, Ignaz. *Ignaz Maybaum: A Reader*, edited by Nicholas De Lange. New York: Berghahn Books, 2001.

Index

Abraham, 116, 152, 175–176, 196–198, 203, 247, 286, 318, 340
Academy of Jewish Studies, 147
Adam, 183, 200, 327–330
Adelmann, Dieter, 88
Adorno, Theodor W., xx, 69, 146n57, 182, 185
Africa, North, 281
agnosticism, 287
Ahad, Ha'am 159
Alfarabi, 53
alterity, 181, 245, 252n18; see also Other
Altizer, Thomas, 289
Altmann, Alexander, 43, 85
America, 93, 148, 154
  North, 9, 267, 281
  South, 281
  United States of, xvii, 12, 35, 48, 211
Amos, 114, 153; see also Bible
Amsterdam, Netherlands, xvii, 14, 27, 154–156
Anderson, Pamela, 338
angst, 181
Anidjar, Gil, 41
Annapolis, Maryland, 148
anthropomorphism, 15, 17–18, 133
anti-Semitism, 83, 177, 291
  anti-Jewish, 81–83, 90, 159, 337
anti-Zionist, 123, 161
Aquinas, Thomas, 14
Arendt, Hannah, xviii, xx, 9–10, 190n48, 292–295, 299n42
Argument from Incomprehensibility, 287
Aristotelianism, 60, 63, 66, 68–69, 332
Aristotle, 53, 55, 57, 148, 152, 162, 166n18, 177–178, 220, 329–330

De Anima, 66
Arkush, Alan, 7, 11
Arnauld, Antoine, 4
Arnold, Matthew, 333
Asia, 281
assimilation, 2, 158–159, 164, 171, 177, 181
atheism, 8, 64–65, 139, 151, 154, 164, 178, 319n13
Athens, 152
Athens and Jerusalem, 2, 139, 152–154, 161
Auerbach, Isaac Levin, xvii
Augustine, Saint, 126
Auschwitz, *see* Holocaust
Austin, J. L., 244, 318n1
autonomy, 7, 38, 91, 151, 192–208, 210, 220, 227; *see also* freedom
  moral, 181, 334
  political, 177
Averroes, 75n51
Avicenna, 75n51, 163

Babel, 183
Bach, Johann Sebastian, 95
Baeck, Leo, 3, 127
Baal, 43
Baal-Shem Tov, 103
Balkans, 126
Barth, Karl, 9, 166n10, 305
Basel, Switzerland, xviii
Batnitzky, Leora, 11, 334, 337
Bayle, Pierre, 149
Beauvoir, Simone de, 12, 331, 336–337
Beethoven, Ludwig van, 95
being
  aesthetic ontology and, 241
  being-in-the-world, 243
  being-toward-death, 130

Other titles in the series *(continued from page iii)*